NATIONAL SOCIETY

OF

DAUGHTERS OF FOUNDERS AND PATRIOTS

OF AMERICA

FOUNDERS INDEX

OF

LINEAGE BOOKS

VOLUMES I THROUGH XXXX

1898-2006

DONNA CHILTON DERRICK
(Mrs. H. Lester Derrick, Jr.)

National President
2009-2012

Published in the United States by Railroad Street Press, St. Johnsbury, Vermont.

ISBN   978-1-936711-23-9

1. Reference
2. American History

Printed in the United States of America

Railroad Street Press
394 Railroad Street, Suite 2
St. Johnsbury, VT 05819
(802) 748-3551
www.railroadstreetpress.com

With love and appreciation, the following National Officers are thanked for their support of this President and the Founders Index

NATIONAL OFFICERS 2009-2012

President
Donna Chilton Derrick

Vice President
Helen Ross Staley

Chaplain
Mary Carolyn Trent

Recording Secretary
Carol Farmer Bower

Corresponding Secretary
Sharla Wilson Luken

Organizing Secretary
Louise Huntoon Heynau

Registrar
Virginia Wood Frost

Treasurer
Judith Haddock Swan

Historian
Ann Fellows Moore

Color Bearer
Harriet L. Edwards

DEDICATION

This Founders Index is dedicated to the National Registrars and Genealogists who have served the National Society. In the early days of our society, applications were verified by the National Registrars. Beginning in 1954, a National Genealogist was retained to verify the applications.

Past and Present National Registrars

Mrs. William L. Mason	1898-1903
Mrs. Peter Perry Pealer	1903-1918
Mrs. Amos G. Draper	1918-1919
Mrs. Fredrick A. Fernald	1919-1920
Mrs. Gaius M. Brumbaugh	1920-1928
Mrs. Albert F. Olson	1928-1931
Mrs. Frank Leon Nason	1931-1934
Mrs. James J. Gilligan	1934-1937
Miss Bessie Porter	1937-1940
Mrs. Herbert E. McQuesten	1940-1943
Mrs. J. Brent Clarke	1943-1944
Mrs. Arthur Beecher Iffland	1944-1946
Mrs. Phillip Wallace Hiden	1946-1949
Mrs. James A. Williamson	1949-1952
Mrs. George H. Bonsall	1952
Mrs. Neil A. Cameron	1953
Mrs. George L. Bennett	1954-1955
Mrs. Ivan T. Johnson	1955-1958
Mrs. William V. Tynes	1958-1961
Mrs. Len Young Smith	1961-1964
Mrs. Michael J. Galvin	1964-1967
Mrs. William Seth Kenyon	1967-1968
Mrs. Alvin A. Kurtz	1968-1970
Mrs. Richard J. Roberts	1970-1973

Miss Margaret I. McKay	1973-1976
Mrs. John G. W. Melbin	1976-1979
Miss Frances V. Flanders	1979-1982
Mrs. William A. Smith	1982-1985
Mrs. Alden A. Lofquist Jr.	1985-1988
Mrs. Boyd M. Lien	1988-1991
Mrs. Robert S. Dean Sr.	1991-1994
Mrs. John J. Lawler	1994-1997
Miss Marguerite F. Fogleman	1997-2000
Mrs. Eugene E. Tibbs	2000-2003
Mrs. Melvin Dale Austin	2003-2006
Mrs. Dale Moore	2006-2009
Mrs. Paul R. Frost	2009-

Past and Present National Genealogists

Jean Stephenson	1954-1957
Katie-Prince Esker	1958-1964
Inez Waldemaier	1964-1966
Margaret Searcy (Mrs. James K.)	1967-1981
William Blount Stewart	1981-1990
John Frederick Dorman	1990-2009
David C. Smith	2009-

ACKNOWLEDGEMENT

The preparation and publishing of this Founders Index grew out of a casual conversation in 2010. Desire was expressed that the National Society of Daughters of Founders and Patriots of America have a volume which would provide easy access to the names of Founders which had been used for admission to our Society. It was felt this would be of great benefit to those seeking membership and for those members seeking a supplemental line as well.

Helen Staley, Vice President 2009-2012, undertook this tremendous project which involved hundreds of hours of compilation over a period of two years. It was first prepared by her in handwritten form. After the pages were typed the cross checking began as well as the proofreading of the typed manuscript.

Assistance in checking the material was given by Harriet Edwards, National Color Bearer 2009-2012, and her contribution to this Founders Index is also acknowledged.

Gratitude and appreciation is expressed to both of these ladies for their extensive time and effort on behalf of the Society and the National President's Project. I am pleased to acknowledge their lasting contribution to our Society through their work on this Founders Index.

Members and prospective members will benefit from this Index both now and for years to come. It will be a valuable tool to be added to our Society's extensive records since 1898.

Donna Chilton Derrick

National President 2009-2012

PREFACE

The National Society of Daughters of Founders and Patriots of America Founders Index is compiled in order to identify every individual FOUNDER accepted by the NSDFPA from 1898 through 2006 as published in the DFPA Lineage Books one through forty.

This Index is the project of National President Donna Chilton Derrick, and has been funded by the generous donations of individual members and the chapters of the National Society.

Included is each FOUNDER'S name, colony or colonies in which he settled; birth, marriage and death years, if known; his wife's birth and death years, if known and; the DFPA Lineage Book Volume number and pages therein.

Every effort has been taken by the compiler, Helen Ross Staley, and the verifier, Harriet Louise Edwards, to make this Index as accurate as possible, but it is realized that errors may appear.

It is hoped the Founders Index will assist the chapters and individuals desiring membership in the National Society of Daughters of Founders and Patriots of America.

Donna Chilton Derrick

National President 2009-2012

Editorial Committee

Helen Ross Staley, Compiler
National Vice President
2009-2012

Harriet L. Edwards, Verifier
National Color Bearer
2009-2012

EXPLANATION

The **DFPA FOUNDERS INDEX** contains as many Founders approved, published given name-surname from the year 1898 through 2006, approximately 4,000 + or – given name-surnames.

For brevity, the Founder's surname, given name, years of birth, marriage and death dates, plus his wife's or wives' birth and death dates and colony or colonies in which they lived are recorded here. Each entry is a composite of all the Vital Records, presented in the 40 volumes of the DFPA Lineage Books, of all the Founders of each different given name-surname. These may be used as a guide, not as proof. Only **complete lineages** are listed, no partial.

Please note: Each surname listing begins with the most recent spelling, i.e. the applicant's, followed by other spellings, including the "immigrant" spelling. The immigrant spelling, if different from the lead surname is usually spelled out after the given name and/or parenthesized there.

ABBREVIATIONS

a before
ae age
ante before
b born
banns
bef before
bet/bt between
bp baptized
bur buried
by = by
c circa/about
ca circa/about
"ca 1636 pb" 40:158
chr children or church record
chrt christened
d death
div divorce
early early in year/century
ESQ Esquire/gentleman lawyer
es estate
es admin estate administration
late late in year?
inv inventory (estate)
int marriage intentions

liv living (in that year)
m married
mid middle of year or century
n.i.w. named in will? Vol. 35, p.103
p after
pb probably
post after
pr probably Vol. 40, p. 148
pre before Vol. 37, p. 262
prior to before
w will
wd will dated
wid widow
w.f. Vol. 25, p. 187
wp will probated/will proved
wr will recorded
In Lineage Book Volume XXXIX,
b means by
a.w. after will Vol. 38, p. 129
The most recent spelling of a surname, in most cases is put first to facilitate individuals seeking a founder surname

ABBE
MA **JOHN** 1613-1689/90
 m1) c 1634
 Mary Loring c 1615/20-1672
 XVIII 102; XX 18; XXXII 198;
 XXXV 299; XXXIX 51; XXXX
 217

ABBOT, see ABBOTT

ABBOTT/ABBOT
MA **GEORGE** 1615-1681
 m 1646/47
 Hannah Chandler 1629-1711
 VI 81/94; X 241; XI 58; XV 117;
 XX 90; XXX 62; XXXI 285;
 XXXIII 160; XXXV 248;
 XXXVI 206; XXXVIII 41;
 XXXIX 285
MA **GEORGE**....-1647
 m c 1630 ____ ____
 ....- a 1647
 XXXV 218

ABELL
MA **ROBERT**....-1663 m ....
 Joanna/Johanna ____ ....-
 p 1682
 XXXIV 71; XXXVII 212; XXXX
 62
MA **SAMUEL, I** c 1650-c1698
 m c 1670 **Ann**____ c 1650-c1700
 XXXX 200

ACKERMAN
NY **DAVID** 1614-1662 m 1640
 Elizabeth DeVillers ...-1679
 XIX 41

ACKISS
VA **JOHN** ...-a 1728 m ....
 Katherine____....-a 1734
 XXXVII 323

ADAMS
CT **DANIEL** 1652-1713 m 1677
 Mary Pinney ....-1715
 XXIII 57
CT **EDWARD** ....-1671 m ...
 Mary____ ....-p 1687
 XXVII 162
MA **GEORGE** ....-1696 m....
 Frances____...-....
 XXXVI 12
MA **HENRY** ....-1646 m ....
 Mary Alexander ....-....
 III 43
MA **HENRY** c 1583-1646
 m c 1609 **Edith Squire** bp 1587-
 1673
 IV 102; IX 44; X 112, 264; XV
 60; XIII 53; XXV 16, 149; XXIX
 72, 318; XXXI 20; XXXIII 290;
 XXXIV 33; XXXV 48; XXXVI
 11, 246; XXXVIII 204; XXXIX
 262
MA **HENRY** ....-1604-1676 m 1643
 Elizabeth Paine ....-1676
 XIV 47, 98; XVII 25
MA-CT **JEREMY ADDOMS**
 1604/05-1683 m c 1636
 Rebecca Greenhill
 ....-....
 XXXIII 156
MA **JOHN**....-1633 m c 1625
 Ellen Newton 1593/98-1681
 XIII 42; XXXX 181
MA **MATTHEW** ....-.... m ....
 ____ ____ ....-....
 XX 82
VA **PETER, I** c 1640-1687 m c 1660
 Anne Nichols c 1642-c 1710
 XXXII 220
MD **PHILIP ADDAMS** c 1650-1696
 m 1670 **Anne Crewe** 1655-
 1687/91
 XXIX 283

ADAMS-Cont.
MA **ROBERT** 1602-1682 m ....
    Eleanor _____ ....-1677
    XVIII 144; XXXV 152; XXXX
    88, 225
VA **ROBERT** "of 1620" m ....
    _____ _____ .... -....
    XXVIII 124; XXXIII 196
MA/ME **SAMUEL** 1602-1652
    m 1623 **Alice Stone** ....-....
    XXXVIII 258
MD **SUMER** a 1659-wp 1687
    m a 1666
    Elizabeth _____ ....-1681
    XXXVIII 321
MA **WILLIAM** 1594-1661 m ....
    _____ _____ ....-....
    XXII 121; XXXX 49

ADDAMS, see ADAMS

ADDISON
MD **JOHN** ....-1706 m ....
    Mrs. Rebecca Dent Wilson ....-
    1729
    XVI 50.
VA **JOHN** 1655-1716/17 m ....
    Barthina _____ ....-p 1716
    XXXI 261

ADDOMS, see ADAMS
ADKINS, see ATKINS

AGEE
VA **MATTHIEU** 1670- .... m ....
    Ann Godwin ....-....
    XXXIII 203

AINSWORTH
CT **EDWARD** c 1652-1740/41
    m 1687/88
    Johanna Hemmingway 1670-
    1748

    XIV 50
ALBEE
MA **BENJAMIN** c 1600-.... m ....
    Hannah Chambers or Miller
    ....-a 1669
    XXVII 51; XXXI 95; XXXIII 67;
    XXXIX 203

ALDEN
MA **HENRY** c 1667-1730
    m1) _____ _____ ....-a 1719
    XXIX 372
MA **JOHN** 1599/1600-1686/87
    m 1621/22 **Priscilla**
    Mullens/Molines 1602/04-
    p 1680
    IX 45; XV 130; XXIX 370;
    XXXIII 264; XXXVI 253;
    XXXVIII 314; XXXX 23

ALDERMAN
CT **WILLIAM, Sr** c 1640-1697
    m 1679 **Mary Case** 1660-1725
    XXXVI 184; XXXVII 34;
    XXXVIII 180; XXX 157

ALDRICH
MA **GEORGE** 1605-1682 m 1629
    Katherine Seald ....-1691
    XXIX 330

ALEXANDER
CT **GEORGE** c 1620-1703 m 1644
    Susan Sage c 1624-1684
    XXVI 181; XXXVII 243;
    XXXVIII 11
MD **JAMES** c 1652/81-1725
    m .... **Jean Wallace** ....-wd 1736
    XXVIII 119; XXXVI 11
CT **JOHN** ....-.... m ....
    _____ _____ ....-....
    XXVI 181; XXX 273

ALFORD, see ALVORD
ANNANSON, see ALLISON

ALLEN/ALLIN/ALLING/
ALLYN
MA/CT **EDWARD** c 1630-1696
  m 1658 **Sarah Kimball**
  c 1635/39-1696
  XVIII 26; XXX 95; XXXI 90;
  XXXVII 118; XXXVIII 155
MA **GEORGE** c 1619-1648 m ....
  Katherine ____ ....-....
  XXIV 72
MA **JAMES** c 1614-1676 m 1638
  Ann Guild c 1616-1673
  XIX 56; XXV 18
MA **LEWIS** c 1630 – 1708
  m1) c 1664 **Sarah Ives**
  1639-....
  m2) .... Mrs **Mary (Sherman)**
  Freeman ....-1703
  XXXV 225; XXXVI 126
CT **MATTHEW ALLYN** 1604-
  1670/71 m ....
  Margaret Wyatt ....-p 1670
  XII 83
CT **ROBERT ALLYN** 1608-1683
  m .... **Sarah** ____ ....-....
  XXI 49; XXV 188
CT **ROGER ALLING** bp 1612-
  1674 m c 1642
  Mary Nash ....-1683
  XII 30; XV 86; XXVII 201;
  XXXI 179, 295; XXXVI 328;
  XXXVII 257
MA **SAMUEL** ....-1669
  m)1 ....**Ann** ____ ....-1641
  XXVII 91; XXVIII 149; XXXV
  256
MA/CT **SAMUEL** c 1588-1648
  m1) a 1634 **Ann** ____ ....-1687
  XXXII 149; XXXIV 200;
  XXXVI 268; XXXIX 255

MA **WILLIAM, Sr** c 1610-
  1681/86 m 1)1638/39
  Ann Goodale c 1600/18-
  1678
  XIII 91; XXXI 100;
  XXXV 108; XXXVII 131,
  247; XXXX 240
MA **WILLIAM** 1602-1678
  m ....
  Alice/Alys Norman ....- 1631/32
  XXIX 312
VA **WILLIAM, I** c 1630-1677
  m .... **Judith** ____ ....-....
  XXX 67
RI **WILLIAM ALLIN** c 1640- 1685
  m .... **Elizabeth** ____ ....-1685
  XXII 136

ALLERTON
MA **ISSAC** 1583/85-a 1659
  m2) 1626 **Fear Brewster** ....-
  1634
  XVIII 44, 69

ALLEY
MA **JOHN** 1575-1653
  m ....**Rebecca Ayres** 1626-....
  VII 46

ALLIN, see ALLEN
ALLING, see ALLEN

ALLIS
MA **WILLIAM** 1613/16-1678
  m 1641 **Mary**____ ....-....
  XIX 22

ALLISON /ALLANSON
MD **THOMAS** 1637-p 1677
  m 1662 **Mary Roberts** ....-p 1673
  XXXI 94

ALLYN, see ALLEN

ALVORD/ALFORD
CT/MA **ALEXANDER** bp 1627-
1687 m 1646
Mary Vore/Vose   ....- a 1687
VI 16/17; X 74, 76; XXXX 80
CT **BENEDICTUS** 1619-1683
m 1640 **Joan Newton** ....-....
XXV 21; XXIX 268

ALWARD
NJ **HENRY** a 1675-1718
m 1693 **Judith Hendrickson** ....-
....
XXX 289

AMBROSE
MA **HENRY** 1613-1658
m ....**Susannah** _____ ....-p 1663
XV 26

AMERMAN
NY **DERICK JANSE** ....-
wp 1723/25 m ....
Altje Paulus Van der   Beck ....-
....
IV 119; XII 98

AMES/EAMES
VA **JOSEPH AMES** ....-wp 1709/19
m .... **Esther Gray** ....-1719
XXIX 20; XXXIII 14; XXXVIII
275
MA **THOMAS EAMES** c 1618-
1680 m1)1640 **Margaret Dean**
....-1660
X 159; XXXVIII 199
MA **WILLIAM** bp 1605/15-
1653/54 m 1640
Hannah (Alden) Niles ....-
1703/4
XV 34; XXIV 53; XXXI 13;
XXXIII 30; XXXVIII 259

AMIDON/AMIDOWNE
MA **ROGER AMIDOWNE** ....-
1673/75 m 2) 1668
Joanna Harwood ....-1711
XXXVI 99; XXXVIII 3

AMSDEN
MA **ISAAC** ....-1659 m 1654
Frances Perriman ....-....
XXXIII 77

ANABLE/ANNABLE
MA **ANTHONY** 1599-1673
m2) 1645 **Ann Clark** ....-
p 1686
XXIV 85; XXVI 255

ANDERSON
NJ **ENOCH, Sr** 1668/69-1741
m c 1690
Tryntje (Catherine) Opdyck
1668/72-1722/41
XXXX 73, 404
VA **ROBERT** c 1640-1712
m ....   **Cecelia Massie** ....-
a 1727
XX 110; XXI 88; XXXIII
22,69; XXXIX 74

ANDREWS/ANDRUS
CT **JOHN ANDRUS** ....-1681
m.... **Mary** _____ ....-1694
XII 103; XIX 83; XX 48; XXI
63; XXII 11; XXIV 78; XXXV
251
MA **JOHN** c 1618/21-1708
m 1645 **Jane Jordan** c 1622-
p 1707
XII 120; XIX 162; XX 31;
XXXX 34, 424
MA **JOHN** ....-1679 m ....
Hannah Jackson 1638- ....
XXXIX 158

ANDREWS/ANDRUS-Cont.
CT **WILLIAM** ....-1675/76
    m1) c 1625 ____ ____ ....- 1663
    XI 39; XXIII 75
CT **WILLIAM** ....-1659 m....
    Mary ____ ....-1639/40
    XXVI 90
CT **WILLIAM** c 1595/1600-1659
    m .... **Abigail (Graves)** ....-
    1682/83
    XXXVII 364; XXXX 316

ANDRUS, see ANDREWS
ANGEL, see ANGELL

ANGELL/ANGEL
RI **THOMAS** c 1618-c 1694
    m 1643 **Alice Ashton**
    bp 1617/18-1694/5
    X 196, 197; XIV 51;XX 17;
    XXIV 58;XXVII 127; XXXI 75

ANNABLE, see ANABLE

APPLETON
MA **SAMUEL** 1586-1670
    m 1616 **Mary Everard** ...-c 1630
    XIII 54; XVIII 13; XXIII 18;
    XXX 26

ARMISTEAD
VA **RALPH** ....-.... m ....
    ____ ____ ....-....
    XXX 189; XXXI 88
VA **WILLIAM** bp 1610-a1660
    m 1632 **Anne Ellis** ....-....
    XXVII 178; XXIX 366;
    XXXVII 153

ARMS
VA **WILLIAM** 1654-1731
    m 1677
    Joanna Hawks 1654-1729

XIII 109

ARMSTRONG
CT **BENJAMIN** ....-1717/18
    m .... **Rachel** ____ ....-....
    XXXIII 315
RI **JONATHAN** a 1650-p 1677
    m .... ____ ____ ....-....
    X 291; XI 17; XV 15; XVI 33;
    XXIX 48; XXXIV 268

ARNOLD, see STEUBEN

ARNOLD
VA **ANTHONY** c 1630/35-....
    w 1689 m c 1659 **Johanna** ____
    ....- ....
    XXVIII 192, 193; XXXVI 18
CT **JOHN** c 1590-wd 1664 m ....
    Susannah ____ ....-p 1670
    XI 69; XII 23; XXI 131; XXV
    113; XXIX 44; XXXV 189, 311;
    XXXX 275
MA **JOSEPH** c 1625-.... m 1648
    Rebecca Curtis ....-1693
    XXV 8; XXXV 294
MA/RI **THOMAS** bp 1599-1674
    m2) 1635/40
    Phoebe Parkhurst
    bp 1612-c 1688
    VII 36; XXIII 20
MA/RI **WILLIAM** 1587-1675/7
    m c 1610 **Christian Peake** 1583-
    1659
    XXX 176; XXXVII 235;
    XXXIX 311

ARRINGTON
VA **WILLIAM** c 1662-1709/25
    m a 1683 **Elizabeth**
    Pedden/Pedin c 1665-c 1725
    XXXII 191; XXXIX 173

ARSDALEN, see VAN ARSDALE
ARUNDEL-HOWARD, see
HOWARD

ASBURY
MD **HENRY, Sr** ....-wp 1707
   m .... **Mary** _____ ....-....
   XXXV 223

ASH
MA **JOHN** ....-1694/95
   m 1667 **Mary Bartlett** 1647-
   p 1706
   XXVI 85; XXXVIII 271

ASHBROOK
NJ **JOHN** 1656-1730
   m2) 1678 **Mary Hamilton** ....-
   ....
   XXVIII 15; XXIX 309

ASHCRAFT
CT **JOHN, I** ....-1680
   m 1670 **Hannah Osborn** ....-....
   XXX 169; XXXIV 199

ASHLEY
MA **JOSEPH** c 1670-c1750
   m1) 1704 **Elizabeth Percival**
   1675-c 1727
   XXXIII 232, 282
MA **ROBERT** a 1618-1682
   m c 1641
   Mrs Mary Horton ....-1683
   XVIII 92

ASHER, see ASHWORTH

ASHWORTH/ASHER/ASHUR
VA **JOHN c** 1682-p 1719 m ....
   _____ _____ ....-....
   XXXX 432

ASHUR, see ASHWORTH

ATHERTON
MA **JAMES** 1626-1710
   m ....
   Hannah _____ ....-1713
   XXX 12

ATKINS/ADKINS
CT **JOSIAH** ....-1690
   m1)a 1650 _____ **Andrews** ....-
   a 1673
   XXXIII 66
CT **THOMAS ADKINS** ....-
   c 1694 m 1672
   Jane Williams ....-....
   XXVII 191.

ATWATER
CT **DAVID** bp 1615-1692
   m 1646 **Damaris Sayre** 1625-
   1691
   XXXVIII 337; XXXX 332

ATWOOD
MA **HARMAN** ....-1651
   m 1646 **Ann Copp** ....-....
   XXX 62
MA **JOHN WOOD/ATWOOD**
   1614-1676 m c 1642
   Sarah Masterson 1620-
   pr 1701/02
   IV 74, 75; XXXVII 266
MA **STEPHEN** c 1620-1694
   m 1644 **Abigail Dunham** ....-....
   XXX 246
MA **THOMAS** ....-1694 m ....
   Elizabeth _____ ....-....
   XXVII 67

AUDLIN, see ODLIN

AULD
MD **JAMES** 1665-1721 m....
 Sarah Elliott 1670-p 1721
 XXVI 224

AUSTIN
MA **ANTHONY** 1635/36-1708
 m 1664 **Esther/Hester Huggins**
 1642/43-1698
 XIV 88; XXXX 346, 358,364
CT **JOHN** ....-1657 m....
 Constance _____ ....-....
 II 40
MA **RICHARD ANTHONY**
 c 1598-c 1639
 m .... _____ _____ ....-....
 XI 38; XIV 52; XVI 132
RI **ROBERT** c 1634-a 1687
 m .... _____ _____ ....-....
 XXIX 57; XXXVI 331

AVERELL, see AVERILL

AVERILL/AVERELL
MA **WILLIAM** c 1611/13-a 1653
 m 1631/32**Abigail Hinton** 1619-
 1655
 XIV 13, 62; XXV 300; XXX
 29; XXXVIII 297

AVERY
MA **CHRISTOPHER** c 1590- 1679
 m 1616 **Margery
 Stevens/Stephens** ....-c 1643
 II 31, 42; X 274, 283; XI 172;
 XVII 7; XIX 35; XXII 145;
 XXIII 66, 81; XXV 209; XXVI
 119; XXVII 61; XXX 26,41
MA **WILLIAM** c 1622-1686/87
 m 1644 **Margaret
 Altright/Albright** c 1628-1678
 XXXI 247; XXXIX 68; XXXX
 207

AXTELL
MA **HENRY** bp 1641-1676 m 1665
 Hannah Merriam 1645-p 1677
 XXIII 31; XXX 197

AYER/AYERS/AYRES/EYRE
MA **JOHN** 1590/92-1657 m ...
 Hannah Evered 1600-1688
 XVI 26; XVIII 20; XXIV 141;
 XXVI 141; XXVII 173; XXXII
 136; XXXV 195; XXXVI 176
MA **JOHN** c 1623-1675 m c 1648
 Susanna Symonds c 1628-
 1682/83
 XXXIX 337
CT **RICHARD AYRES** c 1620-
 c 1719 m ....
 Mary _____ .... -1715/16
 X 244; XVI 6

BABAR, see BABARS

BABARS/BABAR
VA **ROBERT, I** c 1650-p 1718
 m .... **Sarah** _____ ....-....
 XXXII 94

BABB
MA **PHILIP** 1651-c 1670 m ....
 Mary _____ ....-p 1670
 XXV 158; XXVI 242, 250;
 XXXIII 101

BABBITT/BOBET
MA **EDWARD** ... -1675 m 1654
 Sarah Tarne .... - c 1684
 VII 48

BABCOCK/BADCOCK
RI **JAMES** 1612 – 1679
 m 1) 1639 **Sarah** _____ .... – bet
 1664/69
 VI 98/116; VII 42; IX 10; XII

BABCOCK/BADCOCK-Cont.
57; XIII 52; XIX 36; XXV 145;
XXIX 116, 172, 202; XXX 239;
XXXI 17, 133; XXXIII 291;
XXXIX 282; XXXX 362
MA **DAVID BADCOCK** .... - ....
m .... ____ ____ .... -....
XXXV 158; XXXVI 162, 295

BABSON
MA **JAMES, Jr** 1620/25-1683
m 1647 **Elinor Hill** 1631-1713/14
XXVII 52

BACHELDER, see BATCHELDER
BACHILER, see BATCHELDER

BACKUS
CT **STEPHEN** bp 1640/41 – 1695
m 1666 **Sarah Spencer**
c 1644-....
XXXIX 40; XXXX 65
CT **WILLIAM** c 1606-1661/64
m c 1627 **Elizabeth** ____ ....-
1643
XXXIX 40; XXXX 65

BACON
VA **EDMUND** c 1641-1705
m .... **Ann Lyddall** ....-1655
XXXIII 40
MA **GEORGE** 1592-1642
m .... **Margaret** ____ .... -1683
XXV 106
MA **MICHAEL Jr** c 1608-1688
m1) 1624 **Mary** ____ ....-1655
V 130; XI 12
MA **MICHAEL** bp 1579-1648
m ....**Alice/Elizabeth** ____ ....-
1647/48
V 130; XI 12; XX 42; XXV
63; XXXI 102; XXXIV 180
CT **NATHANIEL, I** c 1630-1708

m 1) c 1652 **Ann Miller** ....-1680
m 2) 1682 **Elizabeth Pierpont**
....-a 1705
XVIII 134; XXXV 345
MA **THOMAS** 1640-1701 m 1663
Mary Gamblin 1641-....
XXIV 129

BADCOCK, see BABCOCK

BADGER
MA **GILES/GYLES** ....-1647
m 1642 **Elizabeth Greenleaf**
bp 1622-   ....
XX 161; XXVI 120

BADLAM
MA **WILLIAM** ....-....
m 2).... **Mary French** 1662-
a 1717/18
XXXII 223

BAGBY
VA **JOHN** 1619-1670 m 1640
____ ____ ....-....
XXXII 166; XXXIV 77

BAGG
MA **JOHN** ....-1683 m 1657
Hannah Burt 1641-1680
XXIX 272

BAILDON, see BELDING

BAILEY/BAILY/BAYLEY
MA **JAMES** c1612-1677
m a 1642 **Lydia** ____ ....-1704
XV 27; XIX 76
PA **JOEL BAILY** 1658-wp 1732
m 1687 **Ann Short** ....-....
XXI 95; XXV 177; XXIX 344
CT **JOHN** ....-p1696 m ....
Lydia Backus ....-a 1696

BAILEY/BAILY/BAYLEY-Cont.
　XXXIII 198
MA **JOHN BAYLEY Sr**
　c 1590/96-1651 m ....
　Eleanor Knight ....-....
　IV 138; XXXII 62; XXXVI 28;
　XXXIX 314
MA **JOHN, Jr** c 1613-1690/91
　m 1640 **Eleanor Emery** ....-
　a 1700
　XXXII 62
MA **RICHARD** c 1623-1647/50
　m ....**Edna Holsted** ....-p 1649
　XVII 14
MA **THOMAS BAYLEY** ....-1681
　m .... ＿＿ ＿＿ ....-....
　XXII 16; XXVI 8

BAILY, see BAILEY

BAKER
MA **ALEXANDER, Jr** 1607-1688
　m 1632 **Elizabeth Farrar** 1612-
　1691
　XXV 170; XXVII 140; XXXI
　61, 201; XXXIII 96
MA **CORNELIUS** ....-1716
　m 1652 **Hannah Woodbury**
　bp 1636- ....
　XXII 133; XXXIII 265
MA **EDWARD** c 1610-1687
　m a 1640 **Joan** ＿＿ ....-1693
　XVI 17; XIX 80
MA **FRANCIS** 1611-1696　m 1641
　Isabel Twining 1610- 1706
　XXX 283; XXXIV 80; XXXVIII
　122
CT **JOHN** ....-.... m ....
　Lydia Baysey ....-1700
　X 59
MA **JOHN** 1598-.... m ....
　Elizabeth ＿＿ 1606-p 1666
　XXVII 119

MD **MAURICE** ....-1700
　m .....
　Elizabeth Greenif ....-wd 1703
　XXXII 236
MA **THOMAS**....-1683 m ....
　Elizabeth ....-....
　X 134
MA **THOMAS** 1618-1700　m 1643
　Alice Dayton c 1620-1708/09
　XV 121; XVI 7; XVII 16, 23;
　XXIX 320
MA **WILLIAM** ....-1679 m 1661
　Mary ＿＿ ....-....
　XXXI 73

BALCH
MA **JOHN** 1579-1648 m1) 1625
　Margery Lovell ....- 1630
　VI 45/51; XXXI 180; XXXV
　315; XXXVI 340; XXXVII 35;
　XXXVIII 313

BALCOME
RI **ALEXANDER** ....-1711 m pr
　1654
　Jane (Holbrook) Albree ....-
　a 1711
　XX 143; XXXVIII 298

BALDWIN
MA **HENRY** ....-1697/98 m 1649
　Phebe Richardson bp 1632-
　1716
　XI 164
MA **JOHN** ....-1687 m 1655
　Mary Richardson bp 1638 -
　....
　V 45; XVI 61; XXXIII 239
MA **JOHN, Sr** ....-1681 m1) ....
　Mary ＿＿ -1652
　m2) a 1660 **Mary Bruen** 1622-
　1670
　VI 99/117; VIII 5; XX 132; XXV

BALDWIN-Cont.
    66; XXVII 164; XXX 275;
    XXXI 190
CT **JOHN** c 1630-....m 1653
    Hannah Birchard ....-....
    XXXII 69
CT/MA **JOSEPH, I** c 1609/10- 1684
    m1) 1636/40 **Hannah**
    Whitlock .... c 1645
    XVI 118; XXI 127; XXII 18;
    XXVIII 81; XXXIX 26;
    XXXX 169
CT **NATHANIEL** a 1632-1658
    m c 1649 **Mrs. Joanna Westcoat**
    ....- 1682
    XV 18
CT **RICHARD** bp 1622-1665
    m p 1642/43 **Elizabeth Alsop**
    a 1629-1688
    VI 9/11; IX 16; X 185, 276;
    XI 113; XXVI 199; XXVII 54;
    XXXIII 177; XXXV 105;
    XXXX 35

BALL
CT **ALLEN/ALLING** ....-1716
    m 1646 **Dorothy**
    Fujell/Fogal/Fugill ....-1690
    XXXIII 341; XXXV 213;
    XXXVI 48
NJ **EDWARD** 1644- p 1722/24
    m c 1664 **Abigail Blatcheley**
    1645/54-1699
    XXX 249; XXXX 99
MA **JOHN** c 1585-1655 m ....
    Joanna King ....-....
    XXVI 64; XXVII 17; XXXVII
    62; XXXIX 201; XXXX 183,
    184
VA **RICHARD** ....-.... m....
    Elizabeth Lorton ....-....
    XXXVII 25
VA **WILLIAM** c 1615-1680

    m 1638 **Hannah Atherold** ....-
    wd 1695
    VI 26/29, 28/31; XXXI 173;
    XXXIII 335; XXXIV 195, 198;
    XXXV 293; XXXVI 141;
    XXXVIII 143

BALLARD
MD **CHARLES** ....-1677 m ....
    Sarah Elsey Jordan ....-1734
    XXXIX 324
MA **WILLIAM** c 1603/17-1689
    m1) 1638 **Elizabeth** ____
    c 1609- ....
    m2) 1653 **Grace Berwick** ....-
    1694
    VII 11; IX 23; XIV 126; XX
    28; XXX 63, 104; XXXI 203;
    XXXVII 216

BALLOU
RI **MATURIN** 1610/20-p 1661
    m 1646/49 **Hannah Pike** ....-
    1715
    XVIII 127; XXII 25

BANCKER
NY **GERRIT** ....-1690/91
    m 1658 **Elizabeth Dirkse Van**
    Eps 1623-1693
    XXXIII 226

BANCROFT
MA **JOHN** ....-1637 m ....
    Jane ____ ....-....
    XIV 43
MA **THOMAS** ....-1684 m ....
    Hannah ____ ....-....
    XIV 59
MA **THOMAS** c1622/25-1691
    m 1647/48 **Elizabeth Metcalf**
    bp 1626-1711
    XXXIII 274; XXXVI 70;

BANCROFT-Cont.
   XXXX 116

BANGS
MA **EDWARD** 1591-1678
   m2) .... **Rebecca** _____ ....-....
   XXX 60

BANKESTOK see BANKSTON

BANKS
VA **ADAM** 1645/48-a 1690 m ....
   _____ _____ ....-....
   XXVI 31; XXXIV 273
CT **JOHN** c 1608-1685 m ....
   Mary Taintor ....-c 1640
   XX 72

BANKSTON/BANKESTOK/
BENKESTOK
PA **ANDREW/ANDRE** 1640-1706
   m 1668 **Gertrude Rambo**
   1650-c 1705/06
   XXX 119; XXXI 114; XXXIV
   231; XXXX 239, 370, 429

BANTA
NJ/NY **EPKE BANTA (JACOBS/E)**
   1615-1685
   m a 1655
   Tietske Dircksda/Sitske
   Drucksta c 1624-a 1686
   XXV 38; XXXI 225; XXXX
   226

BARBER
RI **JAMES** ....-.... m ....
   _____ _____ ....-....
   XV 104; XXVI 202
CT **THOMAS** 1614-1662 m 1640
   Jane/Joan _____ ....-1662
   XVI 12; XVII 8, 98; XIX 130

BARDWELL
MA **ROBERT** c 1647-1726 m 1676
   Mary Gull ....-1726
   XV 129; XXXVIII 121

BARKER
CT **EDWARD** ....-.... m ....
   Elizabeth _____ ....-....
   XII 97
RI **JAMES** 1617-1702 m 1644
   Barbara Dungan 1628-1662
   XXVIII 45
VA **JOHN, Sr** c 1604-a 1690 m ....
   _____ _____ ....-....
   XXXVII 186
MA **RICHARD** ....-1692/93 m 1688
   Joanna _____ ....-1687
   XIII 81; XXXVII 349
MA **ROBERT** 1616-1691m ....
   Lucy Williams ....-1681/91
   XXIV 133
DE **SAMUEL** 1648-1720 m ....
   _____ _____ ....-....
   XXVII 135

BARKSDALE
VA **WILLIAM** 1629-1694 m ....
   _____ _____ ....-1675
   XXX 227

BARLOW
MA **GEORGE** ....-1684 m p1667
   Mrs. Jane Besse/Busse/Bussi
   ....-p 1693
   V 134, 135; XII 51; XIV 68;
   XVI 41; XVII 46

BARNABY
MA **JAMES** ....-a 1677 m ....
   Lydia Bartlett 1647-....
   XIX 167; XXVII 171

BARNARD
MA **FRANCIS** c 1617-1698 m 1644
    Hannah Merrill/Marvin
    c 1623-c 1676
    XI 167, 174; XXXIV 67;
    XXXIX 206
PA **RICHARD** 1611-1698 m ....
    Frances _____ ....-....
    XXXIII 186, 315
MA **THOMAS** 1612/14-1677/82
    m .... _____ _____ ....-....
    XXXVIII 357

BARNES
MA **THOMAS** ....-1672 m ....
    Anna _____ ...._....
    XXIX 144
CT **THOMAS** 1615-1688/91
    m1) 1658 **Mary** _____ ....-....
    m2) 1662 **Mary Andrews/**
    Andrus 1643/44-p 1689
    XIV 124; XXXIX 115; XXXX
    265
CT **THOMAS** c 1623-1691/93
    m 1) 1647 **Mary** _____ ....-1676
    m 2) p 1676 **Elizabeth** _____
    ....-1690
    XV 48; XXII 86; XXVIII 24;
    XXXI 159
MA **THOMAS, Sr** c 1636-1679
    m 1661/62 **Abigail Goodenow**
    1642-1734
    III 11; IV 127; XXIV 127;
    XXVIII 188; XXXIII 296;
    XXXV 54
VA **THOMAS** ....-1683 m c 1665
    Diana (Bragg) ....-....
    XXXX 421
NY **WILLIAM** c 1635-1699/1700
    m 1665 **Elizabeth Mulford**
    1643-1723/24
    IV 112; XXXI 170;
    XXXIX 97, 343

BARNEY
MA **JACOB** 1601-1673 m ....
    Elizabeth _____ ....-....
    XXIII 12; XXXII 123

BARNS, see BARNES

BARNUM
CT **THOMAS** c 1625-1695 m2) 1662
    Sarah Hurd 1632-1718
    X 77; XX 46; XXXV 92

BARRELL
MA **GEORGE** ....-1643 m....
    Ann _____ ....-....
    XXXVII 157

BARRET
VA **WILLIAM** 1590-1640 m ....
    Ann Ferrell ....-....
    XXVII 47
VA **WILLIAM** 1623-1705 m ....
    Anne Ludwell 1651-1710
    XXIX 40

BARRETT
MA **HUMPHREY, Sr** 1592-1662
    m .... **Mary** _____ ....-1663
    XXXI 215
MD **JOHN, Sr** c 1651-p 1722 m ....
    Ann Hill ....-p 1722
    XXXI 76
MA **THOMAS** _____-1668 m ....
    Margaret _____ ....-1681
    VI 79/91; XXIX 238

BARRICK, see BARWICK

BARRICKLOW/ VAN BARKELO
NY **WILLEM JANS VAN**
    BARKELO ....-1683 m 2) 1666
    Leysebet Jansen c1650-....
    XXXVI 317

BARROWS
MA **JOHN** c 1609-1692
   m1) 1634 **Ann Thompson**
   bp 1598-   ....
   XIII 70; XXXVI 260

BARSTOW
MA **JOHN** c 1625-1657 m ....
   Hannah _____ ....-a 1657
   XXXVIII 6

BARTHOLOMEW
NJ/PA **GEORGE** ....-1689
   m2) a 1683 **Jane** _____ ....-....
   XXXVI 338
MA **WILLIAM** 1602/03-1680
   m....**Anna Lord** ....-1682
   XVIII 96; XXXVIII 339;
   XXXIX 226

BARTLETT
MA **HENRY** ....-....
   m .... **Mary Bush** ....-....
   XXIX 223
MA **JOHN** ....-1684 m c 1665
   Sarah Aldrich 1645/46-
   1684/85
   XXXII 124
MA **JOSEPH** c 1630-1701/02
   m 1668 **Mary Waite/Wayte**
   1645-1721
   XXIX 203; XXXIX 186
MA **RICHARD, I** 1575/90-1647
   m c 1608/10 **Joahan** _____ ....-
   1647
   XXII 159; XXX 153; XXXIV
   61; XXXVI 240; XXXIX 146;
   XXXX 259, 307
MA **ROBERT** c 1603/06-1676
   m c 1628/29 **Mary Warren**
   c 1610/12-1677/83
   XV 30; XXXV 288; XXXIX
   11

MA/CT **ROBERT** 1603-1675/76
   m .... **Anne** _____ ....-1676
   XVIII 128; XXXV 157;
   XXXX 454

BARTON
MA/NH **EDWARD** ....-a 1671/73
   m .... **Elizabeth** _____ ....-p 1671
   XXIV 36; XXV 15; XXXI 155
NY **ROGER** 1620-1688 m ....
   Mary Lounsberry ....-.....
   XIX 88
RI **RUFUS** ....-1648
   m .... **Margaret** _____ ....-....
   XXXVII 133

BARWICK/BARRICK
MD **JOHN, Sr** c 1640/44-
   p 1712/17
   m c 1673 _____ _____ ....-....
   XXXVII 49; XXXX 422

BASCOM
CT/MA **THOMAS** ....-1682
   m .... **Avis** _____ ....-1676
   VII 14; XXX 157

BASS/E
VA **NATHANIEL** bp 1589-1654
   m 1613 **Mary Jordon/Jourdan**
   1613-1629/30
   XXXV 247; XXXVIII 52, 82
MA **SAMUEL** 1600/01-1694 m....
   Anne _____ 1600-1693
   XXIII 77; XXXVIII 53

BASSETT
CT **JOHN** ....-1653
   m .... **Margery** _____ ....-....
   XXX 34
CT **THOMAS** c 1597-c 1670 m....
   Lydia Alcock ....-....
   XXIII 31

BASSETT-Cont.
MA **WILLIAM, Sr** bp 1600-
wp 1667 m1) c 1621
Elizabeth Tilden ....-1648
II 47; XVIII 105; XXX 185;
XXXIII 53; XXXIV 162
CT **WILLIAM** 1626-1684
m 1648 **Hannah (Dickerman)**
Ives ....-....
XXXIII 139
MA **WILLIAM** ....-c 1734
m .... **Elizabeth** _____ ....-....
XXXVI 23

BATCHELDER/ BACHELDER/
BACHELER/ BACHILER
BATCHILER
MA **JOSEPH BATCHELLER**
c 1575/1600-1647 m ....
Elizabeth _____ ....-p 1644/57
IV 95; V 105; XVI 133; XXI
43; XXVII 23, 69; XXIX 389
MA/NH **STEPHEN** c 1561-
1656/60
m1) by 1590 **Anna Bate** ....-
c 1610/24
m2).... **Helen** _____ ....-....
X 99; XVII 150; XX 83; XXI
16, 177; XXV 295; XXXII 54;
XXXIII 255; XXXVIII 340;
XXXX 330

BATCHELLER, see
BATCHELDER
BATCHILER, see BATCHELDER

BATE
NJ **WILLIAM** c 1635-1700
m c 1660 _____ _____ ....-....
XXXV 131

BATEMAN
MA **ELEAZER** 1662-1751 m 1686

Elizabeth Wright 1664-....
XXXIV 114

BATES
MA **CLEMENT** bp 1595-1669/71
m .... **Ann Blythe/Bliss** 1595-
1669/74
XXI 28; XXIV 164; XXIX 182;
XXXIV 165; XXXV 59;
XXXIX 54
MA **EDWARD** c 1605-1686
m a 1639 **Susanna** _____
pr 1605/10-p 1686
XXXI 15; XXXIV 68; XXXVII
252
VA **JOHN** c 1598/99-wp 1667
m 1680 **Elizabeth Winston** ....-
....
XXXV 189; XXXVII 43

BATTAILE
VA **JOHN** c 1658-1708
m2)c 1690 **Elizabeth Smith** ....-
....
XXV 90, 130;XXVI 38, 39, 40

BATTLE
VA **JOHN** ....-1690 m ....
Elizabeth _____ ....-....
XXXIV 108; XXXV 307;
XXXVII 108

BAUDOUIN/BOUDOIN/ BOWEN
ME/MA **PIERRE** ....-wp 1719
m a 1676 **Elizabeth** _____ 1643-
wd 1717
XXXV 364

BAUGHN/BAUGHAN
VA **JAMES** c 1625-1672/78
m ....**Thommassie** _____ c 1625-
p 1687
XXXV 337

BAYLDON, see BELDING

BAYLES
NY **JOHN** 1617-1682 m ....
    Rebecca _____ ....-....
    XXXII 138

BAYLOR
VA **JOHN** ....-.... m ....
    _____ _____ ....-....
    XXXVIII 301

BAYLEY, see BAILEY
BAYNE, see BEAN
BAYNHAM, see BYNUM

BEACH
CT **JOHN** 1615/23-1677/80 m 1650
    Mary Staples ....-p 1668
    V 65; XIX 149; XXXII 227;
    XXXIII 303
CT **RICHARD** c 1618-c 1688
    m 1641 **Katherine (Cook) Hull**
    ....-....
    XXIV 10
CT **THOMAS** 1622-1662 m 1652/54
    Sarah Platt ....-1670
    XIV 15; XVII 44; XXI 24;
    XXVIII 77; XXIX 343; XXXV
    85

BEAL, see BEALL
BEALE, see BEALL

BEALL/BEAL/BEALE/BEALS
MD **ALEXANDER** 1649-1744
    m 1685 **Elizabeth Coombs/Dick**
    ....- 1743
    X 66, 90, 102, 270; XXIX 302;
    XXXI 267; XXXVI 263
MD **JAMES** bp 1652-1725 m 1693
    Sarah Pearce 1701-1761
    XXI 108; XXIV 127

MD **JOHN BEALE/S** 1588-1688
    m2)1630 **Nazareth (Hobart)**
    Turner 1600-1658
    XIII 122; XXXI 152
NH **JOSEPH BEALE** ....-....
    m .... _____ _____ ....-....
    XXX 57
MD **NINIAN** c 1625-1717
    m1) c 1649 **Elizabeth Gordon**
    ....-a 1667
    m2) 1670 **Ruth Moore** ....-....
    XIV 106; XXIX 178
VA **THOMAS BEALE, I** c 1621-
    1688
    m 1646 **Alice** _____ ....- wp 1702
    XXXIX 335
ME **WILLIAM BEALS** ....-1653
    m.... _____ _____ ....-....
    X 155, 251

BEALS, see BEALL

BEAN/BAYNE/BEANE
NH **JOHN** c 1634-1718
    m2) c 1660 **Margaret** _____
    c 1640-1714/18
    XXI 15; XXXIV 319
MD **JOHN BAYNE** ....-....
    m .... _____ **Ebsworth** ....-....
    XXVI 198
MA **LEWIS, Sr** ....-1677
    m 1668 **Mary Mills** ....-1689
    XXVII 26
MD **WALTER BAYNE** ....-
    a 1670
    m1) .... _____ _____ ....-....
    m2) 1661 **Eleanor Weston** ....-
    wp 1701
    XXVI 198

BEANE, see BEAN

BEARCE
MA **AUSTIN** 1618-a 1697
m 1639 **Mary Hyanna** ....-....
XXXIII 205

BEARD
CT **JOHN** c 1630-1690 m 1653
Anna Hawley ....-1698
I 44; XII 22; XXXI 214

BEARDSLEE, see BEARDSLEY

BEARDSLEY/BEARDSLEE
CT **WILLIAM** c 1605-wp 1661
m 1631/32
Marie/Mary Harvie/Harvey
1605/09-wp 1661/68
IV 123; V 98; VI 55/62; VIII 16;
IX 35; X 96; XVII 54; XXV 168,
169; XXVI 43, 136, 260, 261,
262; XXVII 183; XXVIII 71;
XXIX 171; XXX 260; XXXI 303;
XXXIII 142, 190, 333; XXXIV
137, 215, 255; XXXVI 47;
XXXVIII 104; XXXIX 325

BEATTY
NY **JOHN** ....wp 1721 m c 1691
Susanna Asfordby ....-1742/45
XXVII 76

BEAUCHAMP
MD **EDMUND** ....-1691
m 1668 **Sarah Dixon** ....-....
XXVII 65; XXXIX 97

BEAUFORD, see BUFORD

BEAVEN/BEVAN
MD **CHARLES** ....-1699 m ....
Mary Marsham/Marshall ....-
c 1712
XIII 98; XVI 22, 81; XIX 19

BECKER/BECKKER
NY **JAN JURGERISON** ....-
c 1697 m a 1660
Maria Adriance ....-....
XII 59; XXIX 132; XXXI 124

BECKKER, see BECKER

BECKWITH
CT **MATTHEW, Sr** 1610-1680/81
m c 1635/37 **Elizabeth** _____ ....-
a 1690
VIII 24; X 301; XXIII 38; XXIX
11; XXXIV 238; XXXVII 28

BEDFORD
VA **WILLIAM** 1600-....
m .... _____ _____ ....-....
XXX 214; XXXII 291

BEDWELL
VA **ROBERT** ----c 1686
m1) **Ann Colby** ....-1669/80
XXXV 244

BEEBE
CT **JAMES** c 1641-1728 m 1679
Sarah Benedict ....-1700
XXXX 112
CT **JOHN, II** 1628-1714 m a 1660
Abigail Yorke c 1638-p 1690
XXXII 122
CT **SAMUEL** 1633-1722 m a 1662
Mary Keeney 1640- p 1683
XX 76; XXXII 294

BEECHER
CT **JOHN** 1590/1600-1637/38 m....
Hannah Potter 1590/1600-1659
XXII 107; XXIII 51; XXIV 120;
XXX 218

BEEKMAN
NY **WILHELMUS** 1623-1707
    m 1649 **Catalina de Boogh** ....-
1733
XII 19

BEEMAN
MA **SIMON** ....-1675 m 1654
    Alice Young ....-1708
XV 139; XIX 150

BEERS
CT/MA **ANTHONY** ....-1676/79
    m.... **Elizabeth** _____ ....-p 1679
XVI 74; XVIII 118; XX 47;
XXXV 55

BELCHER
MA **ANDREW, Sr** 1613/14-1673
    m2) **Elizabeth Danforth** ....-
....
XXXIII 126
MA **GREGORY** 1606-1664/74
    m .... **Catherine** _____ ....-c 1679
X 303; XIII 6; XXXVII 220
MA **JEREMIAH** c 1613-1692/93
    m .... **Mary Clifford** 1610-
1645/52
XII 89

BELDEN, see BELDING

**BELDING/BAILDON/
BAYLDON/BELDON**
CT **RICHARD BAYLDON**
    bp 1591-c1655
    m .... _____ _____ ....-1650
XVII 97; XVIII 147; XXII 138;
XXXI 306
CT **WILLIAM BELDEN** c 1622-
1660/65 m ....
    Tomasin _____ ....-....
IV 118

BELDON, see BELDING

BELKNAP
MA **ABRAHAM** bp 1589/90-1643
    m 1617 **Mary Stallion** bp 1595-
1671
XXXVI 230; XXXIX 130

BELL
CT **FRANCIS** ....-1689/90
    m ..... **Rebecca** _____ ....-1684
XIX 63; XXXII 16
VA **ROBERT** ....-1624
    m .... _____ _____ ....-....
XII 15

BELLINGER
SC **EDMUND, I** 1657-1707
    m c 1680 **Sarah Cartwright** ....-
....
XXXV 104
NY **JOHANNES** c 1660-.... m ....
    Anna Maria Margaretha ....-....
XXXVI 241

BELLOWS
MA **JOHN** c 1623- wp 1683
    m 1655 **Mary Wood** ....-1707
X 293; XXVI 83; XXIX 279;
XXX 147; XXXVII 228, 375

BEMIS
MA **JOSEPH** 1619-1684 m ....
    Sarah _____ ....-c 1712
XXIII 22; XXXI 98

BENEDICT
CT/NY **THOMAS** 1617-1689/90
    m c 1638/40
    **Mary Bridgham/Bridgum/
Bridgman** c 1616/19-1717/1719
X 40, 121, 166; XXVI 78;   XXX
64, XXXVI 24; XXXVII 78, 172,

BENEDICT-Cont.
221, 292

BENHAM
MA/CT **JOHN** ....-1659/61 m ....
Margery Alcott ....-....
XXIX 367; XXXIV 174; XXXVI
257, 269
CT **JOSEPH** ....-1703 m 1657
Winifred King ....-....
XXXIV 174

BENJAMIN
MA **JOHN (WATERMAN)**
BENJAMIN
c 1580/98-1645 m 1619
Abigail Eddye c 1600-1687
XX 22; XXXV 199; XXXVIII 95

BENKESTOK, see **BANKSTON**
BENNET, see **BENNETT**

BENNET/BENNETT
MA **HENRY** c 1629- p 1707
m c 1650
Lydia Perkins ....-1672
XIII 8
CT **ISAAC** 1650-1720 m 1683
Elizabeth Rose 1658/59-1733
X 305
MA/CT **JAMES** ....-1659 m c 1639
Hannah Wheeler ....-....
XIX 136; XXVII 20
VA/MA **JOHN, Sr** 1641-1717
m 1671 **Deborah Grover** 1648-
1717/18
XXXIII 105
VA **THOMAS** c 1590-1634/35
m 1624 **Alice (____) Pierce**
c 1592-....
XXXV 309; XXXVI 16; XXXVII
52
VA **WILLIAM** c 1659-....

m 1684 **Mary Smith** ....-....
XXXX 29
NY **WILLIAM ADRIANCE** ....-
liv 1654 m ....
Mary Ann Badger Thomas ....-
....
XVIII 56

BENSON
MA **JOHN** 1608-1678 m 1633
Mary Williams c 1610-1681
XXXVII 331

BENT
MA **JOHN** 1596-1672 m c 1624
Martha Blanchard 1598-1679
XII 13; XIX 127; XXVII 104;
XXVIII 21; XXXVI 208; XXXX
373

BENTLEY/BENTLY
RI **WILLIAM BENTLY** ....-c 1720
m .... **Sarah Litchfield** ....-....
XVII 100

BENTON
CT **ANDREW** bp 1620-1683
m1) 1649 **Hannah Stocking** ....-
1670
X 13; XXXIV 202; XXXVII 310
CT **EDWARD** c 1620-1680 m....
Anne ____ ....-1671
XXXIX 314

BERGEN
NY **HANS HANSEN** ....-p 1653
m 1639 **Sarah Rapalje** 1625-
c 1685
XXXII 24

**BERGH/VAN DEN BERGH/
VANDENBURG**
NY **GYSBERTSE CORNELIUS**

BERGH/VAN DEN BERGH/
VANDENBURG-Cont.
VAN DEN BERGH
 c 1620- p 1685 m....

 _____ _____ ....-....
XXXX 8

BERKHOVEN, see BREWER

BERNARD
VA **WILLIAM** ....w p 1704
 m .... _____ _____ ....-....
 XXXII 234; XXXIV 250

BERRIEN
NY **CORNELIUS JANTSEN**
 c 1640-1688 m 1664
 Jannetje Strycker 1642-....
 XXXIX 294

BERRY
MD **JAMES** ....-c1685
 m .... **Elizabeth** _____ ....-....
 VI 83/96
MA **THADDEUS** ....-1718 m ....
 Hannah Farrar ....-....
 XII 104; XIV 100

BERRYMAN
VA **JOHN** ....-a 1679/90 m ....
 Jane Tucker ....-....
 XXX 56

BERTHOLF
NY **GUILIAEM** 1656-1724 m 1677
 Martyntje Vermeulen ....-....
 XVI 104; XVII 42; XVIII 70

BETTS
CT **THOMAS** bp 1615-1688
 m c 1643
 Mary _____ ....-p 1723/24
 XXXVII 313; XXXVIII 347;

XXXX 172

BEVAN, see BEAVEN
BEVIER, see BOVIER
BEVILL, see BEVILLE

BEVILLE/BEVILL
VA **ESSEX, Sr** 1637/40- wp 1683
 m c 1669 **Amy (Ann) Butler** ....-
 a 1689/90
 XXXI 95; XXXV 84, 185;
 XXXVI 273; XXXVII 112;
 XXXVIII 268; XXXIX 253

BIBB
VA **BENJAMIN** 1610- a 1702/04
 m .... **Mary** _____ ....-p 1702
 XII 43, 60; XVI 11; XIX 128;
 XX 113; XXII 108; XXIX 16;
 XXXVI 113

BIDDLE
NJ **WILLIAM** c 1630-1712 m 1665
 Sarah Kemp c 1634-1709
 XIII 114

BIDWELL
CT **JOHN** c 1618-1687 m 1640
 Sarah Wilcox (Willcockes)
 c 1618-1690
 VI 31/34; XXXIII 216; XXXIV
 97

BIGELOW/BIGLO/BIGLOW/
BIGLOUGH
MA **JOHN** 1616-1703 m1)1642
Mary Warren (Warner) 1628-
 1691
 IV 158; IX 5; XVII 136; XIX
 89; XXV 199; XXVI 60, 174;
 XXIX 33; XXXI 53, 188;
 XXXIII 339; XXXVII 303

BIGGER
VA **WILLIAM** c 1650-c 1679 m ....
   Martha Woodward c 1657-1727
   XXXIX 218

BIGGS
NY **JOHN** ....-p 1687
   m .... **Mary Hall** ....-....
   XXXI 12

BIGLO, see BIGELOW
BIGLOW, see BIGELOW
BIGLOUGH, see BIGELOW
BIGSBY, see BIXBY

BILL
MA/CT **PHILIP** c 1620-1689
   m .... **Hannah** _____ ....-1709
   XIV 16

BILLING, see BILLINGS

BILLINGS/BILLING
MA **ROGER** 1618-1683
   m .... **Hannah** _____ ....-1662
   XVIII 110
MA **ROGER BILLING** 1620-1683
   m 1640 **Mary** _____ 1622- p 1683
   XXVI 128, 206
MA **WILLIAM** c 1629-1713
   m 1657/58 **Mary** _____ ....-1718
   X 53

BILLINGSLEY
MD **FRANCIS** 1620-1684/95
   m c 1647**Ann** _____ 162_-a 1668
   XXVI 124; XXVIII 37; XXXV
   137, 145; XXXIX 243; XXXX
   93, 324, 360

BILLUPS
VA **GEORGE** c 1625/30-c 1684
   m 1655

   Sarah _____ ....-p 1684
   XV 80; XXXIX 72

BINGHAM
CT **THOMAS** 1642-1729/30
   m 1666 **Mary Rudd** 1648-1726
   XIII 46; XV 102

BIRCHARD
MA/CT **THOMAS** 1595-1657 m ....
   Mary Robinson/Robertson
   1597/1602- c 1655
   XVIII 59; XXXV 187

BIRD
MA **THOMAS** c 1613-1667 m .....
   Anne _____ ....-1673
   XXIV 122; XXXIV 99; XXXV
   279; XXXVII 376

BIRGE
CT **RICHARD** ....-1651 m 1641
   Elizabeth Gaylord ....-1675
   XXXIV 47

BISHOP
MA **EDWARD** ....-a 1715 m a 1646
   Hannah More ....-....
   XXI 18
CT **JAMES** ....-1691 m c 1650
   Mary Lewen ....-1664
   XXXVII 179
CT **JOHN** 1604-1661 m ....
   Anne _____ ....-1676
   XII 49
MA **THOMAS** ....-1670 m ....
   Margaret _____ ....-c 1681
   XVIII 28

BISSELL
CT **JOHN, Sr** 1589/91-1677
   m1).... **Mary Drake** ....-1641
   IV 132; XXIV 112; XXV 214;

BISSELL-Cont.
XXVIII 104, 166; XXXI 294;
XXXIX 214; XXXX 241

BIXBY/BIGSBY
MA JOSEPH bp 1621-1701 m 1647
Sarah (Wyatt) Heard ....-....
XXXIV 291; XXXIX 105

BLACKFORD
NJ SAMUEL c 1640 wp 1711/12
m .... Anna Smalley ....-....
XXXIV 181; XXXV 228;
XXXVI 102

BLACKISTON/E
MD NEHEMIAH p 1635-1693
m 1669
Elizabeth Gerard 1653-1715
XXXX 122

BLACKMAN/ BLACKMUN
MA JOHN c 1625- p 1675
m2) c 1655 Sarah _____ 1630-
1712
XXXVI 322; XXXVII 63;
XXXIX 145

BLACKMER/BLACKMORE
MA WILLIAM c 1636-1676 m 1666
Elizabeth Banks/es c 1640-
p 1687
XXXIV 178, 274; XXXV 28

BLACKMORE, see BLACKMER
BLACKMUN, see BLACKMAN

BLACKWELL
VA JOSEPH 1615-p 1680
m .... _____ _____ ....-....
XI 176, 177; XXXVI 192;
XXXX 128, 141
NJ/NY ROBERT c 1650-1717/19

m 1676 Mary Manningham ....-
....
XVII 68; XXIX 232

BLAISDELL/BLASDEL
ME RALPH BLASDEL c 1600-
1648/51 m ....
Elizabeth _____ ....-c 1667
XVI 106; XX 6; XXII 74; XXV
283; XXVII 29; XXIX 69;
XXXIV 73

BLAKE
NH JASPER 1647-1673/74 m ....
Deborah Dalton ....-1678
XXXI 311
CT JOHN c 1652-1690 m 1673
Sarah Hall ....-1726
XIX 72
VA THOMAS, I ....- bet 1707/09
m ....
Alice/Alise _____ ....-p 1708
XXXII 83
MA WILLIAM bp 1594-1663
m 1617 Agnes (Thorn/e)
Band/Bland bp 1594-c 1678
XIII 117; XXIV 16; XXX 72;
XXXIV 313

BLAKER/BLEEKER/ BLEIKER
PA JOHANNES BLEIKER
c 1660-1741
m .... Judith _____ ....-....
XVIII 38

BLAKESLEE/BLAKSLEE
CT SAMUEL 1620/25-1672 m 1650
Hannah Potter a 1636- 1723
XI 11; XV 133; XVII 129; XX
26; XXII 35; XXVII 123;
XXXVI 293; XXXVIII 80

BLAKSLEE, see BLAKESLEE

BLANCHARD
VA/NC **BENJAMIN, Sr** 1665-
  a 1719 m 1685
  Catherine _____ 1665-a 1719
  XXXIX 298; XXXX 160
MA **THOMAS** a 1620-1654
  m .... **Agnes Brent** ....-1639
  XXIII 55, 64

BLAND
VA **JAMES** ....- wd 1708 m ....
  Margaret _____ ....-p 1708
  XXXVII 218
VA **THEODORIC(K)** bp 1629-1671
  m c 1660/63 **Anne Bennet**
  c 1641-1687
  XXXIV 118; XXXV 133, 134;
  XXXVI 265; XXXVII 139;
  XXXVIII 93
MD **THOMAS** 1634-1700
  m .... _____ _____ ....-....
  XXXVII 312

BLANDEN, see BLANDING

BLANDING/BLANDEN/
BLANTINE/ BLANTON
VA **THOMAS BLANTON** ....-
  wp 1697 m 1670
  Jane Saunders ....-....
  XXXV 52
MA **WILLIAM** ....-1662
  m .... **Phoebe** _____ ....-....
  XXX 271; XXXI 58

BLANTINE, see BLANDING
BLANTON, see BLANDING
BLASDELL, see BLAISDELL

BLAUVELT
NY **GERRIT HENDRICKSEN**
  1620/23-wp 1685 m 1646
  Marretje Lambertse Moll ....-

1674/79
VIII 17; XIV 35; XXX 80;
XXXIV 149; XXXIX 119

BLEDSOE/PLETSOE
VA **GEORGE** ....wp 1705
  m a 1684 **Anne** _____ ....-p 1691
  XXX 205

BLEEKER, see BLAKER
BLEIKER, see BLAKER

BLISH/BLUSH
MA **ABRAHAM** ....-1683
  m .... **Anne** _____ ....-....
  XXVII 125

BLISS
MA **JONATHAN** c 1625/26-1687
  m c 1648 **Miriam Harmon** ....-
  1706
  XXV 289; XXXVII 345
MA **THOMAS** ....-1649
  m .... **Mistress Ide** ....-....
  XVI 99, XXXI 188
MA/CT **THOMAS** c 1580/90-a 1650
  m c 1612/15 **Margaret**
  Lawrence/Hulins 1594-1684
  XXII 149; XXX 115; XXXX 6

BLODGETT
MA **THOMAS** c 1604/05-1642
  m.... **Susan/Susanna** _____
  c 1607-1660/61
  XVI 28; XXIII 6; XXXVIII 201,
  281; XXXX 368

BLOOD
MA **JAMES** c 1605-1682
  m .... **Ellen** _____ ....-....
  XXVI 276; XXVII 63
MA **JAMES** a 1639-1683
  m ....**Elizabeth Wheeler** ....-1674

BLOOD-Cont.
  XVII 38
MA **RICHARD** c 1617-1683
    m 1642 **Isabel** _____ 1606-....
    IX 17; XXIV 59; XXXV 33;
    XXXVI 26; XXXVII 327

BLOOM
NY **BARENT JANSEN** 1611-1665
    m 1641**Styntie Pieters** ....-p 1674
    XXXIII 94

BLOUNT
NC **JAMES** ....-1686 m1) c 1665
    _____ _____ ....-....
    XXXI 172

BLOW
VA **GEORGE** ....-a 1675
    m .... **Marjorie** _____ ....-....
    XXV 206

BLUSH, see BLISH

BOARDMAN/BORDMAN/
BOREMAN
MA **SAMUEL** bp 1615-1673
    m ....**Mary Betts** ....-1684
    XXXIII 322
MA **THOMAS** bp 1601-c 1673
    m .... **Margaret** _____ ...-1679
    XIX 40

BOBET, see BABBITT
BOCHOLTE, see BOOKHOUT

BOCKEE/BOKEE/BOCQUET
NY **JEROME** a 1621-p 1667
    m1)1641 **Anne L'Agache**
    a 1626-a 1644
    XI 42; XII 25

BODDIE, see BODIE

BODDIE/BODIE
VA **WILLIAM BODDIE**
    bp 1633-wp 1717
    m2)1683/84
    Elizabeth _____ 1668-1699
    XXXI 297; XXXV 161; XXXIX
    271

BODFISH
MA **ROBERT** ....-1651
    m .... **Bridget** _____ ....-....
    XXVIII 182, 183

BOGAERT, see BOGART

BOGARDUS
NY **EVERARDUS** 1607-1647/48
    m 1638/42
    Anneke/Annetjen (Webber)
    Jansen 1602/05-1663
    XIII 84; XXIV 39, 162; XXV
    299

BOGART/BOGAERT
NY **TUNIS GYSBERTEN**
    BOGAERT c 1625-1685
    m1) pr 1655 **Sara (Rapalje)**
    Bergen 1625-a 1687
    XXVI 270
NY **CORNELISE JAN BOGAERT**
    a 1661-c 1681 m ....
    Geesje Willemse ....-c1683
    XXXVII 314
NY **JANS LAURENS (LOUE)**
    1630-c 1708 m....
    Cornelia Everts ....-c 1708
    XXXV 244

BOKEE, see BOCKEE

BOLLES
ME **JOSEPH** 1608-1678
    m 1640 **Mary Howell** 1624-p

BOLLES-Cont.
  1684
  XXXIII 48

BOLLING
VA **ROBERT** 1646-1709
  m1)1675 **Jane Rolfe** ....-....
  m2)1680 **Anne Smith** 1654-....
  VII 40; XIII 94; XVII 75;
  XXXIV 19

BOND
MA **JOHN** bp 1624-1674
  m 1649 **Hester Blakeley** ....-....
  XXX 292
MD **PETER** ....-1706
  m.... _____ _____ ....-....
  XXII 49
MA **WILLIAM** bp 1625-1695
  m 1649/50
  Sarah Biscoe ....-1692/93
  XXXIII 318; XXXX 233

BONNELL/ BOUNELL
MA **WILLIAM** ....-p 1669
  m .... **Anne Wilmot** ....-1653/54
  XII 24

BONNER
VA **THOMAS** c 1617- wp 1685
  m .... **Mary** _____ ....-....
  XXXVIII 251

BONSALL
PA **RICHARD** bp 1641-1699
  m ....
  Mary Wood ....-1698
  XXIX 153; XXXIII 326

BOOKER
VA **RICHARD** 1652-1704
  m1)....**Rebecca Leake** ....-
  a 1694

  m2) 1694 **Hannah Hand** ....-
  ....
  XXI 156; XXX 275; XXXIV
  74; XXXVI 149

**BOOKHOUT/BOCHOLTE/
BUCKOUT**
NY **JAN BOCHOLTE** ....-
  a 1694/95
  m .... **Hannah** _____ ....-p 1694/95
  XXXIII 34

BOOMER
RI **MATTHEW** ....-....
  m .... **Eleanor** _____ ....-....
  XXXIV 28

BOONE/BOON
MD **HUMPHREY** ....-1709
  m a 1672
  Rebecca Burle ....-1709
  XXXIX 73
VA **THOMAS BOON** c 1648- 1723
  m .... **Elizabeth** _____ ....-....
  XXXVIII 195

BOOTH/BOOTHE
VA **ADAM** ....-a 1703
  m a 1690
  Miss Barret ....-a 1703
  XXXII 46
NY **JOHN** 1610-c 1689/90
  m .... **Mary** _____ ....-p 1691
  XIV 73; XXV 173; XXXVII
  332
CT **RICHARD BOOTHE** 1607-
  p 1689
  m1)c 1640 **Elizabeth Hawley**
  ....-p 1661
  IV 16; V 61, 86, 218; XVI 139

**BOOTHE, see BOOTH
BORDMAN, see BOARDMAN**

BORDEN
RI **RICHARD** c 1595/1601-1671
 m 1625 **Joan Fowle (Fowler)**
 1604-1688
 XXXVIII 78, 92; XXXIX 117

BOREMAN, see BOARDMAN

BOSCH/TER BOSCH
NY **JAN (TER BOSCH)** 1626-
 c 1678 m 1663
 Rachel Farnelje (Vermilye)
 1637-a 1756
 XXXX 446

BOSTON
MD/VA **HENRY** c 1620-1676
 m c 1655 m1)**Anne Moore** ....-
 1671/73
 XXXVI 300; XXXVII 11

BOSTWICK
CT/NY **ARTHUR** bp 1603- p 1680
 m1)1627/28 **Jane Whittel** ....-
 ....
 VI 27/30; XXXVII 166

BOSWORTH
MA **JONATHAN, Sr** c 1613-
 1687/88 m ....
 Elizabeth ____ 1614-1705
 XXXVI 170; XXXVIII 252;
 XXXX 221
MA **NATHANIEL** c 1615-1693
 m .... **Mary** ___ ....-....
 XVI 13

BOTSFORD
CT **HENRY** bp 1608-1685
 m .... **Elizabeth** ____ ....-1690
 XXIX 126; XXX 52

BOUCQUET, see BOCKEE

BOULDEN
MD **WILLIAM** ....-1677/79
 m .... ____ ____ ....-....
 XXXI 223

BOURNE
VA **JOHN, II** ....-.... m ....
 Elizabeth (Johnson?) ....-p 1721
 XXV 138
MA **RICHARD** bp 1610-a 1682
 m 1637 **Bathsheba Hallett** ....-
 1670
 XXX 138; XXXX 295
VA **WILLIAM, I** c 1650-1716
 m1).... **Miss Crump** ....-....
 m2)....**Mary Vaughn** ....-1711
 XXXVIII 275; XXXX 238

BOUTELLE, see BOUTWELL

BOUTON
CT **JOHN** c 1580-....
 m .... **Alice** ____ c 1610-....
 XXXII 67
CT **JOHN** 1615-wd 1705/p 1706
 m 1656/57 **Abigail Marvin**
 1637/38-p 1680
 X 6; XIII 64; XXXII 67

BOUTWELL/ BOUTELLE
MA **JAMES BOUTELLE** a 1625-
 wd 1651 m ....
 Alice ____ ....-.....
 X 166; XIX 94; XXVII 172;
 XXVIII 106; XXXIII 100

BOVIER/BEVIER
NY **LOUIS** ....-1720 m 1673
 Marie Le Blanc ....-1689
 XXXIII 83

BOWDEN/BAUDOUIN
MA **MICHAEL** c 1652-1740

BOWDEN/BAUDOUIN-Cont.
    m 1669 **Sarah Nourse** ....-....
    XXXVII 326
ME/MA **PIERRE BAUDOUIN** ....-
    wp 1719 m a 1676
    Elizabeth _____ 1643-1720
    XXX 199; XXXIV 34; XXXV
    364

BOWDLE
MD **THOMAS** c 1639-1696
    m1)1676 **Joanna Loftus** a 1640-
    a 1682
    XI 6, 127; XXI 22; XXII 133

BOWDOIN, see BOWDEN

BOWEN
MA **GRIFFITH** 1605-a 1676 m 1629
    Margaret Fleming 1607-1684
    XXII 56
MA **RICHARD** c 1585/1600-
    1674/75 m1)c 1621 **Ann** _____
    c 1600-c 1646
    IV 110; V 67, 261; XX 34; XXI
    67; XXIX 198; XXX 279;
    XXXIV 219

BOWLES
VA **JOHN, I** ....-1664
    m .... _____ _____ ....-....
    XXVIII 86

BOWMAN
MA **FRANCIS** 1630-1687 m ....
    Martha (Palmer) Sherman
    1641-....
    VIII 33
MA **NATHANIEL** 1608-1682
    m .... _____ _____ ....-....
    VIII 33
VA **ROBERT** c 1600-1667/71
    m .... _____ _____ ....-....

XXXVII 336; XXXVIII 197

BOWNE
MA **WILLIAM** ....-1677
    m .... **Ann** _____ ....-a 1669
    XIX 51

BOYCE/BUYS
NY/NJ **ADRIAEN PIETERSE
    BUYS** ....-.... m 1672
    **Tryntie Hendrickse
    Oosteroom** 1654-p 1697
    XXXI 160

BOYD/BOYDE
MD **JOHN** c 1650-1705
    m .... **Mary** _____ ....-c 1772
    XXX 87

BOYDE, see BOYD

BOYDEN
MA **THOMAS** 1613-....
    m .... **Frances** _____ ....-1658
    XVII 142; XXX 129

BOYKIN
VA **EDWARD** .... wp 1728 m ....
    Ann (?Gwaltney) ....-....
    XIX III; XXXVII 65
VA **EDWARD, Sr** c 1650-1725
    m c 1675 **Ann Marshall** 1652-
    1730
    XXI 166; XXV 226; XXXVIII
    126

BOYLSTON
MA **THOMAS** 1615-1653
    m.... **Sarah** _____ ....-....
    XXXVII 167

BOYNTON
MA **JOHN** 1614-1670 m c 1644

BOYNTON-Cont.
Ellen/Helen Pell ....-p 1660
IV 57; VI 35/40; XXI 128; XXV
203; XXIX 222
MA **WILLIAM** 1606-1686 m ....
Elizabeth Jackson ....-1687
XXXIX 66

BRACEY/BRESSIE
VA **WILLIAM BRESSIE** c 1615-
p 1700
m .... _____ _____ ....-....
XXXVIII 20

BRADBURY
ME/MA **THOMAS** 1610-1695
m 1636 **Mary Perkins** 1620-
1700
I 31,40; II 34; XVII 143;
XVIII 89; XXXIV 240

BRADFORD
MA **ROBERT** c 1627-1707
m .... **Martha** _____ ....-....
XV 17
MA **WILLIAM** c 1652-1717 m 1676
Rachel Rayment/Raymond
....-....
XXXV 143; XXXIX 41, 169
MA **WILLIAM** bp 1589-1657
m2)1623 **Alice (Carpenter)**
Southworth c 1590-1670
IX 50; XXIV 104; XXV 43;
XXVIII 164; XXXVII 249;
XXXVIII 202; XXXIX 1;
XXXX 419

BRADLEY
CT **FRANCIS** ....-1689
m .... **Ruth Barlow** ....-....
XIV 122; XXVI 173
MD **HENRY** ....-a 1679
m .... **Mary** _____ ....-p 1679

XX 120
CT **ISAAC** 1650-1712/13 m ....
Elizabeth _____ 1656-1712/13
XII 92; XXXV 218
CT **STEPHEN** 1642-1702
m1) 1663 **Hannah Smith** ....-
169_
XI 150; XX 80; XXXI 147
CT **WILLIAM** c 1620-1691 m 1645
Alice Prichard a 1635-1692
VI 23/25; XI 71; XXI 92; XXVII
28; XXX 233

BRADSTREET
MA **SIMON** bp 1603/04-1697
m c 1628 _____ _____ c 1612-1672
XXXIV 70

BRADT/BRATT
NY **ALBERT ANDRIESSEN**
BRATT 1607-1689 m c 1630
Annetje Barentse van Rolmers
....-c 1662
XXXI 224; XXXVII 123;
XXXVIII 115; XXXX 105

BRAGDON
ME **ARTHUR** c 1597- p 1665
m .... **Mary** _____ ....-....
XXXIV 241

BRAINARD, see BRAINERD

BRAINERD/BRAINARD
CT **DANIEL** c 1641-1715
m c 1663/64
m1)**Hannah Spencer** c 1641-
a 1691
V 59; X 290; XI 7, 112, 113;
XII 104; XXI 58, 86; XXIX
156; XXXI 148, 212, 291;
XXXIV 87, 316; XXXVIII 228;
XXXX 94

BRAMAN/BRAYMAN
MA **THOMAS BRAYMAN**
 1620/30-a 1666
 m .... **Jane** _____ ....-....
 XXXV 147

BRAMHALL/BRIMHALL
NH/ME **GEORGE, I** ....-1689
 m a 1671 **Martha Beard** ....-....
 XXXIX 167, 326

BRANCH
VA **CHRISTOPHER** 1595-1681/82
 m 1619 **Mary Addie** c 1600-1630
 XIV 20; XXVI 151; XXXIII
 137
MA **JOHN** 1628-1711
 m 1652 **Mary Speed** ....-....
 XXXX 395

BRASHEARS
VA/MD **BENJAMIN** c 1611/15-
 a 1662 m c 1645
 Mary Radford c 1621-....
 XXXVI 216

BRATT, see BRADT

BRAY
NJ **JOHN** ....-1716
 m .... **Susanna** _____ ....-....
 XXXIV 129
MA **THOMAS** 1604-1691
 m 1646 **Mary Wilson** ....-1707
 XXXVIII 345

BRAYTON
RI **FRANCIS** 1611/12-wp 1692
 m .... **Mary** _____ ....-p 1692
 XVII 106; XXV 44, 182, 282
RI **FRANCIS** ....-1718
 m 1671 **Mary Fish** ....-1774
 XXIX 233

BRAZER/BRAZIER
MA **EDWARD BRAZIER** 1602-
 1689
 m .... **Magdelen** _____ ....-....
 XXXII 213

BRAZIER, see BRAZER
BREYANDT, see BRYANT

BREED/BREAD
MA/NY **ALLEN BREAD** 1600/01-
 1690/92
 m1)1622 **Elizabeth Wheeler**
 m2)1656 **Elizabeth Knight**
 XX 75; XXV 31; XXXVII   184;
 XXXVIII 188

BRESSIE, see BRACY

BRETT
MA **WILLIAM** 1618-1681
 m .... **Margaret Ford** ....-....
 XVI 112

**BREWER/BROUWER/
BROWER**
NY **ADAM BROUWER
 BERKHOVEN** ....-w 1692
 m 1645 **Madalena Jacob
 Verdon** c 1624-p 1698
 XXIX 326; XXXIII 183;
 XXXVII 90
MA **DANIEL** 1605- 1646 m ....
 Joanna _____ 1601-1688/89
 XXXVIII 81
VA **GEORGE** c 1680-1744 m c 1705
 Sarah Lanier c 1686-1724/29
 XXXIX 213, 237
MA **JOHN** ....-....
 m a 1642 **Anne** _____ ....-....
 XXXI 105
MA **JOHN** 1642-1690 m ....
 Elizabeth Rice 1648-1739/40

BREWER/BROUWER/
BROWER-Cont.
  XXXI 21
VA **JOHN, I** c 1575-1635
  m 1615 **Mary Drake** ....-....
  XXXVII 288
VA **JOHN** 1565-1635
  m .... **Mary Grove** ....-....
  XXXVI 90

BREWSTER/BRUSTER
NH **JOHN BRUSTER** 1627-1693
  m .... **Mary** _____ ....-....
  XXXVI 20
MA **LOVE** ....-wp 1650/51
  m 1634 **Sarah Collier** ....-1691
  V 119
NY **NATHANIEL** ....-1690
  m .... **Sarah Ludlow** ....-....
  XVII 67
MA **WILLIAM** 1566/67-1644
  m 1591 **Mary** _____ c 1569-1627
  V 119; XI 116, 152, 153, 154,
  156; XXVI 37, 211; XXVIII
  148; XXX 222; XXXIX 235

BREYANDT, see BRYANT
BRIANT, see BRYANT

BRICK
NY **JOHN, Sr** ....-wp 1752/53
  m ....**Hannah Davis** ....-....
  XXXIII 151

BRICKEY
SC/MD **JOHN** ....-....
  m .... _____ _____ ....-....
  XXXII 105

BRIDGE
MA **JOHN** ....-1665
  m .... _____ _____ ....-a 1631
  XXXIV 214, 317

BRIDGES
MA **EDMUND** 1612-1684
  m1).... **Alice** _____ ....-....
  m2).... **Elizabeth** _____ ....- 1664
  XVIII 22

BRIDGHAM
MA **HENRY, Sr** 1573-1641
  m 1610 **Ursula Brett** ....-1644
  XXXII 282

BRIDGMAN
CT/MA **JAMES** ....-1676
  m .... **Sarah** _____ ....-1688
  XXIX 325; XXX 284

BRIGGS
MA **CLEMENT** c 1600-1648
  m1) c 1630/31 **Joanne Allen**
  ....-....
  m2) .... **Elizabeth** _____ ....-....
  XXXIV 36
MA **HUGH** ....-.... m 1682/83
  Martha Everson ....-....
  XXVII 36
MA **JOHN** ....-1641
  m .... _____ _____ ....-....
  XXVI 137
RI **JOHN** ....-1644
  m .... **Catherine** _____ ....-....
  XXXVII 290

BRIGHAM
MA **THOMAS** c 1603-1653
  m c 1637 **Mercy Hurd** ....-1693
  X 192; XIX 105; XXIV 154;
  XXVIII 204; XXX 82; XXXV
  156; XXXIX 33

BRIMHALL, see BRAMHALL

BRINCKERHOFF
NY **JORIS DERICKSON** 1609-

BRINCKERHOFF-Cont.
    1661 m ....**Susanna Dubbels** ....-
    a 1677
    XXXII 55

BRINSMADE/BRISMADE
MA/CT **JOHN** ....-1673
    m a 1640 **Mary** _____ ....-.....
    VI 46/52

BRINTNALL
MA **THOMAS, I** ....-....
    m .... **Esther** _____ ....-....
    XXXV 15, 183

BRINTON
DE **WILLIAM** 1636-1700
    m 1659 **Anne Bagley** 1635-1699
    XXXI 120; XXXVI 183

BRISCOE
MD **JOHN, I** 1590-....
    m .... **Elizabeth DuBois** ....-....
    XXIX 31, 230; XXXI 138

BRISMADE, see BRINSMADE

BRISTOL/BRISTOW
CT **HENRY BRISTOW** c 1625-
    1695 m2) **Lydia Brown(e)**
    1636/38-c 1719
    XIV 27; XVIII 120; XXXV 316,
    333

BROCK
VA **JOSEPH, I** c 1668-1742
    m1)c 1699 **Elizabeth** _____ ....-
    .....
    m2).... **Mary Clayton** ....-....
    XXV 230

BROCKETT
CT **JOHN** 1609-1690 m 1640/46

    _____ _____ ....-....
    X 164; XXX 100; XXXIII 257,
    345; XXXIV 257

BRODHEAD
NY **DANIEL** 1631-1667 m 1661
    Ann Tye ....-1710/14
    XII 27; XXV77; XXVII 73;
    XXVIII 9, 114

BROKAW/BROUCARD
NY **BOURGON BROUCARD**
    1645-.... m 1666
    Catherine LeFebre ....-....
    XXX 246

BROME, see BROOME

BROMLEY
RI **LUKE** ....-a 1700
    m .... _____ _____ ....-....
    XXXVI 342

BRONDIG, see BRUNDAGE
BRONDISH, see BRUNDAGE

BRONSON
MA/CT **JOHN** 1600-1680
    m .... _____ _____
    XII 15; XVII 115, 145; XVIII
    80; XXI 126; XXXII 78;
    XXXIII 61

BROOK, see BROOKS
BROOKE, see BROOKS
BROOKING, see BROOKINGS

BROOKINGS/BROOKING
ME **HENRY** 1641-a 1712
    m3)a 1686 **Sarah** _____ ....-....
    XXXI 248
VA **WILLIAM BROOKING**
    c 1630-1702 m ....

BROOKINGS/BROOKING-Cont.
   Martha ____ ....-p 1704/05
   XXXVII 190

BROOKS
MA **HENRY** 1591-1683
   m2)a 1623 **Susanna** ____ ....-
   1681
   XXXV 53; XXXVI 325;
   XXXIX 321; XXXX 12
MA **JOHN** c 1623-1691 m 1649
   Eunice Mousall ....-1691
   XXIX 150
CT **JOHN** 1650-1695
   m 1685 **Sarah Peat** ....-1694
   XXXI 242
MD **ROBERT BROOKE** 1602-1655
   m1) 1627 **Mary Baker** ....- 1634
   m2) 1635 **Mary Manwaring**
   ....-1663
   XVIII 85; XXXI 220; XXXX
   383
MA **THOMAS** ....-1667
   m .... **Grace Concord** ....-1664
   VI 43/48; X 121; XXXX 39
CT **THOMAS** 1617-1668
   m 1662 **Alice Spencer** ....-....
   XXVI 14
MA **WILLIAM** 1610-1688
   m 1654 **Mary Burt** ....-1680/89
   XXXVIII 290; XXXIX 21

BROOME/BROME
MD **JOHN** ....-1689
   m .... **Margaret** ____ ....-....
   XIX 140

BROUCARD, see BROKAW

BROUGHTON
MA **JOHN** 1615-1662 m 1650
   Hannah Bascom a 1639-1681
   XXXII 109

BROWER, see BREWER

BROWN/BROWNE
MA **ABRAHAM BROWNE** ....-....
   m .... **Lidia** ____ ....-....
   XXX 252
RI **CHAD** 1600-1650/63 m 1626
   Elizabeth Sharparrow ....-
   1663/72
   XX 97; XXIII 11
MA **CHARLES** ....-1687
   m 1647 **Mary Acy** ....-1683
   XIX 7; XXII 39
MA **EDWARD** 1591-1659
   m ....**Faith Bartholomew** ....-....
   VIII 17
RI **HENRY BROWNE** p1600/25-
   1702/03
   m .... **Waite Waterman** ....-....
   XV 72; XVI 18
MA **HENRY BROWNE**
   1615-1701
   m .... **Abigail** ____....-1702
   XXX 32; XXXIV 25
PA **JAMES** 1656-1715/17
   m 1679 **Honour Clayton** ....-....
   XXVII 44; XXXII 128
MA **JOHN, Sr** ....-1677
   m1)a 1657 **Mary** ____ ....-....
   XXXII 161
MA **JOHN BROWNE** 1584-1662
   m .... **Dorothy** ____ c 1583-
   1673/74
   XI 55; XXXX 385, 386
NH **JOHN** 1588/89-1687 m a 1640
   Sarah Walker 1618-1672
   XVI 101
MA **JOHN BROWNE** bp 1601-1637
   m ....**Dority/Dorothy** ____ ....-....
   IX 15; XIV 95; XVII 154;
   XXIII 48
MA **JOHN** c 1628-1714
   m1) 1659 **Elizabeth Osgood**

BROWN/BROWNE-Cont.
....-....
m2) 1681 **Sarah** ____ ....-p 1714
XI 73; XII 86; XXIII 10;
XXXVIII 68
MA **JOHN** c 1631-wd 1697 m 1655
Esther Makepeace 1631-p 1699
XXVIII 151, 207; XXXI 246
MA **NICHOLAS BROWNE** ....-
1673 m ....**Elizabeth Lide** ....-
1674
IX 12; XX 58; XXVI 161; XXXII
292; XXXIV 323
RI **NICHOLAS** ....-1694
m2) .... **Frances Parker** ....-1669
XXIV 106; XXIX 322
MA/CT **PETER** ....-1633
m2) .... **Mary** ____ ....-....
III 35
NY **RICHARD** bp 1623-1686
m c 1650/51 **Hannah King**
1629-....
XXVIII 157
MA **THOMAS** 1605-1688
m .... **Bridget** ____ ....-1680/81
XI 63; XXVIII 11; XXXVI 323
MA **THOMAS BROWNE** c 1607-
1686/87 m .... **Mary** ____ ....-
1654
X 253; XXI 165
MA **THOMAS BROWNE** c 1628-
1693
m ....**Mary Newhall** 1637-1683
XXXIII 38
MA **THOMAS** a 1638-1690 m 1656
Mrs. Martha Oldham ....-
p 1668
VI 13/15

BROWNE, see BROWN

BROWNELL
RI **THOMAS** c 1618/19-1665

m c 1638 **Ann** ____ ....-1665
XVIII 12; XXI 61; XXXIV 61

BROWNING
VA **JOHN** c 1588-....
m 1614 ____ ____ ....-....
XXII 90; XXIV 13; XXVI 42;
XXXIV 190

BROWNSON, see BRUNSON

BRUEN
MA **OBADIAH** 1606-p 1681
m 1632/33 **Sara** ____ 1609-
p 1681
X 210

**BRUNDAGE/BRONDIG/
BRONDISH**
NY **JOHN BRONDISH/BRONDIG**
c 1632-1697 m a 1685
____ ____ ....-....
XXXIV 123; XXXIX 168
CT **JOHN** c 1597-inv 1639
m .... **Rachel Hubbard** ....-....
XXXIV 239

BRUNSON/BROWNSON
CT **RICHARD BROWNSON, I**
c 1637-....
m .... ____ ____ ....-....
XXXII 76; XXXVI 111
CT **RICHARD BROWNSON**
c 1617-wd 1684
m1)c 1640
Abigail Wilborne 1620-1666
XXXVI 231

BRUSH
NY **RICHARD** c 1640-1711/14
m c 1668 **Joanna Sammis**
c 1648-a 1707
XXXIII 312

BRYAN
CT **ALEXANDER** bp 1602-1679
  m a 1630 **Ann Baldwin** ....-1661
  XXIX 134
VA **WILLIAM SMITH** ....-....
  m.... _____ _____ ....-....
  XXX 190

BRYANT/BREYANDT
MA **ABRAHAM** 1647-1720
  m1)1664 **Mary Kendall**
  1647/48-1688
  XXVIII 131,132
NY **CORNELIUS AERTSZEN**
  BREYANDT 1607- .... m a 1650
  Belitje Hendricks ....-a 1662
  XXXIV 43; XXXVIII 24
MA **JOHN** ....-1674 m 1643
  Mary Lewis c 1623-1655/65
  XXXI 164; XXXIV 270;
  XXXV 67
MA **STEPHEN, Sr** a 1632-....
  m .... **Abigail Shaw** ....-....
  XXXI 232

BUCK
CT **EMANUEL** c 1623-c 1700
  m1) 1645/54 **Sarah Ryley** ....-
  1656/58
  m2)1658 **Mary Kirby** 1637-
  1711/12
  XV 94; XXV 70; XXVII 206;
  XXX 178
MD **JOHN** ....-1687/88 m ....
  Catherine Acton ....-1734
  XXXIV 338; XXXV 114

BUCKHOUT, see BOOKHOUT

BUCKINGHAM
CT **THOMAS** c1610-wd 1657
  m .... **Hannah** _____ ....-1646
  V 86; X 109, 160; XXV 117

BUCKLIN
MA **WILLIAM** 1613-1683 m ....
  Mary Bosworth 1614-1687
  XXXVII 75

BUDD
CT/NY **JOHN** ....-1670
  m.... **Kathlene Browne** ....-....
  XXXIV 252

BUDDINGTON
CT **WALTER** ....-1713
  m2) .... **Mercy Haynes** ....-....
  XXXIII 300

BUDLONG
RI **FRANCIS** ....-1675 m 1668/69
  Rebecca (Lippitt) Howard
  ....- 1675
  XXXV 359

BUELL
CT **WILLIAM** c 1610-1681
  m 1640 **Mary** _____ ....-1684/89
  VI 8/10; X 192; XXI 156; XXII
  137; XXXVI 329

BUFFINGTON, see BUFFINTON

BUFFINTON/BUFFINGTON
MA **THOMAS BUFFINGTON** ....-
  1725/29 m 1670
  Sarah Southwick 1644-p 1733
  XVI 60

BUFORD/BEAUFORD
VA **RICHARD BEAUFORD** 1617-
  ....
  m 1640 **Dora Vausi** ....-....
  XXXIV 259

BUGBEE
CT **EDWARD** c 1594-1669

BUGBEE-Cont.
    m .... **Rebecca** _____ ....-c 1602
    XIV 22; XV 108

BUGG
VA **SAMUEL** 1640-1716
    m c 1688 **Deborah Sherwood**
    ....-1715
    XXXVIII 254

BUILE, see GILE

BULFINCH
MA **ADINO** ...-1746
    m 2)1727 **Susanna Green** ....-
    1743/45
    XXXIII 256

BULKELEY
MA **PETER** 1582/83-1659
    m2) 1633/35**Grace Chetwood**
    (Chetwode) 1602-1669
    XVIII 145; XIX 98; XXXII 123

BULL
MA **ISAAC** 1654-....
    m ..... **Mary** _____ ....-....
    XXXIV 164
CT **THOMAS** c 1605/15-1684
    m 1643 **Susan/Susannah** _____
    c 1610-1680
    V 58; X 133; XXXVII 297

BULLARD
MA **BENJAMIN** 1630/34-1689
    m1) 1655/59 **Martha Pidge**
    1642-1676
    VI 101/119; XV III 60; XXXVIII
    256
MA **GEORGE** c 1607-1688/89
    m p 1640 **Beatrice Hall** ....-1652
    XXXX 37
MA **JOHN** 1601/02-1678 m ....

    Magdalene _____ ....-1661
    XXV 281
MA **ROBERT** 1594/99-1634/39
    m .... **Anne** _____ ....-liv 1644
    VI 101/119; XVIII 60; XXXVIII
    256

BULLEN
MA **SAMUEL** ....-1691/92 m 1641
    Mary Morse ....-1691/92
    XXVI 303; XXXII 256

BULLOCK/BULLUK
MA **RICHARD** c 1622- 1667
    m1) 1647 **Elizabeth**
    Ingraham ....-1659
    m2).... **Elizabeth Billington**
    ....-....
    X 203; XXXVII 114
VA **RICHARD** 1641-1667 m a 1662
    Dorothy _____ ....-....
    XXXI 36; XXXIV 337

BUNKER
ME **JAMES** bp 1633/34-1697/98
    m .... **Sarah Nute** ....-....
    XXXIX 332

BUNNELL
CT **WILLIAM** .....-p 1654
    m .... **Ann Wilmot** ...-1653/54
    XVII 5

BURBANK
MA **JOHN** ....-1681
    m1).... **Ann** _____ ....-....
    VI 31/35

BURDETT, see BURDICK
BURDGE, see BURGESS

BURDICK/BURDETT
RI **ROBERT** c 1630-1692

BURDICK/BURDETT-Cont.
  m 1655 **Ruth Hubbard** 1640-
  1691
  XIII 86; XXII 98; XXV 263;
  XXVI 189; XXX 118; XXXII
  272; XXXIV 303; XXXVI   145;
  XXXIX 119; XXXX 328

BURGESS/BURDGE/BURGIS
NY **JONATHAN BURDGE**
  ....-p1698
  m....**Hannah/Sushannah**____
  1685-1714
  XXIII 24
MA **THOMAS** 1603-1685
  m .... **Dorothy** ____ ....-1687
  XXXIII 42
MD **WILLIAM** 1622-1686
  m1) c 1649
  Elizabeth Robins   ....-....
  XXVII 159

BUGIS, see BURGESS

BURHANS
NY **JACOB** ....-a 1677
  m .... ____ ____ ....-....
  XXVI 149

BURLEIGH/BURLEY
MA **GILES** ....-1668 wp 1669
  m 1656
  Rebecca/Elizabeth Fitts....-
  a1680
  XIX 23; XX 140; XXXVI 215;
  XXXVII 350; XXXIX 131;
  XXXX 19, 77

BURLEY, see BURLEIGH

BURLINGHAM
CT/RI **ROGER** 1620-wp 1718
  m .... **Mary** ____ 1626- p 1718

XI 56

BURNAP, see BURNETT

BURNETT/BURNAP
MA **ROBERT BURNAP** c 1595-
  1689 m c 1624
  Ann (Agnes) Miller 1600- 1681
  XXXI 219; XXXII 100
MA **ROBERT BURNAP, Jr** 1627-
  1695 m2) 1662 **Sarah Brown**
  ....-a 1703/13
  XXXI 219; XXXIX 257
MA/NY **THOMAS** 1630-1691
  m1) a 1663 **Mary Pierson**
  1643-1690/91
  XIX 49; XXII 100; XXX 277

BURNHAM
MA **JOHN, I** 1618/26-1694
  m .... **Mary** ____ ....-....
  XXXIII 158
MA **THOMAS** 1623-c 1694
  m 1643/45 **Mary (Lawrence)**
  Tuttle 1624-1685/1715
  X 29; XVIII 126; XXI 35;
  XXXIV 109

BURPEE/BURKBY
MA **THOMAS BURKBY** c 1613-
  1701
  m2).... **Sarah Kelly** 1640- 1713
  XII 114

BURR
CT **BENJAMIN** .... -1681/82 m....
  Ann/Anna ____ ....-1683
  XXI 36, 129; XXIII 63; XXXX
  142
CT **JEHUE** c 1600-1672 m a 1624
  ____ **Cable** ....-....
  XXII 92
MA **JOHN** a 1600-p 1635

BURR-Cont.
   m ... ____ ____ ....-....
   XVI 30

BURRAGE, see BURRIDGE

BURRIDGE/BURRAGE
MA **JOHN BURRAGE** 1616-1685
   m2)1654/55 **Joanna Stowers**
   1624-1689
   XXXI 244

BURRITT
CT **WILLIAM** ....-inv 1651
   m .... **Elizabeth** ____ ...-wd
   1681
   XI 120; XII 53; XXXII 99

BURROUGH
NJ **SAMUEL** ....-c 1692/93
   m.... **Hannah** ____ ....-....
   XXX 94

BURROWS
CT **ROBERT** ....-c1682/83 m....
   Mrs. Mary Ireland....-1672
   V 74; XII 20

BURSON
PA **GEORGE, Sr** ....-1715/16
   m .... **Hannah Gouda** ....-....
   XXXI 268
PA **JOSEPH** 1650-1700 m ....
   Gemima Stroud 1652-1710
   IX 24; XIII 59

BURT
MA **HENRY** c 1590/96-1662 m 1619
   Eulalie Marche c 1600-1690
   XVII 33; XX 136;XXVII 116,
   132; XXVIII 191; XXXII 263;
   XXXVII 253; XXXIX 173;
   XXXX 310, 388, 392

MA **RICHARD** ....-a 1647
   m .... ____ ____ ....-....
   XXXI 24

BURTON
VA **JOHN** 1632-1689
   m .... ____ ____ ....-....
   XXIX 309
VA **ROBERT** ....-1725
   m1) 1676 **Catherine Cotton**
   ....-....
   XXXVI 147
CT **SOLOMON** c 1660-c 1720
   m 1687 **Mercy Judson** 1665-
   c 1736
   XXXII 86
VA **THOMAS** 1634-1686
   m 1655 **Susannah Lockett** ....-....
   XXXIX 93
VA **THOMAS** ....-c 1686
   m a 1664 **Susannah Allen** ....-....
   XXXI 51; XXXIII 168; XXXVII
   45
VA **WILLIAM** ....-wp 1695
   m .... **Anne Stratton** ....-....
   XXXIV 246

BURWELL
MA/CT **JOHN** 1602-1649
   m .... **Alice** ____ ....-1666
   XXV 132
VA **LEWIS** 1621-1658
   m .... **Lucy Higginson** ....-1675
   XII 122

BUSH
VA **ABRAHAM** c1622/23-a 1687
   m p 1668/70
   Ann Alexander 1628-c 1690
   XXXX 183, 255, 276
NY **JAN WOUTERS (VAN DEN**
   BOSCH) 1638-....
   m 1654 **Arentje Arends** ....-

BUSH-Cont.
 1660
 XXXII 19
ME **JOHN** 1613-1670 m ....
 Grace Walker ....-....
 XXX 287
MA **JOHN** c 1628-1662 m ....
 Elizabeth ____ 1632-....
 XXXX 423
MA **JONATHAN, I** c 1650-1738/39
 m 1679 **Sarah Lamb** 1660-....
 XXXI 146; XXXIV 155
MA/CT **SAMUEL** 1647-1733 m ....
 Mary ____ ....-1687
 XXIV 6
VA **WILLIAM, Sr** c 1645-1716
 m a 1670/73
 Martha ____ c 1645/50-p 1728
 XXXVI 306

BUSHNELL
CT **FRANCIS** c 1580-w p1646
 m 1605 **Ferris Quenell** bp 1587-
 1627/38
 XXXIV 86; XXXV 142;
 XXXVI 58; XXXVII 72, 348;
 XXXVIII 244; XXXX 211
CT **JOHN** bp 1615-1667 m c 1650
 Ja ___ ....-....
 XXXVI 58
CT **WILLIAM** bp 1610/11-1683
 m a 1643 **Rebecca Chapman** ....-
 ....
 XXXV 142; XXXVII 234

BUSS
MA **WILLIAM** c 1613-1698
 m1).... **Ann** ____ ....-1674
 m2)....**Dorcas Jones** ....-....
 XXVIII 177

BUTCHER
PA **JOHN** ....-1707

m ... **Hannah** ____ ....-....
XII 12

BUTLER
MA **JAMES, Sr** c 1630-1681
 m 1670 **Mary** ____ ....-p 1724
 XIX 96, 160; XX 100; XXIV
 36; XXVII 204; XXXIX 302
MA **JOHN** bp 1624-p 1658 m c 1650
 Mary Lynde c 1629-1658
 XVIII 11; XXVIII 133
CT **JOHN** .....-1733 m ....
 Katherine Houghton ....- 1728
 IX 41
MA **NICHOLAS** 1595/1600-1671
 m2)1623/24 **Joyce Baker**
 bp 1602-1680
 XVII 82; XVIII 11; XXIV 151;
 XXV 172; XXVIII 133;
 XXXII 147; XXXIII 77
MA **PETER, I** ....-1654/1660
 m .... **Mary Alvord** ....-1693
 XVIII 59; XXIX 268; XXXI
 161; XXXIII 90; XXXIV 199,
 218
MA **RICHARD** ....-1684
 m2).... **Elizabeth Biglow** ....-
 1656/57
 XIX 59; XXVII 156; XXXI 320

BUTMAN/BOSTMAN
MA **JEREMIAH BOOTMAN**
 c 1631-1693/94
 m1) 1659 **Hester/Esther**
 Lambert ....-....
 XXXV 43

BUTT
VA **ROBERT, Sr** ....-1675/76 m ....
 Jane ____ ....-p 1675
 XXXI 254, 319

BUTTERFIELD
MA **BENJAMIN** ....-1687/88
   m1).... **Ann** _____ ....-1660/61
   m2)1663 **Hannah Whitmore**
   ....-1677
   III 38, 60; IV 82, 113; XVIII
   127; XXI 137; XXIV 90;
   XXIX 89

BUTTON
MA **MATTHIAS** bp 1607-1672
   m2)1653/54 **Teagle** _____ ....-
   1662/63
   XI 60; XII 29; XXII 123

BUTTS
VA **THOMAS** 1675-.... m 1713
   Catherine Maclagelee ....-....
   XVI 14

BUXTON
MA **ANTHONY** 1601-1684 m ....
   Elizabeth _____ ....-p 1684
   XXV 112, 205; XXXVII 58

BUYS, see BOYCE

BYNUM/BANUM/BAYNHAM
VA **JOHN BANUM** 1569- p 1624
   m .... **Elizabeth** _____ 1580-....
   XV 62

CADMUS/CUYPER/DE CUYPER
NY **THOMAS FREDERICKSEN**
   de CUYPER
   1611-1702 m 1646
   Marretje Adriam/Adriance
   1628-1702
   XIV 81; XV 9; XIX 47; XX
   125; XXVII 113, 114

CADWELL
CT **THOMAS** ....-1694 m 1658

   Elizabeth Stebbins (Wilson)
   ....-....
   XXXIII 107

CADY
MA **NICHOLAS** ....-a 1712
   m c 1648 **Judith Knapp** ....-....
   XIII 105; XXVI 112; XXVIII
   178; XXXIV 94; XXXVIII 351,
   369; XXXX 326

CAHOON
RI **WILLIAM** ....-1675
   m .... _____ _____ ....-....
   XX 167

CALDWELL
MA **JOHN** 1624-1692 m c 1654
   Sarah Dillingham 1634-
   1721/22
   XXXV 270

CALKINS
CT **HUGH** 1600-1690
   m .... **Ann** _____ ....-....
   XVIII 30; XXXIV 31

CALLAWAY
VA **JOSEPH, Sr** 1648-1727
   m c 1674 _____ _____ ....-....
   XXXVIII 54

CAMFIELD, see CANFIELD

CAMP/CAMPE
CT **EDWARD** bp 1617-1659
   m c 1645 **Mary Canfield** c 1622-
   p 1680/81
   IV 108; V 117; XXXI 28, 219;
   XXXVII 302; XXXVIII 91;
   XXXX 180, 210
CT **NICHOLAS** 1597-c 1635
   m .... **Sarah** _____ ....-1645

CAMP/CAMPE-Cont.
    XXX 203
VA **THOMAS** c 1661-1711
    m c 1689
    Catherine Barron c 1672-1715
    XXXV 272; XXXVIII 208
NJ **WILLIAM CAMPE** ....-....
    m 1661 **Mary Smith** ....-....
    X 100

CAMPE, see CAMP
CAMPFIELD, see CANFIELD
CANDE, see CANDEE

CANDEE
CT **ZACCHEUS** c 1640-1720
    m 1670/76
    Rebecca Bristol 1649/50-1739
    XVI 55; XVIII 86; XIX 38;
    XXXIII 50

CANFIELD/CAMFIELD/
CAMPFIELD
CT **MATTHEW CAMFIELD**
    bp 1604-1673 m a 1643
    Sarah Treat bp 1620-c 1673
    XXVIII 60; XXXIII 89; XXXIV
    39; XXXV 249
CT **THOMAS** bp 1623-1689
    m 1649 **Phebe Crane** ....-1690
    III 17; XV 49; XXXIV 297

CANNON
MD **JAMES** ....- w p 1712
    m .... **Mary** _____ ....-p 1711
    XXII 156; XXX 124

CANTINE/QUANTAIN
NY **MOSES QUANTAIN** c 1660-
    1744 m 1691
    Elizabeth Deyo LeFevre
    c 1653-1702
    XXXV 342

CAPEN
MA **BARNARD** 1562-1638
    m 1596 **Joan Purchase** c 1578-
    1653
    XXI 125; XXXVII 275

CAPPS
VA **WILLIAM** c 1585-p 1630
    m .... _____ _____ ....-....
    XXIX 319

CAPRON
MA/RI **BANFIELD, Sr** 1660/66-
    1752
    m1) 1681 **Elizabeth Callender**
    1662-1733/35
    XXV 265; XXIX 227; XXXI 124

CARD
RI **RICHARD** ....-a 1674
    m a 1648 Rebecca _____ ....-....
    III 71

CARDWELL
VA **THOMAS** c 1614-1687
    m .... **Mary** _____ ....-....
    XXXVIII 360

CAREY, see CARY

CARHART
NY **THOMAS** c 1650-1696
    m 1691 **Mary Lord** 1668-....
    XXXIII 313

CARLETON
MA **EDWARD** a 1605/bp 1610-
    a 1661 m 1636
    Ellen Newton/Eleanor Denton
    bp 1614-....
    IV 111; XX 13; XXVI 110;
    XXVII 100; XXVIII 75; XXXIV
    24

CARLTON, see CARLETON

CARMAN
MA/NY **JOHN** 1606-1653
m 1629/30
Florence Fordham 1629-1661
XXIV 112; XXXVIII 162

CARPENTER
RI **RICHARD** c 1550-1625
m .... _____ _____ ....-....
XXXX 270
RI **WILLIAM** 1605-1685
m a 1635
Elizabeth Peake Arnold 1611-
1683
XXXX 270, 375
MA **WILLIAM** 1593/1605-1659
m a 1628 **Abigail** _____ 1606-
1687
VI 6/7, 19/21, 94/111; X 39; XI
190; XIII 102; XIV 6; XVII 35;
XVIII 14; XXII 54; XXV 273;
XXVII 141, 223; XXVIII 31, 32,
33, 34, 35; XXIX 92, 131, 185;
XXX 187; XXXI 145; XXXIII
95, 207, 208; XXXV 257;
XXXVII 136, 347; XXXVIII 270;
XXXX 354
MA **WILLIAM** 1576-....
m .... _____ _____ ....-....
XXIX 92; XXXIII 208

CARR
RI **CALEB** 1616-1695 m ....
Mercy Vaughan 1630-1675
XXX 248
MA **GEORGE** 1599-1682
m2)1640 **Elizabeth Oliver**
c 1618/27-1691
XI 35; XXI 142
RI **ROBERT** 1614-1681
m .... _____ _____ ....-....

XXXI 205

CARRIER
MA **THOMAS** c 1625-1735 m 1664
Martha Allen ....-1692
XXIV 64

CARRINGTON
CT **PETER** ....-wd 1726 m 1691
Ann Wilmot Lines 1669/70-
p 1727
XXXII 89

CARTER
PA **EDWARD** ....-....
m .... **Margaret** _____ ....-....
XXII 126
VA **GILES** 1634-1699/1700
m .... **Hannah** _____ ....-....
XXX 226
VA **JOHN**, I ....-1669 m 1662
Sarah Ludlow ....-....
XXXII 87
MA **THOMAS** ....-1676
m .... **Mary** _____ ....-....
XVIII 54
MA **THOMAS** c 1603/10-1684
m a 1640
Mary Parkhurst bp 1614-1687
X 118, 297; XVIII 54; XXV 101;
XXXVII 250; XXXX 321, 322,
337, 345, 347
VA **THOMAS**, Sr c 1630/31-1700
m2) 1670
Katherine Dale c 1652-1703
XI 62; XIV 114; XV 52; XVI
57; XXIV 168; XXXII 187;
XXXIII 281; XXXIV 17, 172;
XXXIX 227
VA **WILLIAM** c 1660- wp 1751
m2) 1691 **Mary
Goodlow/Goodloe**
c 1667- wp 1744

CARTER-Cont.
    XXXVII 182; XXXX 9

CARTWRIGHT
VA **ABRAHAM** ....-....
    m .... _____ _____ ....-....
    XXXIX 129
MD **MATTHEW** 1634-1688
    m .... Sarah _____ ....-....
    XXVI 285; XXIX 15; XXXVI
    333

CARVER
MA **ROBERT** c 1594-1680
    m .... **Christian** _____ ....-1658
    XVI 65; XXV 45; XXXIII 247
PA **WILLIAM, I** ....-1736
    m1) 1689 **Joan Kinsey** ....-
    by 1723
    XXXVI 179; XXXIX 242

CARY/CAREY
MA **JOHN** c 1610-1681 m 1644
    Elizabeth Godfrey 16__- 1680
    XXVI 109; XXXIV 193, 230,
    305; XXXVIII 59, 137; XXXX
    382, 389
VA **MILES** 1622-1667
    m 1640 **Anne Taylor** ....-....
    XXXVII 187
VA **RICHARD** ....-1682
    m .... _____ _____ ....-....
    XXVIII 101

CASE/CASS
CT **JOHN** c 1616-1703/04
    m1) c 1657
    Sarah Spencer c 1636-1691
    XVIII 124; XXV 239; XXIX
    182; XXX 132; XXXI 143
NH **JOHN CASS** c 1620-1675
    m 1647/48 **Martha Philbrick**
    1633-1694

    IX 22; XI 76; XXIX 298; XXX
    14; XXXI 321;XXXV 306

CASEY
RI **THOMAS** c 1637- c 1711
    m .... **Sarah** _____ ....-....
    XXI 71; XXIV 40

CASH
VA **WILLIAM** c 1653-1707/08
    m 1677 **Elizabeth** _____ ....-....
    XXXX 275, 314

CASS, see CASE

CASTLE
CT **HENRY** 1613-1697
    m 1666 **Abigail Dickerson** ....-....
    XXIX 261

CATE
NH **JAMES** c 1634-1677
    m .... **Alice** _____ ....-....
    XXXVII 30

CATLIN/CATLING/CATTEL
CT **JOHN** ....-wp 1644
    m .... **Isabella** _____ ....-1676
    XXXVII 125
CT **THOMAS** 1612-1690
    m2) .... **Mary Ellison** ....-....
    XIX 87

CHAFFE, see CHAFFEE

CHAFFEE/CHAFFE
MA **THOMAS** c 1615-wp 1683
    m c 1637 **Dorothy** _____ c 1620-
    ....
    IX 44; XIX 19; XX 118;
    XXVI 23, 94, 201; XXVIII 72;
    XXXVI 252; XXXVIII 15;
    XXXX 157, 343

CHAIRES/ DE LA CHAIRE
NY/MD **JAN de LA CHAIRE**
  c 1625-c 1690 m c 1658
  Dame Elizabeth Adee c 1630
  XXXIII 212, 377
MD **JOHN, Sr** 1668-wp 1718
  m c 1689 **Catherine Collins**
  c 1670- p 1728
  XXXIII 337

CHAMBERLAIN/
CHAMBERLIN
MA/CT **EDMUND** ....-1696
  m1) 1646/47
  Mary Turner ....-1669
  XXX 19; XXXVI 154
MA **HENRY** c 1595/96-1674
  m c 1615
  Jane/Joan _____ ....-1674/86
  VI 51/58, 54/60; XV 93; XVI 79;
  XVII 19, 66; XXIX 43; XXXVII
  362
MA **RICHARD** c1620-inv 1673
  m2) c 1652
  Sarah Bugby 1630-a 1672
  XXXV 304; XXXIX 94
MA **WILLIAM** ....-1678/79
  m2) .... **Sarah Jones** ....-
  p 1678/79
  VI 51/58, 54/60
MA **WILLIAM CHAMBERLIN**
  c 1620-1706 m a 1648
  Rebecca Shelley/Addington
  1625-1692
  IV 160; XXV 298; XXVII   174;
  XXXI 315; XXXIV 107

CHAMBERS
NJ **JOHN, Sr** ....-....
  m .... _____ _____ ....-....
  XXX 276
NH **JOHN, Jr** ....-p 1740
  m .... _____ _____ ....-....

XXX 276

CHAMPION
VA **EDWARD** ....-.... m ....
  Elizabeth ....-p 1668/69
  XXXV 232

CHAMPLIN
RI **JEFFREY** ....-a 1695
  m .... _____ _____ ....-....
  XXIX 399

CHANDLER
MA **EDMOND** 1588/89-1662
  mc 1625 _____ _____ ....-....
  XXXIX 261
MA **EDMUND** ....-liv 1684
  m .... _____ _____ ....-....
  II 25, 26
MA **THOMAS** c 1630-1703 m ....
  Hannah Brewer 1630-1703/17
  XIX 39; XXX 250
MA **WILLIAM** bp 1595-1641
  m2) 1621/25 **Annis** _____
  1603-1683
  XIX 95; XXII 103; XXIII 83;
  XXVI 107; XXX 250; XXXIV
  78, 277; XXXIX 289

CHANEY, see CHENEY

CHAPIN
MA **SAMUEL** bp 1598-1675 m 1623
  Cicely Penney bp 1601-
  1682/83
  VI 29/32, 32/36; X 113, 114, 272;
  XI 143; XVI 34; XVIII 39; XX
  104; XXIII 26; XXVI 214;
  XXIX 349; XXXIV 256;
  XXXVI 292; XXXVIII 168;
  XXXIX 259; XXXX 13, 90

CHAPLIN/CHAPLINE
MA **HUGH** 1603-wp 1657 m 1642
    Elizabeth ____ ....-1694
    XXVII 134; XXXVI 89, 296;
    XXXVII 29
MD **ISAAC CHAPLINE** 1584-....
    m 1606 **Mary Calvert** 1586-....
    XII 82

CHAPMAN
CT **EDWARD** ....-1675 m ....
    Elizabeth Fox ....- p 1677
    IV 164; XI 92
MA **EDWARD** c 1620-1678
    m1) c 1642
    Mary Symonds ....-1658
    XIX 84
CT **ROBERT, Sr** 1616-1687
    m 1642 **Ann Bliss (Blith)**....-
    1685
    XI 144; XXXI 293; XXXIV
    167; XXXVI 89, 296
VA **THOMAS, I** c 1590-....
    m 1618 **Ann** ____ ....-....
    XXXVII 85
CT **WILLIAM** ....-wd 1669/99
    m .... ____ ____ ....-....
    XXXVII 76, 120

CHAPPELL
VA **THOMAS** 1612-....m 1648
    Mary Bannister ....-....
    XXXVII 358

CHASE
MA/NH **AQUILA** 1618-1670
    m 1639/46 **Anne Wheeler**
    1620/30-1687
    X 105, 190; XII 122; XIII 73;
    XIV 46;XV 82; XVII 59;
    XVIII 49, 62, 78, 125; XX 10,
    148; XXVI 210, 278, 289; XXX
    114; XXXI 84, 192; XXXIV 228;

    XXXVI 189; XXXVII 142, 267;
    XXXVIII 107, 242; XXXX 215
MA/ME **WILLIAM, Sr** c1584/1605-
    1659 m c 1620/27
    Mary Townley ....-c 1659
    VIII 9; XXXIV 148; XXXV
    35; XXXVI 45; XXXIX 55;
    XXXX 310, 423, 426

CHATFIELD
CT **GEORGE** 1624-1671
    m2)1659/60 **Isabel**
    Nettleton ....-....
    XIII 67; XVI 72; XX 131;
    XXXVI 134; XXXIX 83, 99

CHEASBRO, see
CHESEBROUGH

CHEATHAM
VA **THOMAS** c 1640/49-wd 1726
    m 1681 ____ ____ ....-....
    XX 128; XXXVI 312; XXXVII
    51

CHEESEBROUGH, see
CHESEBROUGH

CHEEVER
MA **DANIEL** 1621/22- wp 1703/04
    m.... **Esther (Hester)** ____ ....-
    ....
    X 233; XXXI 134

CHEINE, see CHENEY

CHENEY/CHANEY/CHEINE/
CHEYNEY
MA **JOHN** c 1605-1666
    m .... **Martha** ____ a 1607-
    c 1684
    VI 65/74; XVIII 50; XXVI 7;
    XXVII 78; XXXIV 282;

CHITTENDEN-Cont.
XIV 113

CHOATE
MA **JOHN** bp 1624-1695
m 1660 **Anne** _____ 1637-1727
XV 26; XXXIV 172

CHRISTANCE
NY **CHRISTIAN** ....-.... m ....
Maritie Ysbrantse Elders ....-
....
XXVII 158

CHRISTIE
NJ **JAMES** 1670-1768 m 1703
Magdalena Demarest 1685-
1749
XXXIX 99

CHURCH
CT/MA **RICHARD** 1610-1667
m 1627 **Ann Marsh** 1600/27-
1684
XVIII 90; XXIV 139; XXVII
9; XXVIII 137; XXXI 294, 311

CHURCHILL
CT **JOSIAH** ....-a 1686 m 1638
Elizabeth Foote 1616-1700
VIII 23; XI 194, 196, 197, 200;
XXXIII 116; XXXVII 249
NY **WILLIAM** ....-a 1714 m 1672
Susannah Brayser ....-p 1714
XXV 271

CILLEY/SEALEY/SEELEY
NH **RICHARD SEALEY** a 1632-....
m .... _____ _____ ....-....
VI 62/70
MA/CT **ROBERT (SEELEY)** 1601-
1668 m 1626
Mary Mason ....-1646

XXXIII 23

CLAFLIN/MACKCLAFLIN/
MACKCLOTHAN/
MACKCLOTHIAN/
MACKCLOTHLAN/MCCLAFLIN
MA **ROBERT MACKCLOTHLAN**
....-bef 1686 m 1664
Joanna Warner ....-1680/90
XXVI 67; XXVII 115; XXXI
231; XXXX 295, 320

CLAGETT
MD **THOMAS** c 1635/44-wp 1703
m1)1674 **Mary Nutter (Hooper)**
....-....
m2)1683 **Sarah Patterson**
1665-....
XXVI 241; XXXII 278;
XXXX 256

CLAIBORNE
VA **WILLIAM** c 1587-1676 m ....
Elizabeth Butler 159_-....
X 101

CLAP, see CLAPP

CLAPP
MA **NICHOLAS** 1612-1677/79
m1)....**Sarah Clapp** ....-1650
IV 168; XV 116
MA **ROGER** 1609-c 1691 m 1633
Joanna Ford 1617-1695
VI 14/16; XV 140; XVI 5; XX
35; XXXI 121; XXXX 404
MA **THOMAS** 1597-1684 m ....
Abigail _____ ....-a 1657/84
XIV 10; XXVIII 115; XXXI
274; XXXIV 59, 176; XXXVI
160

CLARK/CLARKE

VA **BENJAMIN CLARKE, I** ....-
a 1717/19
m2) .... **Mary** _____....-1718
XXXX 58

CT **DANIEL CLARKE** 1622-1710
m 1644 **Mary Newberry** 1626-
1688
XXVII 107; XXXII 286;
XXXIX 160; XXXX 71,
374

MA **EDMUND** ....-1666/67 m a
1651 **Agnes Tybbot** ....-1682
XXXVIII 71

NY **EDWARD** ....-1683/1700
m 1678
Dorothy Raynell ....-liv 1700
XXV 191

MA **EDWARD** c 1622-1695/1710
m1)a 1648/53 **Dorcas
Bosworth** ....-1681
II 36; XXII 107; XXXI 208;
XXXIII 346; XXXVI 297;
XXXVIII 368

CT **GEORGE CLARKE, I** 1610-
1690 m .... **Sarah** _____ ....-1689
IV 114; XIV 122; XV 183; XVI
102; XXIV 29; XXIX 323;
XXXIII 280; XXXVIII 7;
XXXIX 24; XXXX 427

MA **HUGH CLARKE** 1613-1698
m ..... **Elizabeth** _____ ....-1692
XXXVI 215

CT **JOHN** ....-inv 1648/49
m .... **Mary** _____ ....-1648/49
XXVII 43; XXVIII 67, 69

CT **JOHN, Jr** 1625/35-1677
m 1650 **Rebecca Porter** 1623-
1683
XVIII 50; XXXIII 261

CT **JOHN, Sr** 1608-1673/74 m ....
Mary Cooley ....-.....
XVIII 50; XXXIII 261

CT **JOHN** ....-1712   m ....
_____ _____ ....-p 1680
XXXIV 252

MA **JOSEPH, Sr** c1597-1684
m c 1640/41
Alice Fenn Pepper/Peppit
1623-1710
XI 187; XXI 100; XXXX 132,
421

RI **JOSEPH CLARKE** 1618-1694
m1)c 1641 _____ **Saunders** ....-
p 1660
m2).... **Margaret** _____ 1694
VI 88; IX 37; X 284,285; XV 96;
XVII 160; XXIV 69; XXXIV
243; XXXVII 210; XXXX 442

MA **NATHANIEL** 1642-1690
m 1663 **Elizabeth Somerby**
1646-1716
XV 103

NY **RICHARD** ....-1697 m 1660
Elizabeth _____ 1630/40-c 1724
XXII 109

CT **SAMUEL CLARKE, Sr** c 1619-
1690 m ....
Hannah Fordham ....-....
XXXI 170; XXXIII 86; XXXVI
138

MA **THOMAS** ....-.... m c 1637
Abigail Cogswell ....-....
XVIII 24

MA **THOMAS CLARKE** 1599-
1697 m 1634
Susanna Ring .... a 1664
XIII 103; XV 44; XXVI 69

MA **WILLIAM CLARKE** c 1609-
1690 m .... **Sarah** _____ ....-1675
XX 93; XXV 157; XXIX 93;
XXXX 36

CT **WILLIAM, Sr** 1645-1712
m .... _____ _____ ....-....
XXXV 298

CLARKE, see CLARK

CLASON
CT **STEPHEN** ....-c 1699 m 1654
    Elizabeth Periment ....-....
    XVIII 151

CLAY/CLAYE
VA **JOHN CLAYE** c 1587-wp 1675
    m 16?3 **Ann** _____ ....-p 1638
    XXI 174; XXVI 187; XXVII 46;
    XXXI 227; XXXVII 16;
    XXXVIII 195
MA/NH/ME **JONAS** ....-1660 m ....
    Mary Batson ....-p1673
    XXXI 217

CLAYE, see CLAY

CLAYES/CLOYES
MA/ME **JOHN** bp 1604-1676
    m a 1637 **Abigail** _____ ....-....
    XXXV 349; XXXVI 44; XXXX
    244

CLAYPOOL
DE **NORTON** ....-1688
    m1) .... **Edith** _____ ....-....
    m2) .... **Rachel** _____ ....-....
    XXXVII 82

CLAYTON
DE/NJ/PA **WILLIAM, I** ....-a 1689
    m .... **Prudence**_____ ....-1728
    XXXIV 310; XXXV 235;
    XXXVI 75, 82; XXXVII 226;
    XXXIX 80

CLEAVLAND, see CLEVELAND

CLEMENT
VA **JEREMIAH** ....-.... m ....
    Edey _____ ....-....

    XXVI 32
MA **ROBERT** c 1590-1658
    m1)a 1615
    Lydia _____ a 1615-1642
    XII 56; XXI 7; XXIII 13; XXVII
    25; XXXI 207

CLEMENTS, see CLEMENT

CLEVELAND/CLEAVLAND
MA **MOSES** c 1624-1701/02 m 1648
    Ann Winn c 1626-1682
    I 45; XI 26; XVIII 71; XXVII
    153; XXXI 291; XXXIII 246,
    278; XXXX 384

CLIFT
MA **WILLIAM** 1666-1722 m ....
    Lydia Wills 1676-1761
    V 97

CLINTON
MA **LAWRENCE** 1643-p 1704
    m p 1690 **Margaret (Painter)**
    Morris
    c 1667- p 1743
    XXIII 56

CLIZBE
NJ **JAMES** c 1670-a 1712 m ....
    Elizabeth Burwell/Burrell ....-
    ....
    XXIX 327

CLOPTON
VA **WILLIAM** 1655-1733
    m 1673/80
    Ann (Booth) Dennett 1646-1716
    XX 63; XXXI 156

CLOSE
CT **JOHN** c 1600-1653 m ....
    Elizabeth _____ ....-1656

CLOSE-Cont.
XXVIII 184
CT **THOMAS** 1636-1709 m 1669
Sarah Hardy 1650-1727
XXII 44

CLOUD
PA/DE **WILLIAM** 1620-1702
m 1647 **Susan James** ....-....
XXXV 96; XXXVII 220;
XXXVIII 239

CLOUGH/CLUFF/CLOW
MA **JOHN** c 1613-1691
m1)c 1641 **Jane? Macomber?**
c 1620-1679/80
XIX 73; XX 122; XXIV 107;
XXXI 222; XXXIII 70, 174;
XXXIV 30, 180, 188; XXXV 175

CLOW, see **CLOUGH**

CLOW
MA **JOHN CLOW** ....-1668
m .... _____ _____ ....-a 1652
XXXV 49

CLUFF, see **CLOUGH**
CLOYES, see **CLAYES**

CLUTE/KLEUT
NY **JOHANNES** ...-1725 m 1672
Baata Van Slichtenhorst ....-
p 1722
XXIV 83; XXVI 17

COALBORNE, see **COLBURN**

COATE
NJ/PA **JOHN** ....-1699/1700 m 1663
Elizabeth Humphreys ....-1720
XXXI 233
NJ **MARMADUKE** 1651-1728

m 1670 **Ann Pole** 1653-1729
XXXVIII 346

COBB/COBBS
VA **AMBROSE COBBS** 1603-
a 1654/56 m 1625
Ann White c 1608-....
XXXV 334; XXXVIII 32;
XXXIX 270
MA **HENRY, Sr** 1596-wp 1679
m1) 1631 **Patience Hurst** ....-
1648
m2) 1649 **Sarah Hinckley**
bp 1629-1679
XXIV 113; XXXVI 169, 200;
XXXVIII 63, 220, 299; XXXIX
5; XXXX 338

COBORN, see **COLBURN**
COBURN, see **COLBURN**

COCHRANE
NH **JOHN** ....-.... m ....
_____ _____ ....-....
XXII 51

COCK, see **COCKE**

COCKE/COCK/COX
NY **JAMES COCK** ....-1690 m ....
Sarah Clarke ....-1715
XII 27
MD **JOHN COCK (COX)** ....-c 1702
m2) c 1672 **Margaret** _____ ....-
....
XXVIII 89
VA **RICHARD COCKE** c 1600-
wd 1665
m1)a 1639 **Temperance Baley**
1617-a 1647
XXXII 15; XXXV 117; XXXVIII
147
VA **WALTER COCKE, I** ....-1738

COCKE/COCK/COX-Cont.
m .... **Anna Hamlin** ....-....
XI 29; XXV 237

CODDINGTON
NJ **JOHN** ....-1655 m ....
Emma _____ ....-....
XXVII 126
MA **STOCKDALE** ....-1650 m ....
Hannah _____ ....-1644
XXXVII 150
RI **WILLIAM** 1601-1678 m3) 1649
Ann _____ 1628-1708
XIV 36; XV 46

CODMAN
MA **ROBERT** ....-c 1687 m ....

_____ _____ ....-....
XV 106

COE
MA **HENRY** 1555-1630 m c 1588
Mary _____ ....-a 1631
XVII 143
MA/CT **ROBERT, Sr** bp 1596-
c 1685/89
m1)c 1623
Mary Crabbe 1591-1628
m2) .... **Anna** _____ 1591-1674
VI 10/12, 63/72;VII 15, 16, 17;
XVII 126; XIX 114; XXVI 251;
XXVII 21; XXXI 27,189;
XXXIV 142,277; XXXV 215;
XXXVIII 293
CT **ROBERT, Jr** bp 1626-1659
m c 1650
Hannah Mitchell bp 1631-1702
XXXX 457 (see XXXV 215 and
XXXVIII 293)

COEVERS, see COVERT

COFFIN
MA **TRISTRAM** 1605-1681/91
m c 1630
Dionis Stevens (Stephans)
bp 1609-1682/84
XVII 29; XX 65; XXXII 222;
XXXVI 189

COGGESHALL
MA/RI **JOHN** 1601-1647 m ....
Mary c 1604-1684
XXXI 230; XXXIV 122

COGSWELL
MA **JOHN** 1592-1669 m 1615
Elizabeth Thompson ....-1676
XXXVI 12

COIT
MA/CT **JOHN** a 1600-1659 m ....
Mary Jenners c 1596-1676
XI 199; XXXV 57; XXXX 235

COLBURNE, see COLBURN

**COLBURN/COALBORNE/
COBORN/COLBURN**
MA **EDWARD COBORN** 1618-
1712 m a 1642
Hannah? Rolfe? ....-p 1666
XIII 6, 21; XXIII 37; XXIV 102;
XXVI 95; XXVIII 111; XXIX
217; XXXV 24; XXXX 105
MA **NATHANIEL COALBORNE**
....-1691 m 1639
Priscilla Clarke ....-1692
XXIV 96; XXVII 34; XXX 283

COLBY
MA **ANTHONY** 1590-1660/61
m1)1632
Susannah? Sargent ....-1689
XXVIII 201; XXX 66; XXXIII

COLBY-Cont.
305

COLCORD
NH **EDWARD** 1611/15-1681
m a 1640 **Ann Mudd Page** ....-
1688
XXXVI 251

**COLE/COOL/KOAL/KOHL/
KOOL**
NY **BARENT JACOBSEN COOL**
bp 1610-p 1684 m a 1636
Marretje Leenderts de Grauw
c 1605/18-1668
XXXII 182, 293; XXXIV 346;
XXXX 274, 356
MA **DANIEL** c 1614/15-1694 m ....
Ruth Chester 1627/28-1694
X 117, 260
CT **HENRY** c 1621-1676 m 1646
Sarah Rusco c 1623-1687
XXXIX 283
MA **JAMES** c 1600-p 1698
m1)1624/25 **Mary
Lobel/?Tibb(e)s**
1600/06-p 1659/60
m2)**Abigail Davenport** ....-....
VII 13; XI 159; XXXX 49, 382
CT **JAMES** c 1580/90-1652
m1).... ____ ____ ....-a 1625
XXXII 116
MA **THOMAS** ....-p 1678 m ....
Ann/Eunice ____ ....-a 1681
XVIII 106; XXI 75

COLEMAN/COLMAN
VA **HENRY** ....-.... m ....

____ ____   .....-....
XVI 53
VA **JAMES** c 1640/42-1691 m ....
Sarah ____ ....-....
XV 127; XVI 48, 64

VA **ROBERT** 1656/57-1713 m ....
Ann (Spilsbe?)-by 1717
XXVIII 52
CT/MA **THOMAS** c 1598/1600-
1674 m a 1635
____ ____ ....-c 1640/41
IX 37 XXXX 337
MA/NH **THOMAS** 1602-1685
m2).... **Susanna** ____ ....-1650
XXXIII 172
MA **WILLIAM** 1619-1680
m1) ____ ____ ....-....
m2)1662 **Widow Bridget Roe**
XXIX 149
NY **WILLIAM** c 1650-1706
m .... **Mary or Sarah Mapes**
1662-1707
XXXII 85; XXXX 140

COLEY
MA/CT **SAMUEL** ....-1684 m 1640
Ann Pruden ....-c 1689
XIX 67

COLLAMER/COLLAMORE
MA **ANTHONY** ....-1693 m 1666
Sarah Chittenden 1646-1703
XXXVI 194; XXXX 63

COLLAMORE, see COLLAMER

COLLIER
VA **CHARLES** 1660-1735 m ....
Mary ____ ....-....
IX 40; X 44
VA **WILLIAM** 1620-1682 m 1655
Sallie Collier 1636-1680
XVI 43; XXXI 132

COLLINS
MA **BENJAMIN** a 1660-1683
m 1668 **Martha Eaton** 1648-
p 1686

COLLINS-Cont.
XXXX 4, 30, 343
MA **HENRY** 1606-1687
m c 1629
Ann _____ 1605-1691
XIV 120; XXVII 122, 154, 155
MA **JOHN, Sr** 1616-1670 m c 1640
Susannah _____ ....-....
XXXIV 258; XXXV 15, 221
MA **JOHN, Jr** 1640-1704 m 1662
Mary Trowbridge ....-1668
XXXI 105
RI **PAUL COLLIN** c 1666-....
m .... _____ _____ ....-....
XXXVI 269

COLMAN, see COLEMAN

COLTON
MA **GEORGE** c 1610/20-1699
m1) c 1644 **Deborah Gardner**
....- 1689
V 120; X 145; XI 198; XXII 104

COLVER, see CULVER

COLVIN
MA **JOHN** c 1657-a 1729
m c 1678 **Dorothy Allen** 1659-
c 1724
XXXVII 175

COMBS/COOMBS/COOMES
ME **ANTHONY** c 1642/50-
p 1710/28 m 1688
Dorcas Wooden a 1661/71-
....
XVI 46; XXXVIII 324
VA **JOHN** c 1600/04-1675 m p 1625
Margaret Archdale c 1605-....
XXXVI 186; XXXVII 22
MD **RICHARD, I** c 1655-1752 m ....
Anne Shercliffe ....-....

XXXVII 169

COMBSTOCK, see COMSTOCK
COMEE, see COMEY

COMEY/COMEE
MA **DAVID COMEE** ....-1676
m1) c 1660
Elizabeth _____ ....-1671
XXXVII 328

COMINGORE/KAMMINGA/
CAMMENGA
NY **HENDRICK JANSE
KAMMINGA** .....-....
m .... **Anna Maria
Verveelen/Vervele**
1666-a 1717
XXXIX 164

COMLY/COMLEY
PA **HENRY COMLEY** 1635-1684
m2)1673 **Joan Tyler** ....-1689
XIX 34; XXXVII 137; XXXIX
188

COMPTON
MD **JOHN** ....-wp 1718 m c 1675
Mary Clark Douglas ....-....
XXXVII 36
NY **WILLIAM** 1622-p 1679
m .... _____ _____ ....-....
XXXVI 36

COMSTOCK/COMBSTOCK
CT **WILLIAM** c 1590/96-1680/83
m2)a 1624 **Elizabeth Daniel(s)**
1608/10-p 1665
IV 100, 106; X 218; XXIV 15;
XXVII 192; XXIX 61, 211, 385;
XXXIII 195, 304; XXXIV 147,
157 210; XXXVI 197; XXXVII
316

CONABLE/CUNNABELL
MA **JOHN CUNNABELL** c 1650-
1724 m2)1687/89
Sarah Clays 1666/67-1700
XXXVIII 334; XXXIX 38

CONANT
MA **ROGER** bp 1590/92-1679
m 1618 **Sarah Horton** ....-p 1666
XX 70; XXV 141; XXIX 28;
XXXIV 322; XXXVI 37

CONARD/KUNDERS
PA **THONES KUNDERS** 1648-
1729 m ....
Eliza Streypers ....-....
XXXI 266

CONE
CT **DANIEL** 1626-1706 m 1660/62
Mehitable Spencer 1642-1691
XI 20; XIX 116; XXXII 150;
XXXV 150; XXXVIII 35; XXXX
375

CONEY
MA **NATHANIEL** bp 1677-1742
m 1711 **Abigail Skinner Ager**
1685-1728/36
XXXV 207

CONGDON
RI **BENJAMIN** c 1650-1718 m ....
Elizabeth Albro ....-1720
XXVII 89; XXXIII 324

CONGER
NJ **JOHN CONGER/**
BELCONGER 1633/42-wp 1712
m1)1666/67 **(Mary) Sarah Kelly**
1641-1686/90
m2).... **Sarah Cawood** ....-....
XXV 180; XXVI 100; XXVII 92;

XXVIII 87; XXIX 124; XXX 39,
255; XXXV 201, 362; XXXIX
224

CONKLIN/CONKLING
MA/NY **ANANIAS** c 1600-1657
m 1630/31 **Mary Lavendar** ....-
1657
XXXIII 59
NY **JOHN** ....-a 1700 m ....
Helena _____ ....-a 1700
XXXIV 132; XXXVIII 182
MA/NY **JOHN** 1600-1683/84
m 1625/26
Elizabeth Allseabrooke ....-....
XVIII 138; XIX 20; XXII 150;
XXV 128; XXIX 148

CONKLING, see CONKLIN

CONOVER/COUWENHOVEN/
COVENHOVEN/VAN
COUWHOVEN/VAN
KOUWENHOVEN
NY **WOLFERT GERRETSEN**
VAN KOUWENHOVEN c 1584/88-
1661/62 m 1605
Neltje Jans(e)/Neeltje Jansen
....- ....
XXIV 70; XXVI 154; XXIX 357;
XXXII 275; XXXIII 19; XXXIX
315

CONSTANT
See Lineage Book Vol. XXXIV p.
321-322 2nd generation of Smith
adopted by Aunt and Uncle
CONSTANT, see DFPA Index 1975
p. 55

CONVERS, see CONVERSE

CONVERSE/CONVERS
MA **EDWARD** c 1588/90-1663
    m2)c 1615
    Sarah ____ c 1595-1662
    V 43; XXII 135; XXXII 35, 170,
    233; XXXIII 36; XXXIX 82
MA **JAMES** 1620-1715
    m 1643 **Anna Long** ....-1691
    V 43; (see XXXIII 36)

CONWAY
VA **DENNIS** a 1641-1709
    m .... _____ ____ ....-....
    XXXI 227
VA **EDWIN** c 1610-1675 m1) ....
    Martha Eltonhead ....-1640
    VII 34; X 206; XIII 74; XXV
    242, 269, 270; XXXVII 79

CONWELL
VA/DE **FRANCIS** 1615-....
    m .... ____ ____ ....-....
    XXI 77

COOK/COOKE
MA/CT **AARON COOKE** c 1610-
    1690 m1).... ____ **Ford**
    (Thomas) ....-1643/50
    V 121; VI 17/20, 24/26; X 70,
    170; XVIII 62; XXIV 171; XXVI
    142
MD **ANDREW COOKE** ....-....
    m .... **Elizabeth** ____ ....-....
    XXI 134
MA **FRANCIS COOKE** 1583-1663
    m 1603 **Hester Mahieu** ....-
    p 1666
    XXXX 118
MA **GREGORY COOKE** ....-
    1690/91
    m1) ....**Mrs Susannah Goodwin**
    ....-....
    m2).... **Mary Constable** ....-

1680/81
    XXIX 19; XXXIV 289
MA **HENRY** c 1615-1661m 1638/39
    Judith Birdsall ....-c 1689
    XXIX 304; XXXIV 170; XXXV
    22; XXXVI 30, 194
MA **JOSEPH** c 1608-p 1665
    m .... **Elizabeth** ____ ....-....
    V 123
MA **JOSIAH COOKE** c 1610-1673
    m 1635 **Elizabeth (Ring) Deane**
    ....-....
    XXXII 72
MA **JOSIAH** 1645-1732 m 1668
    Deborah Hopkins 1648-1727
    XXXV 300
VA **MORDECAI COOKE** ....-
    a 1667 m 1648
    Susanna Peasley ....-....
    XXXII 94
MA/CT **NATHANIEL** ....-1688
    m 1649 **Lydia Vore** ....- wd 1700
    XXXVIII 53
CT **SAMUEL COOKE** 1641-1703
    m 1667 **Hope Parker** 1650-....
    XXX 179
MA/RI **THOMAS COOKE** c 1603-
    1677 m c 1626
    Mary ____ 1605-....
    XXVI 28; XXXVI 277
VA **WILLIAM, II** 1633-wp 1689
    m .... **Joan (Jane) Roper** ....-1720
    XXXVIII 345

COOKE, see COOK
COOL, see COLE

COOLEY
MA **BENJAMIN** c 1617-1684 m ....
    Sarah Tremaine ....-1684/94
    XIV 67, 85; XVII 98; XIX 75;
    XXI 178; XXXIX 230

COOLIDGE
MA **JOHN** bp 1604-1691 m 1628
   Mary Mattox 1603/04-1691
   XVI 82; XX 21; XXVII 212;
   XXXVI 201; XXXX 277

COOMBS
ME **ANTHONY** c 1642/50-p 1710
   m 1688 **Dorcas Wooden** 1671-....
   XXXVIII 324

COOPER
MA/NY **JOHN** 1594-1662 m 1618
   Wilbroe Griggs 1593/95-a 1662
   XI 179; XXXIII 132; XXXX 301

COPE
PA **OLIVER** c 1647-1697 m ....
   Rebecca _____ ....-a 1728
   XXXVII 306

COPELAND
MA **LAWRENCE** 1588/89-1699
   m 1651 **Lydia Townsend** ....-
   1688
   XII 67; XIII 63

CORBIN
MA **CLEMENT** 1626-1696 m 1655
   Dorcas Buckmaster 1629-
   1721/22
   XVII 140

COREY/CORY
NY **JOHN, I** 1611/19-1685
   m 1638 **Margaret/Ann/Hannah**
   _____ ....-p 1680
   XXII 70; XXV 229; XXXII 237;
   XXXX 262
MA **THOMAS** ....-p 1667 m .....
   _____ _____ ....-....
   V 84
MA **THOMAS** c 1618-1706

   m 1655/65 **Abigail Gould** 1649-
   1719
   XII 40; XVI 93; XXIX 387
RI **WILLIAM** ....-wp 1682 m ....
   Elizabeth _____ ....-wp 1718
   XXXIX 296

CORLISS
MA **GEORGE** c 1617-1686 m 1645
   Joanna Davis ....-....
   IV 169; XII 58; XXV 100; XXIX
   20; XXXI 196

CORNELISE, see CORNELL

CORNELL/CORNELISE/
CORNELIUS
NY **GUILLIAME CORNELISE** ....-
   a 1666 m ....
   _____ _____ ....-a 1666
   XXXI 128
VA **ROWLAND CORNELIUS**
   c 1650/59-a 1727 m ....
   Martha _____ ....-p 1727
   XXXV 77, 117, 308
MA/RI **THOMAS** c 1595-1655
   m 1620 **Rebecca Briggs** 1600-
   1672/73
   XXV 293; XXVII 42; XXXIV
   106

CORNELIUS, see CORNELL

CORNING
MA **SAMUEL, Sr** a 1616-a 1694/95
   m a 1675 **Elizabeth** _____ 1603-
   1688
   XXVIII 99, 141; XXXX 222

CORNISH
CT **JAMES** c 1612/15-1698
   m2)1662
   Mrs. Phebe Larabee ....-1664

CORNISH-Cont.
XXIX 207

CORSA, see CORSON
CORSEN, see CORSON

CORSON/CORSA/CORSEN/
COURSEN/see also JANSEN
NY **PETER CORSEN** ....-....
   m .... _____ _____ ....-....
   XV 10; XXI 61; XXIV 125
NY **CORS PIETERSEN** 1612-1655
   m .... **Tryntje Hendrickse** ....-
   p 1657
   XXXVII 191

CORTELYOU
NY **JAQUES** c 1625-1693
   m c 1655/56
   Neeltje Van Duyn ....-1695
   XXXIII 273; XXXIV 278

CORTRIGHT, see COURTRIGHT
CORTTIS, see CURTIS

CORWIN/CURWEN
MA/NY **MATTHIAS CURWEN**
   1590/1600-1658 m ....
   Margaret Merten ....-....
   XXI 79; XXIV 111; XXIX 247;
   XXXI 88; XXXX 204

CORY, see COREY

COSBY
VA **JOHN** 1630-1695 m c 1660
   Sarah _____ ....-wd 1740
   XIV 7

COSSART, see COZAD

COTTINGHAM
MD **THOMAS** c 1635-1688 m 1666

Mary Dixon c 1650-1692
XXXVI 167

COTTLE
MA **EDWARD** c 1628-c 1710
   m .... _____ _____ ....-p 1668
   XXXVI 162

COTTON
MA **JOHN** 1585-1652
   m2)1632 **Sarah (Hawkridge)**
   Story 1601-1676
   XIV 42; XXIV 140; XXIX 297;
   XXXV 98;
NH **WILLIAM** c 1614/1628-1678
   m c 1650
   Elizabeth Ham c 1630-1678
   XXIV 158; XXVI 18, 63, 82;
   XXVIII 13; XXXI 76

COUCH
ME **JOSEPH** c 1645-1712
   m1).... **Joanne Dearing** ....-
   c 1700
   XXXIX 248
CT **SIMON** c 1633-wp 1687/89
   m .... **Mary Andrews** p 1639-
   1689/91
   VI 70/82; XIII 17; XX 99;
   XXXX 78

COULT/COULT-KIRK
MA/CT **JOHN** 1625-1730
   m2).... **Anne Skinner** 1639-....
   XXXVIII 318

COUNCILL
VA **HODGES** ....-1699 m c 1665
   _____ _____ ....-....
   XXIX 281

COURSEN, see CORSON

**COURTRIGHT/CORTRIGHT/
VAN KORTRIGHT/VAN
KORTRYK**
NY **JAN BASTIAENSEN VAN
KORTRYKE** 1618-....
    m .... ____ ____ ....-....
    XIX 158; XXII 37; XXXI 107

**COUWENHOVEN, see
CONOVER**

COVELL
MA **JAMES, I** ....-c 1690 m ....
    ____ ____ ....-....
    XXXII 215; XXXVII 106
MA **NATHANIEL** 1640-1686
    m 1663
    Sarah Nickerson c 1644-....
    XXXIV 230; XXXV 97; XXXVI
    257

COVENHOVEN, see CONOVER

COVERT/COEVERS
NY **TUNIS JANSZE** c 1625-
    1690/1700 m ....
    Barbara Lucas c 1630-1700
    XIV 117; XV 77; XXXX 170,
    204

COVINGTON
VA **WILLIAM, I** ....-wp 1697
    m .... **Dorothy** ____ ....-....
    XXVI 137; XXXI 134

COWARD
VA **JAMES** ....-a 1717 m a 1687
    Mrs. Mary Collidge ....-....
    XXXV 324

COWDREY
MA **WILLIAM** 1602-1687
    m .... **Joanna** ____ ....-1666

XXXI 234

COWING
MA **JOHN** ....-.... m 1656
    Mrs. Rebecca Man ....-....
    XII 31; XIII 86

COWLES
MA **JOHN** c 1598/1600-inv 1675
    m .... **Hannah** ____ c 1596/1613-
    1683/84
    XV 38, 75; XXXIV 294; XXXV
    20; XXXX 379

COX/COCK/COCKE
NY **JAMES COCK** ....-1690 m ....
    Sarah Clarke ....-1715
    XII 27
MD **JOHN** ....-1702/03 m 1672
    Margaret ____ ....-....
    XXII 49, 93; XXVIII 89
VA **RICHARD COCKE** c 1600-
    w 1665
    m1)a 1632 **Temperance Baley
    Brown** (wid.) 1617-a 1647
    XXXII 15; XXXV 117; XXXVIII
    147
NJ **THOMAS** ....-1681 m 1665
    Elizabeth Blashford ....-p 1672
    XII 95; XV 137; XVI 49, 115
VA **WALTER COCKE** ....-1738
    m .... **Anna Hamlin** ....-...
    IX 29, 40; XXV 237

**COYKENDALL/VAN
KUYKENDALL**
NY **JACOB LEURSZEN** ....-....
    m .... ____ ____ ....-....
    XXXV 42

COZAD/COSSART
NY **JACQUES** 1639-c 1685 m 1656
    Lea/Lydia Willemyns ....-1702

COZAD/COSSART-Cont.
XXXIV 64

CRAFT, see CRAFTS

CRAFTS/CRAFT
MA **GRIFFIN** c 1600-1686/89
   m .... **Alice** ____ ....-1673
   XXXV 268; XXXIX 50; XXXX
   101

CRAMPTON
CT **DENNIS** 1638-1689 m 1668
   Sarah Munger 1644-c 1690
   XXIV 103

CRANDALL
RI **JOHN** 1609/12-1675/76
   m .... **Mary Opp(s)** ....-1669/70
   XXXI 112; XXXV 266

CRANE
CT **BENJAMIN** 1630-1691 m 1655
   Mary Backus ....-1717
   XXV 155
MA **HENRY** c 1621-1709
   m1) .... **Tabitha Kinsley** ....-
   p 1681
   m2) 1655 **Elizabeth Kinsley** ....-
   ....
   VI 84/98; XV 17; XXXII 155
CT/NJ **JASPER** 1590/1635-c 1681
   m ....
   Alice/Allis ____ c 1645-p 1681
   III 52; V 115; XI 117, 136, 155;
   XII 70, 76; XIX 131; XXV 102
MA **JOHN** a 1630-1637 m ....

   ____ ____ ....-....
   XXXII 139
NJ **STEPHEN** 1635-c 1709
   m 1663 ____ ____ ....-....
   XIX 28

CRANNELL
NY **WILLIAM** ....-.... m ....

   ____ ____ ....-....
   XXXIV 270; XXXVI 94

CRANSTON
RI **JOHN** 1625-1679/80 m 1658
   Mary Clarke c 1641-1711
   XXVII 181; XXXI 237, 238;
   XXXIV 175

CRARY
MA/CT **PETER** c 1645-1708
   m1) 1677
   Cristobel Gallup c 1660-....
   XXXIII 328

CRAWFORD
VA **JOHN** 1600-1676 m ....
   ____ ____ ....-a 1643
   XI 183; XXXIII 230; XXXIV 246

CREGIER
NY **MARTIN** 1614-1713 m 1642
   Lysbeth Jans ....-....
   XXXVI 241

CREHORE
MA **TEAGUE** 1640-1695 m 1665
   Mary Spurr 1637-1697
   XXXII 100

CRESSY
MA **MIGHILL/MIGEL** 1628-1670
   m 1658
   Mary Batchelder bp 1640-1659
   XXXV 301

CRISPIN
PA **SILAS** 1655-1711
   m2) 1697 **Mary (Stockton)**
   Shinn 1676-p 1729
   XXX 280; XXXI 112

CRISSEY
CT **WILLIAM** c 1630-.... m ....

_____ _____ ....-....
XXXVI 207

CRITTENDEN/CRITTENTON
CT **ABRAHAM** c 1610-1683
    m1)c 1630 **Mary (Hickson)** ....-
    1664/67
    V 128; VI 82/95; XI 21; XV 64;
    XXXI 270; XXXIX 277

CRITTENTION, see
CRITTENDEN

CROCKER
MA **WILLIAM** c 1612-1692
    m1) c 1635/36
    Alice _____ ....-liv 1683
    XVIII 64; XIX 161; XXVI 98;
    XXXIV 164

CROCKETT
ME **THOMAS** bp 1610/11-1679
    m a 1642 **Anne** _____ ....-1712
    XXXIV 68

CROSEN, see CRUSER
CROESON, see CRUSER
CROM, see CRUM

CROMWELL
MD **WILLIAM** ....-wp 1680
    m2)a 1677 **Elizabeth Trahearne**
    ....-....
    XXX 46; XXXI 16

CROOK, see CROOKE

CROOKE/CROOK
MD **JOHN, I** c 1660-c 1698
    m c 1686
    Wid. Sarah Powell c 1666-

c 1699
XXXVIII 71

CROSBY
MA **ANTHONY** 1635-1672/73
    m 1659 **Prudence Wade** 1638-
    1711
    XV 109
MA **SIMON** c 1608/09-1639
    m 1634
    Anne Brigham 1608/11-1675
    XXIV 71; XXXX 46

CROSMAN, see CROSSMAN

CROSSMAN/CROSMAN
MA **ROBERT CROSMAN** c 1622-
    1692 m 1652
    Sarah Kingsbury c 1635-1686
    IV 122; XXXIII 122; XXXVIII
    248

CROWELL
MA **YELVERTON** c 1620-1683
    m c 1640 **Elizabeth** _____ ....-
    1703
    XVIII 91; XXIV 153; XXIX
    129; XXXI 144; XXXIV 40;
    XXXVI 65

CRUM/CROM
NY **FLOTIS WILLMSE CROM**
    ....-wp 1706 m 1670
    Catalyntze Ariens ....-....
    XXXII 204

CRUMB
RI **DANIEL** ....-1713
    m 1676
    Rachel Roberts ....-1682
    XXX 281

CRUSEN, see CRUSER

CRUSER/CROESEN/CRUSEN/
KROSEN
NY **GARRET DERECKSON
CROESEN** 1640-1680 m 1661
    Neeltie Jans ....-.....
    XVI 6; XXXIII 111

CULVER/COLVER
MA **EDWARD COLVER**
    c 1600/10-1685 m 1638
    Ann Ellis ....-c 1675/78
    IV 165; VI 87/100, 89/104; XI
    102; XVI 29, 105; XVII 86;
    XVIII 61; XIX 113; XXIV 128;
    XXXIII 119; XXXIV 333;
    XXXV 81; XXXVIII 217

CUMMINGS
MA **ISAAC** c 1600/01-c 1677
    m .... _____ _____ ....-....
    VIII 30; XI 191; XIV 89; XIX
    155; XXIX 347; XXX 43; XXXII
    103

CUNNABELL
MA **JOHN** c 1649/50-1724
    m 1688/89
    Sarah Clayes (Cloise) 1666/67-
    a 1700
    XXXV 334

CURREY, see CURRY

CURRIER
MA **RICHARD** c 1616-1686/87
    m1) a 1643 **Ann Goodale** ....-
    1662/76
    XVIII 12; XXV 110; XXXI 48,
    69; XXXVI 13; XXXIX 214

CURRY, see CURREY

CURREY
NY **RICHARD CURREY, Sr** ....-
    1720/22
    m1) 1680 _____ _____ ....-....
    m2) 1706 _____ **Stiver** ....-....
    XXX 102; XXXV 68

CURTICE, see CURTIS

CURTIS/CURTICE/CURTISS
MA **DEODATUS** ....-.... m ....
    _____ _____ ....-....
    XXX 140
MA **FRANCIS CURTICE** ....-1717
    m 1671 **Hannah Smith** 1641-
    1723/24
    XXXIX 67; XXXX 125, 225
MA **HENRY** c 1620-1676/88 m ....
    Jane _____ ....-1694
    XXXX 363
MA **JOHN** 1577-c 1639/40 m 1610
    Elizabeth Hutchins ....-1658
    XXVIII 142; XXXIX 291
CT **JOHN, Jr** 1611/14-1707
    m c 1640/41
    Elizabeth Welles ....-1681/82
    XV 33, 133; XVI 70; XXVIII
    142; XXXI 43; XXXVIII 191;
    XXXX 127, 151, 152
MA **RICHARD CURTICE** ....-
    1671/72 m c 1645
    Sarah Carwithey ....-1739/61
    XXXVII 370; XXXIX 194
MA **WILLIAM** 1592-1672 m 1618
    Sarah Eliot 1600-1673
    XXIV 145
MA **ZACCHEUS CURTICE** 1619-
    1682 m ....
    Joanne _____ 1619-w 1706
    XXV 262

**CURTISS, see CURTIS
CURWEN, see CORWIN**

CUSHING
MA **JOHN** 1627-1708
 m 1658 **Sarah Hawkes** c 1641-
 1678/79
 XXXI 52
MA **MATTHEW** bp 1589-1660
 m 1613 **Nazareth Pitcher** 1586-
 1682
 XXIII 54; XXX 293; XXXI 210;
 XXXIV 302

CUSHMAN
MA **ROBERT** 1577/86-1625/26
 m1) 1606/08 **Sarah Rider** ....-
 a 1614/17
 IV 167; X 146; XVII 64; XIX 74;
 XX 52; XXV 137; XXXI 28, 260,
 279
MA **THOMAS, Sr** 1607/09-1691
 m c 1636 **Mary Allerton**
 1609/16-c1699/1700
 XXXVI 29, 68; XXXX 243

CUSTER/KUSTER
PA **PAULUS KUSTER** c 1630/40-
 1707/08 m c 1670
 Gertrude Streypers 1635-
 1707/18
 XXV 36; XXXV 201; XXXVI
 25; XXXVIII 207

CUTLER
MA **JAMES** 1606-1684/94
 m 1645 **Mary King** ....-1654
 XXII 31

CUTT, see CUTTS

CUTTER
MA **RICHARD** c 1621-1693
 m1) a 1644
 Elizabeth ____ c 1619-1661/62
 XXXII 66; XXXVIII 101

CUTTING
MA **RICHARD** 1613/23-1685/96
 m c 1644 **Sarah** ____ c 1625-
 1685
 XXII 83; XXIV 160; XXXII 107;
 XXXIV 160; XXXVII 132

CUTTS/CUTT
ME **ROBERT CUTT** bp 1619-1674
 m2).... **Mary Hoel** ....-....
 XXXII 162; XXXVIII 114

CUYPER, see CADMUS

DABNEY
VA **CORNELIUS** c 1640-
 c1694/1701 m 1666
 Susannah Swann ....-1724
 XXXVIII 97; XXXIX 147

DAGGETT/DOGGET/DOGGETT
VA **BENJAMIN** 1636-1682
 m 1664 **Jane Garrard** (wid)....-
 ....
 XXXIX 13; XXXX 142, 216
MA **JOHN DOGGETT** bp 1602-
 1663/73 m1) ....
 Hepzibah ____ 1604-c 1651
 XI 75; XV 125; XXXV 203;
 XXXVII 333

DAKIN
MA **THOMAS** 1624-1708 m 1660
 Susanna (____) **Stratton** ....-
 1697/98
 XXXI 178

DAMON
MA **JOHN** 1620-1708 m 1645
 Abigail Sherman a 1635-1713
 XXXIII 233
MA **JOHN** 1621-a 1676
 m1) 1644 **Katherine Merritt** ....-

DAMON-Cont.

....

m2) 1659 **Martha Howland** ....-
1732
XXXVIII 102
MA **THOMAS** ....-p 1723
m .... _____ _____ ....-....
IV 73, 77; XXVIII 28

DAMERON
VA **LAWRENCE** 1620-1660
m c 1645
Dorothy _____ c 1625-1691
XXXIX 336

DANA
MA **RICHARD HENRY** 1612/20-
1690 m c 1648
Anne Ballard ....-1711
I 42; II 43; X 200, 201; XXVI
268; XXX 238; XXXI 65;XXXVI
30

DANFORTH
MA **NICHOLAS** bp 1589-1638
m c 1617/18
Elizabeth _____ ....-1628/29
XXII 113; XXXI 18; XXXIV 232

DANIEL, see DANIELS
DANIELL, see DANIELS

DANIELS/DANIEL/DANIELL
VA **JOHN** ....- wp 1689
m .... **Mary Williams** ....-....
XXXVII 185
MA **ROBERT DANIELL**
c 1592/95-1655
m1) a 1630 **Elizabeth Morse** ....-
1643
XXVII 33; XXXI 217; XXXVIII
15
SC **ROBERT** 1646-1718

m2) 1701 **Martha Wainright** ....-
1742
XXIX 72; XXXI 77
MA **WILLIAM** c 1600-1678
m c 1640-45
Catherine Greenway ....-1680
XXX 28; XXXVIII 262, 348
VA **WILLIAM** ....-bef 1687 m ....

_____ _____ ....-....
XXII 44; XXXI 133
VA **WILLIAM** 1626-1698 m a 1665
Dorothy Forth ....-....
XXXV 262

DANIELSON
RI/CT **JAMES** 1648-1728
m1) .... **Abigail** ....-....
m2) 1700 **Mrs. Mary Tosh** ....-
1752
X 199; XXIV 123

DARBY
MD **SAMUEL** ....-.... m ....

_____ _____ ....-....
XXI 152

DARCEY, see DORSEY
DARCY, see DORSEY
D'ARCY, see DORSEY

DARE
PA/NJ **WILLIAM** ....-1719/20 m ....

_____ _____ ....-....
XXXIV 301

DARLING
MA **DENNIS (DENICE)** c 1640-
1715 m 1662
Hannah Francis ....-p 1687
XXXVI 263

DARROW
CT **GEORGE** ....-.... m ....

DARROW-Cont.
   Mary Sharswood ....-1698
   XXXII 119

DART
CT **RICHARD** ....-1724 m 1664
   Bethia _____ ....-....
   XIII 53

DASHIELL
MD **JAMES** c 1634-1697 m 1659
   Anne Cannon 1639-1697/1705
   XIII 26; XVIII 44; XIX 21;
   XXIV 54; XXXII 118; XXXIX
   103

DAUGE, see DOZIER

DAVENPORT
VA **JOHN** ....-1684 m ....
   Margaret _____ ....-....
   XXXIII 173
CT **JOHN** 1597-1669/70
   m .... **Elizabeth Wolley** 1603-
   1676
   XX 50; XXXV 239
VA **JOSEPH, Sr** ....-1720 m ....
   _____ _____ ....-....
   XXX 135
MA **THOMAS** 1605-1685 m ....
   Mary Forth bp 1587-1691
   XX12; XXXII 60, 287

DAVID, see DAVIS
DAVIDSON, see DAVISON

DAVIS/DAVID/DAVITS
RI/MA **AARON** ....-.... m ....
   Mary _____ ....-....
   XXI 145
MA **BARNABAS** 1599-1685
   m2) .... **Patience** _____ 1608-1690
   XX 82

NY **CRISTOFFEL/**
   CHRISTOPHER DAVITS
   c 1616- c1680
   m1) c 1642 **Cornelia DeVos** ....-
   p 1661
   m2) p 1657 _____ **Martens** ....-....
   XXXVII 169; XXXX 29
MA **DOLOR** c 1593/1600-1673
   m1) 1624 **Margery Willard**
   bp 1602-1656/70
   XXIII 66; XXVI 15, 132; XXVIII
   206; XXXIII 169; XXXV 355;
   XXXX 365, 391
NY **FOLK/FOULK/FULK** c 1615-
   1686/92
   m1) 1639 _____ _____ ....-....
   m2)1660 **Mary** _____ ....-a 1699
   XXII 14; XXXI 244; XXXII 227
MA **FRANCIS** ....-1710 m 1673/74
   Mary Taylor ....-....
   XXII 9
MA **GEORGE** ....-1667 m ....
   _____ _____ ....-....
   XX 90
VA **JAMES** c 1575/80-a 1633/34
   m .... **Rachel** _____ ....-....
   XXXVI 180
MA **JAMES, Sr** c 1583-1678/79
   m 1618
   Cicely Thayer/Tayer 1600-1673
   XXX 176; XXXIV 183
VA **JOHN** 1599-1646 m ....
   Mary _____ ....-....
   XV 132
MA **JOHN** 1660-1710 m 1684
   Elizabeth Bowden 1661-1700
   XXXX 354
VA **JONATHAN** ....-.... m ....
   Martha Drayton Vernon ....-....
   XIV 113; XV 37
PA **MORGAN DAVID** c 1622/23-
   1694/95 m ....
   Catherine _____ ....-1741

DAVIS/DAVID/DAVITS-Cont.
XXX 253; XXXVI 41; XXXVII
288; XXXVIII 139
VA **NATHANIEL** ....-.... m 1680
Elizabeth Hughes ....-....
XXXIV 117
MA **ROBERT** 1608-1693
m2) 1646/57 **Anne** _____ ....-1701
III 12; XXXV 119
VA **THOMAS** c 1632-a 1698
m 1670 **Judith Bost/Best** ....-
a 1698
XXX 149, 181; XXXI 283
MA **WILLIAM** 1617-1683
m1) a 1643
Elizabeth _____ ....-1658
V 55,95; VI 68/78, 69/79; XXIII
50

DAVISON/DAVIDSON
MA **NICHOLAS** c 1611-wp 1664
m .... **Joanna/Joan Hodges** ....-
.....
XIII 71; XXVII 208; XXX 110;
XXXIII 130
NJ **WILLIAM** c 1655-1723
m 1690/99
Margaret Oliphant c 1655/70-
p 1723
XXXVII 215; XXXIX 182

DAWSON
MD **NICHOLAS** ...-1727 m 1706
Mary Doyne 1682/83-c 1734/35
XIX 68
MD **RALPH** c 1635-1706 m c 1660
Mary Archer 1640?-p 1706
XXIV 149

DAY
MA **ANTHONY** c 1616-1707
m 1650 **Susanna Matchet**
c 1623-1717

XIX 104; XXVI 103; XXXI 240
NJ **GEORGE** c 1640-a 1685
m c 1664
Mary Riggs c 1644-....
XXXV 234
MA **MANUEL/EMANUEL** ....-....
m .... **Hannah** _____ ....-....
XXXI 260
MA **RALPH** ....-1677
m 1647 **Susan Fairbanks** ....-
1659
XXX 50; XXXIV 179; XXXIX
342
MA/CT **ROBERT** c 1604-1648
m1) .... **Mary** _____ 1614-....
m2) 1634/40 **Editha Stebbins**
c 1606/13-1688
III 45; XIII 26, 64; XVI 23, 70;
XXX 24; XXXIX 116; XXXX
253, 352

DAYTON
NY **ABRAHAM** a 1684-p 1696
m .... _____ _____ ....-....
XVII 134
CT/NY **RALPH** c 1588-wp 1658
m 1617
Alice (Goldhatch) Tritton
bp 1587/97-a 1655/56
XIV 111; XXIX 194; XXXI 283;
XXXIII 249; XXXVIII 172;
XXXIX 178; XXXX 341

DEAKINS
MD **JOHN** c 1647-1744
m2) 1718 **Priscilla** _____ ....-
p 1744
XVIII 136

DEAN/DEANE
MA **JAMES** 1647-1726 m 1693
Sarah Tisdale ....-....
XXI 82

DEAN/DEANE-Cont.
MA **JOHN, I** c 1600-p 1660 m ....
    Alice ____ 1630-1677
    XXI 150; XXVI 279, 281, 282
MA/NY **SAMUEL** a 1653-1707
    m 1667 **Elizabeth** ____ ....-....
    XXXX 304
MA **WALTER DEANE** c 1615/20-
    p 1693 m ....
    Eleanor Cogan/Strong ....-
    p 1693
    V 62; X 230, 256; XIII 111; XIX
    29

DEANE, see DEAN

DEARBORN
NH **GODFREY** bp 1603-1686
    m1)...."**Miss Goody**" c 1605-
    1662
    XVIII 7; XXIII 23; XXIX 274;
    XXXVII 315; XXXX 218

DEARMAN/DORMAN
VA **RICHARD** c 1634-a 1684
    m c 1657/58 **Elinor Harris**
    c 1636-....
    XXXIX 122

DEAVER
MD **RICHARD** c 1627-1701 m c
    1657 **Grace Fitzmorris** c 1628-
    1702
    XXXIV 293

DEBERRY
VA **PETER** a 1664-a 1679 m ....
    ____ ____ ....-....
    XXXVII 222

DE BOIS, see DUBOIS

DECKER
NY **JAN GERRETSEN** ....-....
    m 1664
    Grietje Hendricks Westercamp
    ....-....
    XXXII 26

DE CUYPER, see CADMUS
DE DUYTSCHER, see DUTCHER

DEE/DEVILLE
MA **WILLIAM DEVILLE** 1615-
    1680
    m2) 1639 **Isabel Anderson** ....-....
    XXXVIII 216

DEEKS, see DIX
DEFOREST, see DE FREES

DE FREES/DE FOREST
NY **ISAAC** bp 1616-1672/74
    m 1641 **Sarah Du Trieux** ....-
    1692
    XXXVI 316; XXXVII 54

DE GRAAF
NY **ANDRIES** ....-.... m ....
    ____-____ ....-....
    XXIII 34

DE GROOT
NY **JACOB PIETERSZEN** ....-....
    m 1652 **Grietie Jans Eggert** ....-
    ....
    XXV 222
NY **WILLEM PIETERSZEN** 1659-
    .... m .... **Lysje Gerrits** ....-....
    XXVIII 95

DE KAY/DE KEY
NY **GUILLAUME T. (WILLEM)**
    DE KEY 1575-1624 m ....
    ____ ____ ....-....

DE KAY/DE KEY-Cont.
XXXVII 73

DE KEY, see DE KAY
DE LA CHAIR, see CHAIRES

DE LA GRANGE/LA GRANGE
NY **JOHANNES DE LA GRANGE**
1630-.... m ....

____ ____ ....-....
XXI 37
NY **OMIE DE LA GRANGE** 1660-
.... m ....
Amelie De Vries ....-1735
XXI 37

DE LA MATER/LE MAISTRE
NY **CLAUDE LE MAISTRE** 1620-
1683 m 1652
Hester Du Bois 1625-1707
XIX 52; XXXX 137

DELANO/DE LA NOY
MA **PHILIPE DE LA NOY** 1602-
1681
m1) 1634 **Hester Dewsbury** ....-
....
m2) 1657 **Mary Pontus Glass**
....- ....
XII 80; XXXIV 251; XXXV 285;
XXXVI 212

DE LA NOYE, see DELANO

DE LA PLAINE
NY **NICHOLAS** ....-.... m 1658
Susanna Cresson ....-1690
XXXVIII 18

DELKE
VA **ROGER DELKE** ....-1635
m .... **Alice** ____ ....-a 1663
XXXIX 247

DE LOACH
VA **MICHAEL** 1649-1727 m 1671
Jane Griffith 1650-....
XXVI 193

DE LONG
NY **ARIE LANGE (LANGART)**
c 1655-1699 m 1680
Rachel Jansen Pyer? c 1657-....
XXXVIII 85

DE MANDEVILLE, see
MANDEVILLE
DEMAREE, see DEMAREST

DEMAREST/DEMAREE/
DES MAREST/DES MARETS
NY/NJ **DAVID des MARETS** 1620-
1693/95 m 1643
Marie Sohier ....-c 1677/78
XIII 81; XXX 73; XXXIII 12,
167, 185, 237; XXXIV 261

DE MERRIT
NH **ELI/ELEY** ....-1747 m 1695
Hopestill Runnels ....-....
XIX 24

DEMING
CT **JOHN** c 1615/16-c 1692/1705
m c 1637 **Honor Treat** bp 1616-
....
XXII 91, 95; XXXVI 142;
XXXVII 160

DENISE/NYSSEN
NY **TEUNIS DENISE (NYSSEN)**
1610-1685?   m 1640
Phoebe (Femmetje Jans) Felix
1614-....
XXX 35

DENISON
CT **GEORGE** 1618/bp 1620-1694
m2) c 1645 **Ann Borodell** 1615-
1712
XII 42; XVI 32; XIX 137; XX
150; XXXIX 220, 227
MA **WILLIAM** 1568/86-1653
m 1603 **Margaret (Chandler)
Monck/Monk** ....-1645/46
II 29; III 30; XIII 103; XVI 32;
XIX 137; XX 150

DENNEN, see DENNING

DENNING/DENNEN
ME/MA **NICHOLAS** 1645-1725
m1) .... **Eme Brown** 1645-1697
XXXI 203

DENT
MD **JOHN** ....-wp 1712
m2) a 1678 **Mary Hatch** ....-
inv 1726
XXXIV 271; XXXVIII 336
MD **THOMAS** ....-1676 m ....
Rebecca Wilkinson ...-wp 1726
XXXIV 60

DENTON
NY **RICHARD** c 1586-c 1662
m c 1623 **Mary** ____ ....-....
XIV 8; XXX 98

DE POLLOK, see POLK

DE PUY/DUPUIS/DU PUY
NY **NICHOLAS DUPUIS** ....-
wp 1691 m ....
Catrina/Catalina deVaux/deVos
....-wp 1705
XI 163; XII 119; XXXII 214;
XXXV 209; XXXVI 59

DE RAPALIE, see RAPELYEA
DE RAPALJE, see RAPELYEA

DERBY
MA **JOHN** ....-.... m ....
Alice ____ ....-....
XXV 124

DES MAREST, see DEMAREST
DES MARETS, see DEMAREST
DE VILLE, see DEE

DEVOL
MA/RI **WILLIAM** ....-p 1680 m ....
____ ____ ....-....
XXV 37

DE WANDELAER, see WANDEL

DEWEY
MA **THOMAS** c 1587/97-1648
m 1638/39
Mrs. Frances Clark c 1610-1690
IV 121; VI 61/69; XIII 96; XIV
90; XXVIII 128, 171; XXIX 173;
XXXVII 324

DE WITT
NY **TJERCK CLAEZEN** c 1630-
1700 m 1656
Barbara Andrieszen c 1636-
1714
XXIX 391

DE WOLF/DOLPH
CT **BALTHASAR** ....-p 1695 m ....
Alice ____ ....-p 1695
VI 41/46; XXXV 282, 342

DEXTER
RI **GREGORY** 1610-1700 m....
Abigail ____ ....-....
VI 57/64; X 213, 214; XI 53;

DEXTER-Cont.
  XXVI 213

DEYO
NY **CHRISTIAN** 1620-1693
  m 1643 ____ ____ ....-....
  XIII 22

DICKERMAN
MA **THOMAS** c 1600-1657/59
  m 1623 **Ellen** ____ ....-1663
  XIII 77; XIV 79; XVI 113;
  XXXIX 42

DICKINSON
NY **JOHN** ....-.... m 1651
  Elizabeth (Howland) Hicks ....-
  ....
  XVII 67
CT **NATHANIEL** c 1600-1676
  m c 1630
  Anna Gull/Gall (wid.) c 1608-....
  IV 128; V 129; XX 73; XXIV
  156; XXVI 91; XXVII 14; XXXII
  111; XXXV 122
MA **THOMAS** ....-1662 m ....
  Jennet ____ ....-1686
  XXXII 155

DIGGES
VA **EDWARD** 1620/21-1675/76
  m 1653 **Elizabeth Page** 1639-
  1691
  XXXIII 168; XXXIX 269

DILLAWAY
MA **WILLIAM** ....-.... m ....
  Sarah ____ ....-1708
  XXXVI 19

DILLE, see DILLEY

DILLEY/DILLE
NJ **JOHN DILLE, Sr** 1649-1683/84
  m .... **Sarah** ____ ....-....
  XXI 74; XXII 96; XXVI 245;
  XXVIII 41

DILLON/DILLWYN
PA **WILLIAM DILLWYN** ....-....
  m .... **Sarah Fuller** ....-....
  XXX 259

DILLWYN, see DILLON

DIMAN/DYMONT
NY **THOMAS DYMONT** ....-1682
  m 1645 ____ ____ ....-....
  XXV 7

DIMICK/DIMMOCK/DIMOCK
MA **THOMAS DIMOCK** 1604/10-
  1657/59 m ....
  Ann Hammond 1616-c 1686
  IV 97; XXXIII 144; XXXVIII
  179; XXXX 247

DIMMOCK, see DIMICK
DIMOCK, see DIMICK

DINGEE
NY **ROBERT** ....-.... m ....
  Rebecca ____ ....-....
  VIII 10

DINGLEY
MA **JOHN** c 1594/1608-c 1658
  m c 1635 **Sarah Chillingworth**
  ....-....
  XXIV 34; XXXII 243; XXXV 13

DISBROW
CT/NY **PETER** 1631-1688 m 1667
  Sarah Knapp 1639-....
  XXII 48

DIX/DEEKS
MA **ANTHONY** ....-1636 m ....
   Tabitha ____ ....-....
   XIII 24
MA **EDWARD DEEKS** c 1615-1660
   m1) 1635/36
   Jane Wilkinson 1615-a 1660
   XXI 73

DOANE
MA **JOHN** c 1590-1685 m ....
   Abigail ____ ....-....
   XXX 21; XXXV 129; XXXVIII
   10

DOBYNS
VA **DANIEL** 1653/54-1712 m3) ....
   Elizabeth Billington ....-p 1712
   XXXVI 205; XXXIX 15

DOD, see DODD

DODD/DOD
CT **DANIEL DOD, I** bp 1615-
   1665/66 m ....
   Mary (Wheeler) ....-1657
   XIII 62; XVI 79; XXVII 221;
   XXX 40; XXXVI 121

DODGE
MA **RICHARD, Sr** c 1602-1671
   m c 1631 **Edith Woodbury**
   1603-1677/78
   X 187; XVIII 15; XX 52, 145;
   XXX 119; XXXV 173, 177;
   XXXX 45
RI **TRISTRAM** c 1628-1700/18
   m a 1644 ____ ____ ....-....
   IX 27; XIII 90; XXXII 231;
   XXXIV 136
MA **WILLIAM** 1604/08-1695/94
   m .... **Elizabeth** ____ ....-....
   XVIII 68; XXXX 400

DODSON
VA **CHARLES** c 1649- wp 1705
   m .... **Ann** ____ -1703/p 1706
   XXXII 144; XXXIII 219;
   XXXVII 44, 58

DOGGET, see DAGGETT
DOGGETT, see DAGGETT

DOLE
MA **RICHARD** bp 1622-wd 1705
   m 1647 **Hannah Rolfe** 1630-
   1678
   XXXVIII 84

DOLLIVER/DOLYER
MA **SAMUEL** bp 1608-1683
   m2) 1654 **Mary Elwell** ....-....
   XIX 117

DOLPH, see DE WOLF

DONNELL
ME **HENRY** c 1602/08-1680 m ....
   Frances Gooch c 1636-....
   XXXX 304, 334, 418

DONOHO/DONOHOE
MD **DANIEL** a 1666-wp 1704
   m a 1691 **Arcadia Turville** ....-
   a 1701
   XXXVI 255

DONOHOE, see DONOHO

DOODES, see also GARRETT MINER
VA **MEINDORT DOODES** ....-1678
   m .... **Mary** ____ ....-1687
   XXIX 271

DOOLITTLE
CT **ABRAHAM** 1619/20-1690

DOOLITTLE-Cont.
m1) 1639 **Joan Allen** 1617/26-
c 1661
m2) 1663 **Abigail Moss** 1642-
1710
XI 9; XV 45; XVII 112; XIX 121;
XXIV 67; XXVI 57,58; XXVIII
57

DORLAND/DORLANDT
NY **JAN GERRETSE DORLANDT**
1625-.... m .... _____ _____ ....-....
XXXVIII 221
NY **LAMBERT JANSE**
DORLANDT 1639/40-1720
m 1665
Herminia Janse Peters c 1645-
....
XXXV 322; XXXVIII 117

DORMAN
MA **THOMAS** 1592/1600-1670
m .... **Ellen Bradley** ....-....
XXXII 205

DORSEY/DARCY/D'ARCY
VA/MD **EDWARD** ....-1659/81
m .... **Ann** _____ ....-p 1659
V 106; XII 96; XXII 94, 117;
XXV 152, 153; XXVI 104; XXIX
256; XXXI 319; XXXVI 256;
XXXVIII 333
MD **JOHN** 1641-1714 m ....
Pleasance Ely 1640/50-a 1734
V 106; XXXI 319

DOSWELL
VA **JOHN, Sr** ....-1718 m ....
Catherine _____ ....-1710
XII 112; XXXVI 88

DOTEN, see DOTY

DOTY/DOTEN/DOUGHTY
MA **EDWARD** c 1599-1655
m 1634/35 **Faith Clarke** c 1619-
1675
XII 100; XXII 35; XXXI 265;
XXXIV 22; XXXV 62, 135;
XXXVI 132; XXXVII 269;
XXXIX 135; XXXX 107, 199
444
MA/NY **FRANCIS** 1605-1695
m c 1629 m1) **Bridget Stone**
....-....
VI 20/23

DOUD, see DOUDE

DOUDE
CT **HENRY DOUDE** ....-1668/88
m .... **Elizabeth** _____ ....-
1684/1713
XXII 24; XXVI 74; XXX 241;
XXXV 178, 208, 323, 326;
XXXVI 334; XXXVII 147, 199;
XXXVIII 289

DOUGHTY, see DOTY

DOUGLAS
MA/CT **WILLIAM** c 1610-1682
m c 1636 **Ann Mattle** 1604/10-
1685
III 56; VII 22,23; VIII 22; XIII
12; XVIII 103; XXV 235; XXIX
365; XXXI 140

DOW
MA/NH **HENRY** bp 1605-1659
m1) 1630 **Joan/Jane Need/Nudd**
1602/07-1640
m2) 1640/41 **Margaret Cole** ....-
adm 1676
XVIII 46; XXVI 284; XXVIII
143; XXXV 338

DOW-Cont.
NH **JOSEPH** 1639-1703 m 1662
    Mary Sanborn ....-1703/04
    XXVIII 88

DOWD, see DOUDE

DOWLING
VA **WILLIAM** ....-.... m ....

    ____ ____ .....-....
    XXXVII 251

DOWNER
MA **JOSEPH** 1638-1715 m 1660
    Mary Knight ....-1719
    XI 91; XXVI 265; XXX 281;
    XXXVI 133

DOWNES, see DOWNS

DOWNING
NH **JOHN** 1659-1744 m 1684
    Susanna Miller 1664-1733
    XXIX 49
VA **WILLIAM** a 1651-1683
    m1) .... ____ ____ ....-....
    XXXVI 182

DOWNS/DOWNES
CT **JOHN** ....-.... m ....

    ____ ____ ....-....
    XIII 107; XV 113; XIX 37;
    XXIX 158

DOZIER/D'OZIER
VA **LEONARD, I** ....-1693
    m a 1683
    Elizabeth ____ .....-p 1702
    XXXIII 138; XXXIV 281;
    XXXV 142; XXXVII 135;
    XXXIX 172

D'OZIER, see DOZIER

DRAKE
MA/CT **JOHN** ....-1659 m ....
    Elizabeth Rogers 1581-1681
    VII 34; IX 31; XIII 66
MA **THOMAS** bp 1635-1691
    m1) c 1656/59
    Jane Holbrook ....-c 1677/80
    XXXI 151; XXXV 264; XXXVII
    340

DRESSER
MA **JOHN** c 1605-1672 m ....
    Mary ____ ....-....
    XXIV 51; XXXIX 7

DREW
NH **WILLIAM** c 1627-1669 m ....
    Elizabeth Mathews c 1628-....
    XXXX 71

DRIESSEN/VAN DRIEST/see also
JOHN & PETER JOHNSON
NY **BARENT** ....-1656 m ....
    Aeltie ____ ....-1656
    XXIII 46

DU BOIS/DE BOIS
NY **JAQUES** 1625-1676/77 m 1663
    Pierronne Bentyn ....-....
    XXVI 46
NY **LOUIS** 1626/27-1695/96 m 1655
    Catharine Blanchan c 1629-
    1713
    XX 86; XXI 80; XXXIV 237;
    XXXVII 20; XXXVIII 257

DUBOSE
SC **ISAAC** c 1665-1718/43
    m c 1688/89 **Suzanne**
    Couillandeau
    c 1665/68-a 1733/42
    XXVIII 150; XXXII 190;
    XXXIX 333

DUDLEY
VA **EDWARD** ....-a 1655 m ....
   Elizabeth Pritchard ....-....
   XXX 211; XXXIII 116
MA **FRANCIS** 1640-1703 m 1665
   Sarah Wheeler ....-1713
   XX 40
CT **JOHN** ....-1690 m 1673
   Martha French 1654-....
   XIX 65
MA **THOMAS** bp 1576-1653
   m1) 1603/a 10
   Dorothy Yorke c 1582-1643
   VI 22/24; IX 21; XXXVIII 177
CT **WILLIAM** 1610-1683/84
   m 1636 **Jane/Jean**
   Lutman/Gutman ...-   1674
   II 39; XXIX 53, 145; XXXIII 137

DUKE
VA **WILLIAM** ....-1678 m ....
   Hannah Grendon ....-a 1672
   XXXIII 80

DUMONT
NY **WALLERAND** ....-1713 m 1664
   Grietje Hendricks ....-1728
   XXIX 168

DUNBAR
MA **ROBERT** c 1630-1683/93
   m .... **Rose** ____ ....-1700
   XXIII 8; XXXX 131

DUNCKLEE/DUNKLEY
MA **ELNATHAN DUNKLEY** ....-
   1669 m 1656 **Silence Bowers** ....-
   ....
   XXV 139

DUNGAN
RI **THOMAS** 1634-1687 m c 1663

   Elizabeth Weaver 1645/47-1697
   XXIX 122

DUNHAM
MA **JOHN** 1588/89-1668/69
   m1) 1619 **Abigail Wood** ....-....
   m2) 1622 **Abigail Balliou** ....-....
   XIII 37; XVIII 111; XXVIII 16;
   XXX 14; XXXIII 179, 283;
   XXXIV 63

DUNKLEY, see DUNCKLEE
DUN, see DUNN

DUNN/DUN
NJ **HUGH, Sr** c 1640-1694
   m 1670/71
   Elizabeth Drake 1654-1711
   XVIII 7; XXXIV 92; XXXIX 323
VA **JOHN** a 1654- p 1682 m 1677
   Obedience Burgess c 1654-....
   XXV 178
NH **JOHN DUN** ....-.... m ....
   ____ ____ ....-....
   XXXV 63

DUNNELL, see DWINNELL

DUNNING/DOWNING
MA **THEOPHILUS** 1611-a 1642
   m .... **Hannah Lindell** ....-....
   XVIII 40; XXXII 41

DUPUIS, see DEPUY
DU PUY, see DEPUY

DURANT
MA **GEORGE** ....-1687 m ....
   Elizabeth (____) **Blake** (wid) ....-
   1691
   XXXVII 253
MA **JOHN** ....-1692 m ....
   Susanna Dutton 1626-1684

DURANT-Cont.
  II 53

DURDEN
VA **STEPHEN** 1611-1681 m ....
    Mary ____ ....-....
    XXII 125; XXXII 172

DURFEE
RI **THOMAS** 1643-1712 m 1664

    ____ ____ ....-....
    XXXV 120

DURIE, see DURYEE
DURGY, see DURKEE

DURKEE/DURGY
MA **WILLIAM DURGY** 1630/32-
    1726/27 m 1664
    Martha Cross 1642/43-1725/27
    XI 5; XXXVI 237; XXXVIII 354

DURLAND, see DORLAND
DURYEA, see DURYEE

DURYEE/DURIE/DURYEA
NY **JOOST DURIE** a 1635/37-
    wp 1727 m1) a 1660____ ____ or
    m2) 1672
    Magdalena La Febve ....-....
    XI 77; XXX 197; XXXIV 177

DUSTIN/DUSTON
NH/ME **THOMAS DUSTON**
    c 1605/06-a 1662 m a 1648
    Elizabeth Wheeler ....-1690
    XXXI 24; XXXV 77; XXXIX
    162

DUSTON, see DUSTIN

DUTCH
RI **OSMAND** ....-1684 m ....

    Grace ____ ....-1694
    XXXVII 111

**DUTCHER/YE DUITCHER/DE
DUYTSCHER**
NY **JAN WILLEMSZEN ye
DUITCHER** ....-.... m a 1662
    Grietje Cornelisse ....-....
    XXVI 280

DU TRIEUX, see TRUAX

DUTTON
MA **JOHN** ....-.... m ....

    ____ ____ ....-....
    XXXI 53
PA **JOHN** 1647-1693 m 1674
    Mary Darlington ....-....
    XXIX 23; XXXI 290

DUVALL
MD **MAREEN** c 1629/30-1694
    m1) 1653/58 ____ ____ ....-....
    m2) 1673/74 pr **Susannah
    Brassier** ....-1688/92
    XXXII 93; XXXV 105, 278;
    XXXVII 280, 295

DWIGHT
MA **JOHN** c 1600-1660
    m1) .... **Hannah** ____ ....-....
    X 14; XXXIII 153

DWINEL, see DWINNELL

**DWINELL/DUNELL/DWINNEL/
DWINNELLE**
MA **MICHAEL DUNNELL**
    c 1625/40-1713/17 m c 1668
    Mary ____ c 1644-....
    VIII 11; XIX 109; XXXVI 301

DYCKMAN, see DYKEMAN

DYE/DEY/DUYTS/DUYTSZEN
RI **WILLIAM ("The Elder")** 1654-
    1720/30 m 1681
    Sarah _____ 1660-....
    V 80
NY **LAURENS DUYTSZEN** 1610-
    1688 m1) .... **Ytie Jansen** ....-....
    XXXVIII 261; XXXX 254

DYER
MA **THOMAS** 1612-1676 m 1640
    Agnes Reed ....-1667
    XXXI 175
RI **WILLIAM** 1587-1677
    m1) ..... **Mary Dyer** ....-1660
    X 17
MA **WILLIAM** 1653-1738 m 1686
    Mary Taylor 1660-1738
    XXXIV 88

DYKEMAN/DYCKMAN
NY **JOHANNES** c 1619-1672
    m .... **Marritje Cornelis (Bosyn)**
    ....- ....
    XXXI 252

DYMONT, see DIMAN

EAGON/HAGAN/HAGOE
MD **THOMAS HAGOE** ....-
    wp 1716 m ....**Mary _____** ....-....
    XXXV 314

EAMES
MA **THOMAS** c 1618-1680
    m1) 1640/60
    Margaret _____ ....-....
    m2).... **Mary (Blandford)**
    Paddleford ....-1676
    X 159; XXXV 353

EARLE
VA **JOHN** 1612/20-wp 1660

m 1635/37 **Mary Symons** 1619-
    1655/60
    XI 61; XIII 78; XXI 39; XXV
    163; XXVIII 158; XXIX 39, 289;
    XXXI 239; XXXIV 269;
    XXXVIII 218
RI **RALPH** a 1634-1678 m 1631
    Joan (pr. Savage) ....-....
    XVII 153
VA **RICHARD, I** ....-.... m ....
    _____ _____ ....-....
    XVIII 20

EASLEY
VA **ROBERT** 1655/80-wp 1712
    m 1679/84 **Anne Parker** ....-
    wp 1720
    XXXVI 48; XXXVIII 138

EASTERLING
MD **HENRY** 1676-wp 1702
    m c 1696 **Elizabeth Vines**
    (Vinnes) ....-a 1702
    XXXIX 329

EASTMAN
MA **ROGER** 1610/11-1694/95
    m a 1640
    Sarah Smith 1620/21-1690/98
    IX 25, 35; XII 48; XIII 20; XV
    115; XVII 92; XXI 87; XXII 60;
    XXIX 80; XXXI 79; XXXIII 46,
    252; XXXV 90; XXXVIII 212

EASTON
MA/CT **JOSEPH, I** c 1602-1688
    m _____ _____ ....-....
    XI 68; XV 58; XXI 116
CT **JOSEPH** 1648-1711 m c 1669
    Hannah Ensign ....-....
    XXV 107

EATON
MA **JOHN, I** c 1595-1668 m c 1617
    Anne ____ c 1595-1660
    XVIII 143; XXVII 219; XXX
    144; XXXIX 105
MA **WILLIAM** c 1604-1673
    m 1627/28
    Martha Jenkins bp 1605-1680
    XXXII 102; XXXVI 281

EAVENSON
PA **RALPH** c 1625-1665 m 1650
    Cicely Orton 1630-....
    XXXVII 25

ECHOLS
VA **JOHN** ....-p 1706 m ....
    Mary Cave ....-1720
    XXXVII 265; XXXVIII 125

EDDY
MA **JOHN** ....-1695 m 1672
    Deliverance Owen 1654-1726
    XXII 69
MA **JOHN** bp 1597-1684 m p 1619
    Amie Doget bp 1597-....
    XXVIII 62
MA **SAMUEL** bp 1608-1687
    m a 1637 **Elizabeth Savery**
    1607/09-1687/89
    XVII 58; XXII 81, 96; XXIV
    116; XXX 133; XXXVII 279;
    XXXX 144, 145, 146, 147
MA **ZACHARIAH** 1639-1718
    m .... **Alice Paddock** 1640-1692
    XXX 133

EDES
MA **JOHN** 1575-1658 m ....
    ____ ____ ....-....
    XXV 147

EDGCOMBE, see EDGECOMBE

EDGECOMB, see EDGECOMBE

**EDGECOMBE/EDGCOMBE/
EDGECOMB**
CT **JOHN EDGCOMBE** a 1640-
    1721 m1) 1673
    Sarah Stallion/Stallon bp 1674-
    ....
    X 304
ME **NICHOLAS EDGECOMB** ....-
    wr 1681 m 1642/43
    Wilmot Randall 1620-1684
    XXXIII 92

EDGERLY
NH **THOMAS** ....-p 1715 m 1665
    Rebecca (Ault) Hallowell 1641-
    p 1711/12
    XXIX 317

EDGERTON
CT **RICHARD** a 1633-1691/92
    m 1653/63 **Mary Sylvester** ....-....
    X 252; XX 98; XXI 5; XXV 40;
    XXXX 100

EDMONSTON
MA **THOMAS** ....-p 1686 m ....
    ____ ____ ....-....
    XXXVI 306

EDSON
MA **SAMUEL** bp 1612/13-1692
    m 1638 **Susanna Orcutt** 1618-
    1699
    XIII 101; XXXIX 157

EDWARDS
MA **ALEXANDER** ....-1690 m 1642
    Sarah (Baldwin) Searle ....-....
    XXXVI 42
MA **RICE** 1615-1683 m ....
    Joanna ____ ....-1681

EDWARDS-Cont.
XXXIX 344
VA **WILLIAM, Sr** ....-1624 m ....

____ ____ ....-....
XXXII 263
MA/NY **WILLIAM** ....-c 1685
m .... **Ann Cole** ....-p 1685/1700
XXXVI 187; XXXIX 75; XXXX
409

EELIE, see ELY

EELLS
MA **SAMUEL EELLS** 1640-1709
m 1663 **Ann Lenthall** ....-1687
XXXI 197

EGGLESTON
MA **BYGOD/BEGAT** 1586/87-1674
m1) c 1611 ____ ____ ....-....
m2) .... **Mary Talcott** ....-1657
XXVII 40; XXXIII 181

ELDER
VA **PETER, Sr** ....-1674 m ....

____ ____ ....-....
XXVIII 95, 120; XXIX 16; XXXI
102; XXXIV 328; XXXVII 365

ELDRED, see ELDREDGE

ELDREDGE/ELDRED
MA **ELNATHAN** 1684-1735 m ....
Hannah Chase 1687-1760
XXX 201
MA/RI **SAMUEL** c 1620-1699
m .... **Elizabeth Miller** ....-....
XXX 138; XXXIII 120
MA **WILLIAM ELDRED** ....-c 1679
m .... **Anna Lumpkin** ....-1676
XV 84; XXI 38

ELLEY
VA **ROBERT** c 1620-....
m ....____ ____ ....-....
XXXVIII 49

ELIOT, see ELLIOTT
ELKIN, see ELKINS

ELKINS/ELKIN
VA **RALPH** c 1610-1690 m ....
____ **Ashton** ....-....
XVI 124; XXI 160; XXXIII 349;
XXXIV 26; XXXV 279

**ELLENWOOD/ELLINWOOD/
ELWOOD**
MA **RALPH ELWOOD, I** 1607-
1673/74 m2) 1655 **Eleanor
(Ellen) Lyn(n)** c 1637-p 1677
XXXII 101; XXXVIII 94

ELLICE, see ELLIS
ELLINWOOD, see ELLENWOOD

ELLIOTT
MA **EDMUND** c 1629-wp 1683/84
m c 1659
Sarah Haddon 1639/40-p 1687
XXIII 39; XXIV 134; XXXVII
141

ELLIS/ELLICE
MA **JOHN** c 1619-a 1677 m 1645
Elizabeth Freeman 1623/25-
1692/1714
XVIII 105; XIX 16, 34; XXV
104; XXXII 48
MA **JOHN ELLICE** ....-1697
m2) 1655 **Mrs. Joan ( ) Clapp**
....- 1703/04
XVIII 68
NJ **SIMON** ....-wp 1715 m 1692
Sarah Bate ....-....

ELLIS/ELLICE-Cont.
XXI 98

ELLSWORTH
MA **JEREMIAH** ....-1704 m2) 1689
   Sarah Jewett c 1660-1746
   XXXV 237

ELMER
CT **EDWARD** 1609-1676 m ....
   Mary ____ ....-....
   XXXVII 171

ELSTON
NY **WILLIAM** a 1660-wp 1689
   m 1682 **Elizabeth Cole** ....-....
   XXXIV 264

ELTON
CT **JOHN** ....-1787 m 1671
   Jane Hall 1652-....
   XXXII 66

ELWELL
MA **ROBERT** c 1612-1683
   m c 1631/54
   Joan(e)/Jane/Joanne Dalliber
   ....- 1675
   XXXVI 90; XXXIX 88; XXXX
   267

ELWOOD, see ELLENWOOD

ELY/EELIE
NJ **JOSHUA** 1649-1702 m 1673
   Mary Seinerd/Senoir ....-1698
   XXXIII 146; XXXX 123
CT/MA **NATHANIEL** 1605-1675
   m .... **Martha** ____ ....-1688
   VI 36/41; XIX 107; XX 107, 111
MA/CT **RICHARD** c 1610-1684
   m .... **Joan (Joanne) Phipps** ....-
   1660

XII 99; XXIV 78; XXIX 50;
   XXX 108
VA **ROBERT EELIE** c 1620-....
   m .... **Anne** ____ ....-....
   XXVI 10; XXXVIII 49

EMERSON
MA **THOMAS** 1584-1666
   m 1611
   Elizabeth Brewster ....-p 1666
   I 41; XIII 60; XXXII 212;
   XXXIV 263

EMERY
*ME/RI **ANTHONY** c 1600-p 1680
   m .... **Frances** ____ ....-p 1660
   V 108; XV 23; XXV 143;
*See XXV 143. Also the 1975 Index
MA **JAMES** c 1630-p 1713 m ....
   Elizabeth ____ ....-....
   V 108
MA **JOHN, Sr** 1598-1683 m1) 1650
   Mary (Shatswell) Webster ....-
   1694
   VII 19, 20; XX 37, 108; XXI 138;
   XXIV 163; XXXV 66, 210;
   XXXIX 2
MA **JOHN, Jr** 1628/29-1693 m 1648
   Mary ____ ....-....
   VII 19, 20

EMMONS
RI **THOMAS** ....-1664/67 m ....
   Martha ____ ....-1667
   XVIII 67; XXXX 66

ENDECOTT, see ENDICOTT

ENDICOTT/ENDECOTT
MA **JOHN ENDECOTT** 1588-1665
   m2) 1630 **Elizabeth Gibson** ....-
   p1671
   XXV 93

ENNES
NY **ALEXANDER** ....-.... m ....

_____ _____ ....-....
XXIV 41

ENO
CT **JAMES** bp 1625-1682
m 1648 **Ann Bidwell** (wid.) ....-
1657
XIX 8

ENOCHS/ENOCHSON
PA **GARRETT ENOCHSON**
c 1640-a 1696 m c 1668
Gertrude _____ ....-w 1737
XXXX 40, 114

ENOCHSON, see ENOCHS

ENSIGN
CT **JAMES** ....-1670 m ....
Sarah Elson ....-1676
XXXIX 177

ENSLEY/ILLSLEY
MA **WILLIAM ILLSLEY** 1608/12-
1681 m .... **Barbara** _____ ....-....
XXXVII 237

EPES, see EPPES

EPPES/EPES
VA **FRANCIS EPES, I** 1597-
1668/74 m a 1626
Mary/Marie _____ ....-p 1643/44
XXXVIII 194, XXXIX 109, 169;
XXXX 246
VA **FRANCIS** 1597-1655/58
m .... **Martha** _____ ....-....
XXXVIII 194

**ESSELSTYN, see VAN
ESSELSTYN**

ESSEX
RI **HUGH** ....-.... m ....

_____ _____ ....-....
XXII 143; XXIV 101; XXV 282

ESTEY
MA **JEFFREY** ....-1657 m ....

_____ _____ ....-....
XXXV 184

ESTILL/D'ESTELLE
NJ **THOMAS D'ESTILLE** c 1623-
1688 m 1670
Lucia Wallace ....-....
XXXVII 334; XXXIX 60

EVANS
MA **ABRAHAM** a 1674-1712
m 1680 **Elizabeth** _____ ....-1712
XXXV 328
MA **DAVID** ....-1663 m ....
Mary _____ ....-....
XXIV 45
MA **HENRY** ....-c 1666/67 m ....

_____ _____ ....-....
XXV 267
NH **ROBERT** c 1630-1697
m2) c 1680 **Ann (Thompson)
Hodson** 1645-p 1697
XXXVI 245; XXXX 364
PA **THOMAS, Sr** c 1662-1756
m c 1730
**Sarah Martha Elizabeth
Roberts** 1692-....
XXXIV 339
NJ **WILLIAM** ....-a 1688 m ....
Jane Hodges ....-1697
XIV 114; XVII 137

EVARTS, see EVERTS

EVELETH
MA **SYLVESTER** ....-1689 m ....

EVELETH-Cont.
  Susanna ____ 1594-1659
    XIII 108

EVEREST
ME **ANDREW** ....-a 1711 m ....
    Barbara/Barbery ____ ....-....
    III 37; XXXVI 204

EVERETT/EVERITT
VA **GEORGE EVERITT** c 1635-
  1712 m .... **Mary Taylor** ....-....
    XXXIV 206
MA **RICHARD** c 1600-1682
  m1) a 1637 **Mary** ____ ....-a 1643
  m2) .... **Mary Winch** 1628-....
    X 277; XIV 103, 123; XXIV 79;
    XXVI 179; XXXIV 266; XXXVI
    288

EVERITT, see EVERETT

EVERTS/EVARTS
MA/CT **JOHN EVARTS** 1600/08-
  1669 m c 1631
    Elizabeth ____ ....-....
    X 128, 147; XIII 83; XXV 144

EVERTSZEN, see also WESSELL
NY **WESSEL** ....-.... m 1643
    Goertie Bouwkens ....-....
    XXXII 34

EWER
MA **THOMAS** c 1585-1638
    m .... **Sarah** ____ ....-p 1649
    XXXIII 40; XXXV 252

EYAMS, see IJAMS
EYRE, see AYER

FAIRBANKS
MA **JONATHAN** c 1595-1668/78

  m 1617
  Grace (Smith)(Warley) Lee ....-
  1673/76
    VIII 26; X 207; XXXI 211;
    XXXIII 99

FAIRCHILD
CT **THOMAS** c 1610-1670
  m1) 1639 **Sarah or Ruth
  Seabrook** ....-p 1653
  m2) 1662 ____ ____ ....-....
    VII 29; XI 69; XXIII 27; XXIX
    308; XXX 215

FAIRFIELD
MA **JOHN** c 1610-1646 m 1632
    Elizabeth Knight 1615-....
    XXV 156; XXVII 129, 130;
    XXXVIII 118

FAIRMAN
CT **JOHN** ....-1684 m ....
    Elizabeth ____ ....-liv. 1712
    XXXVII 65

FALES
MA **JAMES** 1635-1708 m 1655
    Ann Brock ....-1712
    XIX 58

FANNING
CT **EDMUND** c 1620-1683
    m c 1649 **Ellen** ____ ....-p 1687
    XIII 123; XXXX 110

FARLEY
MA **GEORGE** c 1615-1693 m 1641
    Christian Births ....-1702
    XXXIV 19, 32
VA **THOMAS, I** 1600/02-....
    m c 1622 **Jane Sefton** 1604-....
    XXXIV 192; XXXV 303;
    XXXVI 31; XXXVII 13

FARMAN/FOREMAN/FORMAN
NY **ROBERT FORMAN** 1605-
1671 m ....**Johanna Pore** ....-
p 1671
IV 79; XIX 62
MD **WILLIAM FOREMAN** c 1658-
wp 1730 m ....
Elizabeth _____ ....-wp 1733
XXXIII 33; XXXX 38

FARMER
VA **THOMAS, I** c 1594-....
m .... _____ _____ ....-....
XXXVI 283

FARNHAM/FARNUM
MA **JOHN** c 1600-c 1684 m 1654
Susanna Arnold 1636-1717
XXXX 79
MA **RALPH** 1603-.... m ....
Alice _____ ....-a 1648
XXIII 26

FARNUM, see FARNHAM

FARNSWORTH
MA **MATHIAS** 1611/12-1688/89
m1) 1647 **Mary Farr** ....-1717
IV 125; VI 93/109; X 58, 103; XI
29; XIII 37; XV 74; XX 106;
XXIV 47

FARR
MA **STEPHEN** ....-.... m 1674
Mary Taylor 1649-....
XIV 40; XXIII 52

FARRAR/FARROW
MA **JACOB** 1620-1677
m c 1640 **Ann** _____ ....-liv 1658
XIV 51
MA **JOHN FARROW** ....-1687
m ....**Frances** _____ ....-1688/89

XXXI 277
VA **WILLIAM** bp 1583-a 1637
m a 1625
Mrs. Cecily Jordan (wid.) ....-....
XII 117; XIII 19; XXXVII 46;
XXXVIII 312; XXXX 445

FARRINGTON
NY **EDWARD/EDMUND** 1588-
1671 m ....
Eliza/Elizabeth 1586-1678
XXVII 103; XXXVII 367

FARROW, see FARRAR

FARWELL
MA **HENRY** 1604/05-1670 m 1629
Olive Welby bp 1604-1691/92
XXXII 159; XXXVIII 74; XXXX
318

FASSETT
MA **PATRICK** 1628-1713
m 1644 **Sarah** _____ ....-1739/40
XXXIV 314; XXXVIII 328

FAULKNER
MA **EDMOND** 1625-1686/87
m 1647 **Dorothy Robinson** ....-
1668
XXIX 88; XXXI 106

FAUNTLEROY
VA **MOORE** ....-a 1665
m c 1648 **Mary Hill** ....-....
XXIV 115

FAXON
MA **THOMAS** 1601-1680
m .... **Joane** _____ ....-1663/70
XXIX 292; XXXVII 57

FAY
MA **JOHN, Sr** c 1648-p 1690
   m1) 1668/69
   Mary Brigham 1638-1676
   XX 62; XXIX 189; XXXV 23;
   XXXX 340

FAYERWEATHER
MA **THOMAS** ....-1638 m ....
   Mary ____ ....-1682
   V 116; XXVII 184

FEARN
VA **THOMAS** ....-.... m ....
   ____ ____ ....-....
   XXX 252

FEARSON
MD **JOHN** ....-1683 m ....
   Grace ____ ....-....
   XIV 94

FEE
MD **GEORGE** a 1670-....
   m .... **Margaret Purnell** ....-....
   XXX 192

FELCH
MA **HENRY, Jr** 1610-wp 1699
   m 1650 **Hannah Sargent** 1629-
   1717
   XXVI 122

FELLOWS
MA **SAMUEL, Sr,** 1619-1698
   m 1641 **Ann/Anne** ____ ....-1684
   XIV 118; XXII 124; XXV 164;
   XXXII 218; XXXV 282
MA **WILLIAM** 1609-1676/77 m ....
   Mary Ayers ....-1677
   XII 78; XXXII 274; XXXX 54

FELT
MA/ME **GEORGE** 1601-1682/93
   m .... **Elizabeth (Wilkinson)**
   1601/12-1694
   XIII 85; XIV 28; XV 6, 30; XVI
   67; XXVI 106

FELTON
MA **NATHANIEL** bp 1615-1705
   m a 1645 **Mary Skelton** bp 1627-
   1701
   XXXI III

FENNER
RI **ARTHUR** 1622-1703
   m1) **Mehitable Waterman** ....-
   1684
   IX 56; XXV 21

FENTON
NJ **ELEAZER** 1655-1704
   m1) .... **Judith** ____ ....-....
   XVIII 35
MA/CT **ROBERT** ....-p 1730
   m a 1668 **Dorothy** ____ ....-
   p 1710
   XXV 171

FERNALD
NH **RENALD** 1595/1605-1656 m ....
   Joanna Warburton ....-1660
   XX 147; XXII 114; XXXIV 147

FERRIS
CT **JEFFREY** c 1610-1666 m ....
   ____ ____ ....-....
   XXXI 22, 171, 236; XXXIII 25

FESSENDEN
MA **NICHOLAS** c 1650-1718/19
   m 1673 **Margaret Cheney** 1656-
   1717
   X 177; XV 122

FIELD
VA **ABRAHAM, Sr** c 1636-wp 1674
m p 1651
Mary Ironmonger ....-p 1674
XXXIII 151; XXXIV 38; XXXV
220
VA **HENRY** c 1611-.... m ....

_____ _____ ....-....
XXV 123; XXX 116
MA **ROBERT** 1613-1675
m a 1635 **Mary Stanley** 1610-
p 1677
XVIII 83
RI **THOMAS** c 1648-1717 m ....
Martha Harris ....-c 1717
XVIII 16; XXXVIII 119
MA **ZACHARIAH** 1596-1666
m c 1641 **Mary Stanley** ....-
c 1670
XIV 70, 78; XXVIII 36;
XXIX 286, 347; XXXV 240

FILKINS
NY **HENRY, Sr** 1651-a 1714 m ....
Katherine Vonck Ruard 1670-
....
XX 128

FILLEBROWN
MA **THOMAS** 1631-1713 m ....
Anna _____ 1631/32-1713/14
XXVII 72

FILLEY
CT **WILLIAM** ....-.... m 1642
Margaret _____ ....-....
XXXV 62

FINCH
MA/CT **ABRAHAM** c 1585-1638
m .... _____ _____ ....-....
XXIX 278

FINCHER
PA **FRANCIS** ....-1687 m ....
Mary Ackley ....-1687
XXXVI 223

FINNELL
VA **JOHN** 1629-a 1688 m ....
Frances Moss ....-....
XXXIX 52

FINNEY, see PHINNEY
FIRMAN, see FURMAN
FIRMIN, see FURMAN

FISH
MA **NATHANIEL** bp 1619-1694
m a 1645/48 _____ _____ ....-....
XXXVIII 320; XXXIX 23
RI **ROBERT** c 1665-wd 1728
m 1686 **Mary Hall** ....-1735
XXXV 172
RI **THOMAS** 1618/19-1687 m ....
Mary (Sherman) ....-1699
XIX 54

FISHER
MA **ANTHONY** bp 1591-1671
m1) c 1616 **Mary Fisk (e)**
c 1592-a 1662/63
XI 79; XIX 85; XXVI 169; XXX
146; XXXI 187; XXXIV 207;
XXXVI 336; XXXVIII 142
PA/DE **JOHN** ....-1685/86 m ....
Margaret _____ ....-liv 1689
V 83
MA **JOSHUA** bp 1585-p 1656 m ....

_____ _____ ....-....
XII 93
MA **THOMAS** ....-1637/38 m ....
Elizabeth _____ ....-....
XXVII 7

FISK/FISKE
MA **DAVID FISKE** ....-a 1660 m ....
    Sarah Smith ....-a 1660
    X 246; XXII 115; XXXV 190
MA **NATHAN FISKE** c 1615-1676
    m .... **Susanna** _____ ....-....
    XV 84; XXII 47; XXV 47; XXVI
    30; XXXII 217; XXXIV 197
MA **PHINEAS** ....-1673
    m1) 1638 **Sarah** _____ ....-1659
    m2) .... **Elizabeth Esterick** ....-....
    XIX 133; XXVIII 199; XXIX 82;
    XXXI 245; XXXIII 93
MA **WILLIAM** c 1613-1654 m 1643
    Bridgett Muskett ....-....
    XVI 38

FISKE, see FISK

FITCH
CT **JAMES** 1622-1702
    m1) 1648 **Abigail Whitfield**
    1622-1659
    XIV 99, 105; XXXI 280
CT **JOSEPH, I** ....-p 1713
    m a 1663 **Mary Stone** ....-....
    XXIX 49; XXXIII 276
CT **THOMAS, I** 1612-w 1704
    m 1632
    Anna Stacey/Steele/
    Stracyor ....-   ....
    VI 64/73; XXX 217; XXXV 83;
    XXXX 14

FITHIAN
NY **WILLIAM** ....-1678 m ....
    Margaret ....-....
    XXXVIII 338

FITTS
MA **ROBERT** c 1600-1665
    m .... **Grace D. Lord** ....-1684
    XVII 148; XXXVIII 75

FITZHEW, see FITZHUGH

FITZHUGH/FITZHEW
VA **WILLIAM** bp 1651-1701
    m 1674 **Sarah Tucker** 1663-
    1701/03
    XVII 122; XXXI 92; XXXIII
    256; XXXVII 359; XXXVIII 253

FITZRANDOLPH
MA **EDWARD** c 1607/14-1675
    m 1637 **Elizabeth Blossom** 1620-
    1713
    XIII 58, 105; XXVI 212; XXXIII
    331

FLAGG/FLEGG
MA **THOMAS** bp 1615-1697/98
    m 1640 **Mary** _____ 1619/20-
    wp 1702/03
    XIII 47; XIV 9; XVII 102; XXV
    245; XXX 267; XXXVII 97, 307

FLANDERS
MA **STEPHEN, Sr** c 1620-1684
    m c 1640/43 **Jane** _____ ....-1683
    XXX 184; XXXVII 240; XXXIX
    190

FLEGG, see FLAGG

FLEHARTY
MD **JOHN** ....-p 1729 m ....
    Frances _____ ....-p 1714
    XXXIV 102

FLEMING
MD **WILLIAM** 1662-1726 m 1691
    Mary Moore 1674-....
    XVI 47

FLETCHER
VA **RALPH** 1632-1698 m 167_

FLETCHER-Cont.
   Elizabeth Sutton ....-1699
   XXVIII 155
MA **ROBERT** c 1592-1677
   m ....
   Sarah _____ ....-liv 1672
   IV 147; X 221; XIV 101, 108;
   XV 58; XVIII 116; XIX 168;
   XXIV 168; XXVII 101; XXXIII
   136; XXXV 319; XXXIX 159
MA **SAMUEL** a 1630/32-1697
   m 1659
   Margaret Hailston(e) ....-....
   IV 147; XXXIX 159
MA **WILLIAM** 1622-1677 m 1645
   Lydia (Fairbanks) Bates ....-....
   XXXV 322

FLINT/FLYNT
VA **RICHARD** ....-1683 m by
   1677/78 **Mary Sharp** ....-....
   XXXIX 175
MA **THOMAS** c 1603-1663 m 1633
   Ann(e) _____ ....-1668
   XVIII 78; XIX 118; XXIII 47;
   XXV 206; XXXV 169, 179, 278;
   XXXVIII 187

FLOYD
MA/NY **RICHARD** ....-c 1700
   m .... **Susanna** _____ 1626-1705
   XXXV 63

FLYNT, see FLINT

FOBES
MA **JOHN** 1610-1662 m 1645
   Constant Mitchell ....-....
   XXX 35

FOGG
NH **SAMUEL** 1600/13-1672
   m1) 1652 **Ann Shaw** ...-1661

   m2) 1665 **Mary Page** c 1644-
   1700
   XXVII 185; XXXV 281; XXXX
   73

FOLSOM/FOULSHAM
MA **JOHN** bp 1615-1681 m 1636
   Mary Gilman bp 1615-1681/92
   XI 168; XVII 111; XVIII 94;
   XXIV 135; XXV 11; XXX 110;
   XXXIII 342; XXXIX 307

FONDA
NY **JILLIS (JELLES) DOUWSE**
   1604/16-1659 m 1641
   Hester (Douwess) Jans 1615-
   1690
   XVI 114; XXIII 9; XXXII 284;
   XXXX 164

FONTEYNE, see VANTINE

FOOKS
VA/MD **JAMES** ....-.... m ....
   Rachel Haydens ....-....
   XXXVIII 170

FOOTE
MA/CT **NATHANIEL** c 1593-1644
   m c 1615
   Elizabeth Deming c 1595-1683
   III 59; X 183, 237; XII 21, 34;
   XIII 16, 34, 38, 79; XIV 112;
   XXIV 167; XXXI 177, 200;
   XXXVI 225; XXXVII 60, 141

FORBES
MA **DANIEL** c 1620-1687
   m2) 1679 **Deborah Rediat** 1652-
   1720
   XXXVI 151
CT **JAMES** ....-1692 m c 1660
   Catherine/Catheran _____ ....-

FORBES-Cont.
  p 1692
  XVIII 52; XXXVII 55

FORD
MA **ANDREW** 1632-1693
  m 1650/56 **Eleanor Lovell**
  c 1633-....
  X 205; XII 111; XIII 11
MD **THOMAS** c 1631-p 1681
  m a 1670
  Elizabeth _____ ....-....
  XXXII 96; XXXIII 72; XXXV
  335
MA/CT **TIMOTHY** ....-1684 m ....
  Gordy _____ ....-1681
  X 40

FOREMAN, see FARMAN
FORMAN, see FARMAN

FORT
VA **ELIAS, I** a 1646-1679 m ....
  Phillis Champion ....-....
  XXX 274; XXXI 85, 125

FORTESCUE, see FOSCUE

FOSCUE/FORTESCUE
VA **SIMON** 1604-1680 m 1630
  Elizabeth _____ 1615-1661
  XXXIV 339; XXXVIII 175

FOSTER
MA/NY **CHRISTOPHER** 1603/08-
  1687 m 1628 **Frances Glover**
  1607/10-1687/a 1703
  XIX 11; XX 151; XXXVII 363
MA **EDWARD** 1610-1643 m 1635
  Lettice Hanford ....-....
  XII 79; XXXIII 23
MA **JOHN, Sr** c 1618/28-wp 1688
  m 1648/49 **Martha Tompkins**

  c 1627/30-p 1688
  XXV 161; XXIX 377; XXXI 269
MA **REGINALD** 1595-1681
  m2)1617/18 **Judith** _____ ....-
  1664
  IX 48; XIII 75; XVI 107; XXVI
  175; XXVIII 138; XXX 104;
  XXXI 259; XXXIII 266; XXXX
  264
VA **RICHARD** 1615/20-p 1679
  m 1642 **Susannan**
  Garnett/Jarnett ....-   ....
  XXXVII 309; XXXX 151
VA **ROBERT** ....-a 1718 m ....
  Elizabeth _____ ....-....
  XXXV 265

FOULSHAM, see FOLSOM

FOWLER
CT/MA **AMBROSE** c 1620-1704
  m 1646 **Jane Alvord** bp 1622-
  1684
  XIX 91; XXXIII 16
MA/RI **HENRY** ....-p 1687 m a 1655
  Rebecca Newell ....-....
  XXIX 135
CT **JOHN** 1635-1676 m 1647
  Mary Hubbard 1645-1713
  XVI 27
MA **PHILIP** c 1590/91-1679
  m1) a 1615 **Mary**
  Winsley/Winslow ....-1659
  III 26; XXV 215; XXXIII 336;
  XXXIV 311; XXXVI 139, 171
CT **WILLIAM** 1572-1660/61
  m2) .... **Sarah** _____ ....-....
  XVI 27; XXVI 84; XXXIV 264

FOX
MA **THOMAS** 1622-1658
  m2) 1647 **Hannah Brooks** 1627-
  1692

FOX-Cont.
    XI 101; XXVI 291

FRANCIS
CT **ROBERT** 1628/29-1711/12
    m 1650/51
    Joan Sibberance c 1629-1704/05
    X 25; XII 84; XV 68; XXII 87;
    XXVII 163; XXXIII 19; XXXIV
    203

FRANKLIN
NY **HENRY** ....-wp 1710
    m2) 1697/8 **Sarah Cox/Cock**
    1672-1750/51
    XX 39; XXIX 45
MA **JOSIAH** 1655-wp 1750
    m2) 1689 **Abiah Folger** 1667-
    1753
    XXXVII 126
MD **ROBERT, I** ....-c 1681 m ....
    Sarah Puddington ....-....
    XXXVI 139

FRAZEE, see **FRAZER**

FRAZER/FRAZEE
NJ **JOSEPH** ....- wp 1714 m ....
    Mary Osborn ....-1718
    XXI 148

FREDERICKSE, see also
MYNDERSE
NY **MYNDERT** ....-1706
    m1) .... **Cataryna Burger** ....-....
    II 48

FREEMAN
MA **EDMUND** pr 1590-wp 1682
    Elizabeth Beauchamp/Bennett
    1600-1675/76
    X 73, 143; XI 134, 192; XVI 136;
    XX 21; XXI 136; XXIX 42;

    XXXV 237
PA/NJ **HENRY** 1669/72-1763
    m 1695 **Elizabeth Bowne** 1673-
    1760
    XXVII 37, 94, 137
MA **JOHN** 1627-1719   m 1649/50
    Mary Prence c 1631-1711
    XVI 136
NJ **JOSEPH** 1639-1682 m 1666
    Elizabeth Gosse 1636-....
    XXI 60
MA **SAMUEL** ....-1639 m ....
    Apphia ____ ....-a 1668
    XXXII 140

FREER/FRERE
NY **HUGO/HUGUE FRERE**
    a 1647-p 1697
    m1) .... **Maria Haye** a 1653-
    1677/78
    XI 18; XXXIII 320; XXXIV 149

FREESE, see **FREEZE**

FREEZE/FREESE
MA **JAMES FREESE** ....-....
    m .... **Elizabeth** ____ ....-....
    XXXVI 330

FRENCH
MA **EDWARD** 1590/98-1674
    m .... **Ann Swayne/Goodale** ....-
    1682/83
    XXV 218; XXIX 157; XXX 144;
    XXXV 219
VA **HUGH** c 1664-a 1701 m 1685
    Margaret (Gaines) Prosser ....-
    1710
    XXXVI 197; XXXVII 357
MA **JOHN** c 1612/15-1692
    m1) .... **Grace** ____ c 1621-1680
    X 176; XXVII 210; XXXIV 236
CT **THOMAS** ....-.... m2) ....

FRENCH-Cont.
    Deborah _____ ....-....
    XXX 42
MA **THOMAS** ....-a 1639 m ....
    Mary _____ ....-....
    XXII 119
MA **WILLIAM** 1603-1681 m ....
    Elizabeth _____ 1605-1688
    XXXIII 235

FRERE, see FREER

FRINK
MA/CT **JOHN, I** c 1600/18-wp 1675
    Mary Nart ....-p 1675
    VII 37; X 80; XIV 59; XXXX
    415
CT **JOHN, II** 1630/39-1717 m 1657
    Grace Stevens/Stephens 1635-
    1717
    XXXV 29, 106, 107; XXXVI 57;
    XXXVII 319; XXXVIII 110

FRISBEE, see FRISBIE

FRISBIE/FRISBEE/FRISBYE
CT **EDWARD FRISBYE** 1620-1690
    m .... **Hannah/Abigail**
    Culpepper a 1635-1687
    XII 5; XXXIII 171; XXXIV 229;
    XXXVI 69

FRISBYE, see FRISBIE

FROST
MA **EDMUND** c 1600-wp 1672
    m1) 1633/5 **Thornazine** _____ ....-
    a 1653
    X 9; XXIV 77; XXX 85; XXXI
    255; XXXIII 90; XXXIV 65;
    XXXV 265, 336; XXXIX 10

FROTHINGHAM
MA **WILLIAM** ....-1651
    m .... **Anna** _____ c 1607-1674
    XXVIII 170

FRYE
MA **JOHN** 1601-1693
    m c 1630/31 **Ann** _____ ....-1680
    XXV 55; XXXI 235

FULKERSON/VOKERTSZEN
NY **DERICK VOKERTSZEN**
    c 1595-1677/83 m c 1630
    Christina Vigne c 1610-1663/77
    XXXVI 214; XXXVII 203

FULLER
MA **EDWARD** bp 1575-1620/21
    m .... **Ann** _____ ....-1620/21
    X 268; XXXII 55; XXXV 286
MA **JOHN** bp 1620-1666 m ....
    Elizabeth Emmerson 1623-1681
    XXIV 121
MA **ROBERT** c 1615-1706
    m1) c 1639 **Sarah Bowen**
    c 1616-1676
    XXXI 273; XXXVI 169;
    XXXVII 340; XXXVIII 111;
    XXXIX 128, 338
MA **THOMAS** bp 1618/19-1698
    m 1643 **Elizabeth Tidd** ....-....
    XXIX 209; XXX 136; XXXVII
    244

FUNTINE, see VAN TINE

FURMAN/FIRMAN/FIRMIN
MA **JOHN FIRMIN** 1588-....
    m .... _____ _____ ....-....
    XXVI 88

GAGE
MA **JOHN** 1601-1672/73 m1) ....

GAGE-Cont.
Anna/Amy _____ ....-1658
XIV 126; XVIII 87; XIX 154;
XXXX 136
MA **THOMAS** ....-c 1695 m a 1648
Joanna Knight ....-....
XX 161

GAILLARD, see GAYLORD

GAINES
MA **HENRY** ....-1642/44 m ....
Jane _____ ....-1644/45
XXVII 189
VA **THOMAS** c 1585/90-....
m .... **Blanche Kemis** ....-....
XXIV 22; XXXVII 322

GAITHER
VA **JOHN** c 1600-.... m ....
Joan _____ 1612-....
XIX 138

GALE
MA **RICHARD** c 1613-1678/79
m 1640 **Mary Castle** ....-1681
XXII 153; XXXVI 148; XXXIX
313

GALLUP/GALLOP
MA **JOHN** bp c 1590/93-1649/55
m 1617/18
Christobel Brushett ....-1655
XVIII 133; XXXVIII 37, 206;
XXXX 156
CT **JOHN** ....-1675 m 1643
Hannah Lake ....-....
XXVI 55

GAMAGE/GAMIDG
MA JOHN **GAMIDG** c 1650-....
m c 1675 **Mary Knight** ....-
a 1734

XXXIX 56; XXXX 56, 272

GAMBRILL
MD **WILLIAM** a 1660-.... m ....
_____ _____ ....-....
XXXIV 125

GAMIDG, see GAMAGE

GANNETT
MA **MATHEW** 1617-1695 m ....
Hannah Andrews 1622-1700
XXXI 302

GANO/GAYNEAU/GENEAU
NY **ETIENNE "FRANCIS"**
GENEAU 1661-p 1680 m 1653
Lydia Mesterlau ....-....
XXXV 345

GANONG, see GENUNG

GANTT
MD **THOMAS** bp 1616-....
m .... **Mary Graham** ....-....
XXI 12; XXIX 218

GARDINER, see GARDNER

GARDNER/GARDINER
RI **BENONI** 1636-c 1731 m 1667
Mary Eldred 1645-1729
XXXX 331, 332
RI **GEORGE GARDINER** bp 1599-
1677/79 m2) c 1640 **Herodias**
(Long) Hicks c 1655-....
XIII 99; XXII 41; XXVI 22;
XXXIII 35
NY **JACOB JANSE GARDINER**
c 1615-a 1688 m ....
Josyna _____ ....-1669
XX 38; 151
CT/NY **LION GARDINER** 1599-

GARDNER/GARDINER-Cont.
1663 m c 1635
Mary Willemson Deurcant
c 1601- 1665
XXXIV 187
MA **THOMAS** 1592-1674 m1) ....
Margaret Friar ....-....
XXIX 354

GARFIELD
MA **EDWARD** 1575-1672
m .... _____ _____ ....-....
IV 83

GARLAND
MA/NH **PETER** a 1622 or 1615-....
m c 1650 **Joan** _____ ....-....
XXXV 125

GARLINGTON
VA **CHRISTOPHER, I** ....a 1677
m .... **Elizabeth Wyatt** ....-....
XVI 110; XXXX 402

GARNETT
VA **JOHN** c 1648-1703/09
m .... _____ _____ ....-....
XXXI 299; XXXVI 289

GARNSEY/GUERNSEY
MA **HENRY** c 1620/25-1692
m .... **Hannah Munnings** ....-
1686
XXX 131; XXXV 167, 168

GARRIS
VA **AMOS** c 1638-1684/86 m ....
Ann _____ ....-....
XXXIX 40

GARRISON
NY **ISAAC** ....-.... m ....
Catherine de Romagnac ....-....

IX 28

GASKELL, see GASKILL

GASKILL/GASKELL
MA **EDWARD GASKILL**
c 1603/09-liv 1690 m ....
Sarah _____ ....-....
XXVI 295; XXX 174

GATES
MA **STEPHEN** c 1605-wp 1662
m 1628
Ann Veare Hill c 1603-1682/83
XIII 51; XXVI 150; XXXIV 186;
XXXVI 275; XXXVIII 8, 91,
319, 366

GATON, see GAYDEN

GAY
MA **JOHN** ....-1688 m c 1637/38
Joanna (____) Baldwicke(ie) ....-
1691
XIII 96; XXXII 288; XXXIX
310; XXXV 255

GAYDEN/GATON
VA **RALPH** c 1660-.... m ....
Joanna Webster ....-....
XVIII 153; XXIX 86

GAYLORD/GAILLARD
MA/CT **WILLIAM** 1585-1673
m1) 1610/20
Joan Ashwood 1586-1657
X 188; XII 87, 108; XVI 117;
XXIX 159; XXXI 26; XXXVII
84

GAYNEAU, see GANO
GEAR, see GEER

GEER
MA/CT **GEORGE** c 1621-1726
   m 1658 **Sarah Allyn** 1642-p 1723
   IX 14; XXXIV 74; XXXVIII 287

GENEAU, see GANO

GENTRY
VA **NICHOLAS, Sr** 1655-p 1743
   m a 1687 _____ _____ ....-p 1702
   VII 8; XII 10; XIV 31; XXXIII
   260; XXXIV 162; XXXVII 242

GENUNG/GANONG/GUENON
NY **JEAN GUENON** c 1640-a 1714
   m 1662 **Margreta Sneden**
   c 1640-1727
   XVI 31; XXI 120; XXIX 191.
   219; XXXII 144; XXXX 243

GEORGE
MA **JAMES** c 1632/36-c 1707
   m 1658 **Sarah Jordon** 1636-
   p 1689
   XXXVII 311;XXXX 250
VA **JOHN** 1604-1678 m 1632
   Jane _____ ....-....
   XXXII 152
VA **NICHOLAS** ....-1661 m ....
   Margaret _____ ....-....
   XXXIV 129

GERE, see GEER
GHULICK, see GULICK
GEROULD, see JERAULD

GETCHELL
MA **SAMUEL, Sr** c 1615-1697
   m c 1640 **Dorcas Wooden** ....-
   1685
   XXXX 199

GIBB, see GIBBES

GIBBES/GIBBS/GIBB
MA/CT **GILES** ....-1641/48
   m .... **Katherine** _____ ....-1660
   XIII 31; XXXVII 269
VA **JOHN** ....-p 1655 m a 1635
   _____ _____ ....-....
   XXXV 188; XXXVI 22
SC **ROBERT** 1594-.... m 1639
   Mary Coventry 1616-....
   XXX 257
SC **ROBERT** 1644-1715
   m2) 1688 **Mary Davis** ....-
   1696/1715
   XII 74, XXX 257
MA **THOMAS** c 1605-c 1693
   m a 1644
   _____ _____ 1625-p 1657
   XXXVII 119

GIBBS, see GIBBES

GIBSON
MA **JOHN, Sr** c 1601-c 1694
   m1) .... **Rebecca** _____ ....-1661
   XVIII 94; XIX 61; XXXV 30

GIDDINGS
MA **GEORGE** 1608/09-1676
   m 1633/34
   Jane Laurence/Lawrence
   1614/15-c 1680
   X 252; XV 57; XXXVII 343;
   XXXIX 320

GIFFORD
MA/NJ **WILLIAM, Sr** 1620-1687
   m2) 1683 **Mary Mills** ....-1734
   XXXIII 114; XXXIX 3

GILBERT
CT **JONATHAN** 1618-1682 m 1650
   Mary White 1626-1700
   XVII 74

GILBERT-Cont.
CT **MATTHEW** 1599-1680 m ....
    Jane Baker ....-c 1706
    X 56; XXVII 105
CT **THOMAS** 1582-a 1650 m a 1618
    Lydia _____ ....-1654/55
    XXXVII 103
MA **THOMAS** ....-1662 m 1655
    Catherine (Chapin) Bliss ....-....
    XXX 190

GILD, see GUILE

GILDERSLEEVE
CT/NY **RICHARD, I** 1601-1681
    m ....**Joanna Appleton** 1601-....
    XXVII 148; XXXVII 296

GILE, see GUILE

GILL
VA **JOHN** ....-1690 m 1645
    Phoebe Bushnell ....-p 1620
    XVII 12, 117, 137
MD **STEPHEN** 1634-1673 m 1669
    Alice _____ ....-....
    XXX 173

GILLET, see GILLETT

GILLETT/GILLET/GILLETTE
MA/CT **JONATHAN** c 1600-1677
    m 1634 **Mary Dolbere/Dolbiar**
    1607-1685/86
    X 75; XI 171, 173; XVI 130;
    XVII 60; XXV 81; XXXII 107;
    XXXIII 202; XXXIV 225;
    XXXVIII 242

GILLETTE, see GILLETT

GILMAN
MA **EDWARD** c 1587/88-1681

    m 1614 _____ _____ ....-....
    XXIV 147

GILSON/JILLSON
MA **JOSEPH** c 1640-1676
    m ....**Mary Cooper/Caper** ....-....
    XII 61
MA **JAMES** ....-a 1712 m ....
    Mary _____ ....-a 1712
    XXXV 289

GIRARDEAU
SC **JEAN** 1665-1720 m ....
    Anne LeSade ....-....
    XXXIV 275

GLADDING
RI **JOHN** c 1640-1726 m 1667
    Elizabeth Rogers 1649-....
    XXXIX 45

GLASCOCK
VA **THOMAS** ....-.... m 1634
    Jane _____ ....-....
    XXXV 154

GLAZIER
MA **JOHN** ....-1688 m c 1662
    Eliza George ....-....
    XIX 99

GLEASON
MA **THOMAS** 1607-1686/88
    m .... **Susannah Page** ....-1691
    XXIX 104; XXXIII 148

GLIDDEN
NH **CHARLES** c 1632-p 1707
    m 1658 **Eunice Shore** c 1640-
    p 1707
    XXIII 73; XXXII 255; XXXVIII
    255

GLOVER
MA **JOHN** bp 1600-1653/54
　　m c 1625 **Anna** _____ ....-1670
　　XIV 28; XXX 226; XXXVII 121
VA **RICHARD** 1611-1696 m 1636
　　Mary Booker ....-....
　　XXX 224

GOAD
VA **ABRAHAM**, Sr ....-1734
　　m a 1693
　　Katherine Williams ....-1741
　　XXXX 161

GOBLE
MA **THOMAS** 1590/1610-wd 1657
　　m a 1629 **Alice** pr **Mousall** ....-
　　1657
　　XXXIII 311; XXXVI 259;
　　XXXVIII 99

GODFREY
NJ **BENJAMIN** ....-p 1705 m ....
　　Mary _____ ....-1714
　　XV 101; XVI 10
CT **CHRISTOPHER, I** ....-1713
　　m .... **Anne** _____ ....-....
　　XVI 100
SC **JOHN** ....-p 1689/90 m ....
　　Mary _____ ....-....
　　XXXIII 154
MA **RICHARD** ...-1691
　　m1) .... **Jane Turner** ....-a 1684
　　VIII 14; XII 96

GOEN, see GOWING

GOFF
MA **ANTHONY** ....-.... m 1686
　　Sarah Polly/Polley 1650-....
　　XXXX 436
CT **PHILIP** 1625-1674 m ....
　　Rebecca _____ ....-1674

XXXVI 159

GOFORTH
DE/NJ **WILLIAM** 1631-1678
　　m 1662 **Anne Skipwith** 1641-
　　1773
　　XXXIX 234

GOLD, see GOULD

GOLDEN
NY/NJ **WILLIAM** ....-p 1686
　　m .... _____ _____ ....-....
　　XXXI 135

GOLDSBOROUGH
MD **NICHOLAS** 1639-1671 m 1659
　　Margaret Howes ....-....
　　XVII 85

GOLDTHWAITE
MA **THOMAS** c 1610-a 1671/83
　　m1) 1636 **Elizabeth** _____ ....-
　　a 1671
　　XXII 58; XXIV 126; XXVIII 61;
　　XXXII 125

GONSALUS, see GUNSAUL

GOOCH/GOUGH
VA **JOHN GOUGH** c 1625-1683/84
　　m1) 1662 **Mary Trussell** c 1649-
　　a 1677
　　XXXIX 37

GOODALE/GOODELL
MA **ROBERT** 1603/04-1683
　　m1)1628/29
　　Katherine Vilham/Kilham
　　1606-1645/46
　　IX 23; XVII 149; XX 160;
　　XXXV 260; XXXVI 143, 229

GOODE
VA **EDWARD** c 1644-p 1708
   m .... **Margaret** _____ ....-....
   XXXX 91
VA **JOHN** 1620/30-c 1709
   m1) c 1650 **(Martha) Frances**
   Mackarness c 1625-c 1662
   m2) p 1661 **Ann Bennett** ....-....
   XII 68; XIV 75; XV 116; XXXIV
   133; XXXVII 224; XXXIX 137

GOODELL, see GOODALE

GOODENOW
MA **EDMUND** 1611-1688 m a 1634
   Ann Berry 1608-1675/76
   XXXX 153

GOODHUE
MA **WILLIAM** 1612/13-1699/1700
   m1) c 1639 **Margery Watson** ....-
   1668
   XI 36; XXXX 85

GOODING
MA **GEORGE** ....-1712 m 1685
   Deborah Walker 1660-1719
   XXXX 172

GOODLOE
VA **GEORGE, Sr** c 1639-wd 1710
   m .... **Mary** _____ ....-p 1710
   XIX 117; XXV 17; XXXI 154;
   XXXIII 211; XXXV 64, 99

GOODMAN
CT **RICHARD** c 1609-1676
   m 1659 **Mary Terry** 1635-
   wp 1692
   X 18

GOODRICH/GOODRIDGE
MA **WILLIAM GOODRIDGE**

   c 1605-1647 m 1632
   Margaret _____ ....-1682/83
   XV 120; XXVII 138
CT **WILLIAM** c 1620/21-1676
   m 1648 **Sarah Marvin** bp 1631-
   a 1702/03
   X 153; XII 12, 85, 116; XII 33;
   XIV 24; XVII 73; XVIII 119;
   XIX 9; XXIX 305; XXXVIII
   282

GOODRIDGE, see GOODRICH

GOODSELL
CT **THOMAS** 1646-1713 m 1684
   Sarah Hemingway/Hemenway
   1663-1725/85
   X 68; XVI 26

GOODSPEED
MA **ROGER** ....-1685 m 1641
   Alice Layton ....-1688/89
   XXIX 394

GOODWIN
MA **CHRISTOPHER** ....-1701/02
   m a 1642 **Mary** _____ 1617/18-
   1682/83
   XXXX 452
MA **EDWARD** c 1632/a 48-p 1668
   m1).... **Bridget** _____ ....-....
   m2) .... **Susanna Stowers** ....-....
   XI 147; XXI 21; XXXVII 92
VA **JAMES** c 1628-a 1678/79
   m1) 1655 **Rachel Porter** 1630-
   1666
   XVIII 79
CT **OZIAS** 1596-a 1683 m a 1629
   Mary Woodward ....-c 1683
   X 263; XII 73; XVIII 33; XXVI
   256; XXVII 53; XXXI 199
MA **RICHARD** ....-1709 m 1666
   Hannah Jones 1645-1725

GOODWIN-Cont.
XXIX 328, 403

GOOLD, see GOULD

GORDON
NH **ALEXANDER** c 1635-1697
  m 1663 **Mary Lysson/Lisson** ....-
  ....
  VI 78/90; XXX 101
NJ **CHARLES** ....-1739 m 1697/98
  Lydia Hampton ....-....
  XX 9

GORHAM
MA **JOHN** 1621-1675/76 m 1643
  Desire Howland 1623-1683
  V 100; XXXIV 120

GORTON
MA/RI **SAMUEL** 1592-1677
  m c 1628/30
  Mary Mayplett 1598-p 1677
  XXXI 223; XXXIV 300; XXXX
  34

GOSS
VA **JOHN** 1640-1694 m ....

  ____ ____ ....-....
  XXXIX 20
MA **PHILIP** 1654-wp 1698
  m2) 1690
  Mary Prescott 1669-....
  XXXIV 217

GOULD/GOLD/GOOLD
MA **JARVIS/JERVICE** 1605-1656
  m c 1644 **Mary** ____ ....-p 1649
  XXXI 185
CT **NATHAN GOLD** ....-w 1693/94
  m 1657/59 **Martha Harvey**
  (wid.) ....-....
  Sarah (Phippen) Yeo (wid.) ....-

1692/93
XIX 101; XXVIII 10
MA **NATHAN** c 1614-1692/93
  m .... **Elizabeth** ____ ....-p 1692
  XXIII 79
MA **ZACCHEUS** 1589-1668/70
  m c 1630
  Phebe Deacon bp 1620-1663
  XIX 18, 151; XXXIV 107

GOVE
MA **EDWARD** 1630-1691 m 1660
  Hannah Partridge 1639/42-1712
  XXXIV 51, 254
MA **JOHN** 1604-1647/48 m 1627
  Mary Sale 1601/04-1681
  VIII 31; XXXIV 254

GOWING
MA **ROBERT** 1618-1698 m 1644
  Elizabeth Brock 1620-p 1698
  XXXX 4

GRANGER
MA/CT **LAUNCELOT** 1624-1689
  m 1653/54
  Joanna Adams c 1634-p 1701
  XXIX 294; XXXIII 159

GRANNISS
CT **EDWARD** c 1630-1719
  m2) 1662 **Hannah Wakefield**
  bp 1644-1711
  X 106; XII 46

GRANT
MA **EDWARD** 1632-1682 m c 1655
  Sarah Weare/Ware c 1629-1690
  XXXX 408
MA/CT **MATTHEW** 1601-1681
  m 1625 **Priscilla Grey** 1601/02-
  1644
  XXIV 89; XXVI 182; XXIX 265;

GRANT-Cont.
XXXVIII 48
MA **THOMAS** c 1630-1690
m c 1667 **Sarah Brook** 1646-....
XXXVII 278

GRAVES
MA **JOHN** ....-p 1645 m a 1635
_____ _____ ....-....
IX 12; XV 118; XVIII 74;
XXXIII 321
CT **JOHN** 1654-1677 m ....
Mary Smith c 1630-1668
XXVII 161
MA **SAMUEL** ....-.... m ....
_____ _____ ....-....
XXXVIII 365; XXXIX 59
VA **THOMAS** c 1580/85-c 1635
m .... **Katharine** _____ ....-....
XXV 207; XXVIII 176; XXIX
65; XXXI 293; XXXIII 108;
XXXVII 93
CT **THOMAS** c 1585-1662 m ....
Sarah _____ ....-1666
XXVII 161

GRAY
MA **EDWARD** bp 1623/30-1681
m1) 1650 **Mary Winslow** 1630-
1663/79
m2) 1665 **Dorothy Lettice** 1643-
1686/1728
XXXIII 245; XXXV 214;
XXXVI 318; XXXVIII 364;
XXXX 260, 330
NH/ME **GEORGE** ....-wp 1693
m 1672 **Sarah** _____ ....-p 1726
XXXV 73
CT **JOHN** ....-.... m ....
_____ _____ ....-....
XXIV 76; XXV 296

GREELE, see GREELEY

GREELEY/GREELE
MA **ANDREW GREELE** c 1617-
1697 m 1643
Mary Moyse c 1622-1703
VIII 15; X 242; XVIII 93;
XXXVII 268

GREEN/GREENE
RI **JOHN GREENE** c 1590/97-
c 1659
m1) 1619 **Joan Tattersall** ....-
p 1643
IV 101; XIII 110; XVIII 109,
XXI 67; XXV 277; XXIX 251;
XXX 40; XXXI 91; XXXIV
27; XXXV 37; XXXVIII 127;
XXXX 154
RI **JOHN GREENE** c 1606-c 1695
m 1642/45
Mrs. **Joan Baggerly** c 1610-1695
XI 80; XIX 46; XXIX 220;
XXXIX 91
PA **THOMAS GREEN(E) Sr.** ....-....
m .... **Margaret** _____ ....-1708
XXXIV 212
MA **THOMAS GREEN** 1606-1667
m1) a 1628
Elizabeth _____ 1610-1658
XII 21, 36; XXVI 194, 195; XXX
125

GREENE, see GREEN

GREENLEAF
MA **EDMUND** c 1574-1671
m1).... **Sarah Dole** .....-1663
XX 24; XXVIII 203

GREENWOOD
MA **THOMAS** 1643-1693
m 1670 **Hannah Ward** 1651-
1687
XVIII 73

GREER
MD **JAMES** 1650-....
   m 1680 **Ann Taylor** ....-....
   XXIX 274

GREGORY
MA **HENRY** ....-p 1647 m ....
   Goody _____ ....-1640/41
   XXXVI 74
VA **THOMAS** ....-1724 m ....

   _____ _____ ....-....
   XXXIX 291

GRENALL, see GRENELL

GRENELL/GRENALL
RI **MATTHEW GRENALL** ....-
   c 1643 m ....
   Rose _____ ....-1673
   XI 115

GRESHAM, see GRISSOM

GRIDLEY
CT **THOMAS** c 1602/bp 1612-
   inv 1655 m 1644
   Mary Seymour ....-....
   XXXIV 127; XXXVI 319;
   XXXVIII 303; XXXIX 245

GRIFFIN/GRIFFING
MA/NY **JASPER GRIFFING**
   c 1648-1718 m c 1674
   Hannah _____ 1653-1699
   VII 31; XXXIX 223
VA **THOMAS** ....-a 1660
   m .... **Sarah** _____ ....-....
   VI 27/29

GRIFFITH
MD **WILLIAM** ....-1699
   m 1687 **Sarah McCubbin** ....-....
   XXXVI 163

GRIGGS
MA **THOMAS** 1585/1603-1646
   m c 1615
   Mary _____ c 1595-1639
   XXXVIII 295

GRISSOM/GRESHAM
MD/VA **JOHN GRESHAM** 1613-
   1656 m .... _____ _____ ....-....
   XXXIX 6

GRISWOLD
CT **EDWARD** bp 1607-1690/91
   m1) c 1630 **Margaret** _____ ....-
   1670
   IV 141; VI 52/59; VII 24; IX 39;
   X 30, 32, 33, 43; XVII 28; XXV
   97,154, 243; XXXIII 202;
   XXXIV 23; XXXV 295, 327;
   XXXVI 129; XXXVIII 150,
   316; XXXIX 91
CT **FRANCIS** 1635-1671 m ....
   Mary Tracy ....-....
   XII 114
CT **MATTHEW** 1620-1698 m 1646
   Anna Wolcott 1621-a 1702
   XVIII 132
CT **MICHAEL** ....-1684 m a 1646
   Ann _____ ....-....
   XXXI 122; XXXVII 41;
   XXXVIII 193; XXXIX 8

GROCE, see GROSS

GROESBOECK
NY **WILLIAM CLASS** c1660-1722
   m 1684
   Gertrury Schuyler ....-....
   XXIX 27

GROOT
NY **SIMON SYMONSE** ....-p 1696
   m .... **Rebecca Du Trieux** ....-....

GURNEY
MA **JOHN** ....-inv 1662/63
    m1) .... _____ _____ ....-1661
    XXXII 164

GUSTAFSSON, see JUSTICE

GUSTIN
MA **JOHN (JOHN AUGUSTINE,
AUGUSTINE, JEAN)** 1647-1719
    m 1677/78
    Elizabeth Browne 1657-p 1719
    XVI 49; XXIX 175

HACKETT
MA **JABEZ** c 1627-1686
    m by 1654 **Frances** _____ c 1632-
    ....
    XXIX 34

HACKLEY
VA **JOHN** ....-wp 1698 m ....
    Elizabeth Andrews ....-....
    XXIX 64

HADLEY
MA **GEORGE** c 1600-1686
    m1) .... **Mary Proctor** 1633-
    c 1667
    XXXVI 276; XXXVIII 152

HADLOCK
MA **JAMES, Sr** ....-1687
    m 1652 **Demais Fosdick** ....-1669
    XXXX 355

HAGAN, see EAGON

HAGAR
MA **WILLIAM** ....-1683/84
    m 1644/45 **Mary Bemis** 1620-
    1695
    XXVIII 47; XXIX 218

HAGOE, see EAGON
HAIGHT, see HOYT
HAILE, see HALE

HAINES/HAYNE/HAYNES
MA **SAMUEL** 1611-1686 m 1638
    Ellenor Neate ....-c 1685
    XXIX 180
MA **WALTER HAYNES** 1583-1665
    m .... **Elizabeth** _____ ....-1659
    VIII 31
MA **WILLIAM HAYNES** ....-....
    m a 1644 **Sarah Ingersoll** 1627-
    ....
    XXXVIII 341
NJ **WILLIAM HAYNE** 1672-1754
    m 1695 **Sarah Paine** 1678-1728
    XIII 119; XXXI 64

HAIT, see HOYT
HAIKES, see HAWKS

HALE/HEALD/HEALE
VA **GEORGE HEALE** c 1632-
    wp 1698 m .... **Ellen Rogers** ....-
    wp 1710
    XXXIV 343
MA **JOHN HEALD** ....-1662 m ....
    Dorothy _____ ....-1689
    XXII 63; XXIII 80; XXXVI 220
VA **NICHOLAS HEALE** a 1634-
    c 1670/78 m ....
    Mary (or Ellen) Travers? ....-
    1671/72
    X 231; XII 24; XXXIV 22, 343;
    XXXV 295, 343; XXXIX 267
RI/MA **RICHARD HAILE** ....-1720
    m 1640 **Mary** _____ 1652-
    1729/30
    VII 25
MA **ROBERT** 1610-1659 m a 1636
    Jane/Joanna (Knight?) ....-1679
    XX 79; XXXIII 271

HALE/HEALD/HEALE-Cont.
CT **SAMUEL** c 1610/15-1693
   m1) a 1643 **Mary Smith** c 1624-
   1711/12
   XXX 199; XXXIII 326,; XXXIX
   222
MA **THOMAS, I** bp 1606-1682
   m 1632 **Thomasine Dowsett** ....-
   1682/83
   X 88; XXII 78; XXIII 78; XXVI
   293; XXXI 300; XXXIV 237;
   XXXVI 154; XXXIX 78
MA **THOMAS** 1650-1725 m 1675
   Priscilla Markham 1654-1712
   XVI 140; XXIX 60
CT **TIMOTHY** ....-1689 m 1663
   Sarah Barber bp 1646-....
   XXXI 129

**HALENBECK, see
HALLENBECK**

HALL
MA **CHRISTOPHER, Sr** ....-a 1690
   m1) a 1672 **Sarah** _____ ....-1682
   XXXIII 288
MA **EDWARD** ....-1670
   m .... **Hester** _____ ....-....
   I 28
MA **GEORGE** 1600-1669 m ....
   Mary _____ ....-....
   XXVIII 56; XXIX 97
CT **JOHN** 1584-1673 m ....
   Esther _____ ....-....
   XXIII 70
CT **JOHN, Sr** 1604/05-1676
   m 1641/44
   Jane/Jeanne Woolen (Wollen)
   ....- 1690
   X 186; XVII 30; XXII 84;
   XXVIII 14, 185; XXXIV 34, 76
MA **JOHN HALL** a 1609-1696
   m2) **Elizabeth Learned/Larned**

   bp 1621-p 1651
   XI 178; XII 68; XIX 30; XXXV
   245
NH **JOHN** 1617-1692 m ....
   Elizabeth Leighton 1624-....
   XV 76
MA **RICHARD** ....-1691 m ....
   Elizabeth Collicott bp 1628-
   1693
   XXIX 299
MD **RICHARD** 1600-1688 m ....
   Elizabeth Wingfield ....-....
   III 18
CT **WILLIAM** ....-1668/69 m ....
   Hester _____ ....-1683
   XXXI 235
RI **WILLIAM** 1613-1675 m ....
   Mary Stephenson 1617-1680/81
   XXXII 175

HALLAM
CT **JOHN** 1662-1700 m 1683
   Prudence Richardson 1661/62-
   1716
   III 24

HALLENBECK/HALENBEEK
NY **CASPER JACOBSE** c 1635-
   1703 m 1660 _____ _____ ....-....
   XXVIII 22

HALLETT
MA **ANDREW, Sr** ....-1647/48
   m .... **Mary Gorham** ....-
   c 1654/59
   XXXI 81; XXXIV 284; XXXV
   109

HALLEY
VA **THOMAS** 1662-1750 m ....
   Sara Hawley ....-....
   XXXI 86; XXXIV 182

HALLOCK
NY **PETER** 1600-.... m ....
   wid. Howell ....-....
   XXV 280

HALLOWELL
PA **JOHN** 1650-1706 m 1675
   Mary Holland ....-1727
   XXXIII 75

HALSEY
NY **THOMAS** bp 1592-1678/79
   m1) a 1627 **Phoebe** _____ ....-1649
   m2) .... **Ann Johnes** ....-1699
   XII 30; XIII 122; XVI 137;
   XXVII 66; XXXII 235

HALSTEAD
NY **JONAS** c 1610/11-c 1682/83
   m c 1632 **Sarah** _____ ....-....
   XXVIII 179; XXIX 101

HAM
NH **JOHN** 1649-1727 m 1668
   Mary Heard 1650-1706
   V 124; X 254

HAMBELTON/HAMILTON
MD **ANDREW** ....-1678/79
   m .... **Elizabeth Elliott** ....-.....
   XXXVII 308; XXXVIII 224

HAMBLIN, see HAMLIN
HAMERSLEY, see
HAMMERSLEY

HAMILTON
ME/NH **DAVID** 1620-1691
   m 1662/63 **Anna (Jackson)** ....-
   ....
   XXI 104
MD **JOHN** ....-1682
   m c 1677

Elizabeth Burdit/Burdett
   c 1659-a 1686
   XX 102; XXI 34; XXXX 268
MA **JOHN** 1635-.... m ....
   Christian _____ ....-....
   XXVIII 158; XXIX 345; XXXX
   132

HAMLIN/HAMBLEN
CT **GILES** 1622-1689
   m c 1655 **Hester Crow** 1628-
   1700
   XXXVI 341; XXXX 2
MA **JAMES HAMBLEN, I**
   1603/15-1690
   m .... **Anne** _____ ....-....
   XXX 159; XXXVIII 331;
   XXXIX 268; XXXX 323

HAMM, see HAM

HAMMERSLEY/HAMERSLEY
VA **HUGH** 1565-.... m ....
   Mary Derham ....-....
   XVI 40, 111

HAMMOND
MA **BENJAMIN** 1621-1703 m 1650
   Mary Vincent 1633-1705
   X 16; XXV 264; XXXI 14;
   XXXIV 307
MD **JOHN** 1643-1707 m 1667
   Mary Howard 1648-1721
   XXV 32; XXXIII 48; XXXIV
   100
MA **THOMAS, I** bp 1603-1675
   m 1623 **Elizabeth Cason** a 1604-
   p 1675
   X 202; XXXIX 258; XXXX 5, 56
MA **WILLIAM** bp 1575-1662
   m 1605
   Elizabeth Paine 1587-1670/77

HAMMOND-Cont.
　　X 23; XIX 135; XXVIII 17;
　　XXXVI 78, 124
MA **WILLIAM** ....-1729 m 1672
　　Elizabeth Battlecome ....-1705
　　XV 88

HANCHETT
MA/CT **THOMAS** c 1620-1686
　　m c 1642 **Deliverance Langton**
　　(Laughton) ....-1718
　　XXIV 21; XXXVIII 350

HANCOCK/HANDCOCK
NJ **JOHN** ....-1709/10 m .....
　　Mary Champnes/Chambless ....-
　　inv 1713
　　XXXVI 233; XXXVIII 267
VA **SYMON HANDCOCK** 1610-
　　1654 m 1647
　　Sarah Gay/Gaye ____ ....-1689
　　XXXX 249

HAND
MA/NY **JOHN** 1611-inv 1660
　　m a 1633
　　Alice Gransden bp 1613-p 1662
　　XXXV 102; XXXVI 225

HANDY/HENDY
CT **RICHARD HENDY** 1611-1670
　　m .... **Hannah Elderkin** ....-....
　　XXIII 40
MA **RICHARD** c 1620-a 1719 m ....
　　Hannah ____ c 1643-1732
　　VII 25; XXXI 25
MD **SAMUEL** 1651-c 1721
　　m 1675/79 **Mary Sewall** ....-....
　　XXXIII 176; XXXX 66

HANFORD
MA/CT **THOMAS** 1621-1693
　　m2) 1661 **Mary (Miles) Ince** ....-

1730
XXIX 249

HANSCOM
ME/MA **THOMAS** c 1623-
　　1697/1713 m 1644/64
　　Ann ____ ....-p 1720/24
　　XXII 52; XXXIV 212; XXXX
　　371

HANSFORD
VA **JOHN** ....-1661 m ....
　　Elizabeth ____ ....-p 1661
　　XXVII 188

HANSON
MD/DE **JOHN** 1630-1713/14
　　m .... **Mary** ____ ....-a 1713
　　XX 159; XXXVII 294
NH **THOMAS** c 1586-wp 1666
　　m c 1641 **Mary Paul** ....-1689
　　XXX 22; XXXI 96

HARBER/HARBOUR
VA **THOMAS HARBOUR** 1675/80-
　　.... m .... ____ ____ ....-....
　　XXXIII 73

HARBOUR, see HARBER

HARDEN/HARDIN
NY **MARTIN HARDIN** c 1645-....
　　m banns 1671
　　Madeline duSauchoy bp 1658-
　　....
　　XXXIV 331; XXXVI 227;
　　XXXVII 128

HARDENBERGH
NY **GERRIT JANS** 1647-1696
　　m 1666 **Jeapie Schepmoes** ....-....
　　XXVI 27

HARDESTY/HARDISTY
MD **GEORGE HARDISTY, Sr**
   ....-1694/95 m ....
   Cecilia Lingan ....-p 1695
   XXXVII 258

HARDIN, see HARDEN
HARDISTY, see HARDESTY

HARDING
MA **ABRAHAM** 1615/17-1655/85
   m c 1639 **Elizabeth Harding**
   c 1622- 1655/85
   XIV 53; XXVI 230, 259; XXVIII
   63
MA **JOHN** 1567-1637 m ....
   ____ ____ ....-....
   XXV 69
MA **JOSEPH** ....-1630 m 1624
   Martha Doane ....-1633
   XXI 161; XXII 57; XXV 286
MA/RI **RICHARD** c 1580-....
   m .... ____ ____ ....-a 1630
   XVI 94

HARDWICK
VA **JAMES** c 1647-1698 m 1669
   Ann Armsby/Armsley a 1641-
   p 1698
   XXXI 167; XXXX 187

HARDY
VA **GEORGE** ....-wp 1665
   m .... ____ ____ ....-....
   X 63,64
VA **GEORGE** 1633-1693
   m .... **Mary Jackson** ....-a 1693
   IX 32
VA **JOHN** 1613-1670/77 m 1632
   Olive Council ....-p 1670
   XXXI 115, 210; XXXIII 308;
   XXXIV 125; XXXVII 299
VA **JOHN** c 1645/50-c 1719

   m 1670/72
   Charity O'Dyer 1659/60-a 1695
   XXXIX 124
CT **RICHARD** ....-1683 m 1650
   Ann Husted c 1623-1707
   XXXV 196
MA **THOMAS** c 1605/06-1677/78
   m1) c 1630 **Elizabeth Hollete**
   c 1609-....
   m2) c 1636 **Lydia** ____ 1607-
   1649/67
   II 49; XXVIII 195; XXIX 245;
   XXX 93; XXXI 84; XXXIV 41,
   161; XXXV 357

HARLAN
PA/DE **GEORGE** bp 1650-1714
   m 1678
   Elizabeth Duck c 1661-a 1714
   XXXIV 35; XXXV 263; XXXVI
   185; XXXVIII 145; XXXIX 304
PA **MICHAEL** c 1660-1729
   m c 1690
   Dinah Dixon c 1670-p 1707
   XXXIV 205; XXXVII 22

HARMENSEN, see
HENDRICKSEN

HARMON
MA **JOHN** 1617-1683 m 1640
   Elizabeth ____ 1617-1699
   XIV 44, 119

HARRINDEEN, see
HARRINGTON

HARRINGTON/HEARNDEN/
HARRINDEEN
RI **BENJAMIN HEARNDEN** ....-
   1687 m ....
   Elizabeth White ....-liv 1701
   XXVI 87

**HARRINGTON/HEARNDEN/
HARRINDEEN**-Cont.
MA **ROBERT** 1616-1707 m 1647/49
    Susanna George 1632-1694
    XIV 69; XXVI 207; XXX 177;
    XXXIX 4

HARRIS
MA **ARTHUR** ....-w 1673 m ....
    Martha ____ ....-....
    XXV 54
CT **JAMES** c 1640-1714/17
    m c 1666
    Sarah Denison 1647-p 1715
    XIII 50; XVII 107; XVIII 36;
    XXV 95; XXXVII 144; XXXX
    215
VA **JOHN** 1588/89- a 1638 m ....
    Dorothy ____ ....-1684
    XXXV 137; XXXVII 191;
    XXXVIII 140, 358
VA **ROBERT** c 1630-c 1700
    m c 1650
    Mary (Claiborne) Rice ....-....
    XIV 30; XVI 57; XXX 46;
    XXXX 403
VA **THOMAS** 1586-1679 m 1626
    Joane Osborne 1580-....
    XXXIX 30
RI/NY **THOMAS** ....-a 1681 m ....
    ____ ____ ....-p 1681
    XXXI 48; XXXV 340
RI **THOMAS** 1600-1686 m ....
    Elizabeth ____ ....-1687
    XXVII 190
MA **THOMAS** c 1615-1687 m 1647
    Martha Lake ....-a 1700
    XX 53
MA **THOMAS** ....-a 1680 m ....
    Elizabeth ____ ....-1669/70
    XXVI 254
MA **WALTER** .... -1654 m ....
    Mary Fry ....-1655

XXXVII 329

HARRISON
VA **BENJAMIN, I** 1600-c 1645/49
    m .... **Mary Stringer** ....-1688
    I 39; XXVIII 38; XXXII 252;
    XXXV 197; XXXVII 162
CT **RICHARD** ....-1653 m ....
    Sarah ____ ....-....
    VIII 20, 25; IX 17; XI 125; XII
    22

HART
NY **EDWARD** ....-.... m ....
    ____ ____ ....-....
    XVII 71
VA **HENRY** ....-.... m ....
    Elizabeth ____ ....-....
    XXXX 456
MA **ISAAC** c 1614-1699/1700
    m c 1650
    Elizabeth Hutchins ....-1700
    XXXI 117
NY **JOHN** ....-1671 m ....
    ____ ____ ....-1659
    XXIX 362
PA **JOHN** 1651-1714 m 1683
    Susannah Rush ....-....
    XXV 121
MA/CT **STEPHEN** c 1605-1682/83
    m1) .... ____ ____ ....-p 1652
    m2) .... **Margaret Smith** (wid.)
    ....- ....
    VIII 8; XII 45; XIII 47; XXI 66;
    XXXIV 209; XXXVIII 363
VA **THOMAS, Sr** ....-p 1685 m ....
    ____ ____ ....-....
    XXX 97; XXXII 192; XXXVIII
    351; XXXIX 47
MA **THOMAS** 1606-1673 m ....
    Alice ____ 1612-1682
    XXX 163

HARTSHORN
MA **THOMAS** 1614/20-wp 1683
    m1) 1647 **Susanna Buck** ....-
    1659/60
    XII 44; XXII 74; XXXIII 289

HARTWELL
MA **WILLIAM** 1613-1689/90
    m ....
    Susan/Jazan ____ c 1608-
    1675/95
    XXII 60; XXVI 143

HARTY
NY **HAN JACOB** c 1640-1685
    m 1668
    Geertje Lamberson 1648-p 1712
    XXXVII 196

HARVEY
MA **JOHN** 1654-1706 m 1685/86
    Sarah (Barnes) Rowell 1650-
    1720
    XXXIV 227
MA **THOMAS** 1617-1651 m 1642
    Elizabeth Andrews 1614-1717
    V 113; XXXX 1, 271, 297, 347
MA **WILLIAM** c 1614-1691
    m 1639
    Joanne Hucker ....-a 1691
    X 184
MA **WILLIAM** c 1614-1658
    m2) c 1650
    Mrs. Martha Slocum Copp ....-
    ....
    III 32, 33, 34; XXXIV 227;
    XXXVIII 266

HARWOOD
MA **NATHANIEL** 1626-1715/16
    m .... **Elizabeth** ____ ....-1715
    XIV 90; XV 19; XXI 81; XXVI
    102; XXXI 183; XXXIX 175

VA **THOMAS** ....-c 1652
    m2) p 1620 **Ann** ____ ....-1685
    XXVIII 122

HASBROUK
NY **ABRAHAM** 1650-1717
    m 1676/79 **Maria Deyo** 1653-
    1741
    XXV 240; XXXIII 273; XXXX
    149
NY **JEAN/JOHN** 1642/43-p 1714
    m a 1664 **Anna Deyo** 1644-1694
    XXXIII 173; XXXIV 205

HASCALL, see HASKELL
HASELTINE, see HAZELTINE

HASKELL/HASCALL
MA **ROGER HASKELL** bp 1613-
    1667
    m2) a 1639 **Elizabeth Hardy**
    c 1623-1682
    XXXIII 115; XXXIV 100, 178
MA **WILLIAM, I** 1617-1693
    m 1643 **Mary Tybbot** ....-1693
    XXX 195; XXXVIII 173

HASKINS/HOSKINE/HOSKINS
VA **BARTHOLOMEW HOSKINS**
    1601-....
    m .... ____ ____ ....-....
    XVII 36
MA **WILLIAM** c 1604/15-1695
    m c 1638
    Ann Hinde/Hinds c 1616/17-....
    XII 11; XXX 265; XXXIV 170,
    213

HASSELTINE, see HAZELTINE
HASSEN, see HAZEN

HASTINGS
MA **ROBERT** 1653/54-wp 1721

HASTINGS-Cont.
   m 1676 **Elizabeth Davis** 1653-....
   XXXIV 53
MA **THOMAS** c 1605-1685
   m2) 1651 **Margaret Cheney** ....-
   p 1683
   V 80; XV 5; XXXVIII 341;
   XXXX 261

HATCH
VA **ANTHONY** ....wp 1688/89
   m .... **Elizabeth** ____ ....-....
   XXXI 29
ME **PHILIP** 1616-1674
   m .... **Patience (?Edge)** ....-1709
   XXXIX 207
MA **THOMAS** c 1596-a 1646
   m c 1622 **Lydia** ____ ....-....
   XXXIV 41
MA **THOMAS** c 1603-1661
   m c 1624 **Grace** ____ ....-....
   XXII 105; XXV 131; XXVIII 146
MA **WILLIAM** c 1598-1651
   m1) .... ____ ____ ....-....
   m2) 1624 **Jane Young** c 1596-
   1658
   XIV 110; XVI 99; XX 57

HATCHER
VA **WILLIAM** c 1613/14-c 1780
   m .... ____ ____ ....-....
   XXXX 305

HATCHETT
VA **JOHN** a 1675-1756
   m .... **Elizabeth Bass** ....-....
   XXXX 162, 163

HATHAWAY
MA **ARTHUR** c 1630-1711
   m 1650/52
   Sarah Cook(e) 1635-a 1710
   XXXVI 28; XXXIX 263

MA **JOHN** c 1629/30-1704/05
   m1) c 1649 **Martha Shepard** ....-
   1683/92
   VII 35; XXXIII 39
MA **NICHOLAS** c 1595-....
   m1) c 1628 ____ ____ ....-....
   XXVIII 55; XXXI 120; XXXV
   140, 272; XXXVII 104; XXXIX
   279

HAUGHTON
NC **THOMAS** ....-a 1707
   m ....**Sarah** ____ ....-1702
   XXIX 27

HAUKSIE, see HOXIE
HAULEY, see HOLLEY

HAVEN(S)
MA **RICHARD** c 1620/44-c 1701/08
   m a 1646
   Susanna Newhall 1624-1682
   XIII 7; XVII 156; XXXIII 53;
   XXXV 153
RI **WILLIAM HAVENS** c 1600-
   wp 1683
   m 1639 **Dionis** ____ 1623-p 1692
   XXXVI 125, 287

HAVENS, see HAVEN
HAWARD, see HAYWOOD

HAWES
MA **EDWARD** ....-1687
   m 1648 **Eliony Lombard** ....-....
   XXXII 239

HAWKINS
MA/NY **ROBERT** 1610-1704 m ....
   Mary/Marie ____ 1611-1704
   XVIII 51; XXI 10; XXXII 241;
   XXXIII 319; XXXIV 266
RI **WILLIAM** 1609-1699 m ....

HAWKINS-Cont.
    Margaret Harwood c 1612-....
    XXV 294; XXXVII 165

HAWKS/HAKES
CT/MA **JOHN HAKES** ....-1662
    m .... **Elizabeth** _____ ....-1685/89
    X 257; XXXIV 45; XXXVI 196

HAWLEY
CT **JOSEPH, I** 1603-1690 m c 1646
    Catherine Birdsay ....-1692
    V 60; VI 94/112; XIV 102; XVI
    63; XIX 60; XXVIII 42;
    XXXVIII 240

HAY, see HAYES

HAYDEN/HEYDON
VA/MD **FRANCIS HEYDON** 1628-
    1694
    m .... **Thomasine Butler** ....-1701
    XXIX 165
MA **JOHN** ....-1678
    m .... **Susanna** _____ ....-....
    XVI 98
MA **WILLIAM** 1600-1669
    m1) .... _____ _____ ....-1655/65
    XII 16; XIV 88; XVII 141; XXXI
    30

HAYES/HAY/DE LA HAY/HAYS
CT **GEORGE, Sr** 1655-1725 m ....
    m2) 1688 **Abigail Dibble** 1666-
    p 1725
    XXIX 359; XXXV 99
NH **JOHN** ....-1708 m 1686
    Mary Horne 1667/72-p 1708
    XXV 57; XXXIV 76
VA **JOHN DE LA HAY** 1620-1676
    m .... **Mary Wade** ....-....
    XXXVIII 219

HAYNE, see HAINES
HAYNES, see HAINES
HAYS, see HAYES

HAYWARD/HAWARD/
HAYWOOD/HEYWARD/
HEYWOOD, see also HOWARD
MA **JOHN HEYWOOD, Sr**
    1612/15-1700/07
    m1) 1656 **Rebecca Atkinson**
    c 1637/38-1665
    X 266; XII 57; XVII 77; XVIII
    42; XXXII 282; XXXIII 314;
    XXXV 129, 185
MA **THOMAS** ....-1681
    m .... **Susanna** _____ ....-a 1678
    XIX 165; XXV 59; XXXIX 150

HAZARD
RI **THOMAS** 1610-1680 m c 1634
    Martha _____ c 1610/17-1669
    XXXX 41, 57

HAZELTINE/HASELTINE/
HASSELTINE
MA **JOHN** c 1620-1690
    m .... **Jane Auter** ...-1698
    XXVIII 8
MA **NATHANIEL** 1656-1723/24
    m2) 1688 **Ruth (Plumer) Jaques**
    1660-....
    XXVIII 8
MA **ROBERT HASSELTINE**
    1615/18-1674
    m 1639 **Ann** _____ ....-1684
    VII 19, 20; XI 105

HAZEN/HASEN
MA **EDWARD HASSEN** bp 1614-
    1683 m2) 1650 **Hannah Grant**
    bp 1631-1715/16
    XIV 115; XXX 116; XXXII 105;

HAZEN/HASEN-Cont.
XXXIII 27, 84

HEAD
NH **ARTHUR** a 1671-a 1708
    m c 1677
    Sarah Reynolds ....-a 1718
    XVII 80, 107; XXXX 260
VA **JAMES** ....-c 1748
    m .... **Betty** _____ ....-....
    XXXIV 308

HEALD, see HALE
HEALE, see HALE

HEARD
NJ **JOHN** c 1601-1688
    m 1643 **Elizabeth Hull** 1628-
    1706
    XXXVI 35

HEARMANS, see HERMANEE
HEARNDEN, see HARRINGTON

HEARNE
MD **WILLIAM** 1627-1691
    m 1683 **Mary Cuthbert** ....-
    p 1691
    XXX 285

HEATH
VA **ABRAHAM** ....-1688
    m .... **Ursula** _____ ....-....
    XXXI 313
MA **BARTHOLOMEW** c 1615-
    1681 m c 1640
    Hannah Moyce 1623-1677/78
    XXII 82; XXXVIII 294
MA **WILLIAM** ....-1652
    m .... **Mary Spear** ....-1659
    V 93
VA **WILLIAM** ....-w 1681
    m .... **Margery (n.i.w.)** ....-....

XXXV 103

HEATON
MA **NATHANIEL** 1602-1643/50
    m 1630 **Elizabeth Wight** 1606-
    1671
    XI 186; XXXX 458

HEBARD, see HIBBARD
HEDGE, see HEDGES

HEDGES/HEDGE
NJ **SAMUEL HEDGE** c 1650-
    a 1714 m by 1676
    Anne Fenwick c 1654-p 1714
    XXIII 29; XXIV 109
NY **WILLIAM** ....-1674
    m .... _____ _____ ....-....
    XXXV 273
DE **WILLIAM** .... -1678
    m .... **Mary Caldwell?** ....-....
    XXXIV 79

HEERMANCE, see HEERMANS

**HEERMANS/HEERMANCE/
HERMANEE**
NY **FOCKE JANSZ** ....-a 1671
    m ....
    Margriet Hendricks ....-....
    XXXVIII 213
NY **JAN FOCKEN** c 1641-....
    m 1676
    Engeltje Breestede bp 1654-....
    XXXVI 15

HELM, see HELMS

HELMS/HELM
PA **ISRAEL HELM** 1627-1701/02
    m 1655/56 _____ _____ ....-....
    XXXV 27

HEMENWAY/HEMMENWAY
MA **RALPH** 1583-1678 m 1634
   Elizabeth Hewes 1603-1684/85
   XXIX 192; XXXVII 20

HEMMENWAY, see
HEMENWAY

HENDERSON
VA **THOMAS** ....-....
   m .... ____ ____ ....-....
   XXVIII 49; XXXVII 86

HENDRICK/HENDRICKS
PA **ALBERTUS** bp 1641-1715
   m .... **Lysbeth** ____ ....-....
   XXXVII 207
NH **DANIEL** c 1610-1700
   m 1642 **Dorothy Pike** c 1617-
   1659
   XVII 39

HENDRICKS, see HENDRICK

HENDRICKSEN/HARMENSON/
HENDRICKSON
NY **HENDRICK HARMENSEN**
   ....-a 1677
   m 1658 **Egbertie Jans** ....-p 1683
   XXV 174
NY **HENDRICK** 1636-....
   m a 1663 **Jane Luitgirt** ....-....
   XXXIX 115
NY **JACOB HENDRICKSON** ....-
   .... m1) a 1677 **Geesje Bartell**
   ....-1684
   XXXVIII 99

HENDY, see HANDY

HENLEY
VA **REYNOLD** ....-p 1673
   m .... **Susan Turner** ....-....

XXXVI 238

HENNION
NY **NATHANIEL PIETERSEN** ....-
   .... m 1664
   Anneken Ackerman ....-....
   XXX 209

HENSHAW
MA **JOSHUA** 1642/44-1688/1723
   m 1670 **Elizabeth Sumner** 1652-
   1728
   XXVI 271, 273, 274; XXXIX
   204; XXXX 83

HERBERT
NJ **WALTER** ....-....
   m .... **Bridget** ____ ....-....
   XXX 146

HERICKE, see HERRICK
HERMANEE, see HEARMANS

HERNDON
VA **WILLIAM** 1636/37-1699/1722
   m 1677 **Catherine Digges** 1654-
   1727
   XXVIII 97; XXXI 49; XXXIII
   69; XXXV 87

HERRICK/HERECKE/
MA **HENRY/HENERIE HERKKE-
HIRECK** 1604-1671
   m a 1629
   Editha Laskin 1614-liv 1674
   XXII 98; XXV 87; XXVI 36, 96;
   XXIX 258; XXXI 278; XXXII 80

HERSEY
MA **WILLIAM** 1596-1657/58
   m ....**Elizabeth Croad**e ....-1671
   XXII 148; XXXIX 149

HEWES/HUGHES
NJ **WILLIAM THOMAS** 1623-
1698 m 1660
Deborah Pedrick 1640-p 1705
XXXX 283-293

HEWINS
MA **JACOB** a 1650-1711
m .... **Mary** ____ a 1650-1715/16
XVII 18; XXVIII 112, 113

HEWIT, see HEWITT

HEWITT/HEWIT/HUGHITT
CT **THOMAS** ....-c 1662/70
m 1659 **Hannah Palmer** 1634-....
XXVI 79, 228; XXVII 128;
XXXV 52

HEWOOD/HEYWOOD/HOAR
MA **JOHN HOAR** 1619-1704
m 1645 **Alice Lisle** ....-1696
XXXVI 175

HEYDON, see HAYDEN
HEYWARD, see HAWARD or
HOWARD

HIBBARD/HEBARD
MA **ROBERT** bp 1613-1684
m .... **Joanna Luff/Love** ....-1696
XXXII 253; XXXV 112, 177;
XXXVI 235

HICHBORN
MA **DAVID** a 1621-1650
m .... **Catherine** ____ a 1639-
1661
XI 33

HICKES, see HICKS

HICKOX
CT **SAMUEL** a 1638-inv 1694
m .... **Hannah Upson** ....-1655
XXVI 163

HICKS/HICKES/HIX
MA/NY **ROBERT** 1580-1647
m1) 1596 **Elizabeth Morgan** ....-
1607/09
XX 27; XXV 110, 111ʂ XXXII
39; XXXIV 320; XXXVI 164
MA **THOMAS HIX/HICKES** ....-
wd 1653
m .... **Margaret** ____ ....-p 1666
XXXIV 249; XXXVI 137;
XXXIX 266

HIGBY/HIGBEE
CT/NY **EDWARD** 1615/16-1699
m c 1647
Jedidiah Skidmore 1624-c 1660
XXI 46; XXIX 384, 390

HIGDON
VA **RICHARD** c 1625-c 1665
m c 1651
Jane Brookes c 1633-p 1703
XXIX 208; XXXVIII 31

HIGGINS
MA/NJ **RICHARD** bp 1603-c 1675
m1) 1634 **Lydia Chandler** 1616-
a 1650
m2) 1651 **Mary Yeates/Yates**
....- p 1702
XV 19; XX 141, 142; XXIX 246;
XXX 44; XXXII 75; XXXIV
145, 228; XXXX 380

HIGH
VA **JOHN**, Sr c 1655-1740
m c 1676
Sallie ____ ....-p 1685

HILTON-Cont.
MD **JOHN** ....-....
    m .... _____ _____ ....-....
    XXXII 216; XXXIII 78
MA/NH/ME **WILLIAM, I**
    c 1580/85-1655/56
    m2) c 1650 **Frances** _____ ....-
    p 1656
    XXII 150; XXVIII 102; XXXII
    14
NY **WILLIAM** 1665-1749
    m2) 1693 **Anna Brouwer**
    (Berkhoven) c 1670-1748
    XXXII 276

HINCKLEY
MA **SAMUEL** bp 1589-1662 m 1617
    Sarah Soule/Soole 1600-1656/65
    XIII 11; XXXI 184; XXXIX 210
MA **THOMAS** 1618-1705/06
    m1) 1641 **Mary Richards** ....-
    1659
    m2) 1660 **Mary (Smith) Glover**
    1630-1703
    XXXI 184; XXXIV 141; XXXV
    127; XXXIX 210

HINE
CT **THOMAS** a 1646-1694/98
    m 1652 **Elizabeth** _____ ....-
    p 1673/1698
    X 91, 131, 132; XX 11, 137;
    XXII 128; XXVI 298; XXXII 37

HINMAN
CT **EDWARD, Sr** 1609-1681
    m c 1651/52
    Hannah Stiles ....-1677
    IX 15; XVII 20; XVIII 47; XIX
    43; XXV 272, 275; XXVIII 201;
    XXXV 25; XXXVI 129;
    XXXVIII 287

HINSDALE
MA **ROBERT** ....-1675
    m1) a 1636/37 **Ann Woodward**
    1616-1666
    III 13, 39, 65; XXXX 448

HITCHCOCK
CT **LUKE** ....-1659
    m ....
    Elizabeth Gibbons 1596-1696
    XIII 60; XXVI 167
CT/MA **LUKE** 1655-1727
    m 1677
    Sarah (Burt) Dorchester 1656-
    1746
    XXXV 171
CT **MATTHIAS** c 1609/10-1669
    m ....
    Elizabeth Rogers 1621-1676
    IV 92; XI 143; XIX 38; XX 116;
    XXI 101; XXIII 76

HIX, see HICKS

HIXON
MA **RICHARD** ....-inv 1718 m 1686
    Margaret Watkins/Wadkins ....-
    p 1721
    XXXVIII 295

HOADLEY
CT **WILLIAM** c 1630-1709
    m1) .... **Mary** _____ ....-a 1686
    X 15

HOAGLAND/HOAGLIN/
HOGELAND/HOOCHLANDT/
HOOGLAND
NY **CORNELIS DIRCKSEN**
    HOOCHLANDT 1599-1675/76
    m c 1638 **Aeltie Ariaens** ....-....
    XXXVIII 73
NY **DIRCK JANSEN HOOGLAND**

HOAGLAND/HOAGLIN/
HOGELAND/HOOCHLANDT/
HOOGLAND-Cont.
 c 1635- c 1707/33
 m1) 1662 **Annetje Hansen**
 Bergen bp 1640-1678
 XXIX 401; XXXI 182

HOAR/HORR
MA **JOHN** c 1614-1704
 m .... **Alice Lisle** ....-1696/97
 XXXIV 221; XXXVIII 106

HOBART, also see HUBBARD
MA **EDMUND** c 1570/74-1646
 m1) 1597-1600 **Margaret Dewey**
 ....-1641
 XV 59; XVI 16; XXX 290;
 XXXIV 169

HOBBIE, see HOBBY

HOBBS
MA **JOSIAH** 1649-1741
 m 1683 **Mary** _____ ....-....
 XIV 8
MA/NH **MORRIS** c 1615-1706
 m .... **Sarah Estow** ....-1686
 XXVII 121; XXIX 402

HOBBY/HOBBIE/HUBBY
CT **JOHN, Sr** 1630/32-1707
 m .... _____ _____ ....-....
 XXIX 277

HOBSON, see HOPSON

HOCKER
MD **JOHN** c 1635-1696
 m a 1659 **Mary Green** 1637-
 p 1685
 XXX 229

HODGDON/HODGSON/
HODSDON
MA/ME **NICHOLAS HODSDON**
 1616?-p 1679
 m1) 1639 **Esther Wines?** ....-
 1647
 XXXI 68, 296
NY/RI **ROBERT HODGSON** 1626-
 1696
 m 1665 **Rachel Shotten** ....-....
 XIV 65

HODGES
VA **JOHN** ....-1622/23
 m .... **Mary** _____ ....-....
 XXXIV 290; XXXV 296
MA **JOHN** 1650-1719 m 1672
 Elizabeth Macey ....-1718/19
 XXXIII 184
MA **WILLIAM** ....-1654
 m 1628/30
 Mary Andrews c 1625/30-
 p 1700
 IX 51; XV 111; XVI 45; XXI
 144; XXXIII 184; XXXIX 330

HODGKINS, see HOTCHKISS

HODGMAN
MA **JOSIAH WEBBER** 1668-1749
 m1) 1691 **Elizabeth** _____ ....-
 1712
 XIII 120 NOTE; Jan. 7 JOSIAH
 WEBBER was adopted by Thos.
 Hodgman; XXXIII 241

HODGSON, see HODGDON
HODSDON, see HODGDON

HOFFMAN
NY **MARTIN HERMANZEN**
 c 1625-p 1711
 m2) 1664 **Emerentje Classen**

HOFFMAN-Cont.
    DeWitt ....-p 1711
    XXXVII 78

HOLBROOK/HOLBROOKE
MA **JOHN** ....-....
    m .... _____ _____ ....-....
    XIX 159
NY **JOHN HOLLBROOK** ....-....
    m .... _____ _____ ....-....
    X 93
MA **JOHN** 1618-1699
    m1) .... **Sarah French** ....-
    1643/44
    m2) .... **Elizabeth Stream** ....-
    1688
    XVIII 65; XXXX 11
MA/NY **RICHARD/JOHN**
    c 1601/17-c 1670
    m .... **Agnes** _____ ....-p 1670
    IX 18; X 93; XIII 32; XXIX 35;
    XXXX 221, 351
MA **THOMAS, Sr**, 1601-c 1674/76
    m 1623 **Jane Kingman** 1601-
    a 1677
    IX 30; XII 26; XV 8, 15; XXV
    268; XXXV 192
MA **THOMAS** c 1624/25-1697/1705
    m3) 1668/69 **Margaret Potter**
    Bouker ....-1690
    VII 26; X 271

HOLBROOKE, see HOLBROOK

HOLCOMB/HOLCOMBE
MA/CT **THOMAS HOLCOMBE**
    1590/1601-1657
    m 1631/33 **Elizabeth Ferguson**
    ....-1679
    VII 13; XXXI 198; XXXX 108,
    231

HOLCOMBE, see HOLCOMB

HOLDEN
RI **RANDALL** c 1612-1692
    m .... **Frances Dungan** ....-1697
    XXII 65
MA **RICHARD** c 1609-c 1695/96
    m 1640/41 **Martha Fosdick**
    1620-1681
    XXVIII 180; XXXVI 76;
    XXXVII 16; XXXVIII 171

HOLLAND
MA **NATHANIEL** ....-p 1709
    m2) 1661 **Sarah Streeter** ....-....
    XXIV 156; XXXVI 146

HOLLEY/HOLLY/HAULEY
MA **SAMUEL** ....-wp 1643
    m .... **Elizabeth** _____ ....-....
    XXVII 215

HOLLIS
MA **JOHN** c 1640-....
    m .... **Elizabeth Priest** ....-c 1638
    XXV 125

HOLLISTER
CT **JOHN** 1612-1665 m 1640
    Joanna Treat bp 1618-1694
    XI 109, 181; XIII 72; XVII 88,
    131; XXX 150; XXXIII 75, 102;
    XXXVIII 356

HOLLOWAY
MA **WILLIAM** c 1586-1664/65
    m1) **Elizabeth** _____ ....-1679/80
    XXXI 249; XXXX 102, 302

HOLLOWELL, see HALLOWELL
VA **THOMAS** c 1628-....-
    m .... **Elizabeth** _____ ....-....
    X 181

HOLLY, see HOLLEY

HOLME
PA **JOHN** ....-1702/03
 m c 1686 **Mrs. Nicholas More**
 ....-....
 XXX 58

HOLMES
CT **FRANCIS** ....-p 1671
 m .... **Ann** _____ ....-1675/76
 XVII 56; XXXII 31
MA **GEORGE** 1594-1645
 m .... **Deborah** _____ ....-1662
 XIII 40; XX 101; XXIX 55;
 XXXVIII 342
MA **JOHN** ....-1667
 m .... **Sarah** _____ ....-1650
 XX 68
NH **JOHN** c 1641-1712/13 m a 1666
 Mary Peverly c 1646-1712
 XXIX 313
CT **ROBERT** ....-1670
 m .... **Frances Wainwright** ....-....
 VII 44; XXIX 253; XXXIII 187;
 XXXV 164, 176
MA **WILLIAM** ....-1678
 m ....
 Elizabeth _____ ....-1688/89
 XXXII 223

HOLSTON/HOULSTON
PA **JOHN HOULSTON** ....-1699
 m ....
 Elizabeth Serrill ....-1702
 XXXIX 322

HOLT/HOLTE
MA **NICHOLAS** c 1602-1685
 m1) c 1632 **Elizabeth Short** ....-
 1656/58
 XV 36; XVII 47; XVIII 89; XXI
 20; XXIX 375; XXX 121, 162;
 XXXIII 270; XXXV 347;
 XXXVI 260; XXXVIII 202

VA **RANDALL** 1606/07-1639/50
 m 1626/36
 Mary Bailye c 1610-c 1650
 XXXV 213; XXXIX 86
CT **WILLIAM** 1610-1683
 m .... **Sarah** _____ ....-1717
 X 57, 224; XII 33; XXX 266

HOLTE, see HOLT

HOLTON
MA/CT **WILLIAM** 1610/11-1691
 m .... **Mary Pierce** ....-1691
 XI 188; XXXII 131

HONEYWELL
NY **ISRAEL** 1660-1720
 m a 1687
 Mary Spofford 1656-1735
 XXVI 22, 116

HOOD
MD **BENJAMIN** ....-....
 m .... _____ _____ ....-....
 XXXIII 338
MA **JOHN** c 1600-....
 m .... **Elizabeth** _____ ....-....
 XXIV 62; XXXIII 268

HOOE
VA **RICE** c 1599-c 1655 m a 1640
 Sarah _____ ....-c 1665
 XXXVI 280; XXXIX 166

HOOGLAND, see HOAGLAND

HOOK/HOOKE
MD **THOMAS** c 1645-1697/98
 m c 1679
 Annaple _____ c 1658-c 1720
 XXIX 199

HOOKE, see HOOK

HOOKER
CT **THOMAS** c 1585/86-p 1647
　　m .... **Susan/Susannah**
　　Garbrand ....-p 1647
　　IV 70, 71; XXX 255

HOORNBEECK/HOORNBEEK/
HORNBECK
NY **WARNAER**
　　HOORNBEECK....-....
　　m2) .... **Grietge Tyssen** ....-....
　　XXXVIII 98

HOPKINS
MD **GERRARD, I** ....-w 1691
　　m 1658 **Mrs. Thomsin Welch**
　　(wid.) ....-p 1691
　　m 1671 **Thomasine (Eard)**
　　Baker (wid.) ....-p 1691
　　XXV 40; XXXII 156, 260;
　　XXXIII 307; XXXVIII 64
MA **JOHN** c 1613-inv.t.1654
　　m 1633
　　Jane Strong ....-c 1679
　　XI 119; XV 71; XVII 116;
　　XXVII 180; XXIX 46
MA **STEPHEN** ....-1644 m ...
　　Constance Dudley ....-a 1617
　　XXXVIII 322

HOPPIN/HOPPING
NY **JOHN** c 1642-1722
　　m .... **Rebecca Hand** c 1660-1715
　　XXIX 252

HOPPING, see HOPPIN

HOPSON
CT **JOHN** pr 1610-1701
　　m3) c 1673 **Elizabeth Alling**
　　1653-1689
　　XXXI 263; XXXIII 129;
　　XXXVII 248

HORNBECK, see HOORNBEECK

HORNE
NH **WILLIAM** ....-1689
　　m .... **Elizabeth Clough** 1642-
　　1707
　　XIX 119

HORNEY
MD **JEFFERY** c 1682-1738
　　m .... **Margaret** _____ ....-....
　　XXIX 360; XXXII 261

HORNOR
NJ **JOHN** ....-1699
　　m .... **Mary Robinson** ....-....
　　XVIII 129

HORR, see HOAR

HORTON
CT/NY **BARNABAS** 1600-1680
　　m1) 1622 **Anne Smith** ....-a 1640
　　m2) .... **Mary Langton** ....-....
　　V 44; XXX 131; XXXI 176;
　　XXXIII 97; XXXV 230; XXXIX
　　145
NH/NY **JOSEPH** c 1625-a 1696
　　m c 1655 **Jane Budd** ....-....
　　XXX 131
CT/MA **THOMAS** 1602-1641
　　m .... **Mary Eddy** ....-1683
　　XXV 42; XXVII 75
MA **THOMAS** ....-c 1700
　　m1) .... **Rachel** _____ ....-1693
　　XI 66; XII 8

HOSFORD/HORSFORD
MA/CT **WILLIAM HORSFORD**
　　c 1595-c 1660
　　m1) .... **Sara** _____ ...-1641
　　m2) .... **Mrs. Jane Fowkes** ....-
　　a 1671

HOSFORD/HORSFORD-Cont.
XVIII 103; XX 19; XXXIX 256

HOSKINE, see HASKINS

HOSKINS/HASKINS
MA **ANTHONY, I** c 1632-1706/07
   m1) 1656 **Isabel/Jesabel Brown**
   c 1635-1698
   XXXV 20, 181
CT **JOHN** c 1585-1648
   m 1630 **Ann Filer/Fyler** ....-1662
   XXXV 181

HOSLEY
MA **JAMES** 1649-1677 m 1674
   Martha Parker 1649-a 1686
   XXXVIII 67

HOSMER
MA **JAMES** bp 1605-1685
   m2) .... **Mary** ____ ....-1641
   m3) p 1641 **Alice/Elinne** ____
   ....- 1664/65
   XXVII 117, 118, 150; XXXI 103;
   XXXVII 255
MA/CT **THOMAS** bp 1603-1687
   m .... **Frances** ____ 1602-1675
   XXXI 317

HOTALING/HOUGHTAILING
NY **MATTHIAS**
   HOUGHTAILING 1644-1706
   m .... **Marie Hendricksee** ....-....
   XVIII 146

HOTCHKISS/HODGKINS
CT **JOSHUA** 1651-1722 m 1677
   Mary Pardee 1658-c 1684
   XXXV 356
CT **SAMUEL** 1620/23-1642/63
   m 1642/48
   Elizabeth Cleverly ....-1681

IV 68; XI 48; XII 35; XV 88;
XVII 11; XXV 49; XXXIII 28;
XXXIV 140, 172, 345; XXXV
31; XXXVII 360; XXXVIII 46

HOUGHTALING, see HOTALING

HOUGHTELIN/
HOOGHTEYLINGH
NY **JAN WILLEMSEN**
HOOGHTEYLINGH
   c 1630-....
   m .... **Barbara Jans** ....-p 1671
   XXXVIII 281

HOUGHTON
MA **JOHN, Sr** 1624-1684
   m 1647/49
   Beatrix Walker 1622-1711/20
   XVI 9; XX 117; XXX 74; XXXX
   237
MA **RALPH** c 1623-1700/05 m c
   1647 **Jane Stowe** c 1626-1700/01
   XXV 266; XXVII 146; XXXIV
   220; XXXVIII 236; XXXX 72

HOULSTON, see HOLSTON

HOUSE
MA **SAMUEL** 1610-1661 m c 1636
   Elizabeth Hammond c 1619-
   1661
   XXXX 414
CT **WILLIAM** c 1642-c 1703/04
   m a 1670 **Sarah Bidwell** c 1653-
   a 1703/04
   XXXVII 106

HOUSTON
VA **ALFRED** 1572-....
   m 1607 **Ruth Scence** ....-....
   XXXII 267

HOVEY
MA **DANIEL** 1618-1692 m 1641
　　Abigail Andrews ....-1676/1683
　　XXIX 167; XXX 69

HOW, see HOWE

**HOWARD/ARUNDEL-
HOWARD/HAYWARD/
HEYWOOD**
CT **HENRY** ....-1708/09
　　m 1648 **Sarah Stone** ....-....
　　XXII 21
VA **JOHN HEYWARD** 1610-
　　wp 1661 m c 1650
　　Margaret Clarke ....-....
　　XXXIV 309; XXXVI 107
MA **JOHN** c 1620/28-c 1700
　　m c 1645/50
　　Martha Haywood c 1620/30-
　　a 1703
　　X 240; XXVIII 144; XXX 278;
　　XXXVII 199; XXXVIII 6
VA/MD **MATTHEW ARUNDEL-
HOWARD** 1609-a 1659
　　m c 1625/30
　　Ann? Hall? ....-....
　　XXIX 279; XXXIII 213;
　　XXXVIII 285; XXXX 412
MA **SAMUEL** c 1613-....
　　m c 1645 **Sarah Stowers** ....-
　　a 1686
　　XXIX 177
MA **THOMAS** ....-1686
　　m .... **Susanna** _____ ....-....
　　XXXV 269
CT **THOMAS** ....-1675
　　m 1666 **Mary Wellman** ....-....
　　XXXX 51
MA **WILLIAM HAYWARD** ....-
　　1659
　　m 1636 **Margery** _____ ....-1676
　　XXX 155

HOWE/HOW
MA **ABRAHAM** ....-1676
　　m .... _____ _____ ....-1645
　　XV 126; XXXI 83
MA **EDWARD** 1585-1639
　　m 1613/14 **Elizabeth** _____ 1585-
　　1672
　　XXX 191
MA **JAMES** c 1605/06-1702
　　m 1628 **Elizabeth Dane** ....-
　　1693/94
　　XXVI 275; XXXI 262; XXXIV
　　280; XXXVIII 134
MA **JOHN HOW** 1602/17-p 1680/87
　　m c 1638/40
　　Mary _____ ....-c 1698
　　IV 93; IX 14; X 137; XIII 66;
　　XVII 10; XVIII 37; XX 144;
　　XXII 34, 120; XXX 22; XXXV
　　19; XXXIX 312

HOWELL
MA/NY **EDWARD** bp 1584-1655
　　m1) c 1617 **Frances** _____ ....-
　　1630
　　m2) .... **Eleanor** _____ ....-a 1632
　　X 82; XII 72; XIII 85; XX 5;
　　XXIX 162
MA/NY **JOHN** bp 1624/28-1696
　　m c 1647
　　Susanna Townsend c 1628-1711
　　XXIX 162

HOWES
MA **THOMAS** c 1590-1665
　　m a 1630 **Mary Burr** ....-1682/95
　　XXXIII 163

HOWLAND
MA **HENRY** c 1600/09-1661/71
　　m 1637 **Mary Newland** ....-1674
　　XXX 159; XXXVI 53; XXXVII
　　87

HOWLAND-Cont.
MA **JOHN** 1592-1672/73
  m 1623 **Elizabeth Tilley** 1607-
  1687
  XXXII 56

HOWLETT
MA **THOMAS** c 1606-1678
  m 1635 **Alice French** bp 1610-
  1666
  XXXVI 272; XXXVII 42

HOXIE/HAUKSIE
MA **LODOWICK HAUKSIE** ....-
  p 1702 m 1664
  Mary Presbery/Presbrey 1641-
  ....
  IV 162; X 10; XV 41

HOYT/HAIGHT/HAIT/HOYTE
MA **JOHN** 1610/15-1687/88
  m1) c 1635 **Frances** ____ ....-
  1642/43
  m2) .... **Frances** ____ ....-1687
  IX 45; XVI 95; XXI 151; XXIX
  102, 146
MA **JOHN, Jr** c 1638-1696
  m 1659 **Mary Barnes** ....-p 1704
  XXXVI 38
MA/CT **SIMEON/SIMON** 1590/95-
  a 1657
  m1) 1612 **Deborah Stowers**
  bp 1593-1625
  m2) 1618/35 **Susanna Smith** ....-
  a 1674
  X 116, 198; XII 91; XIII 68; XV
  21, 90; XVI 35; XXII 158; XXVI
  144, 245, 247, 248, 249; XXIX
  73, 201, 250, 378; XXXIV 88;
  XXXV 60, 341; XXXVII 176;
  XXXVIII 227

HOYTE, see HOYT

HUBBARD/HUBBERT
MA **CALEB HUBBERT**
(HOBART) c 1622-1711
  m 1675
  Elizabeth Ffackson (wid.) 1655-
  ....
  XXXVIII 77
MA/CT **GEORGE** 1594/1604-1683
  m a 1625/27
  Mary Bishop 1610-1673/75
  X 296; XX 20, 123; XXII 45;
  XXV 51; XXVIII 118; XXIX
  127; XXXII 194; XXXIX 190
CT **GEORGE** 1601-wp 1681/84
  m 1640/47
  Elizabeth Watts 1622-1702
  V 126; XV 68, 82; XXX 20;
  XXXIII 221; XXXIV 240;
  XXXVII 94
MA **RICHARD** 1631-1719
  m ....
  Martha Allen 1645-1718
  XXXIX 317
MA **THOMAS HOBART** 1606-
  1689 m 1629
  Anne Promer/Ptomer ....-....
  XXXX 87, 133, 155
MA/CT **WILLIAM** ....-1694
  m2) .... **Mrs. Ann Allen** ....-1687
  X 38
MA **WILLIAM** 1594- p 1670
  m .... **Judith Knapp** 1610-....
  IX 34

HUBBELL
CT **RICHARD** a 1626/28-1699
  m1) 1650/51
  Elizabeth Meigs 1635-1664/65
  m2) .... **Elizabeth** ____ ....-1688
  V 88; XV 53; XXIII 36; XXIV
  52; XXVIII 82; XXIX 22;
  XXXIII 59

HUBBERT, see HUBBARD
HUBBY, see HOBBY

HUCKINS
NH **ROBERT** c 1620-1694/96
m .... _____ _____ ....-....
XXXVIII 272
MA **THOMAS** 1617-1679
m2) .... **Mrs. Rose Hyllier** 1616-1687
II 50

HUDSON
MA **DANIEL** 1617-1697
m ....
Joanna Everton 1620-1697
XXIX 79
MA **THOMAS** a 1595-....
m .... _____ _____ ....-....
XXIX 194
MA **WILLIAM** 1590-1690
m .... **Susan** _____ ....-1650
XXIX 79

HUESTED, see HUSTED

HUFF/HOUGH
PA **JOHN HOUGH** c 1651-1743
m c 1681
Hannah Spofforth 1645-....
XXXVIII 250

HUGHES/HEWES
NJ **WILLIAM, I** 1635-1698
m c 1660
Deborah (Pedrick) c 1640-a 1692
XXXIX 199

HUGHITT, see HEWITT

HULBERT/HURLBURT/
HURLBUT
CT **THOMAS HURLBUT** c 1610-1671/89
m .... **Sarah Greson** ....-....
XV 50, 70; XXII 8; XXVII 83;
XXVIII 74; XXXVII 270;
XXXVIII 58; XXXIX 106;
XXXX 253

HULIN/HULING/HULINGS
RI **JAMES HULING** 1620-1697
m a 1646
Margaret _____ 1632-1706/07
XXIV 142
NJ **MARCUS LAWRENCE**
(HULINGS) 1640/45-1689
m 1680 **Brigitta Danielsson** ....-a 1685
XXXX 173

HULING(S), see HULIN

HULL
MA **GEORGE, I** 1590-1659 m 1614
Thamzen/Thomasene Mitchell
...-a 1655
XVI 46; XXIX 245; XXX 109;
XXXI 110; XXXVIII 329
MA **JOSEPH** 1594/95-1665
m1) 1618/19 **Joanna** _____ ....-1632/33
m2) a 1635 **Agnes** _____ 1610-....
X 217; XV 51; XVIII 43; XXXIII
127, 244; XXXIV 21; XXXV 336
MA/CT **RICHARD** 1590-1662
m .... _____ _____ ....-....
I 29
MA **THOMAS** ....-....
m .... **Joan Peson** ....-....
XXXX 393

HUMISTON
CT **HENRY** c 1629-....
    m .... _____ ___ ....-....
    XXVI 10

HUMPHREY
MA **JOHN** 1595-1661
    m3) .... **(Lady) Susan Fiennes**
    1630-....
    XXX 208
MA **JONAS** c 1587-1661/62
    m 1607 **Frances Cooley** ....-
    a 1659
    XXVIII 105; XXXVII 38
CT **MICHAEL** c 1620-a 1697
    m 1647
    Priscilla Grant 1626-....
    XVIII 112; XXVI 231

HUNGERFORD
CT **THOMAS** ....-1663
    m1) .... _____ _____ ....-....
    XIV 61; XXXV 138

HUNN
MA **GEORGE** ....-wd 1640
    m .... **Ann** _____ ....-....
    X 60
CT **JONATHAN** ....-1735
    m .... _____ _____ ....-....
    XX 134

HUNT
RI/MA **ENOCH** ....-1645/52
    m .... _____ _____ ....-....
    XXIII 67; XXVII 88
MA **EPHRAIM** 1610-1687
    m ....
    Anna Richards ....-1650/55
    XII 14
MA **JONATHAN** 1637-1691
    m .... **Clemence Hosmer** ....-....
    X 46

NY **RALPH** c 1613- p 1677
    m .... **Elizabeth Anne Jessup** ....-
    a 1677
    XVIII 46; XIX 91; XXII 157;
    XXVIII 7; XXXVII 36
MA **WILLIAM** 1605-1667
    m a 1635/46
    Elizabeth Best ....-1661/a 1706
    XXIX 47; XXX 141; XXXV 80;
    XXXVII 47

HUNTER
VA **WILLIAM** ....-1718
    m 1678 _____ _____ ....-....
    XIV 83

HUNTINGTON
CT **CHRISTOPHER, Sr** 1624/28-
    1691
    m 1652 **Ruth Rockwell** ....-....
    XXX 71; XXXV 126
CT **SIMON** 1629-1706/07 m 1653
    Sarah Clark(e) c 1633-1721
    XIII 116; XVII 124; XXI 157;
    XXIV 25; XXV 26, 74; XXVI
    226, 227; XXX 232; XXXI 156;
    XXXIV 16, 282; XXXIX 287
CT **WILLIAM** a 1625-c 1689
    m a 1643 **Joanna Bayley** ....-
    c 1663
    XXXII 27

HUNTLEY
MA **JOHN** ....-1676
    m .... **Jane** _____ ....-....
    XV 44

HUNTON/HUNTOON
NH **PHILIP** c 1664-1752
    m1) c 1687 **Betsey Hall** ....-
    c 1697/1700
    XXXVI 344; XXXIX 260

HURD/HEARD
CT **ADAM** c 1611-c 1671/73
    m a 1640
    Hannah Bertram/Barbraum ....-
    ....
    XI 81; XVI 68; XXXI 169;
    XXXIII 149; XXXX 171
CT **JOHN** pr c 1585-....
    m .... _____ _____ .....-....
    XXXVII 289
NH **JOHN HEARD** 1601-1689
    m c 1643
    Elizabeth Hull c 1648-1706
    XXXIX 171

HURLBURT, see HULBERT
HURLBUT, see HULBERT

HURST
VA **TOBIAS** 1596-c 1656
    m .... _____ _____ ....-....
    XXXVI 61
HURT
VA **WILLIAM, Sr** c 1620/30-p 1704
    m a 1655 **Margaret** _____ ....-....
    XXXVII 262; XXXIX 290

HUSE
MA **ABLE** 1602-1690
    m2) 1663 **Mary Hilton Sears**
    ....-....
    XXXVII 282

HUSSEY
MA/NH **CHRISTOPHER** 1595/96-
    1686 m c 1630
    Theodate Bacheler ....-1644/49
    XXXIII 64

HUSTAD, see HUSTED

HUSTED/HUESTED/HUSTAD/
HUSTIS

CT **ANGELL** 1620-1706 m a 1685
    Rebecca Sherwood 1625/26-....
    XII 66; XX 14; XXXIII 147
CT **ROBERT** 1579/96-1652
    m 1624-1632/a 35
    Elizabeth Miller c 1595/a 1609-
    1654
    X 228; XII 66; XX 14; XXII 141;
    XXV 115, 116; XXIX 161, 321;
    XXXIII 147; XXXIV 120

HUSTIS, see HUSTED
HUTCHING, see HUTCHINS

HUTCHINS/HUTCHING
ME **ENOCH** ....-1698
    m 1667
    Mary Stevenson 1651-1698
    XXV 165
MA **JOHN HUTCHINS(ON)**
    1604/08-1685/86 m 1638
    Frances Gibbons (Alcock(e))
    1610/12-1694
    XXVII 193; XXIX 212; XXXI
    162; XXXVIII 234; XXXIX 33;
    XXXX 321
MA **NICHOLAS** 1637/38-c 1693
    m 1666 **Elizabeth Farr** ....-....
    XXXIII 263

HUTCHINSON
VA **ANDREW** 1687-....
    m 1710 **Jane Browning** ....-
    a 1732
    XXXIX 41
MA **RICHARD** c 1602-wp 1682
    m1) 1627 **Alice Bosworth** ....-
    a 1688
    XXXV 284

HUXFORD
MA **SAMUEL, I** c 1660-....
    m c 1683 **Esther Norton** ....-1771

HUXFORD-Cont.
XXXX 399

HUYCK
NY **JANS HANSE** c 1600-1654
m ....**Lizabeth Pieters** ....-....
XXXIV 321

HYATT
MD **CHARLES** ....-1726
m .... **Sarah** _____ ....-....
XXX 219

HYDE
CT **WILLIAM** c 1600-1681/91
m ....
_____ _____ ....-p 1637/59
IV 109; XIV 60; XV 66; XVI 21;
XVII 146; XXIV 49; XXV 67;
XXVIII 58; XXIX 37; XXXI 276

IJAMS/EYAMS
MD **WILLIAM EYAMS** c 1650-
1703 m 1669 **Elizabeth Cheney**
1652-....
XXV 29

INGALLS
MA **EDMUND** c 1598-w 1648
m 1620/21 **Ann Tripp** ....-p 1648
X 156; XXVI 305; XXXV 198,
227; XXXIX 96, 343; XXXX 89

INGERSOLL
CT/MA **JOHN** 1615-1684
m3) 1667 **Mary Hunt** ....-1690
X 71; XIV 63; XXXIII 227;
XXXVII 318; XXXVIII 176
CT **JOHN** 1640-1695 m 1673
Jane Skidmore Whitehead ....-
....
XXXVIII 69

INGHAM
CT **JOSEPH** ....-....
m 1655 **Sarah Bushnell** ....-....
XXXVIII 79

INGRAM
VA **JOHN** 1600-1654
m .... **Jane** _____ ....-....
XXXVI 340

INNIS
VA **JAMES** ....-wp 1710/11
m .... _____ _____ ....-....
XXXIII 316

INSLEY, see ENSLEY
IRELAN, see IRELAND

IRELAND/IRELAN
NY **THOMAS** c 1625-wp 1669
m c 1647
Joan (Ireland) Lattin ....p 1671
X 250, 269; XX 164; XXI 69;
XXV 222; XXXV 226, 250

IRISH
MA **JOHN** ....-p 1677/78
m .... **Elizabeth** _____ ....-
p 1673/74
XXXX 315

IRONMONGER
VA **THOMAS** c 1650-1724
m .... **Mary Scale** ....-....
XXXII 179

ISHAM
MA **JOHN** 1654-1713 m 1677/78
Jane Parker 1664-1719/20
XXXI 172

IVES/JOES
CT **WILLIAM JOES** 1607-1648

IVES/JOES-Cont.
  m a 1638/39
  m1) **Hannah** ____ ....-p 1682
  XXII 23; XXIV 73; XXIX 52;
  XXX 81; XXXI 301; XXXIII 204

JACKMAN
MA **JAMES** c 1618-1694
  m1) .... **Joanna** ____ ....-....
  XVII 151; XVIII 17, 112; XXX
  11

JACKSON
MA **ABRAHAM, Sr** ....-1714
  m 1657
  Remember Morton 1637-1707
  XIII 14; XXXI 44
MA **EDWARD** 1602/bp 04-1681
  m1) .... **Frances** ____ ....-1648
  XXIX 21; XXXI 165; XXXVII
  276
NY **ROBERT** c 1620-1684 m 1671
  Agnes Washburn 1620-1683
  XXX 223
MD **SAMUEL** ....-1688
  m 1672 **Ann Clark** ....-....
  XXX 182

JACOB, see JACOBS
JACOBISSEN, see JACOBUS

JACOBS/JACOB
MA **NICHOLAS** c 1605/08-1657
  m 1628 **Mary Gilman** ....-1681
  XV 110; XXVII 8

JACOBUS/JACOBISSEN/JANSE/
JANSZ/JANZ
NY **JACOBUS JANZ/JANSE** ....-....
  m .... **Judik Franse (Clauw)** ....-
  ....
  XXVII 226; XXVIII 212

JANES/JEANES
CT/MA **WILLIAM** 1610-1690
  m1) 1637 **Mary** ____ ....-1662
  m2) .... **Hannah Bascom
  Broughton** (wid.) ....-1681
  XIV 30; XXV 29; XXVIII 94;
  XXXVII 374

JANSE, see JACOBUS

JANSEN, see also CORSON
NY **CARSTEN JENSEN** ....-....
  m .... **Barbara** ____ ....-....
  XXIX 275

JANZ, see JACOBUS
JANZ, see WESTBROOK

JAQUETTE
DE **JEAN/JOHN PAUL** c 1615/20-
  c 1685 m p 1655
  Maria de Carpentier 1628-
  p 1655
  XI 13; XXXX 179

JAQUITH
MA **ABRAHAM, Sr/I** c 1620-1676
  m c 1643 **Ann Jordan** ....-....
  XXX 186; XXXIV 279, 333

JAYNE(S)
CT **WILLIAM** c 1610-1690
  m1) ....**Mary** ____ ....-....
  XIV 30
NY **WILLIAM** 1618-1714
  m2) 1675 **Anna/Annie
  (Jennings) Biggs/Briggs**
  1653/58-1692/94
  XIV 94; XXXVIII 56; XXXIX
  224

JEANES, see JANES
JEFFERIS, see JEFFRIES

JEFFERSON
VA **THOMAS** ....-wp 1687
    m a 1678 **Mary Branch** ....-....
    XXXVI 246

JEFFRIES/JEFFERIS
PA **ROBERT** 1656-1739
    m2) 1729 **Anne Archer** ....-....
    XXVI 233

JENCKS, see JENKS

JENKINS
MD **APP** ....-.... m ....
    ____ ____ ....-....
    XVI 122
MA **EDWARD** 1618-1699
    m1) p 1643/50 **Lettice (Hanford)**
    Foster 1617/18-p 1664/84
    XXXIV 182; XXXX 325
MA **JOEL** c 1614-wp 1688
    m 1640 banns
    Sarah Gilbert 1624-a 1688
    XXIX 175; XXXVI 174
MA **JOHN** 1609-1684
    m 1653 **Mrs. Mary Ewer** ....-....
    XIV 48

JENKS/JENCKS
MA **JOSEPH, Sr** 1602/03-1683
    m1) 1630/32 **Mary Tervyn**
    bp 1611-1643
    m2) a 1648 **Elizabeth** ____ ....-
    1679/97
    XII 47; XIII 80; XX 168; XXIV
    131; XXX 113; XXXI 301;
    XXXVI 53; XXXVII 96, 204;
    XXXVIII 307; XXXX 81

JENNESS
NH **FRANCIS** c 1634-1716
    m1) 1671 **Hannah Swine** ....-
    1700

XXXV 285

JENNINGS
VA **JOHN** ....-1669
    m a 1652
    Margaret ____ ....-1684
    XXI 168
CT **JOSHUA** c 1620/25-c 1675
    m 1647
    Mary Williams ....-p 1697/98
    XIII 90; XXII 53; XXIX 368;
    XXXI 258

JENNISON
MA **ROBERT** 1605-1690
    m2) a 1637 **Grace** ____ ....-1686
    XXXIV 104, 128

JENSEN, see JANSEN

JERAULD/GEROULD
MA **JAMES** c 1660-.... m ....
    Martha Dupee c 1685-1763
    IV 156

JEWELL/JUEL
MA **THOMAS** 1608/12-1654
    m a 1639
    Grisell/Gressell ____ ....-....
    XXV 64; XXIX 54

JEWETT
MA **EDWARD** c 1580-1614/15
    m 1604 **Mary Taylor** ....-....
    XVIII 150
MA **JOSEPH** bp 1609-1660/61
    m 1634 **Mary Mallinson** ....-
    1652
    XXI 178; XXXX 44, 165, 339
MA **MAXIMILLIAN** bp 1607-1684
    m1) c 1638 **Ann Cole** c 1609-
    c 1667
    IX 46; XIII 58; XXXIII 38;

JEWETT-Cont.
XXXIV 138; XXXVII 109;
XXXIX 297

JILLSON, see GILSON

JOBE
PA **ANDREW, Sr** ....-1699
m .... ____ ____ ....-....
XXXIV 268; XXXVI 332

JOCHEMSEN, see also GEORGE ANDERSON
NY **ANDRIES** ....-c 1663
m ....
Seletje Arens/Fredericks ....-
c 1630
XXVI 16

JOES, see NES

JOHNSON
CT **EBENEZER** 1645-1726
m .... **Hannah Tomlinson** ....-....
XII 117
NH **EDMUND** 1612-1650
m .... **Mary** ____ ....-1663
XXXII 231
MA **EDWARD** bp 1598-1672
m c 1620
Susan Munter c 1597/98-
1689/90
XI 94; XXVII 13, 112; XXXIV
139; XXXVIII 42
MA **ISAAC** ....-1673
m c 1637 **Elizabeth Porter** ....-
1683
XXVIII 169
CT **JEREMIAH** ....-....
m .... **Sarah Hotchkiss** ....-....
XXII 42
MA **JOHN** a 1600-1659
m1) 1613 **Mary Heath** ....-1629

m2) .... **Margery** ____ ....-1655
m3) .... **Grace Fawer** ....-....
XIX 77; XXIII 69; XXVIII 125,
169; XXXVII 259; XXXX 24,
111
CT **JOHN** ....-w 1716 m ....
Susannah ____ ....-....
XXXVIII 306
MA **JOSEPH** bp 1636/37-1714
m 1666 **Hannah Tenney** 1642-....
XXVII 39
CT **PETER** ....-a 1654
m .... **Elizabeth** ____ ....-....
XI 107, 108
VA **RICHARD** ....-1699 m ....
Susana Dunscomb 1664-1686
XXVI 86
NJ **RICHARD** c 1649-1719
m 1682 **Mary Grover** ....-1714
III 47; IV 80
MA **SOLOMON** ....-1687
m .... **Ellinor** ____ ....-....
XVI 87; XXIX 57
MA **STEPHEN** 1640-1690
m 1661 **Elizabeth Dane** ....-1722
XXX 167; XXXII 290
VA **THOMAS, Sr** 1621-1704
m 1688 **Mary Baker** ....-....
XXV 255; XXVIII 187
MA **TIMOTHY** ....-1688
m 1674 **Rebecca Aslett** 1652-....
XXIII 44
CT **WILLIAM (WINGLE
JANSEN)** ....-1716
m 1664 **Sarah Hall** bp 1646-....
X 165; XXXVI 249; XXXVIII 26
MA **WILLIAM** c 1601/03-1667/77
m 1630
Elizabeth ____ ....-1684
XXVII 39, 139; XXVIII 140, 209

JONES
MA **HUGH** bp 1636/37-c 1688

JONES-Cont.
   m2) 1672 **Mary Foster**
   bp 1649/50-1717
   XII 55; XXVI 97; XXXIII 31
VA **JAMES, I** 1635/40-1719
   m .... **Sarah** _____ ....-....
   XXXX 194, 278
NJ **JOHN** ....-.... m .... _____ _____
   ....-....
   XVI 30
MA **JOHN** c 1615-1673
   m .... **Dorcas** _____ ....-1709
   XXIV 14
MD **JOSEPH** c 1652-1708 m a 1670
   Elizabeth Clark ....-p 1701
   XXIX 96
MA **LEWIS** c 1600-1684 m ....
   Ann/a Stone c 1602/24-1680
   IV 46; XXXII 186; XXXVIII 5;
   XXXX 53
PA **MALACHI** 1651-1729
   m .... **Mary** _____ ....-1743/44
   XXI 154; XXXVIII 150
VA **MATTHEW, I** a 1620/1640-
   1712 m 1652
   Elizabeth Albrighton ....-....
   XIX 54; XX 103; XXVII 80;
   XXXII 20
CT **NATHANIEL** c 1654-1691
   m 1684 **Abigail Atwater** 1660-....
   V 62
VA **PETER** 1599-1662
   m .... **Margaret Wood** ....-p 1660
   VII 37; X 232
VA **PETER, Jr** 1651-1726
   m .... **Mary Wood** ....-....
   VII 37
VA **RICHARD** 1660/63-1747
   m1) by 1687 **Amy Batte** c 1671-
   1691
   XXXV 152
PA **ROBERT** ....-1746
   m 1693 **Ellen Jones** ....-....

XXVI 15
VA **ROGER** 1625-1701 m ....
   Dorothy Walker 1642-....
   XXV 121
MA **THOMAS** 1598/1600-1667
   m .... **Ann** _____ ....-....
   XXVII 48
MA **THOMAS** 1598-1671
   m .... **Mary North** 1611-1681
   XXVII 179
CT **THOMAS** c 1618-1654
   m 1639 **Mary?** ....-1650
   XXXIX 27
VA **THOMAS** c 1635-a 1675
   m c 1655 **Mary (Repps?)** ....-
   a 1710
   XXXI 12
MA **WILLIAM** c 1587-1677
   m .... _____ _____ ....-....
   XXII 112; XXXIV 303
VA **WILLIAM** 1608-1669 m a 1639
   Elizabeth _____ 1619-a 1668
   XXXI 108
CT **WILLIAM** 1624-1706 m ....
   _____ _____ ....-....
   V 62

JORDAN
VA **ARTHUR** 1629-1696
   m 1654 **Elizabeth Bevins** ....-
   1699
   XXXIX 29
MA **JOHN** c 1650-1728
   m1) c 1672 _____ _____
   ....-....
   XXXII 71
ME **ROBERT** 1612-1679
   m c 1643/50
   Sarah Winter ....-p 1686/87
   VI 92/108; XXXII 16
VA **SAMUEL** 1575/78-1623
   m1) 1595 _____ _____ ....-....
   m2) .... **Cicely Reynolds** ....-....

JORDAN-Cont.
XXX 202; XXXIII 347; XXXVII
300; XXXX 68
VA **THOMAS, I** c 1600-1644
m .... _____ _____ ....-....
XXXIX 274

JOSLIN/JOSSELYN
MA **THOMAS JOSSELYN** 1592-
1660/61 m 1614
Rebecca Marlow 1592-p 1664/
a 1669
XVIII 23; XXVIII 198; XXIX
229

JOSSELYN, see JOSLIN

JOY
MA **THOMAS** c 1611-1678
m 1637 **Joan Gallop** ....-1691
XXIII 75; XXIX 192; XXXI 249;
XXXIV 51

JOYNER
VA **THOMAS** 1619-1694 m 1646/47
Elizabeth Robbins ....-1683
XXX 248

JUDD
CT **THOMAS** ....-1688
m2) 1679 **Clemence Mason** ....-
1696
XXXIX 237

JUDSON
CT **JOSEPH** c 1619-1690
m .... **Sarah Porter** c 1626-1696
XIII 107
CT **WILLIAM** .... -1622
m1) .... **Grace** _____ ....-1659
XVII 159; XIX 80; XXVI 157

JUEL, see JEWELL

JUSTICE/GUSTAFSSON
DE **JOHN GUSTAFSSON** c 1620-
c1699 m c 1655
Brita Mounsdatter ....-1724
XXXVII 121

KEELER
CT **RALPH** 1613-1672
m p 1651
Mrs. **Sarah Whelply** (wid.)
c 1615-a 1672
X 144; XIX 162; XX 158

KEELING
VA **THOMAS** c 1608/13-by 1664
m .... **Ann** _____ ....-a 1688
XXXVIII 196

KEEN/KYN/KEENE
PA **JORAN** 1620-pr a 1693
m .... _____ _____ ....-....
XXXI 94
MA **JOHN KEENE** 1578-1649
m .... **Martha** _____ ....-....
XXIX 67

KEENER, see KENNER

KEEP
MA **JOHN** c 1639-1676 m 1663
Sarah Leonard 1643-1676
XVI 62

KEESE
RI **JOHN** ....-1700
m 1682 **Ann Manton** ....-1728
XXVI 269

KEITH
MA **JAMES, Sr** c 1643-1719
m1) 1668 **Susanna Edson** 1640-
1705
XXXIV 287; XXXIX 251

KELLOGG
CT **DANIEL** 1630-1688
   m2) 1665 **Bridget Bouton**
    c 1642-1689
    VIII 26; XIV 96; XVI 44, 74;
    XVIII 104; XXIII 41; XXVIII
    139; XXXI 206; XXXII 285;
    XXXIII 88
MA **JOSEPH** bp 1626-wp a 1708
   m1) a 1651 **Joanna Foote**
    c 1628-1666
   m2) a 1667 **Abigail Terry** 1646-
   w p 1726
    XIV 42, 54, 87, 108; XVI 128;
    XVII 90; XXI 59; XXII 104;
    XXIX 141; XXXIII 194; XXXIV
    222; XXXV 319; XXXIX 327;
    XXXX 22, 154, 218
MA **SAMUEL** p 1630-1711 m 1664
   Sarah (Day) Gunn ....-1677
   XXXX 195

KELLY
MA **JOHN** ....-1644
   m .... ____ ____ ....-....
   XXXI 189

KELSEY
MA/CT **WILLIAM** c 1600-c 1680
   m 1625/28
   Bethia Hopkins 1605/10-1636
   XIV 36; XVII 15; XXII 12;
   XXVII 175; XXXIII 67; XXXVII
   306

KEMBALL, see KIMBALL
KEMBLE, see KIMBALL and
KIMBLE

KEMP
MD **ROBERT** c 1650-1702 m 1678
   Elizabeth Webb ....-a 1702
   VII 7,10

MA **SAMUEL** ....-p 1692
   m 1662 **Sarah Foster** c 1645-....
   XXII 118; XXXVII 80

KEMPTON
MA **EPHRAIM** bp 1591-1645
   m 1617
   Elizabeth Wilson 1590-1620/40
   XVIII 76; XXXX 242

KENDALL
VA **JOHN** 1617-1679 m 1667
   Susanna Savage 1649-1729
   XXXIII 342; XXXIV 343

KENERSON/KENNISTON
NH **JOHN KENNISTON** c 1620-
   1677 m by 1646
   Agnes ____ ....-....
   XXXII 65; XXXVI 71

KENNE, see KINNEY

KENNER/KEENER
VA **RICHARD, Sr** 1599/1600-1649
   m .... ____ ____ ....-....
   XXXIV 248
VA **RICHARD, Jr** c 1640-1692
   m 1664/71
   Elizabeth Rodham ....-....
   XXX 220; XXXIV 248; XXXX
   294

KENNEY, see KINNEY
KENNICOTT, see KINNICUTT
KENNISTON, see KENERSON

KENNON
VA **RICHARD** ....-wp 1696
   m c 1676
   Elizabeth Worsham ....-....
   XXXIX 340; XXXX 19, 52, 397,
   398

KENT
MA **THOMAS** 1590/1600-1656/58
m .... **Mowet (Ann) Noyes**
c 1613-1671
XXV 210; XXXVI 213; XXXX
407

KENYON/KINYON
RI **JOHN** 1655/57-1732 m ....
Anne/Anna Mumford ....-a 1712
XXXI 303; XXXVI 231

KERBY
MD **WALTER** ....-a 1702
m1) .... **Jane** ____ ....-....
m2) .... **Elizabeth** ....-p 1702
XXXIII 21, 344

KETCHAM, see KETCHUM

KETCHUM/KETCHAM
MA **EDWARD KETCHAM**
c 1590/95-1655
m1) 1619 **Mary Hall** ....-....
XXXV 82
CT **JOSEPH** ....-a 1730
m 1679 **Mercy Lindall** 1658-....
XXXIV 115

KEYES/KEYS
MA **ROBERT** ....-1647
m .... **Sarah** ____ ....-1681
XXXX 118, 180
MA **SOLOMON** ....-1702
m 1653 **Frances Grant** ....-1708
VI 77/89

KEY, see KEYES

KIBBE
MA **EDWARD** ....-....
m .... **Deborah** ____ ....-....
XXXIII 217

KIDDER
MA **JAMES** c 1626-1676
m a 1649/50
Anna Moore c 1630-p 1684/91
XXVI 61; XXXVII 152

KILBOURN, see KILBOURN

KILBOURN/KILBORNE/
KILBOURNE/KILBURN
CT **JOHN** bp 1624/64-1703
m1) c 1650 **Naomi** ____ ....-1659
m2) 1660/64 **Sarah Bronson**
c 1641-1711
XX 36; XXVIII 160; XXXX 106
CT **THOMAS KILBORNE**
bp 1578-a 1639 m 1604/07
Frances Moody bp 1584-1650
XXVIII 160; XXXIII 28

KILBOURNE, see KILBOURN
KILBURN, see KILBOURN

KILBY
MA **JOHN** c 1632-1710 m 1662
Elizabeth (Joslin) Yoemans
c 1628-....
XXXII 270; XXXVI 176;
XXXVIII 183

KIMBALL/KEMBALL, KEMBLE,
see also **KIMBLE**
MA **BENJAMIN** 1637-1695 m 1661
Mercy Hazeltine 1642-1707/08
XXXV 271
MA **RICHARD** 1585/95-1675
m1) a 1615 **Ursula Scott**
bp 1597-a 1661/1676
XI 23; XV 125; XVII 139; XXII
16; XXV 192; XXVI 196, 197;
XXIX 170; XXXI 215; XXXIII
20, 113, 224; XXXIV 55, 211,
310; XXXV 57, 271

KIMBERLY
MA/CT **THOMAS** c 1604/17-
   c 1671/72
   m1) 1628 **Alice Atwood/Aywood**
   1619-1659
   VI (21, 69, 75, 76, 80, 81 or 19,
   62, 66, 69, 70); VII 8, 9, 10; X 8,
   84, 85; XIII 121; XXXII 153;
   XXXIV 142

KIMBLE/KEMBLE
MD **ROBERT KEMBLE** ....-1691
   m .... _____ _____ ....-....
   XVI 136; XVII 43

KINCAID
MA/NH **DAVID** 1664-a 1722/23
   m p 1695
   Anne (Tozier) Jenkins c 1660-
   p 1730
   XXXX 55

KING/KINGE
MA/RI **CLEMENT** c 1641-c 1694
   m a 1674 **Elizabeth** _____ ....-
   c 1708
   VI 73/85
VA **HENRY** c 1658-p 1743
   m c 1678/79
   Katherine Clarke ...-1688
   XXXX 39, 313
MA/CT **JAMES, Sr** bp 1647-1722
   m 1674
   Elizabeth Fuller 1652-1715
   XVI 117; XXI 85; XXII 30;
   XXXV 69, 257
MA **JOHN** c 1600-p 1669/70
   m .... **Mary Blucks** ....-1646
   XXX 106; XXXII 104
CT **JOHN** 1629-1703 m1) 1656
   Sarah Holton c 1640-1683
   XXXIV 98; XXXV 37; XXXVI
   51

VA **JOHN** 1570-.... m ....
   Ann Daniel ....-....
   XXXVI 276
VA **MICHAEL** ....-.... m c 1650
   Elizabeth Hiry/Cary? ....-....
   XXXVII 321
MA **PHILIP** c 1645-1710
   m .... **Judith Williams** ....-....
   XXXV 339
VA **ROBERT** 1636-p 1680 m ....
   Hannah/Johanna Scarborough
   ....- ....
   XXII 17, 101; XXXIII 158;
   XXXIX 35
MA **THOMAS KINGE** c 1613-1691
   m 1637/38 **Sarah** _____ ....-1652
   XV 92; XXII 132; XXV 193;
   XXVI 244
MA **WILLIAM KINGE** 1595-1650
   m 1616/17
   Dorothy Hayne 1600/01-p 1684
   XXIX 223

KINGE, see KING

KINGMAN
MA **HENRY** 1595-1667
   m 1614 **Joanna** _____ 1596-1659
   XIX 57, 151

KINGSBERY, see KINGSBURY

KINGSBURY/KINGSBERY
MA **HENRY KINGSBERY** c 1615-
   1687 m ....
   Susan/Susanna ....-1678/87
   VIII 13; XXII 156; XXXVI 63
MA **JOSEPH** 1600-1676 m ....
   Millicent Ames ....-p 1676/80
   XXXI 256; XXXIII 307;
   XXXVII 210; XXXIX 211

KINGSLAND
NJ **ISAAC** 1648-1698 m ....
   Elizabeth _____ ....-a 1698
   IX 18; XXXIX 65

KINGSLEY
MA **JOHN** ....-1678/79
   m1) .... **Elizabeth** _____ ....-....
   XX 43; XXXVI 208

KINICOTT, see KINNICUT
KINNE, see KINNEY

KINNEY/KENNE/KENNEY/
KINNE
MA **HENRY** 1623/24-1696 m a 1654
   Ann Putnam bp 1629/30-1680
   XXX 126; XXXI 101; XXXIII
   286; XXXVIII 311

KINNICUTT/KINICOTT/
KINNICOTT
MA **ROGER KINNICOTT** ....-....
   m 1661 **Joanna Sheperson** ....-....
   XXXIV 42

KINYON, see KENYON
KIP, see KIPP

KIPP/KIP
NY **HENDRICK KIP** 1600-....
   mp 1624
   Tryntie Lubbers ....-p 1657
   XXXII 110
NY **HENDRICK HENDRICKSON,
   Jr** 1633-1660
   m 1660 **Anna de Sille** 1640-....
   XXI 149

KIRBE, see KIRBY

KIRBY/KIRBE
MD **MICHAEL** ....-1724 m ....

   Elizabeth Parrott 1670-1710
   XXXIX 37
MA **RICHARD KIRBE** a 1627-
   1686/88
   m .... **Jane** _____ ....-....
   XXXI 146

KIRTLAND
MA/NY **NATHANIEL** 1616-1686
   m .... **Parnell** _____ ....-wd 1694
   XXXIV 250

KITCHEL, see KITCHELL

KITCHELL/KITCHEL
CT **ROBERT** 1601/04-1672 m 1632
   Margaret Sheaffe bp 1598-1682
   XXV 136; XXXV 101; XXXVI
   188

KITTREDGE
MA **JOHN** 1630-1676 m 1664/65
   Mary Hill Littlefield 1646-1719
   V 52; XX 112; XXV 70; XXVII
   111

KLEUT, see CLUTE

KNAPP
MA/CT **AARON** ....-wp 1674
   m .... **Elizabeth** _____ ....-....
   XXXVIII 277
MA/CT **NICHOLAS** ....-1670
   m1) c 1629/30 **Elinor/Eleanor
   Lockwood (?)** ....-1658
   XII 6; XV 31; XVII 103; XVIII
   18; XXII 50; XXIII 15; XXIX
   333; XXXI 36; XXXX 98
MA **WILLIAM** 1587-1658
   m .... _____ _____ ....-....
   XXII 89; XXX 128

KNEELAND
MA **EDWARD** c 1580-....
m .... _____ _____ ....-....
II 11, 37, 43, 46; IV 98

KNICKERBACKER, see
KNICKERBOCKER

KNICKERBOCKER/
KNICKERBACKER
NY **HARMAN JANSEN** c 1643/48-
1720/21 m 1675
Elizabeth Van de Bogaart 1659-
1723
XXV 251, 257

KNIGHT
MA **JOHN** 1587-1645
m .... **Mary** _____ ....-1676
XXIX 340
MA **JOHN, Sr** bp 1595-1670
m c 1615 **Sara Hawkins** ....
c 1622/23
XXXIV 244; XXXX 95
MA **JOHN** a 1635-1674
m .... **Mary** _____ ....-1676
XXXI 281; XXXVI 319
MA **PHILIP** 1614-1666
m .... **Margery** _____ ....-1709
XXX 230
MA/NH **RICHARD** c 1605-1680
m 1648 **Sarah Rogers**
1625-p 1685
XVI 52; XXXX 177
MA **WILLIAM** c 1596-1655
m .... _____ _____ ....-....
XXX 261

KNOWER
MA **GEORGE** 1609-1674
m by 1630
Elizabeth Kendall a 1625-p 1648
XXXX 213

KNOWLES, see also OULD
NH **JOHN** ....-1705 m 1660
Jemima Asten/Austin bp 1641-
....
XIX 25; XXIII 21
MA **RICHARD** ....-....
m .... **Ruth Bomer** ....-....
XV 123
NH **RICHARD** a 1620-1682
m .... **Ruth** _____ ....-....
XXI 140

KNOWLTON
MA **JOHN** ....-w 1653
m .... **Margery** _____ ....-1654
XXXVII 178
MA **WILLIAM** 1615-1655 m ....
Elizabeth _____ a 1625-p 1649
XI 11: XVIII 98; XXXVII 95

KOAL, see COLE
KOERTS (COERTEN) see
VOORHEES
KOHL, see COLE
KOOL, see COLE
KROSEN, see CRUSER
KUNDERS, see CONARD
KUSTER, see CUSTER
KYN, see KEEN

KUY KENDALL/VAN
KUYKENDALL
NY **JACOB LUURSEN VAN**
KUYKENDALL c 1616-1655
m 1638 **Styrije Douwes** bp 1617-
p 1682
XXXIX 84, XXXX 458

KYN, see KEEN

L'HOMMEDIEU
RI **PETER PIERRE** 1600-1685
m .... **Martha Peron** c 1600-

L'HOMMEDIEU-Cont.
　a 1692
　XXXIX 69

LA BOYTEAUX
NY **GABRIEL** ....-a 1734
　m2) c 1695/96 **Agnes Constance
　Le Brun** ....-p 1734
　XXXVII 155

LACHARN, see LANGHORNE
LAIGHTON, see LEIGHTON

LACY
MA **JOHN** c 1586-1690 (ae 104)
　m .... **Mary**____ ....-....
　XXXVI 123

LA FETRA
NJ **EDMOND** ....-1687 m a 1667
　____ ____ ....-c 1675
　XXXVII 155

LAING
NJ **JOHN** ....-1699
　m 1685 **Margaret Chapman** ....-
　....
　XXXIX 113

LAKE
RI **DAVID** c 1646-p 1709
　m c 1678
　Sarah Earl Cornell ....-c 1690
　XXXII 126
MA **HENRY** ....-....　　m a 1634
　____ ____ ....-....
　XXIV 149; XXVI 172, 243
NY **JOHN, Sr** a 1652-a 1696
　m .... **Anne Spicer** ....-1700/09
　XVII 32, 114; XXV 223; XXIX
　291; XXX 272; XXXIII 121, 269;
　XXXVIII 359; XXXIX 206
MA **THOMAS** ....-wp 1728

　m pr 1685
　Sarah Peate 1665-p 1728
　XXXVIII 100

LAMAR/LE MAR/LEMORE
VA/MD **THOMAS, Sr** c 1640-
　wp 1714
　m1) 1661 **Mary Pottinger** 1644-
　1685
　XXVIII 21; XXXVIII 110

LAMB
ME/CT **JOHN, Sr** c 1625-p 1674/
　a 1695
　m ....**Ann**____ ....-p 1683
　XXXI 304
MD **PIERCE** a 1662-wp 1709
　m .... **Mary**____ ....-liv. 1709
　XXV 238
MA **THOMAS** ....-1646
　m 1640 **Dorothy Harbittle** ....-....
　XXVIII 130

LAMDIN
MD **ROBERT** 1663-c 1685
　m .... ____ ____ ....-p 1685
　XXVII 56

LAMPHERE/LANFEAR
RI **GEORGE** ....-1731
　m .... ____ ____ ....-....
　XIV 111

LAMPREY
MA/NH **HENRY** c 1616-1700 m ....
　Gillyen Morris/Norris ....-1670
　XX 149; XXI 163

LAMSON
MA **WILLIAM** ....-1658/59
　m .... **Sarah Ayers** ....-....
　XXXVI 128; XXXX 393

LANCASTER
NH **HENRY** 1605-1705
    m .... **Sarah** _____ ....-1693
    XXXVI 166
VA **ROBERT** c 1630/39-a 1720
    m1) c 1665 **Sarah** _____ ....-....
    XXXVIII 167

LANCKTON, see LANGDON

LANDERS
MA **THOMAS** c 1613-1675 m 1651
    Jane Kerbie/Kirby c 1630-1707
    XXXX 447

LANDON
NY **NATHAN** 1664-1718
    m 1692 **Hannah** _____ ....-1701
    VII 6

LANE
PA **EDWARD** 1664-wp 1710
    m2) 1694 **Ann Richardson** ....-....
    XXX 227; XXXI 11; XXXIII 47
MA/ME **JAMES** 1620-1676/88
    m .... **Sarah White** ....-....
    XXXIV 291; XXXVIII 39
MA **JOB** c 1620-1697
    m2) 1660 **Hannah Reyner**
    c 1632-1704
    XVII 89; XXX 139; XXXIX 178
VA **RICHARD** ....-....
    m .... _____ _____ ....-....
    XXX 76
CT **ROBERT** ....-1718
    m 1665 **Sarah Pickett** 1648-1725
    XXV 126
MD **SAMUEL** c 1628-1682
    m c 1669
    Margaret (Mauldin) Burrage
    ....- ....
    XVI 135; XIX 72; XXXIX 262
MA **WILLIAM** ....-....

    m 1656 **Mary Brewer** ....-....
    XXIX 307

LANFEAR, see LAMPHERE

LANG, see also LONG
NH **ROBERT** a 1650-1716
    m .... **Anne Williams** ....-....
    XXVI 9

LANGDON/LANCKTON
MA **GEORGE LANKTON** ....-1676
    m a 1625
    _____ _____ ....-a 1648
    XIV 29; XV 94; XXV 85, 86;
    XXXX 113

LANGHORNE/LACHARN
VA **JOHN** ....-1700
    m .... **Ruth Wade** .....-....
    XXX68; XXXVII 209; XXXIX 5

LANGLEY
VA **WILLIAM** c 1620-c 1676
    m .... **Joyce** _____ 1621-1680
    XXXI 119

LANGSTON
VA **JOHN** c 1620-a 1694
    m .... **Katherine** _____ ....-c 1699
    XXXVIII 301

LANIER
VA **JOHN I, Sr** 1631/35-p 1704
    m1) 1654 **Lucrece** _____ ....-....
    XXXII 21, 112; XXXIII 140;
    XXXVI 304; XXXVIII 108
VA **JOHN, II** c 1655-1719
    m .... **Sarah** _____ ....-....
    XIV 25, 97

LANKTON, see LANGDON

LARCOM
MA **MORDECAI** c 1629-1712/13
     m ..... **Elizabeth Clark** ....-a 1708
     XXIII 42

LARKIN
RI **EDWARD** 1630-1716 m ....

     ____ ____ ....-....
     IX 19; XXIII 41

LARNED, see LEARNED
LAROE, see LA RUE

LARRABEE
ME **STEPHEN** ....-1676
     m c 1655 ____ ____ ....-....
     XXXIX 44

LA RUE/LAROE/LARUE
NY **ABRAHAM** ....-1712
     m .... **Magdaline Gille**

     ....-....
     XXXX 159
NY/NJ **JAQUES LA RUE/LAROE**
1657-a 1730
     m 1681 **Wybrecht Hendricks**
     ....- 1728
     XVII 144; XVIII 29, 82

LARUE, see LA RUE

LATHAM
CT **CARY** bp 1613-1685 m 1638
     Elizabeth (Masters) Lockwood
     c 1617-1712
     XXXVI 295; XXXX 451
MA **ROBERT** ....-1688 m c 1649
     Susanna Winslow a 1634-
     1679/83
     XXXI 267

LATHROP/LOTHROP
MA **JOHN** bp 1584-1653

     m 1610 **Hannah House** ....-
     a 1634
     XII 17; XXI 123; XXXVI 164
MA/CT **SAMUEL** c 1615-1700
     m 1644 **Elizabeth Scudder** 1632-
     c 1689/90
     XXVIII 126, 127; XXXI 19

LATIMER
MA/CT **ROBERT, Sr** ....-1671/91
     m 1660/62
     Mrs. Ann (Griggs) Jones ....-....
     XV 114; XXV 75; XXIX 269;
     XXXIII 181

LATTING/LETTIN
MA **RICHARD LETTIN** ....-
1672/73
     m .... **Christian** ____ ....-1669
     XXXV 38; XXXIX 273

LAURENCE, see LAWRENCE

LAW/LAWES
CT **RICHARD** c 1600-1686/87
     m 1636 **Margaret Kilborn** 1612-
     a 1686
     X 216; XVII 27

LAWES, see LAW

LAWRENCE/LAURENCE
MA **GEORGE** 1636/37-1708/09
     m 1657 **Elizabeth Crispe**
     1636/37-1681
     XXXIV 307
MA **HENRY** ....-a 1647 m ....
     Christiana ____ ....-1647/48
     XXX 133
MA **JOHN LAURENCE** bp 1609-
     1667 m1) a 1635
     Elizabeth ____ a 1620-1663
     VI 75/87; X 282; XVII 95; XX

LAWRENCE/LAURENCE-Cont.
   59; XXX 264; XXXI 218;
   XXXIV 15; XXXV 199; XXXVI
   117; XXXVII 67, 245
NY **THOMAS** bp 1619/20-1703
   m1) .... **Mary** _____ ....-....
   I 34, 35; X 219, 220; XII 9; XIX
   132
NY/NJ **WILLIAM** a 1637-w p 1704
   m a 1666
   Hannah Townsend ....-a 1693
   XXV 144; XXIX 382

LAWTON/LOWTON
RI **GEORGE** ....-1693
   m .... **Elizabeth Hazard** ....-.....
   XVII 126
MA/CT **JOHN LOWTON** 1630-
   1690
   m .... **Benedicta** _____ 1639-
   1692/93
   IX 31; XI 130

LAYTON, see LEIGHTON

LEACH
MA **LAWRENCE** c 1580-1662
   ma 1605 **Elizabeth** _____ ....-
   c 1674
   XVI 19; XXI 89, 154; XXIX 127;
   XXXIX 89

LEAMING
NY **CHRISTOPHER** c 1649-1695
   m 1664/74 **Esther Burnet** ....-
   1714
   XI 84; XII 52; XX 99; XXII 91

LEARNED/LARNED
MA **WILLIAM LARNED** 1590-
   1646 m ....
   Judith Goodith (Goodwife) ....-
   1661

IV 166; V 52; VI 37/42; XIII 5;
XVII 121; XXIX 303; XXXVIII
123

LEAVENS/LEVINS
MA **JOHN** c 1581-1647
   m2) 1639 **Rachel Wright** ....-....
   XV 40; XXXVII 64

LEAVENWORTH
CT **THOMAS** ....-1643
   m .... **Graye** _____ ....-....
   IX 55

LEAVITT
MA **JOHN** 1608-1691
   m1) 1637 **Mary Lovit** ....-1646
   m2) 1646 **Sarah Gilman** 1622-
   1700
   XXX 55; XXXIX 76, 81
NH **THOMAS** c 1616-1696
   m a 1644
   Isabella Bland Asten ....-1697
   XVIII 72

LECOMPTE
MD **ANTHONY** a 1635-1673
   m 1661 **Esther Dottando** ....-
   p 1680
   XVI 123

LEE
CT **JOHN** 1620-1690
   m 1658 **Mary Hart** c 1630-1710
   XXX 25; XXXVI 314
VA **RICHARD** ....-c 1654/55
   m 1642 **Ann** _____ ....-....
   VII 28
VA **RICHARD** 1597-1663/64
   m2) .... **Anna Fittsworth** ....-
   1666
   X 295
CT **THOMAS** ....-1740

LEE-Cont.
     m .... **Sarah Kirtland** ....-....
     XIII 89
CT **WALTER** ....-1718
     m1) .... **Mary** ____ ....-1696
     XIX 120; XXIII 5; XXIV 38;
     XXIX 329
NY **WILLIAM** a 1635-a 1701/24
     m .... **Mary Marvin** ....-....
     X 168; XXIX 190

LEEDS
NJ **THOMAS** 1620-w p 1689
     m1) 1676 ____ ____ ....-1677
     m2) .... **Margaret Collier** ....-
     1703
     XXXII 281; XXXIII 286;
     XXXVI 150

LEETE
CT **WILLIAM** 1613-1683
     m1) a 1636 **Anne Payne** ....-1668
     XXVIII 37; XXXV 191

LEFFINGWELL
CT **THOMAS** bp 1622-p 1714
     Mary White ....-1710/11
     X 42

LEFTWICH
VA **RALPH** ....-1689
     m .... ____ ____ ....-....
     XXXX 53

LE GROW
MA **JOHN** ....-p 1716
     m 1699 **Martha Dutch** ....-p 1716
     XXII 24

**LEIGHTON/LAIGHTON/
LAYTON**
NH **THOMAS LAIGHTON** c 1604-
1672

     m .... **Joanna** ____ ....-....
     XXVIII 156

LELAND
MA **HOPESTILL** c 1580-1655
     m c 1624 ____ ____ ....-....
     XXXX 127

LE MAITRE, see DE LA MATER
LEMAR, see LAMAR
LEMORE, see LAMAR
LENT, see VAN LENT

LEONARD
MA **HENRY** c 1618-c 1695
     m c 1644
     Mary ____ c 1620-c 1695
     XXXVIII 189
MA **JAMES** c 1601/16-1691
     m .... **Margaret-Mary Martin**
     ....-c 1701
     XV 39; XXXIII 223; XXXV 17;
     XXXIX 14
MA **SOLOMON** c 1610-1686
     m a 1640 **Mary** ____ ....-1691
     V 50; VI 34/38; X 248; XIX 93;
     XXIX 249

LESTER
MA **ANDREW** ....-1669/70
     m1) 1651 **Barbara** ....-....
     m2) .... **Joanna** ....-....
     m3) .... **Hannah** ....-....
     XII 35; XVIII 32
PA **PETER** ....-c 1742 m1) 1685
     Mary Duncalf/Duncof ....-a 1740
     XXXI 38

LETTIN, see LATTING

LEVERING
PA **WIGARD JOHN** 1648/49-1745
     m 1672/74

LEVERING-Cont.
  Magdalena Bokers c 1650/57-
    a 1717
    IV 87; X 209; XIII 68; XXIX 117

LEVINS, see LEAVINS
LE WAS, see LEWIS
LEWES, see LEWIS

LEWIS/LE WAS/LEWES
CT **BENJAMIN** 1648-....
    m c 1671
    Hannah Curtis 1654/55-1728
    XX 44, 51
MA **EDMUND** 1601-1650
    m 1630 **Mary** _____ 1602-1658
    IX 22; XXXV 204; XXXX 274
MA **GEORGE LEWES** c 1600-
    w p 1662/63
    m1) a 1623 **Sarah Jenkins** ....-....
    XXX 165; XXXI 256
MA **JOHN** ....-1657
    m .... **Mary Browne** ....-....
    XXXVII 127
RI **JOHN, I** c 1630-1690/91
    m1) 1655 **Dorcas** _____ ....-1705
    XXVI 80; XXX 51; XXXI 255;
    XXXII 287
VA **JOHN** 1635/40-1726
    m 1670 **Mary W. Brent** 1650-
    1720
    XXV 183, 184, 185
VA **ROBERT** ....-1645 m a 1635
    Elizabeth _____ ....-....
    XIV 96; XV 80; XXXIII 104
CT/MA **WILLIAM, Sr** 1594-1683
    m 1618 **Felix Collins** ....-1671
    IV 145; XXXIII 46; XXXX 75,
    201, 206, 210
MA **WILLIAM** 1605-1671
    m a 1635 **Amy Weld** ....-....
    XIX 103; XXI 32

LIBBEY, see LIBBY

LIBBY/LIBBEY
ME **JOHN LIBBEY** c 1602-p 1682
    m1) ...._____ _____ ....-p 1663
    XVIII 24; XIX 148; XX 55;
    XXXII 224; XXXIII 16; XXXVII
    195

LIGAN, see LIGON

LIGON/LIGAN
VA **THOMAS** 1586- w p 1675/76
    m2) c 1648
    Mary Harris 1625- 1703/04
    XVI 139; XXXI 54; XXXIV 91;
    XXXVII 219; XXXVIII 136

LILLIE
MA **GEORGE** 1636/39-1690/99
    m1) 1659 **Hannah Smith** ....-
    1666
    X 140; XI 52; XXV 79; XXVIII
    123; XXXVII 275

LINCOLN
MA **SAMUEL** c 1619-1690
    m c 1649 **Martha** _____ ....-1693
    XXI 153; XXIV 97; XXV 159;
    XXXIII 176
MA **THOMAS** 1603- w p 1684/91
    m2) c 1630
    Anis/Avith Lane ....-1682/83
    XIII 115; XVI 35; XXI 57;
    XXXII 92

LINDLY, see LINDSLEY
LINDSAY, see LINDSLEY

LINDSLEY/LINDLY/LINDSAY/
LINSLAY/LINSLEY
VA **DAVID LINDSAY** 1603-1667
    m .... **Susanna** _____ ....p 1665

**LINDSLEY/LINDLY/LINDSAY/
LINSLAY/LINSLEY**-Cont.
XXIV 68
CT/NJ **FRANCIS LINSLEY**
c 1600/25-c 1704
m2) 1655/65 **Susanna
Culpepper** c 1630-a 1691/1704
V 131; IX 6; XV 107; XVI 131;
XVII 91; XXVI 50; XXVII 50;
XXXIX 204, 225

LINNELL
MA **ROBERT** c 1584-1662/63
m .... ____ **House** ....-....
XXXI 181

LINSLAY, see LINDSLEY
LINSLEY, see LINDSLEY

LINTHICUM
MD **THOMAS** 1640-1701
m c 1668 **Jane** ____ ....-....
XXIX 115

LIPPETT
RI **JOHN** ....-1669
m .... ____ ____ ....-....
XXV 134

LIPPINCOTT
NJ **RICHARD** c 1613-1683 m 1640
Abigail ____ c 1620-1697
XXIX 112; XXXIII 62

LITCHFIELD
MA **LAWRENCE** 1614/20-1649/50
m c 1640
Judith Dennis c 1620-1685
XX 89; XXVI 299; XXXV 307,
349; XXXVI 325; XXXIX 336;
XXXX 455

LITTLE
MA **GEORGE** c 1615/20-p 1693/94
m c 1638/50
Alice Poor/e 1618-1680
XIX 144; XXX 18; XXXIV 12;
XXXV 162; XXXVII 66; XXXIX
16
MA **THOMAS** ....-1671/72 m 1633
Anne Warren c 1612-p 1675/76
XXXVIII 267

LITTLEFIELD
MA/ME **EDMUND** 1592-1661
m 1614
Annis/Agnes Austin bp 1596/97-
1677
XXXVII 291

LITTLEHALE
MA **RICHARD** ....-1663
m 1647 **Mary Lancton** ....-1691
XVI 92

LITTLEJOHN
VA **OLIVER** ....-1704
m .... ____ ____ ....-....
XXIX 30; XXXV 18

LITTLEPAGE
VA **RICHARD** ....-1688
m ....
____ ____ ....-....
XXXIII 94

LIVERMORE
CT/MA **JOHN** c 1606-1684/85
m a 1633
Grace Sherman c 1615-1690
XVII 65; XIX 122; XX 32, 95;
XXI 42

LIVINGSTON
NY **ROBERT** 1654-1728

LIVINGSTON-Cont.
   m 1679
   Mrs. Alyda (Schuyler) Van
   Rensselaer 1656-1729
   III 63; IV 129; XXV 10

LIVEZEY
PA **THOMAS** 1627-a 1686
   m 1665
   Ellen ____ ....-1668
   XXXIX 239

LOBDELL
CT **SIMON** ....-....
   m .... ____ ____ ....-....
   XXVIII 73

LOCKE
NY **JOHN** bp 1627-1696
   m c 1652 **Elizabeth Berry** ....-....
   XXXVI 308
MA **WILLIAM, Sr** 1628-1720
   m 1655 **Mary Clark** 1640-1715
   XIII 74; XVIII 5; XXVIII 90, 116

LOCKETT, see LOCKHART

LOCKHART/LOCKETT
VA **THOMAS LOCKETT, I**
   c 1645- w p 1686 m c 1667
   Margaret ____ ....-1708
   XXXX 89, 413

LOCKWOOD
MA **EDMUND** bp 1594-1634/35
   m a 1625 ____ ____ ....-....
   XXXIX 140
MA/CT **ROBERT** bp 1600-inv 1658
   m c 1634
   Susannah Tenison/Norman
   a 1619-1660
   X 172; XVIII 81; XIX 32; XXV
   162; XXVII 18; XXXV 260;

XXXVIII 81

LOFLAND/LOUGHLAND
VA **DORMAN LOUGHLAND**
   c 1647-1687/88   m c 1667
   Mary ____ ....-p 1687/88
   XXXI 281; XXXIII 249

LOKER
MA **JOHN, I** 1607-1653
   m c 1649 **Mary Draper** ....-1678
   XXXIV 195

LOMBARD
MA **THOMAS** c 1610-1664/71
   m 1630 **Joyce** ____ ....-....
   XXXII 95; XXXIV 101

LONG/LANG
PA **CHRISTIAN LANG** 1664-....
   m .... ____ ____ ....-....
   XXXII 266

LONGFELLOW
MA **WILLIAM** 1619-.... m 1646
   Elizabeth Thornton ....-....
   III 21
MA **WILLIAM** 1650-1690
   m 1676/78 **Anne Sewall** 1662-....
   XIV 12

LONGLEY
MA **WILLIAM** c 1610/14-1680
   m .... **Joanna Goff** ....-....
   XV 119; XXIX 152

LONGSHORE
PA **ROBERT** ....-1694/95 m c 1690
   Margaret Cocks ....-1701
   XXIV 108

LOOMIS
CT **JOSEPH** a 1590-1658 m 1614

LOOMIS-Cont.
  Mary (Algar) White bp 1590/99-
  1652
  XII 86; XVI 78; XIX 163; XXII
  106; XXX 117; XXXI 317;
  XXXIII 189; XXXIV 233;
  XXXVI 59, 337, 346; XXXVII
  173; XXXVIII 29; XXXIX 195,
  265

LORD
VA **FRANCIS** ....-1739
  m .... **Sarah** _____ ....-....
  XXXVIII 278
ME **NATHAN** c 1603/30-1690/91
  m1) c 1645/54
  Judith Conley a 1630-a 1674
  XXX 88; XXXIV 197
MA **ROBERT, Sr** 1603-1683
  m 1630 **Mary Wait/Waite** ....-
  1683
  XXXII 202
CT **THOMAS, I** c 1583/85-
  p 1643/44 m 1610/11
  Dorothy Bird 1588/89-1675/78
  XXIX 74; XXXI 126; XXXVI
  191

LORE, see LOREE

LOREE/LORE/LORIAN/LORING
NY **JOHN LORING/LORE** ....-
  1727
  m .... _____ _____ ....-....
  XXXII 18

LORIAN, see LOREE

LORING/LOREE
MA **THOMAS** c 1600-1661
  m .... **Jane Newton** ....-1672
  XXXII 182

LOTHROP, see LATHROP

LOTT
NY **PETER** 1621-p 1687 m ....
  Gertrude Lamberts ....-1704
  XII 16; XXXI 32; XXXIII 210

LOUD
ME **FRANCIS, Sr** ....-....
  m .... _____ _____ ....-....
  XXXII 90

LOUGHLAND, see LOFLAND

LOUNSBERRY
NY **RICHARD** ....-wp 1694
  m 1670
  Elizabeth Penoyer c 1652-....
  XXXIII 283

LOVEJOY
MA **JOHN** c 1622-1690 m1) 1651
  Mary Osgood 1632/33-1675
  VI 138; XXXIII 68, 251

LOVELAND
CT **THOMAS** 1649-1720/23
  m a 1674
  _____ _____ ....-....
  XXI 26, 129;   XXXIII 243

LOVELL
MA **ALEXANDER** 1619-1709
  m c 1664 **Lydia Leland** ....-1700
  XXXVI 221
MA **JAMES** 1662-.... m 1680
  Mary Lumbert/Lombard ....-....
  IV 96
MA **ROBERT** 1595-wd 1651/
  pr 1672 m a 1619
  Elizabeth _____ c 1600-....
  XXVI 71

LOVERING
NH **JOHN** ....-1668
    m .... **Esther** _____ ....-c 1675
    XI 148
MA/ME **WILLIAM** a 1665-
    a 1690/91 or 1723
    m a 1676
    Margaret Gutch ....-1690/91
    VII 32; XVIII 66

LOW/LOWE
MD **JOHN** c 1642/45-1701
    m .... **Rebecca** _____ ....-....
    XXII 143; XXXVIII 156;
    XXXIX 52
MA **THOMAS** c 1605-1677
    m1) 1630 **Margaret Tod** 1597-
    .... m2) .... **Susan/Susanna**
    (Stone) Cotting c 1598-1684
    XVII 84; XXXI 280; XXXIV
    313; XXXVII 331; XXXX 449

LOWE, see LOW

LOWELL
MA **PERCIVAL** 1571-1664
    m 1593 **Rebecca** _____ ....-1645
    XXIX 388

LOWTON, see LAWTON

LUCAS
PA **ROBERT** c 1630-1688
    m .... **Elizabeth Cowgill** ....-
    p 1712
    XXXVIII 186
MA **THOMAS** ....-c 1675
    m .... _____ _____ ....-....
    XXII 147; XXV 285; XXXV 231
MD **THOMAS** c 1650-w 1721/22
    m a 1688 _____ _____ ....-1692/94
    XXXVIII 45

LUCE
MA **HENRY, Sr** 1640/45-c 1687/89
    m c 1666
    Remember Litchfield/Munson
    c 1644-liv 1708
    XVII 147; XX 96

LUCKETT
MD **SAMUEL** c 1650-1683/w 1705
    m 1683/84
    Elizabeth Hussey (Gardiner)
    ....-1749
    XXXVII 99; XXXIX 69

LUDDEN
MA **JAMES** ....-1692
    m .... **Alice** _____ ....-....
    XIII 30

LUDINGTON
MA/CT **WILLIAM** 1607/08-1662
    m 1635/37
    Ellen Moulthrop 1617/19-a 1670
    III 8; XXVI 152, 301

LUFF
DE **HUGH** 1662-1709
    m 1688 **Sarah Hunn** 1674-1741
    XXX 254

LUM
CT/NY **JOHN** c 1620-c 1673
    m 1642 **Hannah Strickland** ....-
    ....
    XIV 72; XXIII 43; XXX 157

LUMBARD
MA **JOHN** ....-1672
    m 1646 **Joanna Pritchard** ....-
    1690
    XV 101

LUND
NH **THOMAS** c 1660-p 1721
    m c 1680/81 **Eleanor** _____ ....-....
    XXX 130

LUNT
MA **HENRY** ....-....
    m .... **Ann** _____ ....-....
    XXVI 258

LURVEY
MA **PEETER/PETER** a 1678-....
    m .... **Mary** _____ ....-....
    XXXIII 124

LUTHER
MA **JOHN** 1600-1644/45
    m a 1635/38
    Elizabeth Turner c 1600-p 1646
    XXIV 18; XXXIII 88; XXXIX
    126; XXXX 431

LUTTRELL
VA **JAMES, I** 1630-c 1698
    m .... **Susanna** _____ ....-....
    XXXVIII 280

LUYSTER
NY **PIETER CORNELIESE** ....-
    1695 m ....
    Jannetje Janse Snediker ....-
    1713
    XXXVI 80

LYFORD
MA **FRANCIS** a 1647-1724
    m2) 1681 **Rebecca Dudley**
    a 1666-p 1724
    X 11, 212; XV 61; XXIII 45

LYMAN
MA/CT **RICHARD** bp 1580-1640
    m c 1610/11

    Sarah Osborne ....-c 1640/42
    X 273; XVIII 108, 131; XXIV
    108; XXV 148; XXX 86, 268;
    XXXII 98; XXXIII 29; XXXV
    12; XXXVII 138; XXXIX 3, 239

LYNDE
MA **THOMAS** 1593-1671
    m1) _____ _____ ....-a 1634
    VII 43
MA **THOMAS** c 1616-1693
    m ..... **Elizabeth** _____ 1612-1693
    VII 43

LYON
NJ **HENRY** 1625-1703/07
    m1) 1652 **Elizabeth Bateman**
    1630/32-a 1689/1703
    VIII 21; XXX 262; XXXII 59;
    XXXVI 285
CT **RICHARD** ....-wd 1678
    m .... **Margaret** _____ ....-....
    XII 77; XVII 74; XXVI 140
CT **THOMAS, Sr** 1620/21-
    wd 1689/90
    m2) c 1654 **Mary Hoyt** ....-....
    XXVI 66; XXIX 226; XXXIV
    131; XXXVI 331
MA **WILLIAM** 1620-1692
    m1) 1646 **Sarah Ruggles**
    bp 1629-1689/94
    XXXI 141; XXXV 280

MACALL
MA **JAMES** ....-1693
    m .... **Anna** _____ ....-....
    V 76

MACDONALD, see MCDONALD

MACK
MA/CT **JOHN** 1653-wp 1721/34

MACK-Cont.
  m1) 1681 **Sarah Bagley** 1663-1733
  V 127; XXII 38; XXVI 200; XXXV 161; XXXIX 53

MACKALL
MD **JAMES** c 1630-1693
  m c 1659
  Mary Grahame c 1639-1718
  XXIX 200

MACKENNEY, see MCKENNEY

MACKERWITHEE/MACRORY/ WITHEE
MA **JAMES MACRORY** c 1630-1700/09
  m 1662 **Mary Everett** 1638-1670
  XXXX 62

MACKGEHEE, see MCGEHEE

MACKINTOSH
MA **JOHN** ....-....
  m 1650 **Rebecca Metcalf** ....-1667
  XXXII 272

MACKCLAFLIN, see CLAFLIN
MACKLOTHAN, see CLAFLIN
MACLOTHIAN, see CLAFLIN
MACKLOTHLAN, see CLAFLIN
MCCLAFLIN, see CLAFLIN

MACOMBER
MA **JOHN** ....-1687/90
  m1) ____ ____ ....-a 1686
  VI 96/114; XIX 15
MA **WILLIAM** 1610-a 1670
  m .... **Ursilla** ____ ....-....
  XXXIII 102

MACON
VA **GIDEON** c 1637-1702
  m c 1680
  Martha Woodward ....-....
  XXXIII 200

MACRORY, see
MACKERWITHEE

MACY
MA **THOMAS** 1608-1682
  m 1633 **Sarah Hopcot** ....-1706
  XXXII 145

MADDEN
MD **JOHN** ....-a 1700
  m .... **Elizabeth** ____ ....-....
  XXXIX 123

MADDOX
MD **SAMUEL** ....-1684
  m 1669 **Ann Notley** ....-1682
  XXXV 339

MADDUX
VA **ALEXANDER** 1613-wp 1659
  m 1651 **Eleanor White** ....-wp/wr 1694
  XXVI 115, 296

MAGGSON, see MAXSON

MAGRUDER
MD **ALEXANDER** 1610-1677
  m1) **Sarah/Margaret Braithwaite** ....-1671
  VI 46/53; XXXIV 111; XXXVI 324

MAIES, see MAYS

MAIN/MAINES/MAYNE
ME **JOHN** 1614-1699

MAIN/MAINES/MAYNE-Cont.
m c 1638/39
Elizabeth Laurie 1623-p 1687
XII 82; XXXVI 157; XXXVII 39

MALLERY, see MALLORY

MALLORY/MALLERY
MA/CT **PETER** ....-1697/99
m ....
Mary Preston bp 1629-1690
XIII 32; XXXIII 85
VA **ROGER, Sr** c 1632-1696
m .... ____ ____ ....-....
XXXX 135, 168

MALTBIE/MALTBY
CT **WILLIAM** 1644/45-1710
m2) 1675/78 **Hannah Hosmer
(Willard)** c 1639-c 1690
m3) .... **Abigail Bishop** ....-....
XVIII 147; XXVI 76

MAN, see MANN

**MANDEVILLE/DE
MANDIVILLE**
NY **GYLES JANSEN de
MANDEVILLE** 1620-p 1700
m 1648 **Elsie Hendricks** c 1624-
....
XXX 224

MANLOVE
MD **MARK** 1620-1666
m .... ____ ____ ....-....
XXXVII 281

MANN/MAN
MA **RICHARD** ....-1655 m a 1644
Rebecca (Cowen) ____ ....-....
IV 161; XXX 183; XXXIV 122;
XXXX 394

VA **THOMAS, I** c 1626-1689
m c 1659/60 **Elizabeth Booth** ....-
....
XXXII 176; XXXIX 85
MA **WILLIAM** 1607-1662
m1) 1643
Mary Jared ....-....
XXIX 377

MANNING
MA **WILLIAM** c 1592-wd 1665
m .... ____ ____ ....-....
XXV 278; XXXV 44
MA **WILLIAM** c 1614-1690
m c 1641
Dorothy ____ c 1612-1692
XV 112; XXXVIII 169

MANSER/MANSUR
MA **ROBERT** c 1638-c 1680/88
m 1670
Elizabeth Brooks c 1647-
1694/95
XV 55; XXIII 32; XXXX 300

MANSFIELD
VA **DAVID** 1604-1672 m 1630
Katherine Clyfton c 1614-1667
XXXII 79
CT **RICHARD** ....1655 m 1636
Gillian Drake a 1621-1669
XI 90; XXI 40; XXIX 393
MA **ROBERT** 1594-1666
m .... **Elizabeth** ____ 1586-1673
XXXVIII 331

MANSUR, see MANSER

MAPES
NY **THOMAS** 1628-1686/87
m 1650 **Sarah Purrier** 1630-....
XVI 71; XX 49; XXXVII 23

MAPLES
VA **THOMAS** c 1640-....
    m c 1665 _____ _____ ....-....
    XXXV 205

MAPP
VA **JOHN** a 1654-liv 1694
    m .... **Ann** _____ ....-....
    XXVI 20; XXXVIII 283

MARBLE
MA **JOHN** c 1605-1695
    m .... **Judith** 1546/47-....
    XXXIX 170

MARCH
MA **HUGH** 1618-1693
    m1) **Judith** _____ ....-1675
    XXXI 60

MARCHANT
MA **JOHN, Sr** c 1600-a 1670
    m .... **Sarah** _____ ....-1638
    XXXV 253; XXXVI 140

MARCY
CT **JOHN** c 1662-1724 m ....
    Sarah Hadlock 1670-1743
    XII 42; XVIII 9

MARION, see MERION

MARIS
PA **GEORGE** 1632-1705
    m .... **Alice** _____ ....-1699
    X 93, 108, 148; XV 51; XVI 116;
    XVII 65

MARKHAM
MA/CT **DANIEL** 1648-1736
    m 1669 **Elizabeth Wetmore** ....-
    ....
    XXX 17

MARSELLUS
NY **JANSE von BOMMEL** ....-
    a 1700
    m .... **Annatie Gerritse** ....-....
    XIX 106

MARSH
MA **JOHN, I** c 1610-1674 m 1635
    Susannah Skelton 1613/14-1685
    XXV 140; XXXIII 92
CT **JOHN** c 1618-1688
    m c 1640
    Ann Webster ....-1662
    XXIX 318; XXXIII 14, 37
MA **JOHN** 1647/49-....
    m .... **Sarah** _____ ....-....
    XXXII 268
CT **WILLIAM** c 1559-1724
    m 1681/82
    Elizabeth Yeomans 1659-p 1690
    XII 38, 60; XXVI 160; XXVII 46

MARSHALL
MA **JOHN** ....-1672 m a 1659
    Ruth Hawkins a 1638-1710
    XXXII 295
VA **JOHN** 1596-p 1660
    m .... _____ _____ ....-....
    VI 33/37; X 45; XXXVII 271
MA **JOHN** 1632-1702
    m2) .... **Mary Burrage** 1641-
    1680
    VII 27
MA **SAMUEL** 1615-1675
    m 1652 **Mary Wilton** 1634-1683
    XXXIII 65
CT **THOMAS** c 1610-1671
    m .... _____ _____ ....-....
    XIII 77
MA **WILLIAM** c 1607-1673
    m c 1656
    Katherine Hebden ....-p 1673
    XXXI 126

MARSHAND, see MERSHON

MARSTON
NH **WILLIAM, Sr** c1592-1672
  m1) 1614/16 **Sarah** _____ ....-
  1651/60
  IX 10; XII 54; XXXI 72; XXXIX
  242

MARTIN/MARTYN
VA **ABRAHAM** c 1645-c 1684
  m .... _____ _____ ....-....
  XXXVII 212
MA **GEORGE MARTYN** ....-c1686
  m2) 1646 **Susan North** ....-1692
  XXIX 351
VA **JOHN** c 1615/18-1666
  m3) .... **Ann** _____ ....-....
  XXXII 87
NH/NJ **JOHN** c 1620/28-1687
  m 1631/52 **Esther Roberts** ....-
  1687
  XXIV 105; XXXIV 260
MA/RI **JOHN, Sr** 1634/35-1713/14
  m 1671
  Johanna Esten 1645-1733/34
  XXXIX 152; XXXX 229
CT **SAMUEL** ....-1683 m 1646
  Phebe Brace/Bracy/Bisby ....-....
  XXV 127; XXXVI 131

MARTYN, see MARTIN

MARVIN
CT **MATTHEW** bp 1600-1678/80
  m1) c 1622
  Elizabeth _____ c 1604-c 1640
  XXVII 169
CT **REINHOLD/REINOLD**
  bp 1594/96-a 1662
  m c 1617 **Marie (Mary)** _____
  ....-c 1661
  XII 110; XV 99; XXXVIII 151

MARYON, see MERION

MASON
VA **GEORGE** c 1629-1686
  m1) c 1651
  Mary Fowke c 1631-c 1665
  XXXII 73
MA **HUGH** 1605-1678 m 1632
  Esther/Hester Wells bp 1611-
  1692
  X 203; XXXVII 102
MA/CT **JOHN** c 1600/01-1672
  m2) 1640
  Anna Peck bp 1619-a 1672
  III 54; IV 105; XI 170; XIII 51;
  XXII 129
CT **JOHN** 1652-1698 m 1676
  Hannah Haws (Hawes) 1654-....
  XXIV 31
MA **ROBERT** 1590-1667
  m .... _____ _____ ....-1637
  I 27; XIII 18
MA **SAMPSON** ....-1676 m 1650/51
  Mary Butterworth ....-1714
  XXV 204; XXXIV 344
MA **THOMAS** ....-1676 m ....
  Margery Partridge 1625-1711
  I 27

MATHER
MA **RICHARD** 1596-1669
  m1) 1624 **Catherine Holt** ....-
  1655
  X 119; XXVIII 19; XXX 30;
  XXXIII 104; XXXVII 237

MATHEWS, see MATTHEWS

MATLACK/MATLOCK
NJ **WILLIAM** 1648-c 1720/28
  m 1682
  Mary Hancock 1664-1728
  XXI 171; XXIV 5; XXIX 12

MATLOCK, see MATLACK

MATTESON
RI **HENRY** 1646-1684/1711
    m 1670 **Hannah Parsons** ....-
    1711
    XXXIII 98; XXXIV 196, 215;
    XXXV 246

MATTHEWS/MATHEWS
VA **EDWARD** ....-1678
    m .... _____ _____ ....-....
    XXVIII 121
VA **EDWARD** 1660-1712
    m 1688 **Sarah Bishop** 1664-1720
    XXV 92
CT **WILLIAM** ....-c 1684 m c 1671
    Joanna/Jane _____ ....-....
    III 51; XVII 15; XXIX 342;
    XXXI 316; XXXIX 47; XXXX
    119, 120, 121

MATTOON
MA **PHILIP** c 1655-1696
    m 1677 **Sarah Hawks** 1657-1751
    XXXV 54; XXXVI 130

MAXCY
MA **ALEXANDER** ....-1723
    m .... **Abigale** _____ 1661-1741
    XXXII 201

MAXON, see MAXSON

MAXSON/MAGGSON/MAXON
RI **JOHN** c 1638-1720
    m c 1665 **Mary Mosher** 1641-
    1718
    XXXX 396
RI **RICHARD**
    MAXON/MAGGSON
    ....-c 1639/43 m c 1630
    Rebecca (Goodwife) Mosher

    ....-....
    XXVI 36; XXXIII 243; XXXVI
    135; XXXX 299

MAY, see MAYS

MAYNADIER
MD **DANIEL, I** ....-1745 m 1720
    Hannah Haskins ....-p 1745
    XXXII 219

MAYNARD
MA **JOHN** c 1610-1672
    m2) 1646 **Mary Axtell** ....-....
    XXI 62; XXXII 106; XXXV 24,
    121

MAYO
MA **JOHN** a 1617-1676
    m .... **Thomasine** _____ ....-1682
    X 265
VA **VALENTINE** 1666-1716
    m 1710 **Ann Mickleborough**
    Jordan ....- 1743
    XXXX 344

MAYS/MAIES/MAISE/MAY/
MEASE/MAYES
MA **JOHN MAY, I** 1590-1670
    m1) a 1640 **May** _____ ....-1651
    XII 105; XIV 109; XXXVII 89;
    XXXX 166
MA **JOHN** 1631-1671 m 1656
    Mrs. Sarah (Brewer) Brown
    1638-....
    XII 105; XIV 109
VA **WILLIAM MEASE** 1574-
    p 1650
    m **Elizabeth** _____ ....-....
    XXVI 221, 288; XXX 103; XXXI
    127; XXXIV 146

MC CALL, see MACALL

MC CLAFLIN, see CLAFLIN

MC COTTER
MD **ALEXANDER, I** c 1630-
c 1702/04 m c 1683
Mary _____ ....-....
XXXX 311

MC DONALD/MAC DONALD
PA **BRIAN/BRYAN**   1645/55-
1707 m 1675/78
Mary Doyle Combs 1655-p 1707
XXIV 8; XXVIII 25, 28; XXXI
41

MC GEHEE/MACKGEHEE
VA **THOMAS MACKGEHEE**
c 1645-p 1724
m 1676 **Ann Bastrop** ....-....
XXXVIII 247; XXXX 451
VA **THOMAS MACKGEHEE**-alias
(JAMES MCGREGOR) c 1635-....
m .... _____ _____ ....-....
XXXVIII 2

MC INTIRE
ME **MICUM** 1625/30-1700/05
m .... **Dorothy Pearce**
Mackaneer ....-p 1684
XXXI 251
MA **PHILIP** ....-p 1719
m 1666 **Mary** _____ ....-....
XXIX 405

MC KENNEY/MAC KENNEY
MA/ME **JOHN** c 1630-a 1697
m 1668 _____ _____ ....-....
XXIV 24; XXXX 78

MC VEIGH
PA **EDMUND** ....-1739 m ....
Allis (Alice) Dickenson ....-1727
XXXVIII 349

MEACHAM
MA **JEREMIAH** 1613/15-1695/96
m1) 1642 **Margaret** _____ ....-
1679
m2) ..... **Alice Dorne** c 1622-1696
X 123; XIV 56; XV 46; XXIX
242

MEAD/MEET
NY **PIETER JANSEN MEET**
c 1630-1698
m1) .... **Christina Jacobs** ....-
c 1697
XXXVI 244
CT **WILLIAM** bp 1592/1600-
a 1657/63 m c 1620/25
Philip _____ ....-1657
IX 20; X 222; XXI 175; XXIII
44; XXVI 191; XXXI 82;
XXXIV 58, 151; XXXVIII 88;
XXXX 327

MEADOR
VA **THOMAS** ....-....
m .... **Sarah** _____ ....-....
XXX 67

MEARES, see MEARS

MEARS/MEARES
MA **ROBERT MEARES** c 1592-
1666/67 m ....
Elizabeth Johnson c 1602/05-
1672/74
XXVII 124

MEASE, see MAYS

MEDBURY
MA **JOHN** ....-....
m .... **Sarah** _____ ....-....
XVIII 21

MEEKER
CT **ROBERT** ....-wp 1684/85
    m 1651 **Sarah Turberfield** ....-....
    XXXVI 149
MA/CT/NJ **WILLIAM, Sr** 1620/25-
    1690
    m1) 1646/47 **Sarah Preston**
    bp 1626-....
    XXXVI 146

MEIGS
MA/CT **VINCENT** 1563-1658
    m .... ____ **Churchill** ....-a 1634
    XXXI 236

MELLOTT/MERLET
NY **GIDEON LA PLANTE**
    MERLET 1620-1683
    m 1644 **Margaret Martin** 1622-
    ....
    XXXX 209

MELVEN, see MELVIN

MELVIN/MELVEN
MA **JOHN MELVEN** c 1636/56-
    1726 m c 1678
    Hannah Lewis c 1655-1696
    XXXV 347; XXXVII 18, 183

MERCER, see MESSER

MERCEREAU
NY **JOSHUA** 1657-1756 m 1693
    Marie/Mary Chadreyne ....-....
    XXXII 257; XXXV 241

MERCHANT, see MARCHANT

MEREDITH
VA **THOMAS, Sr** c 1620-a 1700
    m a 1660
    ____ ____ c 1630/40-a 1700

XXXVI 292

MERIAM/MERRIAM
MA **JOSEPH** c 1600-1641
    m c 1623
    Sarah Goldstone ....-1670/71
    XXIX 260, XXXVI 173

**MERION/MARION/MARYON/
MERYON**
MA **JOHN MERYON** 1619/20-
    1705/06 m 1640
    Sarah Eddy c 1624-1709/10
    XVIII 15; XXVI 130; XXXIV 37

MERIWETHER
VA **NICHOLAS, I** c 1631-1678
    m .... **Elizabeth
    Woodhouse/Wodenhouse** ....-....
    I 33; V 133; VI 7/9; 16/18; X
    179; XXXV 34
VA **NICHOLAS** 1647-1744
    m a 1688/89
    Elizabeth Crawford 1672-1762
    I 33; V 133; VI 7/9, 16/18

MERLET, see MELLOTT
MERRELL, see MERRILL
MERRIAM, see MERIAM

MERRICK
MA **THOMAS** 1620-1704
    m2) 1653 **Elizabeth Tilley** ....-
    1694
    XXX 49; XXXI 174

**MERRILL/MERRELL/
MERRILLS**
MA **NATHANIEL** bp 1601/10-
    1645/65 m 1633/54
    **Susanna Wilterton/
    Wilberton/Wolterton** ....-
    p 1654/73

MERRILL/MERRELL/
MERRILLS-Cont.
　　V 112; XIII 20; XIV 84; XV 131;
　　XXI 68; XXIV 74; XXV 58, 201;
　　XXVII 209; XXVIII 46; XXXI
　　205; XXXII 90; XXXIV 52;
　　XXXIX 159
NY **RICHARD** 1642-1727
　　m .... **Sarah Wells** 1649-1722
　　XXXIX 333

MERRIMAN
CT **NATHANIEL** 1613-1693/98
　　m1) 1649 **Abigail Olney** ....-
　　a 1680
　　m1) .... **Joan** ____ 1628-....
　　XIII 101; XV 24; XXIX 297

MERRITT
MA **HENRY** 1570-1653
　　m .... **Judith** ____ ....-....
　　XXXII 52
NY **THOMAS** 1634-1725
　　m 1656 **Jane Sherwood** 1636-
　　1685
　　XXXVII 42

MESEREAU, see MERCEREAU

MERSHON/MARSHAND
NY/NJ **HENRI MARSHAND** ....-....
　　m .... ____ ____ ....-....
　　XXXIII 109

MERVIN
MA/CT **MILES** 1623-1697
　　m1) 1648 **Mrs. Elizabeth**
　　(Baldwin) Canfield/Powell
　　1624/bp 1630-1664
　　V 67; XIV 39; XVII 83; XXII 13;
　　XXXIII 171; XXXX 97, 168

MERYON, see MERION

MESLER, see MESSLER

MESSENGER
CT **ANDREW** ....-....
　　m .... ____ ____ ....-....
　　XXI 106; XXV 221

MESSER/MERCER
MA **RICHARD MERCER** ....-1671
　　m 1669
　　Hannah Shatswell 1651-1670
　　XXIII 74

MESSLER/MESLER/
METSELAER
NY **JAN ADAMSEN**
MESLER/METSELAER pr/c 1626-
　　1695/1697 m c 1657
　　Geertje Dircksen ....-1697/98
　　XXII 43; XXXI 289

METCALF
VA **ISAAC** ....-wp 1689
　　m .... **Anne Bagwell** ....-....
　　XXXII 188
MA **MICHAEL** 1586-1664
　　m .... **Sarah Elwyn** 1593-...
　　XXXVII 63

METSELAER, see MESSLER

MIDDLEBROOK
CT **JOSEPH, I** c 1610-w p 1686
　　m1) c 1644 **Mary Bateman** ....-
　　c 1647
　　XXV 259; XXX 258

MIDDLETON
VA **JOHN** c 1612-p 1662
　　m .... ____ ____ ....-....
　　XXXVIII 25

MIKELL
SC **EPHRIAM, Sr** ....-1728/29
    m .... **Martha Sealey** ....-....
    XXXVII 105; XXXIX 121

MILES
MA **JOHN** c 1618-1693
    m 1679 **Susanna Rediat** 1647-....
    XIII 100

MILLER/MILLERD
MA **JOHN** ....-1685
    m1) .... _____ _____ ....-a 1653
    XXX 287
NY **JOHN** a 1619-1649/64
    m .... **Mary Pierson** ....-....
    XXV 291, 297; XXVI 29
MA **ROBERT** 1632-1699 m 1662
    Elizabeth Sabin 1642-1717
    XIX 26; XXVI 186
CT **THOMAS** c 1600/bp 1609/10-
    1680
    m2) 1666 **Sarah Nettleton**
    c 1641/46-1728
    XIII 23; XXIII 28; XXXX 117,
    212
MA **THOMAS** c 1624-1675
    m 1642/49
    Sarah Marshfield c 1630/31-
    1708/09
    XXVII 214; XXXII 291; XXXIII
    26; XXXIV 90; XXXV 320
MA **WILLIAM** c 1620-1690
    m 1641/51 **Patience Bacon** ....-
    1716
    XXIX 213; XXXX 444, 448

MILLERD, see MILLER

MILLIKEN
MA/ME **HUGH** ....-p 1684 m ....
    Eleanor Elleson/Allison ....-....
    XXXIII 63, 281

MILLS
CT **PETER (VAN DER MEULEN)**
    1622-1710 m ....
    Dorcas Messenger 1650-1688
    XXII 53
MA **SAMUEL** ....-1694/95
    m 1645 **Frances Pimbroke** ....-
    1684
    XXXI 42
CT **SIMON** a 1637-....
    m .... **Joan** _____ ....-1659
    XI 138, 139, 140, 141
VA **WILLIAM** 1606-a 1698
    m .... _____ _____ ....-....
    XX 119

MINER/MINOR/MYNARD
MA/CT **MANESSAH** 1647-1728
    m .... **Lydia Moore** ....-1720
    II 28
MA/CT **THOMAS, Sr** 1608-1690
    m 1634 **Grace Palmer** 1608-
    1690
    II 28; IV 104; VI 67/77; IX 7; XII
    88; XX 71; XXIII 71; XXIV 130;
    XXV 194; XXIX 335; XXX 112,
    273; XXXVI 329; XXXVII 101;
    XXXVIII 131; XXXIX 125, 143
CT **WILLIAM** ....- c 1709 m 1678
    Lydia Richards bp 1671-p 1711
    XIX 86

MINNE, see MINNERLY
MINNERLAY, see MINNERLY

MINNERLY/MINNE/
MINNERLAY
NY **JOHANNIS**
    MINNE/MINNERLAY ....-
    a 1693
    m1) .... **Rensie Feddes** ....-....
    m2) .... **Magdalena (Rixe)**

MINNERLY/MINNE/
MINNERLAY-Cont.
   Vonck ....-....
   XXVIII 196

MINOR, see MINER

MINTER
VA **EDWARD** 1612-c 1684
   m 1633 **Grace** _____ 1615-1687
   XXVIII 159

MITCHELL
MA **ANDREW** ....-1736 m 1686
   Abigail Atwood c 1662-1714
   XXIV 136; XXVI 236
ME **CHRISTOPHER** c 1639-
   1686/88 m a 1665
   Sarah Andrews c 1641/43-1732
   XXIX 14; XXXIX 112
MA **EXPERIENCE** 1599/1609-1689
   m1) 1628 **Jane Cooke** ....-....
   XXX 206; XXXVI 49
MA/CT **MATTHEW** 1590-1645
   m 1616
   Susan (Wood) Butterfield ....-....
   X 94; XI 184, 185; XVI 119;
   XVIII 98, 109; XXVII 12, 54,
   168; XXX 81

MIX
CT **THOMAS** c 1620/26-p 1691
   m 1648/49
   Rebecca Turner c 1631-1731
   XXVI 178, 234; XXIX 293;
   XXXIX 231

MIXER/MIXTER
MA **ISAAC, Sr** 1602-1655 m 1629
   Sarah Thurston c 1601-1681
   XXXIII 199

MIXTER, see MIXER

MONROE/MUNRO
VA **ANDREW** ....-1668
   Elizabeth Alexander ....-....
   XXXIX 308
MA **WILLIAM MUNRO** 1625/35-
   1717/18
   m1) c 1665 **Martha George** ....-
   a 1672
   XXXIII 272; XXXIX 136

MONTAGUE
VA **PETER** 1603-1659
   m1) 1633 _____ _____ ....-....
   XXIX 52
CT/MA **RICHARD** c 1614-1681
   m c 1636/41
   Abigail Downing ....-1694
   XVII 133; XXX 142; XXXVII 24

MOOAR, see MOORE

MOODY
CT **JOHN** 1593-1655
   m 1617 **Sarah Doe** ....-1671
   XIV 32; XXX 53
MA **WILLIAM** ....-1673
   m .... **Sarah Pierce** ....-1673
   X 169

MOON
MA **ROBERT** c 1620-1698
   m1) .... **Dorothy** _____ ....-....
   XXXVIII 16

MOORE/MOOAR/MORE
MA **ABRAHAM MOOAR** ....-1706
   m 1687 **Priscilla Poore** 1667-....
   X 56
CT **ANDREW** ....-1719
   m 1671 **Sarah Phelps** 1653-....
   XIX 78; XXXI 246
SC **JAMES** 1640/41-1706/29
   m c 1665/66

MOORE/MOOAR/MORE-Cont.
Margaret Yeamans/Berringer
c 1645-1720
XV 135; XX 163; XXXIX 28
MA/CT **JOHN** ....-1677
m 1639
Abigail ____ ....-....
IV 107; XXI 30
MA **JOHN** 1610-1673/74
m2) .... **Elizabeth Whaley** ....-
1690
XVI 25; XVII 158
MA/NY **JOHN** 1620-1657
m c 1641/44
Margaret Howell bp 1622-....
VI 74/86; XXX 170
MA **THOMAS** ....-a 1636
m .... **Ann** ____ ....-p 1668
XXXII 113
MA/NY **THOMAS, I** c 1615-1691
m a 1636 **Martha Younges**
bp 1613-1671/80
XIII 112; XXXVI 271
MA/CT **THOMAS** ....-1645
m .... ____ ____ ....-1639
IV 107; XXI 30

MOORHEAD, see MOREHEAD

MOORMAN/MOORMEN/
MOREMEN
VA **THOMAS** 1641/49-p1690/1713
m a 1685
Elizabeth Clark (Macajak)
Simpson c 1660-....
XXXX 175,176, 228
SC/VA **ZACHARIAH** 1620-a 1672
m 1646
Mary Chandler c 1620-....
XXXIX 127

MORE, see MOORE

MOREHEAD/MOORHEAD
VA **CHARLES** c 1609-a 1705
m .... ____-____ ....-....
m2) .... ____ ____ ....-....
XXXVIII 128

MOREMEN, see MOORMAN

MORGAN
MA/CT **JAMES** 1607-1685
m 1640 **Margery Hill** ....-1685
IV 133; X 26; XVI 42, 55; XXII
19; XXXVI 290; XXXVIII 19
MA **MILES** 1615-1699
m1) 1643 **Prudence Gilbert** ....-
1660/61
m2) 1669/70 **Elizabeth Bliss**
1637-1683
X 225; XX 155; XXXVI 201;
XXXX 67, 178
NH **RICHARD** 1658-1712 m 1660
Rebecca Holdridge ....-p 1714
XXXX 185
MA **ROBERT** 1600/01-1672 m ....
Margaret Norman ....-by 1694
XXXV 45

MORICE, see MORRIS

MORLEY
MA **JAMES** ....-....
m .... **Anne Skenne** ....-....
XVII 70
MA **THOMAS, Sr** ....-....
m .... **Katherine Burnell** ....-....
XVII 70

MORRILL
MA **ABRAHAM** 1605-1662
m 1645 **Sarah Clement** 1625-
1694
XXXIX 127
ME **JOHN** 1640-1723/28

MORRILL-Cont.
   m a 1667 **Sarah Hodsdon**
   1647/50-1710/17
   XXXI 285

MORRIS/MAURICE/MORICE
NJ/PA **ANTHONY** 1654-1721
   m1) 1675 **Mary Jones** ....-1688
   III 22
PA **DAVID** 1660-1720 m 1685
   Mary Philipin 1665-a 1720/21
   XXXV 44
MA **EDWARD** c 1630-1689/90
   m 1655 **Grace Bett** ....-1705
   V 105, 109; XXXI 151
VA **JOHN** c 1633-1713
   m .... **Elizabeth** ____ ....-p 1713
   XXXVI 279; XXXVIII 125
VA **JOHN MAURICE/MAWRICE**
   c 1655-1694 m c 1675
   Christiana ____ ....-1683
   XXXVII 335; XXXVIII 156
NC **JOHN** 1680-1739 m 1703
   Mary Simons/Symonds 1687-
   1745
   XXXVII 26
NY/NJ **LEWIS** c 1655-1694/95
   m ..... **Elizabeth Almy** ....-....
   XXXV 155
RI **RICHARD MORICE** ....-1674
   m 1628 **Leonora Pawley** ....-
   a 1658
   XXXII 181
NY **RICHARD** 1636-1672 m 1669
   Sarah Pole/Poole ....-1672
   XXIV 150
CT **THOMAS** ....-1673
   m ....**Elizabeth** ____ ....-1681
   XXVI 263, 264

MORSE
MA **ANTHONY** 1606-1686
   m1) .... **Mary** ____ ....-....

   m2) c 1626/29 **Anne Cox** or
   Lewis ....-1679/80
   IV 90; VI 79/92; XVII 157; XXI
   25; XXIX 237, 380; XXXIII 52;
   XXXIV 325; XXXVI 21;
   XXXVII 81; XXXX 96
MA **ANTHONY** 1639-1677
   m 1669 ____-____ ....-....
   m2)... **Mary Barnard** 1645-1714
   XXXX 264
MA **SAMUEL** bp 1585/87-1654
   m c 1610
   Elizabeth Jasper 1587/89-1654
   VI 50/57; XIII 36; XIV 77; XV
   54; XX 43; XXI 94, 139; XXV
   30, 248; XXIX 142, 374; XXXIII
   96; XXXVI 250; XXXVII 217;
   XXXIX 118
MA **WILLIAM** 1614-1683
   m 1635 **Elizabeth Titcomb** ....-
   ....
   XXIV 17

MORSMAN, see MOSMAN
MORTENSEN, see MORTON

MORTON/MORTENSEN
MA **EPHRIAM** 1623-1693
   m1) 1644 **Ann Cooper** ....-1691
   XXVII 152
MA **GEORGE** ....-1624
   m 1612
   Juliana (Carpenter) Kempton
   1584-1665/66
   XXII 40; XXVII 152
VA **JOHN** c 1650-a 1721
   m2) 1682 **Joane/Joanne**
   (Hughes) Anes c 1658-a 1721
   XXXII 68; XXXVI 105
PA **MORTON/MORTENSON** ....-
   1712 m .... **Margaret** ____ ....-....
   XII 65
CT/MA **RICHARD** a 1649-1710

MORTON/MORTENSEN-Cont.
    m .... **Ruth** _____ ....-1714
    VII 21
CT **WILLIAM** ....-a 1711
    m 1670 **Mary Burnham** 1642-
    1719
    XXVIII 190

MOSELEY/MOSLEY
MA **JOHN, I** ....-1661
    m2) .... **Cicely** ....-1661
    IV 84, 86; XXVI 93; XXXI 213;
    XXXV 68, 118
VA **WILLIAM** bp 1606/08-1655
    m .... **Susannah Cockroft** or/?
    m a 1634 **Susan (Burnett)**
    Blackmore ....-p 1655
    XVII 135; XXVI 127; XXXIII
    229; XXXV 145, 292

MOSHER
MA/RI **HUGH** 1600-1694 m 1632
    Lydia Maxon/Maxson ....-....
    XXXV 93

MOSLEY, see MOSELEY

MOSMAN/MORSMAN/
MOSSMAN
MA **JAMES** 1626-1722
    m2) .... **Ann** _____ ....-a 1703
    XXI 31; XXV72; XXVIII 147;
    XXXIII 348

MOSS/MOSSE
VA **EDWARD** ....-1646
    m .... **Ann Belt** ....-....
    XXX 161
CT **JOHN** c 1603/19-1707/08
    m .... **Goody Moss** ....-....
    X 23, 24, 83, 171; XIII 113
VA/MD **RICHARD MOSSE, Sr**
    c 1615-1676 m c 1658

    Elizabeth Orrick ....-by 1677
    XXXVIII 279, 323; XXXIX 134
VA **WILLIAM** 1630-1680
    m ....**Jane North** ....-c 1666
    XV 16

MOSSE, see MOSS
MOSSMAN, see MOSMAN

MOULTON
NH/ME **THOMAS** bp 1608/14-
    1699/1700   m c 1638
    Martha _____ c 1606/37-
    c 1703/11
    XXXV 78; XXXIX 134
MA/NH **WILLIAM** c 1617-1664
    m 1651 **Margaret Page** 1621-
    1699
    XVII 49; XXXII 83; XXXIII 240;
    XXXVI 152

MOUNT
NJ **GEORGE** bp 1626/27-p 1702/05
    m c 1662
    Katherine (Borden?) ....-1702
    XXXVI 305; XXXVII 233;
    XXXX 32

MOUNTJOY
VA **EDWARD** c 1660- a 1712
    m2) c 1710 **Mary Crosby** ....-
    1756
    XXXVI 91

MOWER
MA **RICHARD (MORE)** 1612-
    1668/9
    m .... **Alice** _____ .... -1661/62
    XXXX 60

MOWRY
MA/RI **ROGER** a 1610-1666
    m .... **Mary Johnson** ....-1679

MOWRY-Cont.
XXXII 148

MUDD
MD **THOMAS** 1647-1697
m 1677 **Sarah Boarman** ....-
a 1685
XXXI 150

MUDGE
MA **THOMAS** c 1624-....
m .... **Mary** _____ c 1628-....
XXXII 163

MULFORD
NY **WILLIAM, I** c 1620/30-1687
m 1649/53
Susan Akers 1635-p 1687
VIII 24; XXXII 221; XXXIII
131; XXXVI 16; XXXX 345

MULKEY/MULLCAY
DE **ERIC PALLSON** 1636-1726
m 1656 **Inglebord Helm** 1640-
1713
XXI 172

MULLCAY, see MULKEY

MUMFORD
RI **THOMAS, I** c 1625-1692
m 1655 **Sarah Sherman** c 1636-
c 1690
XXXIX 62; XXXX 413

MUNGER
CT **NICHOLAS** c 1630/31-1668/70
m 1659 **Sarah Hall/Hull**
c 1639/40-1689/98
XXIX 285; XXXIV 342;
XXXVII 346; XXXVIII 60, 88;
XXXIX 98

MUNN
CT/MA **BENJAMIN** c 1600-1675
m 1649
Abigail Bent Ball 1623-1707
XVIII 26; XX 152

MUNRO, see MONROE

MUNSEY
MA/NY **FRANCIS** ....-a 1675
m 1659
Hannah Adams c 1639-p 1716
XXXVI 55; XXXX 75

MUNSON
CT **SAMUEL** bp 1643-1692/93
m 1665 **Martha Bradley**
bp 1648-....
XXXV 144
CT **THOMAS** bp 1612-1685
m a 1643
Joanna _____ c 1610/12-1678
XXV 14, 118; XXXI 284;
XXXIII 298; XXXVIII 96, 284;
XXXX 16, 76, 161, 223, 250

MURDOCK
MA **JOHN** c 1660-1750/56
m1) 1686 **Lydia Young** 1664-
1701
V 51; XXXIII 277

MURPHEY
VA **RICHARD** c 1670-....
m c 1700 **Mary Byrd** 1674-....
XXXI 67

MURRAY
CT **JONATHAN** 1665-1747
m 1688 **Anne Bradley** 1669-
1749
XXXVI 72

MUSE/MEWES
VA **JOHN MEWES** c 1633-1723
    m .... _____ _____ ....-....
    XXXVIII 233

MUZZY
MA **JOHN** ....-a 1690
    m a 1635
    Lydia _____ ....-p 1690
    XXXVI 56

MYNARD, see MINER
MYNDERSE, see FREDERICKSE
MYNDERT, see FREDERICKSE
MYNDERTZE (see also
FREDERICKSE)

NASH
CT **THOMAS** c 1590-1658 m ....
    Margery Baker c 1615-1655/58
    XVIII 130; XXXX 433

NASON
ME **RICHARD** bp 1606-wp 1696/97
    m .... **Sarah** _____ ....-....
    XXXII 99

NEALE
VA **DANIEL** 1620-1670/71
    m .... **Eleanor/Ellen** _____ ....-....
    XXI 96; XXXVII 177

NEEDHAM
MA **ANTHONY** 1628-c 1705
    m 1655 **Ann Potter** ....-c 1695
    XV 96; XXXIV 58
VA **CHRISTOPHER** ....-a 1693
    m .... _____ _____ ....-....
    XXXIV 335
MA **EDMUND** 1600/03-1677
    m 1629
    Joan Leazing/Leesonne c 1610-
    1674

XXXIX 63

NEEDLES
VA/MD **JOHN** 1638-1704
    m .... **Frances** _____ ....-1697
    XXXI 195

NELMS
VA **RICHARD, Sr** a 1631-a 1688
    m p 1652
    Ann _____ c 1640-p 1663
    XXIX 76; XXXI 153

NELSON
MA **THOMAS, Sr** ....- c 1648
    m2) .... **Joan Drummer** ....-....
    IX 28; X 104; XXVI 19

NETTLETON
CT **SAMUEL** ....-1655/p 1668
    m .... **Maria** _____ ....-1658
    VIII 16; XV 69

NEVIUS/NEVYUS
NY **JOHANNES** 1627-1672
    m 1653
    Andriaentje Bleijck ....-....
    XXXVI 289; XXXVIII 164

NEWBERRY
CT **BENJAMIN** c 1624-1689
    m 1646 **Mary Allyn** c 1628-1703
    XXIX 75
MA/CT **THOMAS** 1594-1635/36
    m c 1619
    Joane/Jane Dabinott 1600-1629
    V 64; XI 31; XXIX 75

NEWBY
VA **WILLIAM** 1630-....
    m a 1659
    Isabell _____ 1630-p 1684
    XXXX 372

NEWCOMB
MA **ANDREW** c 1618-1686
   m1) .... ____ ____ ....-a 1663
   XX 23; XXIV 60; XXV 227;
   XXX 158; XXXIII 49; XXXV
   225; XXXVI 141
ME/MA **ANDREW** c 1640-p 1706/
   a 1708
   m1) c 1661 **Sarah** ____ ....-
   c 1674
   XXVII 93, 199, 200; XXX 222;
   XXXVI 218
MA **FRANCIS** 1605-1692
   m .... **Rachel** ____ 1615-....
   XXIX 386

NEWELL
MA **ABRAHAM** 1581-1672 m ....
   Frances ____ c 1592/93-1682
   XV 104
CT **THOMAS** ....-1689 m c 1648
   Rebekah Olmstead 1622-1698
   XXVII 77; XXXVII 99

NEWHALL
MA **THOMAS, Sr** ....-1674 m ....
   Mary ____ ....-1665
   V 25/28; XVIII 55

**NEWKIRK/NIEUKIRK, VAN
NIEUWKIRK/VAN
NIEUWKERCKE**
NY **GERRETT/GARRETT
CORNELISSEN** c 1635-1695/96
   m ....
   Chieltje Cornelissan Slecht ....-
   a 1702/09
   XXV 83; XXVI 222, 223; XXVII
   57; XXVIII 92, 167; XXXVII
   77

NEWMAN
VA **JOHN** 1611-1676/77 m 1655

   Mary Woodbridge ....-a 1677
   XXV 196; XXVI 24, 25;
   XXXVIII 149
NY **THOMAS** 1584-wd 1660
   m 1607 **Mary Moorton** ....-....
   XXII 99; XXXIX 78
NJ **WALTER** c 1659-1729 m c 1687
   Mary ____ c 1668-p 1733
   XXXIV 102

NEWSOME
VA **WILLIAM, Sr** 1614-....
   m3) p 1635 **Elizabeth Wilson**
   ....- ....
   XXXVII 223

NEWTON
MA **RICHARD** 1601/bp 1611-1701
   m c 1636/40
   Ann/Hannah Locarr c 1605/18-
   1666/97
   XIX 157; XXIII 72; XXV 176;
   XXVI 215, 238; XXVIII 197;
   XXXVI 127, 315, 343; XXXVII
   149
CT **ROGER** 1610-1683
   m 1644/45
   Mary Hooker p 1610-1675/76
   V 70; X 20; XI 193, 195, 197;
   XVIII 142; XXIII 19; XXV 99

NICHOLAS
VA **ANDREW** ....-wp 1655
   m ....
   Elizabeth ____ ....-wp 1684
   XXXVI 217; XXXX 104

**NICCOLLS, see NICHOLS
NICHOLLS, see NICHOLS**

**NICHOLS/NICCOLLS/
NICHOLLS**
CT **CALEB** ....-....

NICHOLS/NICCOLLS/
NICHOLLS-Cont.
    m 1650 **Ann Warde** ....-1718
    XIX 66; XXVI 73
CT **FRANCIS, II** c 1595/1600-
    inv 1655
    m1) .... _____ _____ ....-....
    m2) 1645 **Ann Wynes** ....-....
    XVI 76; XXVI 72; XXVII 98,
    173; XXXI 90; XXXIII 127, 134;
    XXXIV 293; XXXVII 353;
    XXXIX 295
MD **JOHN** ....-by 1707
    m .... **Margaret** _____ ....-....
    XXXIV 306
MA **RICHARD NICCOLLS**
    1620/30-1674
    m .... **Anna/Annas** _____ ....-1692
    XXX 151; XXXIII 252
RI **THOMAS** ....-1708
    m .... **Hannah Griffith** 1642-....
    XXXIX 110
MA **WILLIAM** c 1599- wp 1695/96
    m 1640
    Margaret _____ c 1629-a 1696
    XXXIX 339

NICHOLSON
NC **CHRISTOPHER** c 1610-p 1680
    m c 1635 _____ _____ ....-....
    XXV 247

NICKERSON
MA **WILLIAM, Sr** c 1604-1689/90
    m c 1630
    Anne Busby bp 1607/08-1686/90
    XXX 261; XXXIV 132;
    XXXVIII 68

NIEUKIRK, see NEWKIRK

NIGHTINGALE
MA **WILLIAM** 1637-1714

    m .... **Bethia Deering** 1649-1687
    XXXII 193

NIMS
MA **GODFREY** c 1650-1704/05
    m1) 1677 **Mary (Miller)**
    Williams ....-1688
    XXXV 168; XXXVI 134;
    XXXVIII 112

NOBLE
MA **THOMAS** c 1632-1704
    m 1660
    Hannah Warriner 1643-
    wp 1717/21
    V 131, 132; XI 131; XII 97; XV
    67, 76; XXII 7; XXV 167; XXIX
    310; XXXVI 87, 243; XXXVII
    154, 227; XXXVIII 29, 367

NOE/NUEE
NY/NJ **PIERRE NUEE** ....-1709
    m 1659
    Margaret Clark ....-p 1709
    XXII 142, 154; XXIV 11;
    XXXIII 313

NOULDS, see OULD

NORCROSS
MA **JEREMIAH** c 1600-1657
    m .... **Adrean** _____ ....p 1657
    XI 67
MA **JOHN** 1590-....
    m .... _____ _____ ....-....
    XXIX 244

NORRIS
MD **JOHN** 1642/52-wp 1710
    m a 1680 **Susannah Heard** ....-....
    XXXX 170
NH **NICHOLAS** c 1640/44-p 1725
    m 1663 **Sarah Coxe** c 1645-....

NYE-Cont.
XI 165; XXV 11, 213; XXVIII 84; XXIX 296; XXX 166; XXXI 193, 202, 204; XXXII 117; XXXIII 139; XXXIV 274; XXXVI 82; XXXX 121, 208

NYSSEN, see DENISE
OCKERSSEN, see OKESON

ODELL
MA/CT **WILLIAM, Sr** ....-1676
m .... ____ ____ ....-a 1644
XXIII 65; XXIX 147

ODIORNE
MA **JOHN** c 1627-1707
m .... **Mary Johnson** ....-p 1707
XIII 92

ODLIN/AUDLIN
MA **JOHN** 1602-1685
m .... **Margaret** ____ ....-a 1685
V 54

OGDEN
NY/NJ **JOHN** 1609/10-1682
m 1637
Jane Bond ....-1663/p 1683
VII 41; XIII 6; X 62; XI 32; XXIV 61; XXXVII 129; XXXIX 14; XXXX 437, 438, 439, 453, 456
CT **RICHARD** 1610-c 1687
m 1639 **Mary Hall** ....-....
XXXIII 32

OKESON/OCKERSSEN
NY **JOHN OCKERSSEN** ....-....
m .... ____ ____ ....-....
XXVI 184, 185; XXIX 210

OLCOTT
MA/CT **THOMAS, Sr** ....-c 1609
bp 1613-1653/54 m c 1635
Abigail Porter c 1613/15-1693
XXVII 195; XXX 240; XXXIII 135; XXXIV 46, 226; XXXX 361
CT **THOMAS, Jr** c 1637-p 1719
m c 1665 **Mary Levitt** ....-1721
XXVII 195

OLD, see OLDS

OLDS/OLD
CT **ROBERT** 1645/a 49-1728
m1) 1669 **Susanna Hanford** ....-1688
m2) 1689 **Dorothy Granger** ....-....
V 68, 98; XXIV 37

OLIVER
ME **DAVID** ....-....
m .... **Grace (Parker)** ....-....
XVII 52
MA **THOMAS** ....-1658
m .... **Ann** ____ ....-1635
XXXX 381

OLMSTEAD/OLMSTED
MA/CT **JAMES** bp 1580-1640
m 1605
Joice Cornish 1582-1621
XVIII 95; XXIV 87; XXVII 144; XXX 160
CT **RICHARD** 1612-1684/86
m1) a 1640 ____ ____ ....-p 1672
XV 32; XXIV 31; XXX 96; XXXIII 152

OLMSTED, see OLMSTEAD

OLNEY
MA/RI **THOMAS** 1600-1682

OLNEY-Cont.
  m 1631
  Marie Small 1605-1679
  XXIX 352; XXXV 32

OMOHUNDRO
VA **RICHARD** ....-wd 1698 m ....
  Ann Moxley ....-....
  XXXVII 88

ONDERDONK
DE **ADRIAEN** 1596-1651
  m p 1637 **Maria Doughty**
  ....-....
  XXXVIII 143
DE **ANDRIES ANDRIANSE**
  1649/53-a 1687 m 1683
  Maria VanderVliet ....-....
  XXXVI 62

OOSTEROM, see OSTROM
OP DYCK, see UPDIKE

ORCUTT
MA **WILLIAM** ....-1693 m 1663
  Mary/Martha Lane 1640-....
  XXXV 165

ORDWAY
NH/MA **JAMES, Sr** 1618/bp 1621-
  p 1702/04 m 1648
  Ann(e) Emery 1623/32-1687
  XXXII 260; XXXIII 65; XXXV
  113; XXXVI 110, 177; XXXX
  205, 223, 229

ORMSBY
ME **RICHARD** c 1602-1664
  m c 1640
  Sarah (Upham) Wanton c 1610-
  1665
  XXXX 192

ORTON
CT **THOMAS** 1613-p 1688
  m 1641 **Margaret Pratt** ....-....
  XIII 109; XVI 36; XXXII 280;
  XXXVII 355

ORVIS
CT **GEORGE** ....-1664
  m 1652 **Elizabeth** ....-1694
  XXXX 313

OSBORN/OSBORNE
CT **JOHN** 1604-1686
  m 1645 **Ann Oldage** ....-1689
  VI 42/47; VII 38; XXV 122
MA **RICHARD** 1611/12-1685/86
  m1) .... _____ _____ ....-a 1677
  XXXIII 259
MA/CT/NY **THOMAS OSBORNE**
  bp 1594/95-1677/86 m 1620/22
  Mary Goatley ....-....
  XXXV 283; XXXIX 216; XXXX
  279, 440, 441
NY **THOMAS** ....-....
  m .... _____ _____ ....-....
  XXIII 60
VA **THOMAS OSBORNE** ....-
  p 1633
  m .... _____ _____ ....-....
  XXXX 16
MA **WILLIAM** ....-p 1727
  m 1672/73
  Hannah Burten(on) ....-p 1735
  XXXIII 84
MD **WILLIAM** c 1628-1704 m 1694
  Mrs. Margaret Walstone ....-
  p 1705
  VI 86/99, 88/102; XXXIII 306

OSBORNE, see OSBORN

OSGOOD
MA **JOHN** 1595-1645/51

OSGOOD-Cont.
　　m c 1627 **Sarah Booth** 1629-
　　1667
　　V 75; XV 12; XXV 24; XXX
　　207; XXXX 150

OSTROM/OOSTEROM
NY **HENDRICK JANSE**
　　OOSTEROM c 1630-....
　　m 1652
　　Tryntje Lubbertje Gysbertszen
　　1666-....
　　XXXI 35

O'SULLIVAN, see SULLIVAN

OTIS
MA **JOHN** 1581-1657　m c 1603
　　Margaret _____ ....-1653/54
　　XVII 99; XXV 68
MA **JOHN** 1621-1684
　　m 1653 **Mary Jacob** ....-....
　　XVII 99
NH **RICHARD** a 1625-1689
　　m 1649 **Rose Stoughton** 1629-
　　1676
　　XXIV 43

OULD/NOLDS/KNOWLES
CT **ROBERT** 1645-1728
　　m1) 1669 **Susannah Hanford**
　　....- 1688
　　XXXIV 253

OUTLAW
VA **EDWARD** c 1650/52-a 1713/14
　　m c 1680 **Elizabeth Dafnell** ....-
　　1727
　　XXXVI 322

OVERTON
NY **ISAAC** ....-1688
　　m c 1670 **Sarah** _____ ....-....

XV 67
VA **WILLIAM** c 1638-p 1690
　　m 1670
　　Mary Elizabeth Waters c 1638-
　　c 1697
　　XXXVI 309; XXXX 203

OWEN
PA **GRIFFITH** ....-1764
　　m .... **Sarah** _____ ....-a 1764
　　XIV 83
CT **JOHN** 1620/24-1698/99
　　m 1650 **Rebecca Wade** ....-1711
　　XXV 249, 250; XXVI 205, 266;
　　XXVIII 93

OWENS
VA **RICHARD** ....-1673
　　m1) .... **Mary** _____ ....-....
　　XXIX 116
VA/MD **RICHARD** c 1630-c 1693
　　m c 1659 **Ann** _____ 1636-1702
　　XXXIX 39

OWINGS
MD **RICHARD** ....-....
　　m .... **Rachael Beale** ....-....
　　XV 121; XXIV 88
MD **THOMAS** ....-....
　　m .... _____ _____ ....-....
　　XV 121

PACE
VA **RICHARD** c 1590-c 1622/28
　　m .... **Isabella Paine/Smyth**
　　c 1595-p 1635
　　XXVIII 20; XXXI 14; XXXIV
　　337; XXXVIII 241

PACKARD
MA **SAMUEL** c 1604/12-c 1684
　　m c 1634 **Elizabeth** _____ ....-....
　　XXXII 139; XXXVII 256

PACKER
CT **JOHN** 1626-1689
  m2) 1676/78 **Mrs. Rebecca**
  (Wells) Latham 1651/52-....
  XVI 39; XXVIII 70

PADDOCK
MA **ROBERT** ....-....
  m c 1634 **Mary** _____ ....-....
  XV 120

PAGE/PAIGE
CT **GEORGE** ....-1689
  m .... **Sarah Linsley** ....-1695
  XVII 6
MA **JOHN** 1614-1687
  m c 1640 **Mary Marsh** ....-
  1696/97
  XVIII 53; XXXV 216; XXXVI
  282; XXXVIII 185, 332
VA **JOHN** 1627-1692
  m 1650/56
  Alice Lucken/Luckin 1625-
  c 1698
  X 189; XVIII 31; XXXVII 159;
  XXXX 239
MA **NATHANIEL PAIGE** c 1645-
  1692
  m c 1677
  Joanna Merriam 1644-1724/
  a 1734
  XII 76; XXXVII 225; XXXIX
  132
MA/NH **ROBERT** c 1604-1679
  m 1629
  Lucy Ward(e) bp 1604/05/07-
  1665
  XVIII 140; XXXX 434

PAIGE, see PAGE

PAINE/PAYNE
VA **JOHN PAYNE** c 1615-c 1690

  m1) 1635/40 **Lettuce Lawson**
  c 1620-c 1652
  m2) .... **Margaret** _____ ....-1690
  XXVI 89; XXXIV 336; XXXV
  86, 151; XXXVI 203
MA **MOSES** bp 1581-1643
  m1) c 1615 **Mary Bennison** ....-
  1617/18
  m2) c 1618 **Elizabeth** _____ ....-
  1632
  IX 56; X 7, 14; XIV 33; XXIX
  186, 228, 404; XXXIII 175;
  XXXIV 130
RI **RALPH** ....-....
  m .... **Dorothy** _____ ....-....
  XXI 167
MA **ROBERT** 1601-1684
  m2) .... **Dorcas** _____ 1603-1681
  XX 69
MA **STEPHEN, Sr** c 1600-1679
  m .... **Rose/Neele** _____ ....-c 1660
  XXIX 107; XXXIII 337
MA **THOMAS PAYNE** ....-p 1650
  m .... _____ _____ ....-....
  XXXII 41; XXXVII 201
MA **THOMAS** c 1612-1706
  m c 1648/50
  Mary Snow p 1628-1704
  XXIX 392; XXXVI 284

PALFREY
MA **PETER** ....-1663
  m .... **Edith** _____ ....-....
  XXXII 103; XXXIII 110

PALMER
MA/CT **HENRY** 1600-1660
  m .... **Katherine** _____ ....-....
  XX 15
PA **JOHN, Sr** 1639/42-....
  m1) a 1686 **Mary Southery**
  ....- 1744/45
  XXXII 57

PALMER-Cont.
MA **JOSEPH** 1643-1715
   m 1664 **Sarah Jackman**
   1647/48-....
   XXV 202
CT **MICAH/MICHAEL** c 1637-
   wd 1681
   m 1662 **Elizabeth Buckley**
   c 1641-....
   XXXIII 295
MA/CT **WALTER** c 1585/98-1661
   m1) .... **Ann** or **Elizabeth** _____
   ....-....
   m2) 1633 **Rebecca Short** ....-
   p 1662/1671
   XIV 76; XXII 28; XXV 96;
   XXIX 240; XXXII 79; XXXIII
   222; XXXX 33, 194
MA **WILLIAM** 1585-1637
   m by 1637 **Mary Trine** ....-....
   XXXV 27
MA **WILLIAM** 1610/15-c 1661
   m 1639/40
   Judith Flake 1612/20-1668
   XXXV 165; XXXIX 154, 216

PALMES
CT **EDWARD** 1638-1715
   m2) c 1678 **Mrs. Sarah Davis**
   ....-....
   XIII 69

PANNILL
VA **THOMAS** ....-wp 1676
   m .... **Katherine** _____ ....-....
   XXXIV 85

PARDEE
CT **GEORGE, I** bp 1624-wd 1700
   m1) 1650 **Martha Miles** ....-
   a 1662
   VI 54/61; X 162; XXI 115;
   XXXVII 338

PARK/PARKE/PARKS
CT **ROBERT PARKE** 1580-c 1664
   m1) 1601/02 **Martha Chaplin**
   bp 1583/84-a 1630/a 1644
   m2) .... **Mary Rose** ....-....
   VI 49/55; X 125, 138; XII 108;
   XVI 21; XXIX 342; XXXII 222;
   XXXIV 38, 135, 317; XXXVIII
   103, 167
CT **THOMAS** 1616-1709 m 1644
   Dorothy Thompson bp 1624-
   p 1709
   VI 49/55; XXIX 342; XXXVIII
   103
MA **THOMAS** c 1628/29-1690
   m 1653 **Abigail Dix** 1637-1691
   XXVI 208

PARKE, see PARK

PARKER
MA **ABRAHAM** c 1612-1685
   m 1644 **Rose Whitlock** ....-
   c 1691
   XXXII 165; XXXIII 71; XXXVI
   120; XXXIX 34
CT **EDWARD** 1598-1662
   m c 1646
   Elizabeth Potter (wid) ....-1677
   XII 74; XXXIV 295; XXXV 160
VA **GEORGE, Sr** 1627-wp 1674
   m .... **Florence Cade** ....- p 1681
   XXXX 148
NJ **GEORGE** ....-a 1686
   m .... **Sarah** _____ 1635-1720
   XXXIV 112
MA **JAMES** 1617/20-1700/01
   m1) 1643 **Elizabeth Long** 1623-
   a 1697
   XI 49; XIII 7; XXIX 356
CT **JOHN** 1648-1711
   m 1670 **Hannah Bassett** 1650-
   1726

PARKER-Cont.
XXVI 267; XXXIII 189
MA **JOSEPH** 1614-1678
m .... **Mary** _____ ....-1692
XXX 17
VA **RICHARD** ....-a 1677
m 1668
Judith Hunt ....-1679
XXX 155
MA **THOMAS** 1605/bp 09-1683
m 1635 **Amy (Amee)** ....-
1689/90
XVIII 142; XIX 27; XXV 198;
XXX 47; XXXIII 329; XXXIV
329
VA **THOMAS** 1629-1695
m .... **Mrs. Montague** ....-....
XIV 105

PARKHURST/PARKIS
MA **GEORGE PARKIS** c 1588/90-
c 1656
m1) ....**Phoebe** _____ ....-....
m2) ....**Rebecca** _____ ....-....
m3) .... **Susanna Simpson** ....-....
XIX 42; XXVI 41, 229; XXIX
154, 255; XXXIII 218; XXXVIII
159

PARKIS, see PARKHURST
PARKS, see PARK

PARLIN
MA **JOHN** 1615-....
m .... _____ _____ ....-....
XVIII 25

PARMELEE
CT **JOHN** 1580-1659
m1) .... **Hannah** _____ ....-....
V 81; XX 166
CT **JOHN** 1618-1688
m1) .... **Rebecca** _____ ....-....

V 81

PARMENTER
MA **JOHN** c 1588-1670/71
m c 1609 **Bridget** _____ ....-1660
XX 143; XXV 195; XXXIII 254;
XXXV 325; XXXIX 114, 180

PARRISH
MD **EDWARD B.** c 1640-1680
m c 1661/64
Clara _____ c 1640/42-a 1720
XXXV 42; XXXVIII 276;
XXXIX 140
VA **JOHN** a 1663-p 1663
m .... **Margaret** _____ ....-....
XXXX 82

PARRITT/PARROT/PARROTT/
PARRUCK
MA **JOHN** ....-1683
m 1663 **Sarah Smith** ....-1722
XXXIII 267

PARROT, see PARRITT
PARROTT, see PARRITT
PARUCK, see PARRITT
PARSE, see PIERCE

PARSHALL
NY **JAMES** ....-1701 m 1678
Elizabeth Gardiner ....-....
XXX 243

PARSONS
CT/MA **BENJAMIN** 1627-1689
m 1653 **Sarah Vore** ....-1675
XXIX 392
(MA **CORNET, see JOSEPH**)
MA **JEFFREY** 1631-1689
m 1657 **Sarah Vinson** 1635-1708
XXV 100
MA **JOSEPH** 1617/20-1683

PARSONS-Cont.
   m2) 1646 **Mary Bliss** 1620-
   1711/12
   XVI 88; XXXI 221, 306; XXXVI
   92, 252; XXXVII 254; XXXVIII
   63; XXXIX 133
CT **PHILLIP** c 1625-a 1697
   m ....
   Sarah Fairfield Needham 1655-
   ....
   IV 163; VIII 11
NY **ROBERT** 1589-1660 m ....
   Joanna/Hannah ____ ....-p 1662
   XXXX 116

PARTRIDGE
MA **GEORGE** c 1605-1682/95
   m 1638
   Sarah Tracy 1621/23-w 1702/08
   XXXV 354; XXXVIII 328
MA **JOHN** 1620/25-1706 m 1655
   Magdalena Bullard ....-1676/77
   XVII 32; XVIII 31, 139; XXVII
   203; XXIX 108; XXXI 278

PASLEY/PEASLEY
VA **WILLIAM** c 1603-c 1635
   m c 1625 **Ann Calvert** c 1605-....
   XXXII 203; XXXIV 151

PATCH
MA **NICHOLAS** bp 1597-a 1673
   m 1623 **Elizabeth Owley** ....-....
   XXX 54; XXXVI 255

PATCHEN
CT **JOSEPH** c 1610-p 1689/90
   m .... **Mary Morehouse** ....-
   p 1658
   XXXIII 60

PATE
VA **THOMAS** 1640-1710 m by 1680

   Elizabeth ____ 1660-1700
   XXIX 63; XXXVI 79

PATTEN, see PATTON

PATTERSON
CT **ANDREW** 1659-1746
   m 1690/91
   Elizabeth Peat/Peet 1669-1765
   XVIII 27, 107; XXXIV 83;
   XXXVII 174; XXXVIII 54

PATTISON
MD **THOMAS** 1654-1701
   m .... **Ann** ____ ....-1702
   XVII 105; XIX 123

PATTON/PATTEN
MA **WILLIAM PATTEN** ....-1668
   m a 1633 **Mary** ____ ....-1673
   XXI 96; XXXIII 73; XXXVI 159;
   XXXVII 53; XXXIX 300

PATTS, see PETTS

PAUL
ME **DANIEL** ....-....
   m 1617 **Elizabeth Lever** ....-....
   XXXVIII 225
MA **WILLIAM** 1624-1704
   m c 1656
   Mary Richmond 1639-1715
   XXXVII 13; XXXX 186, 379

PAXON
PA **JAMES** ....-1722
   m .... **Jane Garden** ....-....
   XXXIII 170

PAYNE, see PAINE

PAYSON
MA **EDWARD** 1613-1691

PAYSON-Cont.
 m 1642 **Mary Eliot** ....-1697
 XXXI 114

PEABODY/PAYBODY
MA **FRANCIS** c 1612/14-1697/98
 m1) a 1640 **Lydia** _____ ....-
 c 1648/49
 m2) c 1649 **Mary Foster** ....-1705
 XXIX 196; XXXVIII 132;
 XXXX 232

PEACOCK
VA **WILLIAM** 1648-1722
 m .... **Catherine** _____ 1652-1738
 XII 39, 121

PEAK, see PEET
PEARCE, see PIERCE
PEARSE, see PIERCE
PEARSON, see PIERSON

PEASE
MA **JOHN** bp 1608-p 1677
 m c 1630 **Mary Browning** ....-....
 XXXIII 87
MA/CT **JOHN** 1630/32-1689
 m1) 1652 **Mary Goodell** c 1629-
 1669
 m2) 1669 **Ann Cummings**
 c 1634-1689
 XXXIV 154, 326; XXXV 164
MA/CT **ROBERT** 1607-est. sett.
 1644 m c 1628
 Marie _____ ....-p 1644
 III 69; XXXIV 327; XXXV 40,
 159, 164; XXXVII 278

PEASLEY, see PASLEY
PEAT, see PEET

PECK
CT **HENRY** ....-p 1651/54

 m c 1638 **Joan Walker** ....-
 p 1670
 X 122; XXVI 12; XXXII 36;
 XXXVIII 175; XXXX 61
MA **JOSEPH** bp 1587-1663
 m1) 1617 **Rebecca Clark** ....-
 1637
 III 9; VIII 21; X 247; XIV 69;
 XVI 90; XXI 132; XXII 134;
 XXXVI 136, 187
CT **JOSEPH** c 1623-1700/03
 m1) 1650 **Mrs. Alice Burwell**
 ....- 1666
 VI 53/65; XVI 75
CT **WILLIAM** 1601-1694
 m1) c 1622 **Elizabeth** _____ ....-
 1683
 X 193; XIV 91; XV 89; XVII
 130; XXIX 284; XXXV 100;
 XXXVII 366

PECKHAM
RI **JOHN** bp 1595-1676/95
 m1) **Mary Clarke** 1607-1648
 m2) .... **Eleanor Weaver**
 bp 1648-....
 XI 65; XIII 9; XV 95; XXX 175;
 XXXIV 223; XXXV 139;
 XXXVI 100

PEEPLES/PEEBLES
VA **DAVID PEEBLES** c 1583/93-
 a 1659 m c 1632/34
 Elspet Mackie ....-c 1644
 XXXVI 226; XXXX 21, 130

PEET/PEAK/PEAKE/PEAT
MA **CHRISTOPHER PEAKE**
 c 1605-1666 m 1636
 Dorcas French bp 1614-1694
 XXXVIII 120
MA/CT **JOHN PEAT** c 1597-1684
 m 1635 _____ **Charles** ....-....

PEET/PEAK/PEAKE/PEAT-Cont.
XXIX 79; XXXIV 254

PEIRCE, see PIERCE

PELL
NY JOHN 1643-1702 m 1684/85
    Rachel Pinckney ....-....
    XIII 70

PELTON
MA JOHN c 1616-1681
    m c 1643 Susanna _____ ....-1706
    XII 101; XXIII 34; XXXIX 36

PENDLETON
MA BRIAN c 1599-c 1681 m 1619
    Eleanor Price c 1600-c 1688/89
    V 117; X 245; XI 10; XIV 66,
    121; XXII 32, 127; XXIV 86;
    XXXV 12; XXXVI 42; XXXVIII
    159; XXXX 236
VA PHILIP 1650-1721
    m2) 1682 Isabella Hurt/Hart ....-
    1721
    XV 136; XVI 88; XVII 12, 119;
    XIX 105

PENFIELD
MA SAMUEL c 1650/51-1710/11
    m 1675
    Mary Lewis c 1651/52-1741
    XXIX 236, 239; XXXIV 245,
    283; XXXX 22

PENGRY, see PINGRY

PENICK
VA EDWARD ....-....
    m .... Elizabeth _____ ....-....
    XXXX 140

PENN
VA WILLIAM a 1636-.... m ....
    Elizabeth (Markham?) ....-....
    XXXIII 165

PENNIMAN
MA JAMES 1610-w 1664 m ....
    Lydia Eliot 1610-wp 1664/65
    XXI 85; XXXIV 267

PENNINGTON
CT EPHRAIM ....-1660/61
    m .... Mary _____ ....-....
    XIX 50

PEPPER
MA ROBERT c 1620-1684
    m 1642/43
    Elizabeth Johnson c 1622-
    1683/84
    XXXII 265; XXXIX 181

PERIN, see PERRINE
PERINE, see PERRINE

PERKINS
NH ABRAHAM c 1611/19-1683
    m c 1638 Mary Wise/Wyeth
    1618/20-1706
    III 25; X 236, 259; XI 28; XXXX
    280
CT EDWARD ....-p 1655 m 1649
    Elizabeth Butcher ....-p 1656
    X 87
NH ISAAC 1612-1685
    m .... Susanna Wise ....-1699
    XXIX 264
MA JACOB 1624-1699/1700
    m1) 1647/48 Elizabeth Lowell
    1629-1665/66
    XV 111
MA JOHN, Sr bp 1583/90-1654
    m 1603/08 Judith Gater/Gates

PETTS/PATTS
MA **JOHN** c 1654-a 1756
    m c 1700/05 **Abigail** _____ ....-
    a 1762
    XXXVI 302

PETTUS
VA **THOMAS** 1610-1660
    m1) .... _____ _____ ....-....
    XXXV 267

PEYTON
VA **HENRY** bp 1630/31-1658/59
    m .... **Ellen Partington** ....-p 1659
    XXIX 339; XXXV 51
VA **PHILIP** 1644/45-....
    m c 1675 **Mary** _____ ....-....
    XXXIX 268

PHELPS
MA **GEORGE** 1606-1686/87
    m 1648
    Frances ( ) Dewey (wid) ....-1690
    XXII 21; XXXX 227
MA **HENRY** ....-1652
    m .... _____ **Tressler** ....-....
    XXXVII 151
MA/CT **WILLIAM** bp 1599-1672
    m1) 1618/19 **Elizabeth** _____
    1600-1635
    m2) 1638 **Mary Dover** ....-1675
    X 249; XI 64; XII 62; XIV 20;
    XVI 109; XVII 26; XX 78; XXI
    52; XXII 14; XXIII 62; XXXI
    230, 268; XXXII 258; XXXIII
    265, 294; XXXIV 17, 53, 298;
    XXXV 80, 277; XXXVII 108;
    XXXVIII 30; XXXIX 264

PHILBRICK/PHILBROOK
MA/NH **THOMAS PHILBROOK**
    bp 1584-c 1667 m 1615
    Elizabeth Knapp bp 1593-

1663/64
XXIII 36; XXXVII 161; XXXIX
254

PHILBROOK, see PHILBRICK

PHILLIPS
MA **GEORGE** c 1593-1643/44
    m2) 1631 **Mrs. Elizabeth**
    Welden/on ....-1681
    XIII 34; XVI 84; XXVI 26, 48,
    68; XXXVIII 308
MA **JOHN** 1602-1692
    m1) .... **Mary** _____ ....-1646/49
    XXXI 30
RI **MICHAEL** ....-1689
    m .... **Barbara** _____ ....-....
    XXV 39
MD **ROGER** ....-1699
    m 1672 **Dorothy Clarke** ....-....
    XXXX 387
VA **WILLIAM** c 1698-c 1721
    m .... **Mary Swann** ....-....
    XXXIV 127

PHINNEY/FINNEY
MA **JOHN, Sr** ....-1688/p 1702
    m .... **Christiana** _____ ....-
    a 1653
    m3) 1654 **Elizabeth**
    Bayley/Bailey ....-1683/84
    XI 3, 151; XXIX 87; XXXIV
    216; XXXVI 327; XXXVIII 50

PHIPPS/PHIPS
ME **JAMES PHIPS** 1612/13-c 1660
    m a 1640 **Mary** _____ ....-1704
    XXXX 51, 163

PIAT, see PYATT

PICKERING
NH **JOHN** c 1590-1669

PICKERING-Cont.
    m .... **Mary** _____ ....-....
    XXXVI 248
MA **JOHN** 1615-wp 1657 m 1636
    Elizabeth Lawrence 1616-1662
    XXXI 312

PICKETT/PICKET
VA **GEORGE** c 1658-p 1745
    m c 1687 **Ida Martin** ....-c 1745
    IX 32; X 65
VA **HENRY** ....-c 1702
    m .... _____ _____ ....-....
    XXIX 137
MA/CT **JOHN PICKET, Sr** ....-1684
    m .... **Margett(e)** _____ c 1622-
    1683
    XXXII 273; XXXVI 313

PIERCE/PARSE/PEARCE/
PEARSE/PEIRCE/PERS
MA **ABRAHAM** c 1600/05-c 1673
    m 1650 **Rebecca** _____ ....-....
    X 69, 127; XXXII 172; XXXV
    259; XXXX 17
MA **ANTHONY PEIRCE** 1609-
    1678
    m1) .... **Mary** _____ ....-1633
    m2) 1638 **Anne** _____ 1619-
    1682/83
    XXVII 213; XXXV 132, 228
MA **DANIEL PEARCE/PEIRCE**
    1611-1677
    m1) a 1638 **Sarah** _____ ....-1654
    XV 11; XXXI 240
PA **GEORGE PEARCE** c 1654-
    1734
    m 1679 **Ann Gainor** 1661-...
    XXVII 202
MA **JOHN PERS/PEIRCE** c 1588-
    1661 m a 1609
    Elizabeth _____ 1591/1601-
    1666/67

    XXVII 213; XXXIII 21; XXXV
    132, 228
RI **JOHN** c 1632-a 1689
    m .... **Mary** _____ ....-....
    XX 96
MA **JOHN** 1643-1720
    m 1663
    Deborah Converse 1647-....
    XXXIX 208
MA **MICHAEL** c 1615-1676
    m1) c 1645 **Persis Eames/Ames**
    bp 1621-1622-....
    m2) c 1663 **Annah James** ....-
    p 1675
    XI 162; XIII 76; XIX 111; XXIV
    100; XXV 292; XXXIV 54;
    XXXVI 101; XXXX 278
RI **RICHARD** 1590-....
    m .... **Martha** _____ ....-p 1629
    X 208
RI **RICHARD PEARCE** 1615-
    a 1678 m 1642
    Susannah Wright 1620/27-
    a 1678
    VIII 12; XXIX 337
MA **THOMAS, Sr** 1583/84-1666
    m .... **Elizabeth Pierce** 1595/96-
    p 1665
    XI 14; XIX 82, 134; XXVII 157,
    217; XXVIII 79, 80; XXXI 308;
    XXXVI 36
MA **THOMAS, Jr** 1608-1683
    m 1635 **Elizabeth Cole** ....-1688
    II 35; XXXI 308

PIERSON/PEARSON
MA/NY **ABRAHAM** 1608-1678
    m .... **Abigail Wheelwright** ....-
    ....
    X 120, 151
PA **EDWARD PEARSON** c 1650-
    1698
    m 1671 **Sarah Burgiss** ....-p 1698

PIERSON/PEARSON-Cont.
XXIX 84; XXXIII 191
MA/NY **HENRY** 1618-c 1680/81
m 1643 **Mary Cooper** c 1622-....
XIII 28; XVIII 97; XXIX 353
MA **JOHN PEARSON** c 1610/15-
1693 m ....
Dorcas (Bryant?) ....-1702/03
XXXVII 115
PA **THOMAS** a 1660-p 1734
m 1683 **Margaret Smith** c 1664-
p 1690/1734
XXVIII 40, 172, 194

PIKE
MA **JAMES** ....-1699
m .... **Naomi** _____ ....-1692
XIII 41
MA **JOHN** 1605-1654
m 1612/13 **Dorothy Day** ....-....
XV 7; XVI 108
MA **ROBERT** c 1615/16-1706
m1) 1641 **Sarah Sanders**
bp 1615-1679/84
XXVI 75; XXIX 169; XXXIV
262

PILLSBURY
MA **WILLIAM** c 1605/15-1686
m 1641
Dorothy Crosby/Crosbey ....-
p 1686
XIV 26; XXIX 204; XXXI 47,
51, 288; XXXX 353

PINGREY/PENGRY
MA **MOSES PENGRY** c 1610/11-
1696 m c 1644/46
Lydia/Abigail Clement c 1618-
1675/76
IX 38; XXX 45; XXXIX 345;
XXXX 102

PINKHAM
NH **RICHARD** ....-p1647/48
m .... **Julia** _____ ....-....
XXIX 257

PINNEY
MA **HUMPHREY** ....-1683
m .... **Mary Hull** 1618-1684
XXIX 70, 195

PIPER
MA **NATHANIEL** chrt 1627-
wp 1676
m 1654/55 **Sarah Edwards** ....-
p 1696
XXXVII 310

PITKIN
CT **WILLIAM** 1635-1694
m 1661 **Hannah Goodwin** 1637-
1724
XXXV 274

PITT
VA **ROBERT** c 1600-w.pr. 1674
m c 1627
Martha Lear p 1600-p 1674
XXVI 49

PLACE
MA **ENOCH** 1631-1695
m 1657 **Sarah** _____ ....-1695
XXII 55

PLANT
CT **JOHN, Sr** ....-1691
m 1677 **Betty Roundkettle** ....-....
XXV 48; XXXIII 146

PLATT
CT **RICHARD** bp 1603/04-1684/85
m 1628/29
Mary (Place) Wood bp 1605-

PLATT-Cont.
1675/76
X 157; XXIV 124; XXV 88;
XXXI 271, 299; XXXIV 83;
XXXV 119; XXXVII 117;
XXXVIII 262

PLATTS
MA **ABEL** ....-1690
m 1672 **Lydia Bailey** ....-p 1690
XV 81; XXXII 136
MA **SAMUEL** ....-....
m1) .... **Sarah** _____ ....-1681
XXXII 136

PLEASANTS
VA **JOHN, I** bp 1644/45-1690/98
m c 1670
Jane (Larcome) Tucker ....-
1708/09
XVI 15; XXIX 56; XXXI 168

PLETSOE, see BLEDSOE

PLUMB
CT **BENONI, Sr** 1670-1754
m2) 1715/16 **Abigail (Todd)**
Gilbert 1689/90-1751
XXXI 314
CT **JOHN PLUMB/E** c 1632/34-
1696 m 1662/66
Elizabeth Green c 1635/40-....
XXXV 352; XXXVI 236

PLUMER, see PLUMMER

PLUMMER/PLUMER
MA **FRANCIS PLUMER** 1594/98-
1672/73
m .... **Ruth** _____ ....-1647
XIX 155; XXVIII 161; XXXII
128

PLYMPTON/PLIMPTON
MA **JOHN PLIMPTON** c 1620-
1677/78 m 1644
Jane Dammin/Dammand 1626-
p 1678
XXIX 17

POILLON
NY **JACQUES** c 1646-1720
m 1677
Andrianna Cocheron ....-....
XXIX 231

POINDEXTER
VA **GEORGE POINDESTRE**
c 1624/37-c 1690/92
m c 1657 **Susanna Nichols** ....-
1693
XXXI 110; XXXVI 22; XXXVII
197; XXXIX 110

POLK/DE POLLOK/
POLLOK/POLKE
MD **ROBERT BRUCE DE**
POLLOK 1632-1704 m 1650/60
Magdalene (Tasker) Porter
c 1635/45-1726/27
XXVII 85; XXIX 155; XXX 188;
XXXVII 15, 45, 139; XXXVIII
135, 235

POLKE, see POLK

POLLAY/POLLEY
MA **GEORGE POLLEY, Sr** ....-
1683
m 1649 **Elizabeth Winn** ....-1695
XXXII 51

POLLEY, see POLLAY
POLLOK, see POLK

POMEROY
MA/CT **ELTWEED/ELTWOOD**
 bp 1585-1673
 m2) 1629 **Marjorie/Mary
 Rockett** ....-1655
 III 50; X 123, 262; XI 34; XIII
 39, 89; XIV 55; XXVII 176;
 XXIX 13; XXXV 302; XXXVII
 174

POND
MA **DANIEL** ....-1697/98
 m1) .... **Abigail Shepard** 1640-
 1661
 m2) 1661 **Anne Edwards** 1640-
 1732
 XXVII 146; XXX 43, 131
CT **SAMUEL** c 1617-1654
 m 1642 **Sara/Sarah Ware**
 c 1621-....
 XXXI 193; XXXVIII 161;
 XXXIX 44, 183; XXXX 269

POOL/POOLE
MA **JOHN** ....-1667
 m1) .... **Judith** ____ ....-....
 m2) .... **Margaret** ____ ....-1662
 XXVI 11; XXVIII 200; XXXVII
 266

POOR, see **POORE**

POORE/POOR
MA **DANIEL** c 1624-1689/90
 m 1650
 Mary Farnum c 1628-1713/14
 XXXVIII 128
MA **JOHN** c 1615-1684
 m .... **Sarah** ____ ....-1702
 XXII 72

POPE
MA **JOHN, Jr** 1628-1686 m ....

Margaret ____ 1628-1702
 XXXIX 156
MA **JOSEPH** .... a 1667
 m .... **Gertrude** ____ ....-....
 XX 178
MD **NATHANIEL** ....-w pr 1660
 m .... **Lucy** ____ ....-....
 XXVI 180
MA **THOMAS** 1608-1683
 m2) 1646 **Sarah Jenney** 1623-
 a 1663
 XXXVII 229; XXXIX 107

PORTER
CT **DANIEL, I** ....-1690
 m .... **Mary** ____ ....-p 1690
 XIII 106; XVII 57; XXIII 80
VA **EDWARD** 1640-w 1705
 m a 1694 **Mary** ____ ....-....
 XXVI 92
MD **JAMES** c 1670-p 1697
 m .... **Junibar** ____ ....-1703
 XVI 60; XVII 13
MA **JOHN** c 1596-1676
 m c 1634/35
 Mary ____ ....-p 1684/85
 XVI 37; XXIX 395; XXXIII 332;
 XXXVI 116; XXXVII 282
CT **JOHN, Sr** 1590/99-1647/48
 m 1620 **Anne/a White** 1600-
 1647
 XXI 53; XXXIX 102
CT **JOHN, Jr** 1621-1688
 m 1650 **Mary Stanley** c 1628-....
 XXVI 145
VA **JOHN, Jr** c 1630-1691
 m .... **Mary Sidney** ....-....
 XXVI 171
MA **RICHARD** c 1611-c 1689
 m .... **Ruth** ____ ....-....
 XXXIX 219
CT **ROBERT** ....-1689
 m1) 1644 **Mary Scott** ....-....

PORTER-Cont.
XXXV III
CT **THOMAS** ....-1697
m 1644 **Sarah Hart** ....-....
XXXVIII 87

POSCHET, see POSEY

POSEY/POSCHET
VA/MD **FRANCOIS POSCHET**
c 1615-1654 m 1645
Elizabeth ____ ....-1730
XXXVIII 86

POST/POSTMAEL
NY/NJ **ADRIAN** c 1600-1677
m .... **Claertje** ____ ....-....
XIV 34; XVIII 19; XX 61; XXI
17, 27; XXVI 159; XXXVIII 4,
85
NY **JANS JANSEN POSTMAEL**
....-p 1684 m .... **Jannetie**
LeSueur ....-....
XXXIV 225
NY **RICHARD** 1617-1689/1717
m c 1640
Dorothy Johnson 1625- p 1689
XII 78; XIII 62
CT **STEPHEN** c 1596-1659
m. int. 1625
Ellen/Eleanor Panton ....-1670
XIV 16; XV 40; XIX 69; XXIX
263; XXXII 176

POSTMAEL, see POST

POTTER
MA **ANTHONY** 1628-1690
m ....**Elizabeth Whipple** 1629-
1712
V 103
RI **GEORGE** ....-....
m .... ____ ___ ....-....

XXI 143
CT **JOHN** c 1607-1643 m 1630
Elizabeth Wood 1606-1677
XXXII 143
RI **NATHANIEL** c 1617-a 1644
m .... **Dorothy** ____ ....-1698
XXVIII 108
MA/RI **ROBERT** c 1606-1653/65
m1) c 1635 **Isabel** ____ ....-1643
m2) .... **Sarah** ____ ....-1686
XIV 98; XXXVI 66; XXXIX 280

POTTINGER
MD **JOHN** 1642-1735
m 1687 **Mary Beall** ....-....
XXV 254

POTTS
PA **JONAS** ....-p 1737
m .... **Mary** ____ ....-....
XVII 37

POWELL
MA **ROWLAND** ....-.....
m .... **Isabelle** ____ ....-....
XXIV 163
MD **WALTER** c 1620/25-1695
m .... **Margaret Berry** or **Beers**
c 1620/25-1679
XXIX 32; XXXVII 86

POWER, see POWERS

POWERS/POWER
MA **WALTER** c 1639-1708
m 1660/61
Trial/Tryall Shepard/Shepherd
1641-....
XI 168; XII 70; XXX 137;
XXXIII 124; XXXIV 332;
XXXV 149; XXXVI 339;
XXXVII 33

PRATER, see PRATHER

PRATHER/PRATER/PRATOR
VA/MD **JONATHAN** 1630/35-
   a 1680/82 m c 1654/58
   Jane MacKay (Smith) c 1635-
   c 1713/15
   IV 126; XXXIII 321; XXXVIII
   247; XXXX 26

PRATOR, see PRATHER

PRATT
PA **ABRAHAM** ....-wp 1709
   m .... **Jane** _____ ....-p 1709
   XXXIII 237; XXXIV 283;
   XXXVI 64
CT **JOHN** bp 1620-1655
   m 1637 **Elizabeth** _____ ....-....
   IV 135; XXVII 145; XXXI 23
MA **JOSHUA** ....-a 1656
   m .... **Bathsheba** _____ ....-p 1667
   XXXX 59
MA **MATHEW** 1600/08-1672
   m .... **Elizabeth Bate/Bates** 1615-
   c 1641/76
   XI 57; XXVI 6; XXIX 373
MA **PHINEAS** c 1590-1680 m 1630
   Mary (Priest) Allerton ....-1689
   XX 85; XXVII 87; XXXIV 50
MA **THOMAS** 1620-inv 1692
   m .... **Susanna** _____ ....-p 1692
   VIII 27; X 280; XVII 156; XVIII
   22; XXIX 364; XXXI 159;
   XXXII 239; XXXIII 291; XXXV
   89
CT **WILLIAM** ....-1678
   m 1636 **Elizabeth Clarke** ....-....
   XXVII 205; XXXV 110

PRAY
MA **QUINTON** 1595-1677
   m .... **Joan** _____ ....-1677

VIII 19
RI **RICHARD** 1630-1693
   m .... **Mary** _____ ....-1686
   VIII 19

PREBLE
MA **ABRAHAM** 1603-1663
   m 1641 **Judith Tilden** ....-liv.
   1663
   III 19

**PRENTICE/PRENTIS/PRENTISE/
PRENTISS**
MA **HENRY PRENTISS** c 1619-
   1654
   m2) .... **Joan Prentice** c 1623-
   1643
   XIX 81; XXXIV 153
MA **THOMAS, Sr** c 1620-1710
   m c 1643 **Grace** _____ ....-1692
   XXVII 79
MA **VALENTINE PRENTISE** ....-
   1633
   m .... **Alice** _____ ....-....
   XVI 96; XXVI 52

PRENTIS, see PRENTICE
PRENTISE, see PRENTICE
PRENTISS, see PRENTICE

PRESCOTT
NH **JAMES** bp 1642/43-1728
   m 1668 **Mary Boulter** 1648-1735
   XXV 105, 241; XXX 282; XXXI
   264; XXXIV 95; XXXIX 58
MA **JOHN** 1604/05-1681/83
   m 1629 **Mary Platts** ....-1681
   III 64; XIII 55; XVII 18; XXVI
   111; XXIX 77

PRESTON
MA **ROGER** 1614-1666
   m c 1640/43

PRESTON-Cont.
  Martha ____ c 1622-1702/03
  XXIX 290; XXXVII 368
MA/CT **WILLIAM** 1590/91-1647/49
  m1) 1613 **Elizabeth Sale/s** 1590-
  1633
  m2) .... **Mary Seabrook** ....-....
  XXX 143; XXXV 261

PRICE
NY **BENJAMIN** c 1621-wp 1712
  m1) a 1669 **Mary Sayre** ....-
  a 1705
  m2) .... **Judy Farrington** ....-....
  XVI 38; XXXVIII 309
PA **EDWARD** 1650-wp 1728
  m .... **Mabley/Mabby Ievan**
  1650-1699
  XXIX 166; XXXIX 220
VA **JOHN, I** c 1584-1636/38
  m a 1621
  Mary Ann Matthews 1603/04-
  by 1666
  XII 31; XIII 114; XXIII 14;
  XXXX 138
MD **THOMAS PRICE** c 1610-1701
  m 1634 **Elizabeth Phillips** 1612-
  ....
  XXXVIII 90

PRIDE
VA **WILLIAM, I** 1638-1724
  m .... **Jane Holcott** ....-....
  XXXVII 242; XXXVIII 198, 209

PRIEST
MA **JOHN, Sr** 1656/57-inv 1704
  m 1678 **Rachel Garfield** 1656-
  1737
  VI 100/118; XXVI 57, 146, 290;
  XXVIII 181; XXXV 233

PRIME
CT **JAMES** ....-1685
  m .... ____ ____ ....-p 1685
  XVIII 48; XXXIV 13
MA **MARK** ....-1683
  m .... **Ann** ____ ....-1672
  XXXII 81

PRINCE
MA **THOMAS, Sr** 1619-1690
  m a 1644
  Margaret ____ c 1626-1706
  XXXIII 301; XXXIV 73

PRIOR/PRYOR
MA **THOMAS PRYOR** ....-1639
  m .... ____ ____ ....-a 1634
  XXXIV 341

PRITCHARD
NH **WILLIAM** ....-1675
  m .... **Hannah** ____ ....-....
  XXXVII 92

PROBASCO
NY **CHRISTOFFEL JURRANSE**
  bp 1649-1707
  m 1675 **Eytie Strycker** 1651-....
  XXXVII 196

PROCTOR
MA **ROBERT** ....-1697 m 1645
  Jane Hildreth c 1627/28-p 1697
  X 275; XXII 70; XXXVI 77

PROUT
MA **TIMOTHY** 1620-1702
  m .... **Margaret** ____ ....-....
  XXXIX 176

PROUTY
MA **RICHARD** 1650/bp 1652-1708
  m 1676

PROUTY-Cont.
Damaris Torrey 1650/51-p 1717
VII 39; XXII 139; XXXII 147;
XXXIII 295

PRUDDEN
CT **PETER** 1600-1656
m .... **Joanna Boyse** a 1620-
p 1681
XI 43

PRYOR, see PRIOR
PUDDINGTON, see PURINGTON
PUDNEY, see PUTNEY

PUFFER
MA **GEORGE** c 1600-1639
m .... ____ ____ ....-1676
XVII 109; XXIII 25; XXXX 387
MA **JAMES** c 1624-1692
m 1656 **Mary Ludden** 1639-
1700
XXXIV 92

PUGSLEY
NY **MATTHEW** ....-p 1730
m 1683 **Mary Hunt** c 1666/67-....
XXXII 33

PULLEN
VA **HENRY** c 1630/58/60-1698
m c 1680
Mary Stott c 1638/62-w 1731
XXXVII 298; XXXVIII 21;
XXXIX 18, 154, 193; XXXX
103, 248

PULLIAM
VA **EDMUND** 1600-....
m .... ____ ____ ....-....
XXXIV 72

PULSIFIER
MA **JOHN** c 1663-1737
m 1684
Joanna Kent 1665-....
XXXI 286

PURCELL
NY **THOMAS** ....-a 1738
m ....
Christiana Van Woggelum
bp 1667-....
XXXIX 64

PURDY
CT **FRANCIS** 1595/1610-w 1658
m by 1642
Mary Brandagee/Brundage
pr 1616-....
XXII 20; XXXIX 120; XXXX
263

PURINGTON/PUDDINGTON/
PURRINGTON
ME **GEORGE** ....-1647/49
m 1630 **Mary Pooke** ....-p 1691
XXX 203

PURINTON
NH **ROBERT** ....-....
m .... **Amy Davis** ....-....
XIX 44

PURNELL
VA/MD **THOMAS** 1613-1690
m 1647
Elizabeth Darman 1625-1671/73
XIV 107; XV 54

PURRINGTON, see PURINGTON

PUTNAM/PUTMAN
MA **JOHN** bp 1579/80-1662
m c 1611/12

PUTNAM/PUTMAN-Cont.
Priscilla Deacon Gould c 1586-
p 1641
VI 24/27; XII 62, 80; XV 20;
XVI 77; XIX 33; XXIV 56;
XXVII 198; XXIX 341; XXX 45,
231; XXXV 231; XXXVI 86,
237, 262; XXXVII 50; XXXVIII
24; XXXIX 316; XXXX 302
MA **JOHN** 1627-1710
m 1652
Rebecca Price ....-....
XII 80; XXXV 231
NY **JAN/JOHANNES** 1645-1690
m ....
Cornelia Andriese 1655-1690
XXXVII 327; XXXVIII 154

PUTNEY/PUDNEY
MA **JOHN PUDNEY, Sr** .....-1712
m 1662 **Judith Cooke** 1643-....
XXXI 150

PYATT/PIAT/PYOTT
NJ **RENE PIAT** c 1650-1705 m 1677
Elizabeth Sheffield ....-....
XXXIII 145

PYLE
PA **ROBERT** bp 1660-w 1730
m1) 1681 **Ann Stovey** ....-1724
XXXIX 102

PYOTT, see PYATT
QUACKENBOS, see
QUAKENBUSH

QUACKENBUSH/QUACKENBOS
NY **PIETER VAN** 1639-p 1696
m c 1658 **Maritje** ____ ....-1682
IX 6; XXXI 191; XXXIII 299;
XXXVI 248; XXXVII 214, 273

QUANTAIN, see CANTINE

QUARLES
VA **RICHARD** ....-....
m .... ____ ____ ....-....
XXXVI 244

QUEEN
MD **SAMUEL** ....-.... m ....
Katherine (Marsham) Brooke
....- ....
XXX 152

QUESENBURY, see
QUISENBERRY

QUICK
NY **THEUNIS THOMASZEN** ....-
p 1666 m 1625
Belijtgen/Belitze Jacobus ....-....
XXXVI 71, 118

QUIMBY/QUINBY
MA **ROBERT QUINBY** c 1625-
1677 m c 1656
Elizabeth Osgood ....-1694
XXX 85, 288

QUINBY, see QUIMBY

QUINCY
MA **EDMUND** ....-1635
m 1623 **Judith Pares** ....-....
XXVIII 152

QUISENBERRY/QUESENBURY
VA **THOMAS QUESENBURY**
1608-1672 m a 1625 ____ ____
....-....
XXXVIII 223

RAGSDALE
VA **GODFREY, Sr** c 1615-c 1644

RAGSDALE-Cont.
 m .... **Mary** _____ ....-c 1644
 XXXIV 144; XXXV 92; XXXVI
 45

RAIFORD
VA **PHILIP, I** ....-....
 m .... **Sarah Alexander** ....-....
 XXV 98

RAMBO
PA **PETER GUNNARSON** ....-1698
 m .... **Bretta** _____ ....-p 1684
 XX 165

RAMEY/REMY
VA **JACOB/JACQUES REMY**
 c 1630-a 1721
 m2) 1671 **Mary Spencer Miles**
 ....-....
 XXXVI 93, 198; XXXVII 27;
 XXXIX 196

RAMSDELL
MA **JOSEPH** ....-1674 m 1645
 Rachel Eaton c 1625-a 1661
 XXXX 115

RAND
MA **ROBERT** ....-1639/40
 m .... **Alice** _____ 1593-1691
 XVIII 107

RANDALL
RI **JOHN, Sr** 1629-c 1684/85
 m c 1663/65
 Elizabeth Morton c 1640-p 1685
 XXI 42; XXIII 58; XXXIV 62,
 340; XXXVI 335; XXXVII 162;
 XXXIX 186; XXXX 367
MA **WILLIAM** 1609-1693
 m c 1639/40
 Elizabeth Barstow ....-p 1693

XVIII 119; XXV 19; XXX 236;
 XXXVI 116, 183; XXXIX 138

RANDOLPH
VA **HENRY** 1623-1673
 m .... **Judith Soane** ....-....
 IX 9
VA **WILLIAM** 1651-1711
 m 1677/80 **Mary Isham** ....-....
 XXVI 53; XXXII 92; XXXIII
 226; XXXVIII 189

RANLET/RUNDLET
NH **CHARLES RUNDLET** c 1655-
 1709
 m c 1675
 Mary (Shatswell) Smith ....-....
 XXIII 59

RANNEY/RANY
CT **THOMAS RANY, I** ....-1713
 m 1659
 Mary Hubbard 1641/42-1721
 XXXIII 12; XXXIX 129; XXXX
 367, 443

RANSOM/RANSON
CT **MATTHEW** 1661-.... m 1682/83
 Hannah Jones ....-....
 XXXX 81
VA **PETER** 1615-wp a 1663
 m .... _____ _____ ....-....
 XXIX 25; XXXI 182
MA **ROBERT** 1636-1694/97
 m c 1660 **Susannah** _____ ....-....
 XXV 200; XXVI 54; XXXIX 18

RANSON, see RANSOM
RANY, see RANNEY
RAPALJE, see RAPELYEA

RAPELYEA/DE RAPALIE/DE
RAPALJE/RAPALJE

RAPELYEA/DE RAPALIE/DE RAPALJE/RAPALJE-Cont.
NY **JORIS JASSEN/JANSEN** 1572-
c 1661/65 m c 1623
    Catalyntie Frisco/Trico c 1605-
1689
    XI 146; XIV 116; XV 78; XXXV
171; XXXX 18

RATHBONE/RATHBUN
MA **JOHN** c 1610-.... m c 1633
    _____ _____ ....-....
    XIX 65
RI **JOHN RATHBUN, Sr** 1629/34-
1702 m 1650/54
    Margaret (Acres) Dodge
bp 1633-p 1702/16
    XXIX 114; XXXVIII 174;
XXXX 26, 197
MA **RICHARD** c 1574-....
    m .... **Marion Whipple** a 1583-
p 1610/16
    XI 78; XVII 102

RATHBUN, see RATHBONE

RAVENSCROFT
MA/VA **SAMUEL** ....-1692/95
m c 1680
    Dionaysia Savage 1649-1703/23
    XXX 270

**RAWLINGS/RAWLINS/
ROLINGS/ROLLINS**
MA/NH **JAMES ROLLINS, I** ....-
wp 1691
    m .... **Hannah** _____ ....-....
    XX 91; XXXIII 24; XXXVI 101,
321; XXXVIII 330
MD **RICHARD** c 1651-1696
m c 1673
    Jane _____ 1655-p 1696
    XVII 105; XXI 54; XXIV 98;

XXX 229; XXXVII 318
RAWLINS, see RAWLINGS

RAWSON
MA **EDWARD** 1615-1693
    m .... **Rachel Perne** ....-....
    XIII 95; XVIII 149; XXII 79;
XXIX 59, 174, 301; XXX 89

RAY/RAYE
MD **ALEXANDER** a 1652-a 1675
    m .... **Joane** _____ ....-p 1689
    XXX 286
MD **JOHN** ....-a 1692
    m .... _____ _____ ....-a 1692
    XXXII 160; XXXIII 128
VA **THOMAS RAYE** c 1605-
1654/55 m a 1636/42
    Mary Elizabeth Christmas ....-
p/w 1654/55
    XXXVII 230; XXXVIII 164;
XXXIX 148; XXXX 245

RAYE, see RAY
RAYMENT, see RAYMOND

**RAYMOND/RAYMENT/
RAYMONT**
MA **JOHN** c 1616-1703
    m1) .... **Rachel Scruggs/Scroggs**
bp 1627-1666
    X 37; XXXIV 93, 124
CT **JOHN** c 1635-pr 1695
    m 1664 **Mary Betts** 1646-....
    XXVI 297
MA/CT **RICHARD** c 1602-1692
    m .... **Judith** _____ ....-....
    XVIII 101; XX 114; XXI 51;
XXIV 28; XXVI 297; XXXIII
348
NH/MA **WILLIAM** c 1637-....
    m .... **Hannah Bishop** 1646-1709
    XXXIII 289

RAMONT, see RAYMOND

RAYNES
ME **FRANCIS** 1610-1706
    m .... **Eleanor** _____ ....-....
    XXXII 219

READ, see **REED**
READE, see **REED**
REDFEN, see **REDFIELD**

REDFIELD/REDFEN/REDFIN
MA **JAMES** 1646-c/pr 1723
    m 1669 **Elizabeth Howe** 1645-
    a 1693
    XXVI 118
MA **WILLIAM REDFEN** c 1610-
    c 1662 m a 1636
    Rebecca _____ ....-p 1667
    VI 35/39; XII 103; XIV 60; XXII
    64; XXV 136; XXVI 118; XXVII
    187

REDFIN, see **REDFIELD**

REED/READ/READE
MA **ESDRAS READE** 1595-1680
    m .... **Elizabeth Watson** ....-....
    XXXIII 149
VA **GEORGE** 1612-1670 m ....
    Elizabeth Martian 1618-1669
    XXII 22
MA **JOHN** 1598-1683
    m .... **Sarah** _____ ....-....
    XXV 35
CT **JOHN** 1633-1730
    m1) .... **Mrs. Ann Derby** ....-....
    XV 113; XXIV 30; XXXII 177
CT **JOSIAH** 1643-1717
    m 1666
    Grace Holloway c 1646/47-1727
    XXII 152; XXXIV 247
VA **PETER READ** ....-c 1688

    m .... **Ann** _____ ....-....
    XXXX 136
MA **THOMAS** c 1610-c 1667
    m .... _____ _____ ....-c 1645/46
    XXXI 287
MA **THOMAS READ** 1627-1701
    m1) c 1648 **Katherine** _____
    c 1628-1667/78
    XIV 17; XVI 138; XXXV 360
MA **THOMAS** a 1630-....
    m .... **Mary** _____ a 1630-....
    XV 63; XVI 69
MA **THOMAS** c 1556-p 1725
    m pr 1679
    Hannah Blanchard 1658/59-....
    XXXV 74
MA **WILLIAM READE** c 1587-
    1656
    m .... **Mabel Kendall** 1605-1690
    X 300; XXIV 33; XXXVII 343;
    XXXIX 136
MA **WILLIAM READE** 1605-....
    m 1635 **Ivis Deacon** ....-....
    XXV 63; XXX 69
MA **WILLIAM** c 1606/07-a 1679
    m1) 1629 **Susanna/Susan**
    Hayme c 1606-1653
    X 81, 92; XX 109; XXXI 307;
    XXXX 281

REEVES
VA **HENRY, Sr** ....-wp 1687
    m .... **Elizabeth** _____ ....-wp 1711
    XXXVII 208
MA/NY **THOMAS** ....-1650
    m 1645 **Hannah Rowe** ....-a 1650
    XXXIX 236
NJ **WALTER** 1650/57-wd 1698
    m 1682 **Ann Howell** ....-wp 1733
    XXIX 206

REGAN
VA **DANIEL** ....-c 1688

REGAN-Cont.
    m c 1650 **Jane Gross** ....-c 1696
    XXXVIII 47

REMBERT
SC **ANDRE** ....-1786
    m .... **Anne Bressan** ....-....
    XXXII 35

REMICK
ME **CHRISTIAN** 1631-1710
    m c 1654 **Hannah** ____ ....-
    p 1703
    XIV 67

REMINGTON
MA **JOHN** 1610-1667
    m1) a 1630 **Elizabeth** ____ ....-
    1657
    XXIX 105
MA **THOMAS** ...-.... m 1687
    Remember Stowell 1662-1694
    XXXIV 185

REMSEN, see also
VANDER BEEK
REMY, see RAMEY
RENALL, see REYNOLDS
RETYE, see RICHEY

REYNOLDS/RENALL
VA **CHRISTOPHER** 1611-1654
    m .... **Elizabeth** ____ ....-p 1654
    XXX 135; XXXVI 228
RI **JAMES** ....-wp 1700
    m a 1647 **Deborah** ____ ....-
    a 1692
    XXI 44; XXII 66; XXXVI 254
MA/CT **JOHN** c 1612-p 1651
    m .... **Sarah** ____ c 1614-1657
    XXIV 57; XXX 64; XXXIX 318
CT **JOHN** ....-1702
    m 1650 **Sarah Backus** 1628-....

    XXXX 356
CT **JONATHAN** c 1635-1673/74
    m c 1656/58
    Rebecca Husted ....-....
    XIX 143; XXIX 51
VA **NICHOLAS** a 1612-....
    m2) a 1642
    Alice Gregory Delk/Delke ....-....
    XXXV 21, 41
VA **RICHARD** c 1575-....
    m 1605 **Ann Harrison** ....-....
    XXXV 21,41; XXXVIII 66
MA **ROBERT** c 1580/90-1659
    m 1600/22 **Mary** ____ ....-1663
    XVIII 122; XXXI 199
VA **THOMAS RENALL** c 1660-....
    m .... **Mary** ____ ....-....
    XXXII 242
PA **WILLIAM** c 1606-....
    m .... **Margaret Exton** ....-....
    XXXIV 105

RHOADES, see RHODES

RHODES/RHOADES
MA **HENRY RHOADES** 1608-
    1675/1703 m ....
    Elizabeth White 1618- 1700
    XXXX 395
VA **HEZEKIAH** 1662-1717
    m 1684 **Elizabeth Nichols** ....-
    1722
    XXXX 14
MA/RI **ZACHARIAH** 1603-1665/66
    m 1646 **Joanna Arnold** 1617-
    1692
    VI 43/49

RICCAR, see RICKER

RICE/ROICE/ROYCE
MA **EDMUND** c 1594-1663
    m1) a 1615/18 **Thomasine Frost**

RICE/ROICE/ROYCE-Cont.
    Hosmer bp 1600-1654
      X 78; XII 41; XIII 40, 117; XV
      25; XVII 108; XXIII 60; XXIV 7;
      XXVI 168; XXX 74; XXXI 174;
      XXXIII 154; XXXVI 119;
      XXXVIII 205; XXXIX 153
CT **ROBERT ROYCE** 1594-a 1676
    m 1624/34 **Mary Sims** ....-1697
      XVI 134; XVIII 75; XX 135
VA **THOMAS** ....-....
    m .... **Marie/Maree** ____ ....-....
      XXXII 275; XXXIII 157;
      XXXIV 286; XXXVII 170

RICH
NH **RICHARD** 1633-1692
    m a 1671
    Sarah Roberts ....-a 1692
      XXIV 23; XXVI 35; XXX 114;
      XXXVII 133

RICHARDS
MA **HUMPHREY** ....-.... m ....
    Mehitable Ruggles bp 1650-....
      XXVII 211
PA **LEWIS** ....-....
    m .... ____ ____ ....-....
      XXXII 289

RICHARDSON
MA/CT **AMOS** p 1618/23-1683
    m c 1642
    Mary (Smith?) ....-c 1683
      XXXII 97; XXXIII 143; XXXVI
      310
MA **EZEKIEL** 1602-1647 m a 1630
    Susannah Richardson ....-1681
      XVII 53; XXXI 250; XXXIII 276
MA **JOHN** ....-....
    m .... **Hannah Tryer** ....-....
      XXX 91; XXXVI 242
MD **LAWRENCE, I** c 1606-1666

    m .... **Sarah** ____ ....-.....
      XXXI 164
MD **ROBERT** 1650-1682
    m .... **Susanna** ____ ....-....
      I 38
MA **SAMUEL** bp 1602/10-1657/58
    m 1618/38
    Joanna ____ bp 1638-w 1666/wp
    1677
      XVIII 133; XIX 70; XXVII 165;
      XXIX 306; XXXI 163; XXXV
      58; XXXX 94, 405
PA **SAMUEL** 1635-1719 m ....
    Ellinor/Eleanor ____ ....-1703
      XII 52; XXVI 30
MA **THOMAS** 1608-1651
    m2) c 1635 **Mary** ____ ....-1670
      V 114; VI 5/6; X 35, 224; XIX
      152; XX 124; XXIX 24
VA **THOMAS** by 1645-wp 1718/19
    m a 1668
    Elizabeth (Valentine?) ....-
    p 1719
      XXVIII 70; XXXIII 74
MA **WILLIAM** c 1620-1657
    m 1654 **Elizabeth Wiseman** ....-
    ....
      V 57; VI 72/84; IX 29; X 195

RICHEY/RETYE
PA **JOHN RETYE** 1655/60-1685
    m .... ____ ____ ....-....
      XXV 73

RICHMOND
RI **EDWARD** 1632-1696
    m1) .... **Abigail Davis** 1635-1675
      XXXIV 328; XXXX 20
MA **JOHN, Sr** c 1594-1664
    m c 1626
    ____ ____ ....-a 1663
      X 111; XVII 34, 78; XXI 141;
      XXV 190; XXX 213; XXXI 264;

RICHMOND-Cont.
XXXX 20

RICKER/RICCAR
NH **GEORGE** ....-1706
    m .... **Eleanor Evans** ....-....
    XXIX 273

RIDDICK
VA **JAMES** ....-1722 m 1689
    Mrs. Shepherd (wid.) ....-....
    XXX 147

RIDGELY
MD **HENRY** ....-1710 m ....
    Sarah Warner ....-a 1696
    XXVII 99
MD **WILLIAM, Sr** 1645-1716
    m .... **Elizabeth** ____ ....-c 1716
    XXVI 267; XXIX 330

RIDGWAY
PA/NJ **RICHARD** c 1650-1722/23
    m1) c 1673 **Elizabeth**
    Chamberlain c 1655-1692
    XXV 236

RIGGS
MA **EDWARD, I** c 1590-wp 1670
    m1) .... **Elizabeth Rooke** ....-1635
    m2) 1635 **Elizabeth** ____ ....-
    1669
    VI 97/115; XVIII 86; XXIII 7;
    XXXII 134; XXXIII 263; XXXV
    17, 48
CT/NJ **EDWARD, Jr** c 1614-
    1664/68 m 1635
    Elizabeth Roosa ....-a 1665/
    p 1667
    VI 97/115; XVIII 86; XXXII 134;
    XXXIII 263; XXXV 17, 48
MA **THOMAS, Sr** 1631-1721/22
    m1) 1658 **Mary Millet** 1639-

1695
XXXIV 288

RING
MA **ANDREW** c 1618-1692/93
    m 1646
    Deborah Hopkins c 1624/25-
    a 1674
    XXXX 191
PA **NATHANIEL** ....-1714
    m .... **Elizabeth** ____ ....-....
    XXVI 146
MA **ROBERT** 1614-1690
    m .... **Elizabeth** ____ ....-....
    XXI 32

RINGO
NY **PHILIP JANSZEN** c 1615/20-
    1662 m 1647/49
    Geertje Cornelis (wid.) ...-1680
    XXV 76; XXXIX 331

RISLEY
CT **RICHARD, I** a 1615-1648
    m 1640 **Mary** ____ ....-a 1680
    X 227; XVI 83; XXV 65

RISING
MA/CT **JAMES, I** 1617-1688
    m 1657
    Elizabeth Hinsdale/Ensdell
    c 1637/38-1669
    XXXV 317, 318; XXXVII 370

ROBBINS/ROBINS
CT **JOHN ROBINS** ....-1660
    m 1640 **Mary Welles** ....-1659
    V 71; XII 118; XXV 103
MA **NATHANIEL** 1648-1719
    m .... **Mary Brazier** ....-....
    XXXV 287, 346; XXXVII 185
VA **OBEDIENCE ROBINS** 1600-
    1662 m 1628/34

ROBBINS/ROBINS-Cont.
    Grace O'Neill (Waters) 1603-
    1682
    XXX 254; XXXI 40, 60; XXXVI
    232; XXXVII 74
MA **RICHARD** 1610-p 1683
    m 1639 **Rebecca** _____ ....-....
    XX 7; XXI 56
MA **WILLIAM** ....-1725 m 1680
    Priscilla Gowing ....-1745
    XIX 17

ROBERT, see ROBERTS

ROBERTS/ROBERT
PA **JOHN** 1648-1742 m 1684
    Gainor Roberts 1662-1722
    XXIV 82
CT **JOHN** c 1660-1721 m 1683
    Sarah Blake 1665-1737
    XXIV 216, 217; XXIX 109
SC **PIERRE ROBERT** 1655/56-
    1715 m 1674
    Jeanne Braye/Brayer 1657-1717
    XXXVI 337; XXXIX 309, 319
CT **SAMUEL** ....-.... m a 1681
    Sarah Hinman 1653-....
    XXIX 118
CT **SAMUEL** c 1664-1739/40
    m 1691 **Mercy Blake** 1673-
    1739/40
    XXXVIII 28
NH **THOMAS** 1600-1673
    m .... **Rebecca** _____ ....-...
    XXXX 214, 298

ROBERTSON
MA/NJ **JOHN** ....-1705 m ....
    Jennelle Coulter/Cutter? ....-....
    XXXI 321

ROBESON, see ROBINSON

ROBIE/ROBY
MA/NH **HENRY ROBY** 1618/19-
    1688 m1) c 1643
    Ruth Moore ....-1673
    XXXII 115; XXXIII 113; XXXV
    191; XXXVII 33

ROBINS, see ROBBINS

ROBINSON/ROBESON
NJ **ANDREW ROBESON, Jr** 1654-
    1719/20 m c 1685
    Mary Spencer 1666-1716
    XXXII 113; XXXV 212; XXXVI
    81; XXXVII 207; XXXIX 8
VA **CHRISTOPHER** ....-a 1662
    m .... **Frances** _____ ....-....
    XXXVIII 171
MA **GEORGE** ....-1699 m 1651
    Johanna Ingraham ....-1699
    XXVII 109; XXXVIII 17
MA **ISAAC** 1610-c 1704
    m1) 1636 **Margaret Hanford**
    c 1619-1649
    m2) 1650 **Mary Faunce** ....-....
    XIX 115; XXX 89; XXXIII 143;
    XXXIV 324; XXXV 135
MA **JOHN** c 1616-1675
    m .... **Elizabeth** _____ ....-....
    XXXVI 54
MA **JOHN, I** bp 1611/12-1675
    m c 1640
    Elizabeth Trickley c 1623-....
    XXXX 84
VA **JOHN** ....-1688
    m .... **Elizabeth Potter** ....-1691
    XXI 84
MA **THOMAS** ....-1665 m 1652
    Mary (Cogan) Woody ....-1661
    XXXX 255
MA **WILLIAM** ....-1668 m1) ....
    Margaret _____ ....- liv. 1664
    X 46; XVIII 80; XIX 13

ROBINSON/ROBESON-Cont.
MA **WILLIAM** 1640-1693 m 1667
    Elizabeth Cutter 1645-p 1682
    XI 115; XXIX 358; XXXVIII 148

ROBY, see ROBIE

ROCKWELL
CT **JOHN, Sr** ....-1676
    m .... **Elizabeth Weed** ....-....
    XIX 141; XXV 261; XXVII 224;
    XXXIII 220
CT **JOHN, Jr** ....-inv. 1673/4
    m .... _____ _____ ....-....
    XXXIV 117
MA **WILLIAM** 1591/95-1640
    m 1624
    Susannah Capen/Chapin 1602-
    1666
    VII 30; XVIII 48; XXXII 242;
    XXXIV 187; XXXV 128, 329;
    XXXVI 18; XXXVII 110

ROCKWOOD
MA **RICHARD** ....-1660
    m .... **Agnes Bicknell** ....-1643
    XV 87

ROE, see ROWE

ROEBUCK
MD **ROBERT** ....-1709
    m .... _____ _____ ....-....
    XXXVII 98

ROGERS
VA **GILES** 1643-1730
    m a 1673 _____ **Iverson** ....-....
    XXXII 206
CT **JAMES** c 1600/15-1687/88
    m c 1640
    Elizabeth Stebbins Rowland
    1601-1699/1709

    X 21, 34; XVII 40; XIX 12
MA **JOHN** ....-1674
    m .... _____ _____ ....-....
    XXX 243
MA **JOHN** 1654-....
    m2) 1679 **Dinah Chiske** ....-....
    XIII 111
MA **NATHANIEL** c 1598-1655
    m .... **Margaret Crane** c 1610-
    1675
    XVI 89; XXVII 131; XXXI 122
MA **ROBERT** 1617-1663 m a 1647
    Susannah _____ 1627-1677
    XXXX 267
MA **THOMAS** c 1586/87-1621
    m .... _____ _____ ....-....
    XXIX 396; XXX 164
NY **WILLIAM** c 1600-1658
    m .... **Anne** _____ 1601-1669
    X 243

ROLFE
MA **HENRY** 1585-1642
    m 1621 **Honor Rolfe** ....-1650
    XVIII 17; XXIX 207; XXXI 100

ROLINGS, see RAWLINGS
ROLLINS, see RAWLINGS

ROMEYN
NY **CLAES JANSEN** ....-a 1730
    m 1680
    Styntje Albertse Terhune ....-....
    XXIV 172

ROOD/RUDE
CT **THOMAS** c 1626-1672/78
    m 1647 **Sarah** _____ ....-1668
    XXIX 254; XXXIII 150;
    XXXVIII 265

ROOSA
NY **ALBERT HEYMANS** ....-1679

ROOSA-Cont.
  m .... **Wyntje Allard** ....-....
  XXX 142

ROOSEVELT, see ROSEVELT

ROOT/ROOTE/ROOTES/ROOTS
CT **JOHN ROOTE, Sr** 1608-
  1664/84
  m1) c 1640 **Mary Kilbourne**
  1619-1697
  XII 71; XIII 119; XXX 134;
  XXXVII 37; XXXIX 12
MA **JOSIAH** ....-w 1683
  m .... **Susannah** ____ ....-....
  XVIII 100; XXVI 134
CT/MA **THOMAS** 1605-1694
  m1) a 1637 **Ann Russell** ....-....
  m2) .... **Elizabeth** ____ ....-....
  XXIV 119; XXIX 40; XXXII
  238; XXXVII 97

ROOTE, see ROOT
ROOTES, see ROOT
ROOTS, see ROOT

ROPER
MA **JOHN, Sr** 1588-p 1664
  m a 1611 **Alles** ____ ....-p 1676
  XXXI 59; XXXVI 178
VA **JOHN, Sr** c 1640-p 1690
  m c 1660 ____ ____ ....-....
  XXXVII 258
VA **WILLIAM** 1606-1670
  m 1643 **Cathrine** ____ ....-....
  XXVIII 66

ROSE
CT **ROBERT** 1594-1664/65
  m1) 1618/19 **Marjorie/Margery**
  ____ 1594-1677
  XVII 57; XXXII 121; XXXIV 90;
  XXXV 236; XXXVI 307

VA **WILLIAM** c 1622-?1671/72
  m c 1650 **Anne** ____ ....-....
  XXXX 189

ROSENKRANS
NY **HERMAN HENDRICK** ....-
  1697 m 1657
  Magdalena (Dircks) Capes ....-
  1697/1703
  XIV 44; XVI 51; XXXVIII 335

**ROSEVELT/ROOSEVELT/VAN
ROSENVELT**
NY **CLAES MARTENSZEN VAN
ROSENVELT** ....-.... m ....
  Jannetje Samuels-Thomas ....-
  ....
  XXV 50

ROSS
CT/NY/NJ **GEORGE** 1635-1702
  m .... **Constance Little** ....-....
  XX 25
MA **JAMES** c 1635-1690 m 1658
  Mary Goodenow 1640-....
  XXXVIII 145; XXXIX 292;
  XXXX 70
RI **WILLIAM** ....-1712
  m .... **Hannah** ____ ....-....
  XVII 41

ROSSITER
MA **EDWARD** ....-1630
  m .... ____ ____ ....-....
  XXV 191

ROUNDS
MA/ME **MARK** ....-wp 1729
  m (int.) 1696
  Sarah Larreford ....-....
  XXXIII 258

ROUNDY
MA **ROBERT** 1656-1715 m 1678
Deborah Plumb 1657-1740
XXXI 216

ROWE/ROE
NY **DAVID** ....-a 1707
m .... **Mary** _____ ....-p 1698
XXIX 32
MA **HUGH ROE** c 1618-1689
m .... **Abigail** _____ c 1620-1689
XXXI 310
NY **JOHN ROE** 1628-1711
m1) c 1655/69 **Hannah**
Purrer/Purrier ....-....
m2) .... **Alice** _____ ....-a 1712
XV 22; XXII 6; XXXVIII 272

ROWELL
MA **THOMAS** ....-1662
m1) .... _____ _____ ....-1649
XXV 279

ROWLAND
CT **HENRY** ....-1691
m .... **Rebecca** _____ ....-....
XIV 78
PA/DE **SAMUEL, ESQ** ...-w 1727
m .... _____ _____ .....-....
XXI 84

ROWLEY
MA **HENRY** ....-1673
m .... **Sarah Palmer** ....-a 1632
XXXVII 299, 344
CT **THOMAS** ....-1708 m 1669
Mary Denslow 1651-1739
XXIX 94

ROWND
MD **WILLIAM** c 1662-wp 1718/19
m .... **Mary Wood** ....-....
XXXIX 334

RUDD
CT **JONATHAN** c 1625-1658/88
m c 1646/47 _____ _____ ....-....
XXXIV 315; XXXV 91; XXXX
428

RUDE, see ROOD

RUE/LA RUE
NY **MATTHEW LA RUE** ....-
a 1722 m .... _____ _____ ....-....
XXXVII 273

RUFFIN
VA **WILLIAM** ....-1677
m .... _____ _____ ....-....
XXXII 130

RUGG
MA **JOHN** a 1634-1696/97
m2) 1660 **Hannah Prescott**
1639-1696
XIV 79; XXXII 246

RUGGLES
MA **JOHN** c 1590/91-1663
m1) .... **Barbara** _____ c 1605-
1638
XIV 58
MA **THOMAS** ....-1658
m 1620 **Mary Curtis** 1589-1675
XXX 103

RUNDLET, see RANLET

RUSH
VA **WILLIAM, I** ....-1708
m 1650 **Ann Gray** ....-....
XXX 188

RUSS
MA **JOHN, I** 1611/12-1691/92
m 1638 **Margaret** _____ 1620/21-

RUSS-Cont.
1687/89
XXIX 140; XXXIII 329; XXXVI
345; XXXVII 272

RUSSELL
MA **GEORGE** c 1595-....
    m .... ____ ____ ....-....
    XXIX 169
MA **JOHN** 1595/97-1680
    m1) .... ____ ____ ....-....
    XXXVIII 367; XXXX 281
MA **JOHN** 1608-1694/95
    m .... **Dorothy** ____ ....-....
    XIV 82; XXXIII 343
MA **ROBERT** 1630-1710 m 1659
    Mary Marshall c 1642-1716
    XXII 85
MA **WILLIAM** ....-1661-62
    m a 1640 **Martha** ____ ....-
    c 1694
    XV 99; XIX 23; XXIV 72; XXXI
    228; XXXIII 161; XXXVII 14
CT **WILLIAM** bp 1612-1664/65
    m 1644 **Sarah Davis** ....-1664
    XXIX 314; XXXVII 263

RUST
MA **HENRY** ....-1684/85
    m a 1638 **Hannah** ____ ....-....
    IX 8; XI 82, 83, 93
VA **WILLIAM** c 1634-wp 1699
    m a 1662 **Anne Metcalf** ....-
    a 1697
    XXXIV 207

RUTHERFORD
VA **ROBERT, Sr** bp 1640-p 1728
    m .... **Margaret Vawter** 1647-
    1735
    XXXVI 258

RUTTY
CT **EDWARD** ....-1714 m 1678
    Rebecca Stevens ....-1737
    XVI 19

RYDER/RIDAR/RIDER
MA **SAMUEL** 1601-1679
    m .... **Ann/e** ____ .... -1695
    XXXII 141; XXXIX 299
MA/NY **THOMAS** a 1614-1699
    m .... **Elizabeth Lane** a 1634-
    1650
    XI 104; XIII 10

SACKETT
MA/RI/CT **JOHN** ....-....
    m .... ____ ____ ....-....
    XXXVII 59
CT **JOHN, Jr** c 1628-1684
    m 1652 **Agnes Tinkham** ....-1707
    XXX 269
MA **SIMON** 1602-p 1635
    m a 1630 **Isabel** ____ ....-p 1636
    XIII 35; XXVI 303; XXXVI 264;
    XXXIX 142

SAFFORD
MA **THOMAS** ....-1666/67 m ....
    Elizabeth Sutton ....-1670/71
    XI 95, 96; XVII 123; XXVIII 30;
    XXXVI 40

SAGE
CT **DAVID** c 1639-1703
    m1) 1664 **Elizabeth Kirby**
    1646-1670
    XXIV 155; XXXI 56, 297;
    XXXX 196

ST. JOHN/SENSION/SENTION
CT **MATTHIAS**
SENSION/SENTION ....-1669
    m .... ____ ____ ....-p 1669

ST. JOHN/SENSION/SENTION-
Cont.
>XI 145; XXI 97; XXXII 119;
>XXXV 316; XXXIX 264

SALISBURY
MA **WILLIAM, Sr** 1622-1675
>m .... **Susannah** ____ ....-p 1677
>VI 95/113; XXXVII 39

SALTONSBALL
MA **RICHARD** 1586-.....
>m .... **Grace Kaye** ....-....
>IX 8

SAMBORNE, see SANBORN

SAMMIS
CT/NY **JOHN** c 1648-c 1693/94
>m1) 1670/72 **Abigail Corey**
>c 1648-1685
>XXIX 259; XXX 30
CT **RICHARD** ....-1650
>m .... **Esther Horsford** ....-....
>XXIX 259

SAMS
VA **JOHN** c 1630-1727
>m .... ____ ____ ....-....
>XXV 186

SAMPSON
MA **ABRAHAM** c 1600/14-1701
>m 1639 Esther Nash ....-....
>XXXV 76; XXXVI 97; XXXIX
>293

SAMSON
MA **JOHN** 1627-1711/12
>m1) .... ____ ____ ....-....
>XXXIII 352

SANBORN/SAMBORNE
NH **JOHN, Jr** 1620-1692
>m1) c 1647 **Mary Tuck** ....-1668
>XI 16; XVIII 45; XXX 87;
>XXXII 43; XXXIII 71; XXXV
>61, 123; XXXVI 113; XXXVII
>304; XXXIX 139, 197
NH **WILLIAM** c 1622-c 1692
>m .... **Mary Moulton** 1624-1686
>XXVI 131; XXX 70; XXXIV 143

SANDERS, see SAUNDERS

SANFORD
MA/RI **JOHN** c 1605-1653/55
>m 1631
>**Elizabeth Webb** ....-1635/36
>XXXVIII 65
CT **ROBERT** 1615-1676
>m 1643 **Ann Adams** ...-a 1682
>XXIV 119; XXXX 113, 450
MA/CT **THOMAS, Sr** c 1607/08-
>1681
>m1) .... **Dorothy Meadows** ....-....
>m2) 1636/37 **Sarah** ____ a 1614-
>1681
>IV 148; XI 124; XIII 120; XIX
>129, 139; XX 74; XXIII 33;
>XXIV 93; XXV 260; XXVI 117;
>XXVII 68; XXX 108; XXXI 31,
>63, 157; XXXIII 63; XXXIV 82;
>XXXVI 56, 109

SARES, see SEARS

SARGENT
MA **WILLIAM** c 1602/06-c 1675
>m2) c 1633/34 **Elizabeth Perkins**
>bp 1609-a 1670
>XXI 146; XXVI 139; XXXIII
>134; XXXV 313; XXXVI 274,
>286; XXXVII 152
MA **WILLIAM** c 1622/24-1717

SARGENT-Cont.
m4) 1651 **Abigail Clark** c 1632-
1711
XIII 27; XXXVIII 20

SATTERLEE
CT **BENEDICT** ....-....
m 1682 **Rebecca Dymond** ....-....
XXX 245

SAUNDERS/SANDERS
VA **EDWARD** 1625-1672 m ....
Elizabeth Webb Hudnall
c 1630-1683/84
XII 55; XXXIII 236
VA **JAMES SANDERS** a 1650/58-
1717 m 1698
Sarah Shrimpshire ....-1716
XXXIV 286; XXXVI 107, 219;
XXXVII 102; XXXVIII 154
MA **JOHN** bp 1613-1643
m .... **Priscilla Grafton** ....-....
IV 91
RI **TOBIAS** ....-1695
m 1661 **Mary Clarke** ....-1695
XXXVII 71

SAVAGE
VA **GRIFFIN/GRIFFITH, I** ....-
1685
m .... **Bridget** _____ ....-....
XXXII 168
CT **JOHN** ....-1684/85 m 1652
Elizabeth Dubbin/D'Aubin
....-....
XXXVI 153
VA **THOMAS** c 1592/94-a 1633/35
m c 1621 **Hannah Tyng** ....-
a 1641
XXVIII 189; XXXIII 103
MA **THOMAS** 1606-1681 m ....
Faith Hutchinson ....-1651
VIII 14

SAWIN
MA **JOHN** ....-1690 m c 1652
Abigail Munning c 1627-p 1667
XXXVII 213; XXXVIII 43

SAWTELL/SARTELL
MA **RICHARD** 1604/11-1694
m 1627/28
Elizabeth Post/Pople ....-1694
XXII 66; XXIX 187; XXX 263;
XXXIX 56

SAWYER
MA **JOHN S.** ....-....
m .... _____ _____ ....-....
XXXX 246
MA **THOMAS** c 1615/23-1706
m 1648
Marie/Mary Prescott 1630/31-
1717/a 20
I 30; XXX 163; XXXI 253;
XXXIX 107; XXXX 282
MA **WILLIAM** 1613-1705
m .... **Ruth Bitfield** ....-p 1705
XXXII 39

SAXTON
MA **JAMES** 1660-1741
m2) 1701 **Anna Bancroft** 1662-
1733
XXXV 186

SAYERS, see SAYRE

SAYLES
RI **JOHN** 1633-1681 m 1650/52
Mary Williams 1638-1681
X 258, 279 292; XXVI 287;
XXIX 139

SAYRE/SAYERS
NY **THOMAS** bp 1597-1670
m ....

SAYRE/SAYERS-Cont.
Margaret Aldrich ...-1652/69
X 152, 161; XXVI 114; XXXI
166; XXXII 266; XXXX 400

SCARBOROUGH, see
SCARBURGH

SCARBURGH/SCARBOROUGH
VA **EDMUND** 1584-1634
m 1615 **Hannah Butler** ....-....
XXXVIII 37

SCENTER, see **SENTER**

SCHAMP
NY **PIETER** 1636-c 1690/93
m 1674 **Jannetje Dircks**
bp 1653-....
XXXV 141

SCHELLENGER
NY **JACOBUS** a 1626-1693 m 1653
Cornelia Melyn Loper 1628/29-
1717
XXV 27, 244

SCHENK
NY **REOLOF MARTENSE**
1619/20-1704/05 m 1660
**Neeltje Van
Couwenhoven/Conover**
bp 1641-1672/75
XXII 46; XXXIX 212

SCHERMERHORN
NY **JACOB JANSEN** 1622-1688
m 1650 **Jannetje
Edgmont/Egmont** 1633-1700
XII 121; XIX 126; XX 105;
XXIX 123

SCHOFIELD
MA **RICHARD** c 1613-c 1670
m .... **Mary** _____ ....-....
XX 126

SCHOL, see **SCULL**
SCHOLL, see **SCULL**

SCHOONMAKER
NY **HENDRICK JOECHEMSEN**
a 1655-a 1682
**Elsie Jans (von Breestede)
Peterson** (wid.) ....-....
IV 150; V 91, 96; XXXI 106

SCOFIELD
CT **DANIEL** c 1595-wp 1670
m .... **Mary Youngs** ....-....
XXIX 346; XXX 13, 65; XXXI
226; XXXIII 42

SCOTT
MA **EDMUND, Sr** 1625-1690/91
m1) 1646 **Hannah Bird** ....-
a 1672
m2) .... **Elizabeth (Fuller) Upson**
(wid.) ....-....
IV 159; V 49; XXX 20
VA **JOHN** ....-1729
m .... **Judith** _____ ....-....
XXXVII 55; XXXVIII 61
MA **RICHARD** 1605-1680 m 1632
Catharine Marbury 1617-1687
XXXII 142
VA **THOMAS** ....-wp 1678/79
m .... _____ _____ ....-....
XXV 233

SCOVELL
CT **JOHN, I** c 1635-1696/1700
m 1666 **Sarah Barnes** ....-c 1712
XXI 122; XXXIX 195

SEARS/SARES
MA **RICHARD SARES** c 1590-
1676 m 1632/35
Dorothy Thatcher Jones c 1603-
1678/79
V 66; X 294; XV 124; XVII 22;
XIX 90; XXI 133; XXVI 43;
XXVII 22; XXX 145; XXXVII
301; XXXVIII 213; XXXX 68
(incomplete)

SEAVER
MA **ROBERT** 1608-1683
m 1634 **Elizabeth Ballard** ....-
1657
XXVI 113; XXXVII 89

SEAVEY/SEAVY/ZEVIE
NH **THOMAS ZEVIE** c 1627-
1707/08 m a 1667
Tamsen ____ c 1641-p 1711
XXXVII 264; XXXVIII 18
NH **WILLIAM, I** bp 1601-c 1688
m .... **Mary** ____ ....-....
XXXIV 222; XXXV 36, 238;
XXXVI 79; XXXVIII 103

SEBRING, see SEBURN

SEBURN/SEBRING
NY **JAN ROELOFSE SEBRING**
c 1631-p 1703 m ....
Adrianna Polhemius c 1644-
p 1685
XXXVI 165; XXXVII 189

SECORD/SICARD
NY **AMBROSE SICARD** 1630/31-
c 1701 m 166_
Jennie Serot ....-1701
XX 162

SEDGWICK
MA **ROBERT** bp 1600/11-1656/73
m c 1628
Joanna/Johanna Blake ....-
p 1667
VI 38/43; VII 17; X 235; XIV 13;
XXXIV 234

SEE/DU CIE
NY **ISAAC DU CIE** 1615-....
m .... **Esther** ____ ....-....
XXXV 330

SEELEY/SEELY/SEELYE
CT **OBADIAH SEELY** ....-1657
m 1648 **Mrs. Mary Miller** ....-....
XXIX 243
MA/CT/NY/NJ **ROBERT** c 1600/01-
est. adm. 1668
m1) 1626 **Mary Mason** ....-1630
m2) 1648 **Mary Walker** ....-....
XI 74; XVIII 33, 74; XXIV 170;
XXIX 98; XXXIII 279

SEELY, see SEELEY
SEELYE, see SEELEY
SEIMAN, see SIMON

SELDEN
CT **THOMAS** bp 1600/20-a 1655
m 1643/44
Hester Wakeman bp 1617-
c 1693
V 87; VI 59/66; XIII 61; XIV 86;
XX 157; XXXVI 266

SELLECK
MA **DAVID** bp 1614-1654
m 1636 **Susanna Kibby** c 1622-
....
XXX 195; XXXVII 229; XXXIX
181; XXXX 329

SELLERS
PA **SAMUEL** bp 1655-1732 m 1684
   Anna Gibbons ....-1742/43
   X 226

SELLMAN
MD **JOHN** ....-1707 m ....
   Elizabeth _____ ....-1728/29
   XXX 186

SEMMES, see SIMMS
SENIX, see SINEXON
SENSION, see ST. JOHN

SENTER/SCENTER
MA **JOHN SCENTER** ....-1700
   m1) a 1666 **Sarah Weeden**
   bp 1666-a 1685
   XX 164

SENTION, see ST. JOHN
SERVAES, see VLERMOME

SESSIONS
MA **SAMUEL** ....-....
   m .... _____ _____ ....-....
   XXII 140

SETH
MD **JACOBUS/JACOB** 1665-1697
   m 1676
   Barbara Beckwith 1656-a 1697
   XXXI 37

SETTLE
VA **JOHN** 1654-1667
   m .... **Elizabeth** _____ ....-....
   XIX 56

SEWALL
MD **HENRY** c 1625-wd 1664
   m c 1654 **Jane Lowe** 1635-1700
   XXXVIII 291

SEWARD
NY **OBADIAH** ....-....
   m .... **Ann Biggs (Dinah)** ....-....
   XXXI 26
MA/CT **WILLIAM** 1627-1689
   m 1651 **Grace Norton** 1632-
   1702
   XI 59; XII 69; XXXV 94

SEXTON
MA **GEORGE** c 1618-1685/90
   m .... **Katherine** _____ ....-1689
   IX 48; XXVII 71

SEYMOUR/SEAMER
CT **RICHARD SEAMER**
   bp 1604/05-c 1655
   m c 1631 **Mary/Mercy**
   Muscoe/Ruscoe/Rashleigh
   c 1610-p 1656/65
   III 28; IV 76; IX 24; X 55; XV
   56; XXI 50; XXIV 12; XXV 212;
   XXXIII 193; XXXX 317, 350

SHACKELFORD
VA **ROGER** bp 1629-p 1704
   m c 1658 **Mary Palmer** ....-....
   XXX 268; XXXIII 231; XXXIV
   202

SHACKFORD
NH **WILLIAM** c 1640-1720
   m c 1673 **Deborah** _____ c 1646-
   1720
   XXIV 94

SHALER
CT **THOMAS** ....-1692
   m1) .... **Marah** _____ ....-....
   m2) .... **Alice (Spencer) Brooks**
   ....-....
   XXIX 183; XXXVI 224

SHAPLEIGH
MA/ME **ALEXANDER** 1585-a 1650
   m1) .... **Marguerite Bloedel** ....-
   ....
XXVII 38

SHARPE
MA **ROBERT** ....-1653
   m .... _____ _____ ....-....
   XIV 23

SHARPLESS
PA **GEOFFREY** ....-....
   m .... **Margaret Ashley** ....-....
   XXXV 47

SHATTUCK
MA **WILLIAM** 1621/22-a 1672
   m c 1642
   Susanna _____ a 1625-1686
   V 101, 102; VI 48/54, 85/98;
   XXXIX 59

SHAW
MA **ABRAHAM** 1589/90-1638
   m 1616
   (Elizabeth) Bridget Best
   bp 1592-c 1635/36
   XII 40; XV 129; XXXV 200;
   XXXVIII 157, 225; XXXX 366
NY **RICHARD** ....-p 1671 m c 1659
   Temperance Garlick ....-....
   XXX 241
MA/NH **ROGER** 1594-1661
   m1) ....**Ann** _____ ....-....
   XXV 34; XXX 153

SHEAFE
MA/NH **SAMPSON** 1650-1724
   m .... **Mehitable Webb Sheafe**
   1656- ....
   II 41

SHED, see SHEDD

SHEDD/SHED
MA **DANIEL SHED** 1620-1708
   m2) 1659 **Elizabeth** _____ ....-....
   XXXIII 125

SHELDON
MA/CT **ISAAC** c 1629-1708
   m1) 1653 **Mary Woodford** 1636-
   1684
   m2) c 1685/86 **Mehetabel**
   (Gunn) Ensign 1644-1720
   VIII 9; XI 46; XXXI 221;
   XXXIII 98; XXXIV 292;
   XXXVII 285; XXXVIII 153;
   XXXIX 66
RI **JOHN** 1629-w 1706
   m 1662 **Sara Palmer** ....-....
   XXXV 116
RI **JOHN** 1630-1708
   m 1660 **Joanna Vincent** ....-....
   XXVI 34
MA **WILLIAM** 1597-....
   m c 1618 **Mary Clarke** ....-....
   XXIX 83

SHEPARD, see SHEPPARD

SHEPPARD/SHEPARD
MA **EDWARD SHEPARD** bp 1596-
   1679/80
   m1) 1620 **Violet**
   Charnold/Wolterton bp 1596-
   1648
   XXXI 197; XXXX 269, 315, 390
NJ **JOHN** a 1665-c 1710
   m .... _____ _____ ....-....
   XXX 161
MA **JOHN SHEPARD** 1673-1756
   m1) 1703 **Elizabeth Woodruff**
   1669/79-1731
   XIV 17, 37; XXXVI 221

SHEPPARD/SHEPARD-Cont.
MA **RALPH** 1603/06-1693 m ....
   Thanks/Thankslord/Thank Ye
   Lord c 1612-1666/81
   II 33; XXXVII 17; XXXIX 61
VA **ROBERT** ....-.... m ....
   Elizabeth Cockersham ....- ....
   XXVI 192; XXXIV 116

SHEPHERD
VA **JOHN** .... -1683 m ....
   Frances Robinson ....-....
   XXXVI 239

SHERARD
VA **JOHN** c 1630-a 1706 m c 1651
   Elizabeth _____ ....-....
   XXIX 338

SHERBURNE
NH **HENRY** 1612-1680 m 1637
   Rebecca Gibbons ....-1667
   XXXIV 304

SHERIFF, see SHREVE

SHERMAN
MA/CT **EDMUND/EDMOND**
   c 1572/85-1641
   m .... **Joan Makin** 1611-....
   XIII 15; XXX 194; XXXIII 11;
   XXXVIII 362
MA **JOHN** bp 1613-1691 m c 1637
   Martha Palmer/Porter ....-1701
   IV 124; XXV 252; XXX 194
MA/RI **PHILIP** bp 1610-1687
   m c 1633 **Sarah**
   Odding/Codding ....-....
   XXXI 212; XXXIV 218; XXXV
   159, 254
CT **SAMUEL** 1618-1700
   m 1640 **Sarah Mitchell** 1621-....
   XX 81; XXXIII 11

MA **WILLIAM** ....-1679
   m 1638 **Prudence Hill** ....-a 1676
   XXVI 203, 204

SHERRILL
NY **SAMUEL** bp 1633/39-1719
   m a 1676/78
   Elizabeth Parsons c 1642-1722
   XI 63; XXIV 48; XXIX 363;
   XXXIX 311

SHERWIN
MA **JOHN** c 1644-1726 m 1691
   Mary Chandler 1659-1745
   XXXV 124, 157

SHERWOOD
MD **HUGH** 1632-1710
   m .... **Mary** _____ ....-....
   XV 38
MA/CT **THOMAS** c 1585/86-
   w 1655
   m1) .... **Alice Seabrook** 1586/87-
   c 1634/38
   m2) c 1640 **Mary Fitch** c 1619-
   1693/94
   V 77; XIII 29; XVII 35; XXI 170;
   XXII 67; XXVI 147; XXX 172,
   244
CT **THOMAS** 1624-1697/98
   m .... **Elizabeth Cable** ....-....
   XXXV 291

SHINN
NJ **JOHN** 1632-wp 1712
   m .... **Jane** _____ .....-1711
   X 97; XXXIV 204; XXXVIII 89

SHIPEE
RI **DAVID** c 1620-1718 m 1664
   Margaret Scranton c 1643-....
   XXVIII 39; XXXVI 103

SHIPLEY
MD **ADAM** ....-c 1696
    m by 1677 **Lois** _____ ....-....
    XXXIX 21

SHORTRIDGE
NH **RICHARD** c 1610-a 1636
    m .... _____ _____ ....-....
    IV 151, 152

SHREVE/SHERIFF
MA/RI **THOMAS SHERIFF**
    c 1620-1675 m a 1649
    Martha _____ ....-p 1691
    XIX 68; XXXIII 242; XXXIX
    252

SHUMWAY
MA **PETER, Sr** 1635-a 1695
    m a 1678 **Frances** _____ ....-
    a 1714
    VI 80/93; IX 53; X 175; XVIII
    57; XIX 31; XXXIII 91, 253;
    XXXX 333

SIBLEY
MA **JOHN** c 1597-1661
    m .... **Rachel Leach** ....-....
    XXXX 271
MA **JOHN** 1614-1661
    m2) 1639 **Rachel**
    Pickworth/Pickford 1646-1717
    V 79; XII 102; XVII 45, 76, 77;
    XXX 83; XXXIII 255

SICARD, see SECORD

SILL
MA **JOHN** ....-1653
    m .... **Joanna** _____ ....-1671
    XVII 81

SILLIMAN
CT **DANIEL** ....-1690
    m1) 1661 **Peaceable Eggleston**
    (wid.) ....-1667
    XXXI 55

SILSBY
MA **HENRY** bp 1613-1700
    m .... **Dorothy** _____ ....-1676
    XXXIV 75

SIMMONS/SIMONDS
MA **MOSES** ....-....
    m .... _____ _____ ....-....
    XXI 23
VA **WILLIAM** 1648-wp 1693/94
    m c 1675
    Elizabeth _____ c 1652-wp
    1696/97
    XXV 92; XXXI 87
MA **WILLIAM** 1612-1672 m 1643
    Judith Pippen Hayward 1617-
    1690
    XXXIX 250

SIMMS/SEMMES
MD **MARMADUKE SEMMES**
    by 1639-1692/93
    m c 1668 **Mrs. Fortuna**
    Metford/Mitford c 1642-1701
    XV 70; XXXX 188

SIMON/SEIMAN
PA **JAN/JOHN SEIMAN** c 1650-
    a 1685 m 1679
    Mercken Lucken a 1652/54-
    p 1717
    XXXIV 121

SIMONDS, see SIMMONS

SIMPSON/SYMPSON
MD **THOMAS SYMPSON** c 1640-

SIMPSON/SYMPSON-Cont.
   a 1699 m c 1662
   Elizabeth ____ c 1640-p 1705
   XXIX 254; XXXI 118

SINCLAIR/SINKLER
NH **JOHN** 1630-p 1699/1700
   m1) .... **Mary** ____ ....-....
   m2) a 1660 **Deborah** ____ ....-
   p 1700
   II 56, 57; VI 30/33; XIV 11;
   XXIX 36; XXXVII 68; XXXIX
   155

SINEX, see SINEXON

SINEXON/SINICKA/SINEX/
SINIE/SENIX
DE **ANDERS SINICKA** ....-....
   m .... **Margaret** ____ ....-....
   XXXIV 163

SINGLETARY
MA **RICHARD** 1585/88-1687
   m a 1639 **Susanna Cook** 1616-
   1682
   X 278

SINICKA, see SINEXON
SINIE, see SINEXON
SINKLER, see SINCLAIR

SINNICKSON
DE **ANDERS** c 1646-1700 m a 1682
   Sarah Gilljohnson ....-1718/19
   XXXX 149

SIPE, see SIPES

SIPES/SIPE
NJ **CLAAS ARIANSE SIPE** ....-
1691
   m1) 1656/57 **Grietje Warnants**

Van Schonevelt ....-....
   XXX 99

SIPPLE
VA **GARRETT** 1653-1718
   m 1674 **Mary Calvert** 1656-1698
   XXXII 169

SKIDMORE
CT **THOMAS** c 1605-1684
   m c 1626 **Ellen** ____ ....-....
   XXXVIII 27

SKIFF
MA **JAMES** 1610-p 1687
   m .... ____ ____ ....-....
   XXXI 298

SKILLMAN
NY **THOMAS** c 1635/40-1697/98
   m 1669/70 **Sarah Petit** ....-p 1699
   XXVI 277; XXIX 248

SKINNER
CT **JOHN** ....-1650
   m .... **Mary Loomis** 1620-1680
   XII 92; XV 64; XXVII 96
MA **THOMAS** 1617-1703/04
   m1) by 1645 **Mary (Pratt)?**
   Gooden ....-1671
   XXXVII 68; XXXVIII 77;
   XXXIX 199
VA/MD **THOMAS** ....-a 1675
   m1) .... **Elizabeth** ____ ....-a 1678
   XX 29; XXI 134

SLACK
MA **WILLIAM** 1659/60-1727
   m .... **Mary** ____ ....-....
   XIX 168

SLADE
RI/MA **WILLIAM** c 1638-....

SMITH/SMYTH-Cont.
CT **GEORGE** c 1620-1662
　m 1640/42
　　Sarah ____ ....-....
　　XVII 28; XVIII 42; XXXVII 350;
　　XXXIX 77, 301
CT **GILES** c 1603-1690
　m1) .... ____ ____ .....-....
　m2) .... **Eunice Porter** (wid.) ....-
　.....
　　XIII 17; XVII 51; XXX 291
CT **HENRY** 1588-1648
　m2) 1622/23 **Dorithy/Dorothy**
　?Cotton? 1590-1694
　　XXV 120; XXX 211; XXXIV 15;
　　XXXVII 117; XXXIX 274
MA **JAMES** ....-1676
　m .... **Joan** ____ ....-1659
　　XXXIII 292; XXXIV 144
ME **JAMES** ....a 1667
　m 1648 **Elizabeth** ____ ....-
　p 1688
　　XXXV 149
NJ **JAMES** c 1665-1727 m ....
　　Mary Baldwin Crane 1693-1727
　　XXXVI 95
NY **JASPER, Sr** a 1667/68-1769
　m a 1699 ____ ____ ....-a 1769
　　XXXIII 287
MA **JOHN** ....-.... m .... **Isabella**
　____ 1579-1639
　　XIV 26
CT **JOHN** ....-1684
　m 1642
　　Grace Hawley ...-1689/90
　　II 38; III 7, 15, 16, 31, 57; XIII
　　42; XV 24; XXIII 68; XXVI 291
MA **JOHN** ....-1727 m 1685
　　Mary Ellen Wood 1664-....
　　XIV 56
MA **JOHN** c 1622-1687 m 1647
　　Sarah Hunt ....-....
　　XXVIII 165

MA/RI **JOHN (the Miller)** 1595-
　1648 m1) .... **Alice** ____ ....-1650
　　XV 72; XXXII 279
MA **JOHN** ....-1676 m ....
　　Mary Partridge ....-....
　　XXXV 154
NY **JOHN "BLUE" SMITH** ....-
　p 1698
　m .... **Sarah Strickland** ....-....
　　XXXVII 330
MA **JOHN** c 1618-1692 m 1665/66
　　Ruhannah Kirby ....-1707
　　XXXX 416
CT **JOSEPH** 1636-1689/90
　m 1656 **Lydia Huit** ....-1711/12
　　III 10; XXVI 59; XXXI 177
MA **MATTHEW, I** ....-....
　m 1655 **Alice Loader** ....-....
　　XII 99
MD **MATTHEW** a 1661-wp 1715
　m 1671 **Elizabeth Thomas** ....-....
　　XXXI 99
MA **MATTHEW, I** c 1610-a 1681
　m .... ____ ____ ....-....
　　XXXX 10
MA/CT **NEHEMIAH** c 1605-1686
　m 1639/40
　　Sarah Ann Bourne c 1615-
　p 1684
　　X 302; XI 19; XII 33; XVII 160;
　　XVIII 8, 66; XXVIII 98
CT **NICHOLAS SEVER** ....-p 1681
　m 1666
　　Mary Tibbals bp 1644-....
　　XI 180
MA **RALPH SMYTH** c 1610/14-
　wp 1685
　m1) c 1638 **Elizabeth Hobart**
　c 1612-....
　m2) .... **Grace (　) Hatch** (wid.)
　....-p 1685
　　XXXI 66; XXXII 70; XXXIV
　　104, 262; XXXIX 151, 248;

SMITH/SMYTH-Cont.
XXXX 377
NY **RICHARD SMYTH** ....-1692/93
m .... **Sarah Folger** ....-1708
IV 78, 130; XV 9; XXXII 183;
XXXIV 115; XXXIX 43
MA **ROBERT** c 1623-1693
m c 1656 **Mary French** 1634-
1719
XIV 19; XXI 103; XXXII 157
NH **ROBERT** c 1611-1706
m .... **Susanna** ____ ....-1680
XXXVI 168, 345; XXXX 138
MA **SAMUEL** 1602-1680/81
m c 1624/33
Elizabeth Chileab c 1602-1686
I 38; XIII 56, 99; XVI 24; XVII
127; XVIII 34; XXII 29, 128;
XXXVI 320
VA **THOMAS** c 1612-w 1669
m .... ____ ____ ....-....
XXXVII 205
MA **THOMAS** ....-1666 m a 1639
Rebecca Stark/e ....-1670
XXXIV 322
SC **THOMAS LANDGRAVE** 1648-
1694
m1) a 1687 **Barbara Atkins** ....-
a 1687
XXIX 62; XXX 38; XXXV 241;
XXXVI 27; XXXIX 167
MA **THOMAS** c 1601-1692/93
m ....**Mary Knapp** ....-....
XIX 32; XXVI 102; XXXIX 35
NY **WILLIAM** ....-a 1670
m .... **Magdalen** ____ ....-p 1670
XXV 267
CT **WILLIAM** c 1669/70 m 1644
Elizabeth Stanley/Standly ....-
a 1678
III 4; XI 72; XV 21; XXXII 254
NY **WILLIAM (TANGIER)** 1655-
1704/05 m 1675

Martha Tunstall ....-1709
XXI 6
PA **WILLIAM** 1669-1743
m2) 1720 **Mercy** ____ ....-1743
XXXII 38; XXXX 262

SMOCK
NY **HENDRICK MATTHYSE** ....-
p 1708
m .... **Geertje Harmens** ....-1708
XXXII 82; XXXV 332

SMOOT/SMUTE
VA/MD **WILLIAM SMUTE**
1596/97-1670 m ....
Grace (____) Wood ....-1666
XXXI 38; XXXIII 199; XXXIV
28, 192

SMUTE, see SMOOT
SMYTH, see SMITH

SNEDEKER/SNEDEGER
NY **JAN SNEDEGER** ....-1689
m ....**Annetje Buys-Rys-Ryssen**
.... -c 1674
XXXVIII 184

SNELL
MA **THOMAS** 1625-1724/25
m c 1668
Martha Harris c 1650-p 1726
XXXII 200

SNOW
MA **NICHOLAS** ....-1676 m 1627
Constance Hopkins 1608-1677
X 47; XXIV 32; XXX 170
MA **WILLIAM** c 1621/24-
1699/1708 m ....
Rebecca Brown 1628/34-p 1699
XXIV 65; XXVIII 83

SNOWDEN
NJ **JOHN, Sr** 1632-1736
   m 1682/83 **Ann Barrett** ....-1688
   IV 144; V 53, 85

SNYDER
NY **JOHN W.** 1654-p 1681
   m .... **Elizabeth** _____ ....-....
   XIV 118

SOMERS
PA **JOHN** 1640-1723 m 1685
   Hannah Hodgkins 1667-1738
   XVIII 144

SOPER
NY **HENRY** ....-a 1699 m ....
   Sarah Wattleson/Simson ....-
   p 1699
   XXXII 269

SOULE
MA **GEORGE** c 1590-wd 1677/80
   m c 1623/27
   Mary Beckett ....-1676/77
   XXI 150; XXIV 48; XXX 184;
   XXXVI 235

SOOPLIS, see SUPPLEE

SOUTHARD
NY **THOMAS, I** c 1615/28-
   c 1688/90 m a 1653
   Annica Jansen c 1632-p 1698
   XIII 44; XXXIV 96, 275; XXXX
   48

SOUTHERLAND/SUTHERLAND
VA **ROBERT SUTHERLAND, I**
   c 1668-p 1722
   m c 1722 _____ _____ ....-....
   XXXIV 280; XXXV 70; XXXVII
   206

NJ/NY WILLIAM SUTHERLAND
   c 1664-a 1728 m c 1690
   Hannah Avery c 1668-....
   XXXVIII 12

SOUTHERNE
VA **JOHN** c 1600-....
   m .... _____ **Tucker** ....-....
   X 182, 215

SOUTHMAYD
MA **WILLIAM** 1607/15-1648
   m 1642
   Millicent Addis/Addez ....-1699
   XXXIV 134; XXXVI 151

SOUTHWORTH
MA **CONSTANT** 1615-1679
   m 1637
   Elizabeth Collier a 1633-....
   XI 149; XXX 33

SPACKMAN, see SPARKMAN
SPAFFORD, see SPOFFORD

SPALDING/SPAULDING
VA/MA **EDWARD SPAULDING**
   c 1600-1670
   m1) a 1633 **Margaret** _____ ....-
   1640
   m2) 1640/43 **Rachel** _____ ....-
   1670
   X 154; XIII 88, 93; XIV 54; XVI
   62, 120; XVII 96; XX 54; XXIV
   9; XXV 13, 78; XXIX 134;
   XXXIII 220; XXXVII 61;
   XXXIX 79

SPARHAWK
MA **NATHANIEL, Sr** c 1598-1647
   m .... **Mary Angier** ....-1643/44
   XVII 138; XXXVIII 355; XXXX
   369

SPARKMAN/SPACKMAN
VA **JOHN** c 1610/12-....
 m a 1635 **Dorothy** ____ ....-....
 XXXV 84, 182, 243

SPAULDING, see SPALDING

SPEAR/SPEARE/SPEERE
MA **GEORGE SPEERE** c 1613/23-
 1688
 m1) .... **Mary Heath** c 1627-1674
 XV 48; XXV 53; XXVII 30;
 XXIX 315; XXXIII 82, 133, 306

SPEARE, see SPEAR
SPEERE, see SPEAR

SPENCER
CT **GERRARD/JARED** bp 1614-
1685
 m1) 1636/37 **Hannah**
 Pratt/Sexton ....-p 1677/c 81
 m2) p 1677 **Rebecca (Porter)**
 Clark 1630-1682
 X 234; XI 99, 141; XXI 48; XXV
 126, 258; XXVIII 96; XXIX 133,
 287; XXXIV 29; XXXX 312
RI **JOHN** a 1646- c 1684
 m 1664/65
 Susannah Griffin ....-1719
 VII 45; XXIX 400; XXXIV 168;
 XXXVI 50
MA/CT **THOMAS** bp 1607-1687
 m1) c 1635 **Ann Derifield**
 c 1610-c 1644
 XVII 50; XXXV 148; XXXX 357
MA/CT **WILLIAM** bp 1601-
 wp 1641m c 1633
 Agnes (Haene) c 1613-a 1647
 IV 69; XXXIX 94
CT **WILLIAM** p 1653-a 1714
 m c 1686
 Sarah Ackley c 1661-a 1712

XXXX 42

SPERRY/SPEARY
CT **RICHARD** c 1618-c 1698
 m .... **Dennise** ____ ....-c 1707
 XXVI 77; XXXIII 215; XXXVI
 266; XXXVII 198; XXXVIII
 296; XXXIX 276

SPOFFORD/SPAFFORD
MA **JOHN, I** 1612-1678
 m .... **Elizabeth Scott** 1625-1691
 XXI 91; XXVI 129; XXXII 178

SPOONER
MA **WILLIAM** a 1622-1684
 m2) 1652 **Hannah Pratt** c 1631-
 1684
 IV 159; XXXVIII 186

SPRAGUE
MA **FRANCIS** c 1600-1666/69
 m .... **Lydia** ____ c 1602-1660
 XXXVIII 210; XXXIX 17;
 XXXX 335, 336
MA **RALPH** 1599/1603-1650
 m 1623 **Joanna/Jean Warren**
 ....- 1679/80
 XV 42; XVII 9; XXX 98;
 XXXVII 168
MA **WILLIAM, I** 1609-1675
 m 1634/35
 Millicent Eames ....-1695/96
 XX 30; XXIV 143; XXXI 137,
 195, 270; XXXIV 285

SPRING
MA **JOHN** 1589-.... m ....
 Eleanor ____ 1588-a 1656/57
 XX 25

SPRINGER
DE **CARL/CHARLES**

SPRINGER-Cont.
CHRISTOPHER 1658-1738
　m 1685 **Maria/Marian**
　Hendrickson ....-1727/28
　XXIX 154; XXXIII 52; XXXVI
　233
RI **LORENTZ/LAWRENCE** 1646-
　1701
　m 1684 **Martha Hicks** ....-....
　XXXVII 286; XXXVIII 23

SPRINGS/SPRINGSTEEN
NY **CASPER SPRINGSTEEN** ....-
　liv. 1687
　m 1663 **Catherine Lothie** ....-....
　XXVI 47

SPRINGSTEEN, see SPRINGS
SPROAT, see SPROUT

SPROUT/SPROAT
MA **ROBERT** ....-1690/1712 m 1660
　Elizabeth Sampson p 1636-
　p 1712
　IV 81, 120; XXII 88; XXXI 308

SQUIRE
MA **GEORGE, Sr** 1618-1691
　m c 1640 **Ann** ____ ....-a 1691
　XVIII 9

STAATS
NY **ABRAHAM/ABRAM** a 1620-
　wp 1694 m ....
　Catrina Jochemse Wessels ....-
　....
　IX 39; X 173

STAFFORD
ME **SYLVESTER STOVER** c 1635-
　1687/90 m by 1655
　Elizabeth Norton ....-1714/22
　XXXIX 234

MA/RI **THOMAS** 1605-1678 m....
　Elizabeth ____ a 1630-p 1678
　X 139
VA **WILLIAM** 1608-1654/55
　m 1640 **Frances Mason** ....-....
　XXXVI 199; XXXVIII 137

STAGG
NJ **THOMAS** ....-1691 m ....
　Margrietje ____ ....-....
　XXXVI 52

STANBERY/STANBOROUGH
MA/NY **JOSIAH**
　STANBOROUGH c 1600-1661
　m1) .... **Frances Gransden** ....-....
　m2) .... **Alice/Alce Wheeler** ....-
　....
　XXXV 26

STANDISH
MA **MILES/MYLES** c 1584/86-
　1656
　m2) 1623/24 **Barbara Allen** ....-
　p 1659
　XXIX 316; XXXIII 123; XXXVI
　270; XXXVII 145, 225

STANHOPE
MA **JONATHAN** ....-1681
　m 1656 **Susannah Ayer** ....-....
　XXIX 71

STANLEY
CT **THOMAS** c 1600/34-1663
　m2) 1630 **Benett (Willarton)**
　Tritton 1609-1664
　XXVI 52; XXXI 148; XXXVIII
　109

STANNARD
CT **JOSEPH** ....-....
　m c 1662 ____ ____ ....-....

STANNARD-Cont.
XXIX 224

STANBOROUGH, see STANBERY
STARNBOROUGH, see
STANSBURY

STANSBURY/STERNBERG/
STARNBOROUGH
MD **DETMAR STERNBERG** ....-
   a 1685 m c 1650
   Catherina (Renske) _____ ....-....
   XXXIX 321
MA **TOBIAS STARNBOROUGH**
   c 1652-1709
   m .... **Sarah Raven** ....-a 1714
   XXXIX 321; XXXX 42

STANTON
CT **THOMAS** c 1615/16-1677
   m 1637 **Ann/a Lord** 1621-1688
   IX 33; X 298; XII 28, 111; XIII
   57; XXXVII 180

STAPLEFORT
MD **RAYMOND** ....-1687 m a 1666
   Mrs. Elinor (Thompson) May
   ....-....
   XIX 124

STAPLES
CT **THOMAS** ....-wp 1688
   m a 1646
   Mary _____ ....-p 1696
   XXXII 33

STAPP, see STEP

STARK
CT **AARON** c 1602/08-1685
   m1) by 1637 **Mary Holt** ....-....
   m2) c 1653 **Sarah** _____ ....-....
   XXIX 100; XXX 61; XXXIX 70;

XXXX 435
VA **RICHARD** ....-1702/03
   m .... **Rebecca** _____ ....-1713
   XXXVII 341

STARKWEATHER
MA **ROBERT** ....-c 1674
   m .... **Jennet Roberts** ....-p 1674
   XIII 49; XVII 47, 132; XXX 220;
   XXXIV 79

STARR
MA **COMFORT** 1589-1659/60
   m .... **Elizabeth** _____ 1595-1658
   XIV 46; XVIII 100; XXI 112;
   XXV 12, 62
MA **COMFORT** 1644-1693
   m .... **Marah Weld** ....-....
   IX 43

STEADMAN
MA **ISAAC** 1605-1678
   m a 1630 **Elizabeth** _____ 1609-
   ....
   XXX 125

STEARNS/STERNS/STEARNES
MA **CHARLES** ....-....
   m2) .... **Rebecca Gibson** ....-1635
   XII 37
MA **ISAAC, Sr** ....-1671/77
   m 1622
   Mary Baker/Barker ....-1677
   XXV 94; XXVII 222; XXVIII
   103, 115, 211; XXXIV 152, 327;
   XXXVI 67
MA **SHUBAEL** a 1600-1630/31
   m .... _____ _____ ....-1630/31
   XXXVI 291

STEBBINS
MA **ROWLAND** c 1592-1671
   m 1618 **Sarah Whiting** 1591-

STEBBINS-Cont.
  1649
  XI 37; XX 15
MA **THOMAS** 1620-1683
  m1) 1645 **Hannah Wright** ....-
  1660
  XXXI 113

STEELE
CT **GEORGE** ....-1663
  m .... _____ _____ ....-....
  XIV 76, 92; XVII 125
CT **JOHN** 1591-1665
  m1) 1622 **Rachel Talcott** ....-
  1653/63
  VI 60/67; XXIV 137; XXV 80;
  XXVII 19; XXXIII 192

STEELMAN
DE **JAMES** ....-....
  m .... _____ _____ ....-....
  XV 35
NJ **JAMES** c 1665-1733/34
  m a 1690 **Susanna Toy** ....-
  a 1730
  XV 35; XXI 147

STEERE
RI **JOHN** 1634-1724
  m1) 1660 **Hannah Wickendon**
  ....- ....
  m2) .... **Eleanor Sheringham** ....-
  ....
  XXV 257; XXVI 69

STEEVENS, see STEVENS

STEP/STAPP
VA **ABRAHAM STAPP** c 1650/57-
  1714 m a 1677/79
  Dorothy Moss ....-....
  XXXVII 48; XXXX 129

STEPHENS, see STEVENS
STERGES, see STEARNS

STETSON
MA **ROBERT** 1613-1702/03
  m .... **Honour** _____ ....-....
  XXX 50

STEUBEN
CT **JOHN ARNOLD** c 1685-c 1664
  m .... _____ _____ ....-....
  XXXX 275

STEVENS
MA **CYPRIAN** 1644/48-1720/22
  m1) 1672 **Mary Willard** 1653-
  c 1685
  XIII 118; XXX 277; XXXI 128
MA **ERASMUS** ....-1691
  m .... **Elizabeth** _____ ....-....
  XXII 80; XXV 175
MA **HENRY** c 1611-1689
  m1) .... **Alice** _____ ....-a 1652
  XXVI 125
CT **HENRY, I** 1639-a 1726
  m 1677
  Elizabeth Gallup 1645-1736
  IX 36; XXXI 243
VA **JOHN, I** 1589-1676
  m .... _____ _____ ....-....
  XXXVII 83
CT **JOHN STEPHENS** a 1608-1670
  m .... **Mary (Anne)** _____ ....-1703
  XI 76; XII 50, 113; XV 109;
  XXXIII 248
MA **JOHN** bp 1605/07-1662 m 1638
  Elizabeth Parker c 1613/14-
  1694
  III 61; X 67; XXIV 91; XXV 290;
  XXIX 95; XXXI 207; XXXIII 58;
  XXXV 66
MA **RICHARD STEPHENS** 1634-
  p 1722 m 1667

STEVENS-Cont.
　Mary (Lincoln) Hacke 1642-
　1716
　XXXIII 350; XXXIV 45, 69
MA **WILLIAM** ....-....
　　m .... ＿＿＿ ＿＿＿ ....-....
　　XVI 103

STEVENSON
MD **EDWARD** ....-wp 1717
　　m .... **Mary** ＿＿＿ ....p 1727
　　XXXV 136

STEWARD
MA **ALEXANDER** ....-1731
　　m3) 1688 **Deborah (Rediat)**
　　Forbes 1652-1720
　　XXXIV 113

STEWARD/STUART
MA **DUNCAN** 1623-1717
　　m 1654/55
　　Anne Winehurst c 1637-1729
　　XIV 5; XXI 121

STICKNEY
MA **WILLIAM** bp 1592-1664/65
　　m ....
　　Elizabeth Dawson 1608-1678/80
　　X 61; XX 33; XXV 129; XXXX
　　36, 134

STILES
MA/CT **JOHN** bp 1595-1662/63
　　m c 1631 **Rachel** ＿＿＿ 1606-1674
　　XI 86; XIII 79; XXXII 96;
　　XXXIII 332; XXXV 60
CT **JOHN** c 1632/33-1683
　　m .... **Dorcas Burt** ....-....
　　XXVI 62

STILLMAN
MA **GEORGE** 1654-1728
　　m1) 1677 **Jane Pickering** 1659-
　　1684
　　m2) 1685/86 **Rebecca Smith**
　　1668-1750/58
　　XIII 48, 104; XIV 14

STILLWELL
NY **NICHOLAS** c 1603-1671
　　m1) .... **Abigail** ＿＿＿ ....-....
　　XXXV 180

STITES
NY **JOHN** 1595-1717
　　m .... ＿＿＿ ＿＿＿ ....-....
　　XIX 5

STOCKBRIDGE
MA **JOHN** 1608-1657
　　m1) 1632/34 **Anne** ＿＿＿ 1614-
　　a 1643
　　XV 6; XXVII 81

STOCKING
CT **GEORGE** c 1582-1683
　　m .... **Anna** ＿＿＿ ....-....
　　IX 49

STOCKMAN
MA **JOHN** c 1653-1686 m 1671
　　Sarah Pike Bradbury 1641-
　　1718
　　XXIII 50

STOCKTON
MA/NY **RICHARD** a 1640-1707
　　m 1652
　　Abigail ＿＿＿ ....-p 1714
　　XI 133, 135; XVII 114; XXIX
　　110; XXXIX 198

STOCKWELL
MA **QUINTON** c 1640-1713/15
　　m 1666 **Abigail Bullard** 1641-
　　1730
　　XXXVIII 292
MA **WILLIAM** c 1650-1727/29
　　m 1685
　　Sarah Lambert 1661-c 1738
　　XXXVII 371; XXXIX 11, 72

STODDARD
CT **JOHN** 1612-1676 m ....
　　Catharine _____ ....-p 1676
　　V 72; XIX 120
CT **JOHN** c 1620-1664
　　m ....
　　Mary Foote c 1623-p 1685
　　XII 94

STODDER
MA **JOHN** .... 1661 m ....
　　Hannah/Anna _____ ....-1675
　　XXIV 138; XXXI 149; XXXVII
　　238

STOFFELSZEN, see VANSANT

STONE
MA **GREGORY** bp 1592-1672
　　m1) 1617 **Margaret Garrad**
　　bp 1597-1626
　　m2) 1627 **Lydia (_____) Cooper**
　　(wid.) 1598-1674
　　IX 50; XIII 113; XVI 122; XIX
　　79; XXIV 75; XXVI 99; XXVIII
　　26; XXX 259; XXXIII 162;
　　XXXVI 33; XXXIX 210, 240
RI **HUGH** 1638- ....
　　m 1665 **Abigail Busecot** ....-....
　　XXXII 256
MA **JOHN** c 1596-p 1667
　　m .... _____ _____ ....-....
　　XXXX 257

MA **SIMON, I** bp 1585/86-1655/65
　　m1) 1616 **Joane/Joanne Clarke**
　　c 1596-a 1654
　　XXX 12, 48, 106; XXXIV 299;
　　XXXV 360; XXXVIII 286;
　　XXXIX 257
VA **WILLIAM** ....-....
　　m .... **Mary Marvel** ....-....
　　XVI 125
CT **WILLIAM** ....-1683
　　m1) .... **Hannah** _____ ....-a 1659
　　IV 142; XXXIV 190
VA/MD **WILLIAM** 1603-1660
　　m .... **Verlinda Cotton** ....-
　　wp 1675
　　XXII 26; XXIII 29; XXXI 139
VA **WILLIAM** 1650-a 1707
　　m .... **Sara** _____ ....-1711/17
　　XXIV 89; XXIX 18, 398; XXI
　　242

STOOPE, see STOOPS

STOOPS/STOOPE/STOPE
VA **CHRISTOPHER** 1612-1672
　　m .... _____ _____ ....-....
　　XXI 169; XXIV 35, 114

STOPE, see STOOPS

STORER
NH **WILLIAM** c 1611-1658/61
　　m1) .... **Sarah** _____ ....-....
　　XXVI 292; XXX 127

STORM
NY **DIERCK** 1630-c 1716
　　m c 1655
　　Maria Pieters Momfort ....-
　　c1701
　　XXV 224; XXIX 325; XXXVI 39

STORRS
MA **SAMUEL** 1640-1719
    m 1666 **Mary Huckins** 1646-
    1683
    XXXV 242
MA **THOMAS** bp 1605-....
    m .... _____ _____ ....-....
    XXXI 275

STORY
MA **ANDREW** ....-....
    m .... _____ _____ ....-....
    XXX 251
MA **WILLIAM** 1614-1702/03
    m .... **Sarah Foster** 1620/28-....
    XXVI 302

STOUGHTON
CT **THOMAS** ....-1661
    m1) .... _____ **Montepeson** ....-....
    m2) .... **Margaret Huntingdon**
    ....- ....
    XIV 18; XXXII 115

STOUT
NY/NJ **RICHARD** 1602/15 wp 1705
    m c 1644/45
    **Penelope Kent (or Lent) Von
    Princes/Printzen (Roth)**
    1622/23-1712/32
    XIV 64; XVII 79, 161; XIX 14;
    XXVI 165; XXXII 121; XXXVII
    70

STOUTENBERG
NY **PIETER** 1610-c 1698/99
    m 1649
    Afegy Van Tiehoven ....-....
    XXXVII 181

STOVALL
VA **BARTHOLOMEW** 1665-
    wp 1721 m 1693

    Ann Burton c 1670-1736
    XXXI 79; XXXV 268; XXXX
    415

STOW/STOWE
MA **JOHN** 1595-1643
    m .... **Elizabeth Bigg** ....-1638
    XIV 71

STOWELL
MA **SAMUEL** 1620-1683 m 1649
    Mary Farrow/Farrar 1633/35-
    1708/15
    XI 85, 86, 87; XII 9; XIII 14;
    XIV 21; XVI 42

STRAIT
RI **HENRY** 1652-1728
    m .... **Mary Long** ....-1757
    XXXII 89

STRATTON
NY **JOHN** bp 1621-1685
    m 1644 **Sarah** _____ ....-....
    XXXIX 49
MA **SAMUEL** c 1592- w 1672
    m1) .... **Alice** _____ ....-a 1657
    VII 49; XXXVIII 192; XXXIX
    306

STREET
MA **NICHOLAS** bp 1603-1674
    m .... _____ _____ ....-....
    XII 84; XXXV 126

STREETER
MA **STEPHEN** 1600-by 1652
    m 1640
    Ursula Adams c 1600/19-
    1673/76
    XXV 197; XXXX 43

STRICKLAND
VA **MATTHEWS, Sr** c 1637-
1698/99 m by 1674
Elizabeth Loreen c 1641-....
XXXIX 295

STRODE
PA **GEORGE** ....-....
m .... **Margaret** ____ ....-1696
XXXIV 265

STRONG
MA/CT **JOHN** 1605/10-1699
m1) .... **Margery Deane** ....-
c 1630/35
m2) 1630/36 **Abigail Ford**
1608/19-1688
IV 88; V 110; VIII 30; XI 128;
XIII 30; XV 43; XVII 24, 93;
XVIII 40; XIX 164; XX 41; XXI
90; XXII 61; XXV 60, 160, 217;
XXVI 21; XXXII 22; XXXIII 55;
XXXV 174; XXXVI 123;
XXXIX 232, 278; XXXX 126

STROTHER
VA **WILLIAM** 1627-wp 1702
m a 1666
Dorothy Savage ....-p 1716
XXIX 138; XXXVII 372

STRYCKER, see STRYKER

STRYKER/STRYCKER
NY **JAN** 1615-1697
m .... **Lambertje Seubering** ....-
liv. 1663/79
XXVIII 65; XXX 112; XXXVI
294; XXXVII 303; XXXVIII 231

STUART, see **STEWART**

STUBBS
VA **JOHN** ....-....
m .... ____ _____ ....-....
XXXVII 111
MA **RICHARD** c 1619-1677
m 1658/59
Margaret Reade c 1636-....
XXXIX 22

STURDEVANT
MA **SAMUEL, Sr** c 1624-1669
m 1643 **Ann** ____ ....-....
XXXVII 75

STURGES
CT **JOHN** 1623-1697/1700 m c 1650
Deborah Barlow c 1620/30-
a 1698
I 35; XVII 87; XXXVI 103;
XXXVII 69

STURGIS
PA **ANTHONY** ....-1702
m .... **Anne** ____ ....-1696
XXVIII 68
MA **EDWARD** c 1613-1695
m1) 1640 **Elizabeth Hinckley**
....- 1679
XIV 22

SUDLER
MD **JOSEPH** ....-a 1700 m a 1682
Cecily Bright ....-wd 1717
XXXVIII 168

**SULLIVAN/O'SULLIVANT/
SULLIVANT**
VA **JOHN** 1638-a 1698
m1) .....____ **Hayes** ....-....
m2) .... **Sara Gore** ....-....
XXVIII 43; XXXIX 205
VA **THOMAS O'SULLIVANT**
1641-....

SULLIVAN/O'SULLIVANT/
SULLIVANT-Cont.
    m .... **Jean Pleasant** ....-....
    XXV 183

SULLIVANT, see SULLIVAN

SUMMERS
MD **JOHN, I** ....-a 1703
    m .... **Rebecca** _____ ....-....
    XXXIX 202

SUMNER
MA **WILLIAM** 1605-1688
    m 1625 **Mary West** ....-1676
    XXII 111; XXIX 188; XXXIII
    268; XXXVI 76

SUPPLEE/SOUPLIS
PA **ANDROS** 1634-1726
    m .... **Gertrude Stressinger**
    1642-p 1737
    XI 103

SUTCLIFFE, see SUTLIFF

SUTHERLAND, see
SOUTHERLAND

SUTLIFF/SUTCLIFFE/SUTLIFFE
/SUTTCLIFFE
MA **NATHANIEL** ....-1676
    m 1665/66
    Hannah Plympton 1645/46 ....
    XXIX 128; XXXI 305

SUTLIFFE, see SUTLIFF

SUTPHEN/VAN SUTPHEN
NJ **DIRK JANSEN VAN**
SUTPHEN c 1645-1702/07
    m 1680
    Elizabeth Jansen Jacobse/Janse

    Van Nuys ....-....
    XIX 100; XXXVIII 146

SUTTCLIFFE, see SUTLIFF

SUTTLE/SETTLE
VA **FRANCIS SETTLE** c 1635-
    wp 1708 m1) ....
    Elizabeth _____ ....-a 1708
    XXXVI 284

SUTTON
MA/NC **GEORGE** c 1613-1669
    m c 1636
    Sarah Tilden 1613-1677
    XXXVIII 327
MA **JOHN** 1619-....
    m .... **Juliana** _____ ....-....
    XXXI 166

SWAIN
MA **JEREMIAH** 1643-1710
    m 1664
    Mary Smith ....-1658
    XXXIII 30; XXXV 23

SWAN
MA **RICHARD** ....-1678
    m1).... **Ann** _____ ....-1658
    XXXVII 40

SWART
NY **TEUNIS CORNELISZE** ....-
    c 1680 m ....
    Elizabeth Van der Linde ....-....
    XXIX 145

SWEET
MA/RI **JAMES** bp 1622-1695
    m c 1654
    Mary Greene bp 1633-....
    XIV 73; XIX 7
RI **JOHN** 1579-a 1637

SWEET-Cont.
m 1619
Mary Periam 1638-1681
XXI 47; XXVIII 85, 175; XXX
172; XXXI 74

SWEETSER/SWEETSTER
MA **SETH** 1606-1662
m1) 1630 **Bethia Cooke** ....-1660
m2) 1661 **Elizabeth Oakes** ....-....
XXX 180; XXXIV 66

SWEETSTER, see SWEETSER

SWETT
MA **JOHN** c 1592-1651/52
m c 1615/17
Sara/Sarah Swett c 1594-1650
XII 63; XVII 86, 110; XXXVII
261; XXXX 230, 231

SWIFT/SWYFT
MA **WILLIAM SWYFT** c 1543-
1642/44
Joan/Joanna ....-pr 1663
XIII 83; XVII 120; XVIII 121;
XX 84; XXXVIII 51

SWITS
NY **CLAUS CORNELIUS** ....-1641
m .... ____ ____ ....-....
XIX 71; XXVI 235

SWYFT, see SWIFT

SYDNOR
VA **FORTUNATUS, I** c 1638-
1683/84 m c 1670
Joanna (Lawson) Stockwell ....-
....
XXXV 183

SYKES
VA **BERNARD** 1620-a 1685
m c 1648
Julianna ____ ....-p 1690
XV 91; XXXVIII 269
VA **BERNARD, Sr** 1633-1682
m 1662
Elizabeth Thomas ....-....
XXXX 224

SYLVESTER
MA **RICHARD** ....-1663
m c 1632 **Naomi Torrey** ....-1668
IX 52; XI 27; XXXV 193, 194

SYMPSON, see SIMPSON

TABER/TABOR
MA **PHILIP, Sr/I** 1605-1672
m1) 1634 **Lydia Masters** ....-....
m2) 1639 **Jane Latham** ....-....
XIX 108; XXVIII 117; XXXIII
238

TABOR, see TABER
TAENTER, see TAINTER

TAFT
MA **ROBERT** c 1640-1725
m c 1665/70
Sarah ____ c 1640- c 1725/26
VIII 7; XV 139; XXI 176; XXXV
39; XXXVIII 163; XXXIX 111;
XXXX 50

TAINTER/TAENTER/TAINTOR
CT **CHARLES TAINTOR** ....-1654
m .... ____ ____ ....-....
XXXV 112
MA **JOSEPH** 1612/13-1690
m 1639/40 **Mary Guy** 1619-1705
XXVII 136; XXXVI 122
CT **MICAEL TAINTOR** c 1625-

TAINTER/TAENTER/TAINTOR-
Cont.
    1672/73 m ....
    Elizabeth Rose c 1621-1659
    XXXV 112

TAINTOR, see TAINTER

TAIT/TATE
VA **JAMES TATE** 1618-1727
    m a 1688 **Ann** _____ ....-p 1743
    XV 42; XXX 150

TALBOT/TALBOTT
MA **JARED** ....-a 1686 m 1664
    Sarah Andrews c 1643-p 1686
    XXVII 90
MD **RICHARD TALBOTT** ....-
    wd/p 1663 m a 1656
    Elizabeth Ewen 1638-1703/04
    IX 11; XXXIII 86

TALBOTT, see TALBOT

TALCOTT
MA/CT **JOHN** a 1600/04-1660
    m a 1630
    Dorothy Mott a 1615-1670
    IV 117; V 56; XIV 41; XXIX
    332; XXXVI 195, 272

TALIAFERRO
VA **ROBERT** bp 1626-c 1682 m ....
    (Sarah) Katherine Deadman ....-
    ....
    XXXV 46

TALLMADGE, see TALMADGE

TALMADGE/TALLMADGE
CT **ROBERT TALLMADGE**
    c 1600-1680 m 1648/49
    Sarah Nash ....-p 1687

    XXII 40; XXXVI 217
MA/NY **THOMAS, Sr** c 1595-1653
    m a 1630
    _____ _____ ....-p 1653
    XXXIV 224

TALLMAN
RI **PETER** chr 1623-1708/09
    m2) by 1665 **Joan Briggs** ....-
    a 1684/85
    XXXIX 229

TANDY
VA **HENRY, Sr** c 1630-1691
    m .... **Rebecca** _____ ....-....
    XXV 287; XXIX 176, 179; XXXI
    72; XXXX 31

TANEY
MD **MICHAEL** ....-1692
    m .... **Mary Phillips** ....-a 1686
    XXII 10

TANNER
VA **JOSEPH** 1630-1668
    m 1661 **Mary** _____ ....-....
    XXXX 129
RI **WILLIAM** c 1659/60-1738/40
    m2) .... **Mary Babcock** ....-....
    m3) c 1707 **Elizabeth Cottrell**
    1666/88-....
    IV 99, 149; X 70; XVIII 77;
    XXIV 83; XXX 93; XXXV 331

TAPPEN
NY **JURIAN TEUNISSE** ....-p 1689
    m1) .... **Wybrecht Jacobse** ....-
    1677
    m2) 1662 **Aariantje Davidts** ....-
    p 1694
    XXV 119; XXXIV 159

TARBELL
MA **THOMAS, I** ....-1678
    m a 1647 **Mary** ____ 1620-1674
    XXVIII 134; XXXII 137; XXXIII
    51

TARBOX
MA **JOHN** a 1619-1674
    m .... ____ ____ ....-p 1674
    XXXII 29

TATE, see TAIT

TAYLOE
NH **WILLIAM** 1645-....
    m 1685 **Anne Corbin** ....-....
    XIII 72

TAYLOR
NH **ANTHONY** 1607/09-1687
    m c 1640 **Phillipa** ____ ....-1683
    XXXV 88; XXXVII 314; XXXX
    189
PA **CHRISTOPHER** 1620-1686/88
    m .... **Elizabeth** ____ ....-....
    XXX 198
VA **JAMES, I** c 1615/40-1698
    m1) c 1667 **Frances (Walker?)**
    ....-1680
    X 54; XVI 125; XXVI 162;
    XXVII 207; XXIX 262
VA **JAMES** 1654-....
    m .... ____ ____ ....-....
    XXXIX 87
CT **JOHN, Sr** ....-wd 1645/47
    m2) 1635/40 **Rhoda** ____ ....-
    c 1694/96
    XXXIII 318; XXXV 362; XXXX
    159
MA **JOHN** c 1639-1713 m 1666
    Mary Selden bp 1648-1713
    XI 183; XV 74
MA **RICHARD** ....-1673

    m 1646 **Ruth Wheldon** ....-1673
    XXII 124
MA **RICHARD (ROCK)** ....-1703
    m 1646 **Ruth Burgess** ....-1693
    XXVI 254; XXVII 11
VA **RICHARD** 1612-1679
    m .... **Margaret Hodges** ....-1679
    XXVII 177
CT **STEPHEN** 1618-1668
    m1) 1642 **Sarah Hosford** ....-
    1648
    m2) 1649 **Elizabeth Newell** ....-
    1717
    XVIII 135; XXXVII 21
PA **THOMAS** bp 1628-1682
    m c 1673
    Frances Yardle 1644-1712
    XXXVIII 34; XXXIX 147
MA **WILLIAM** 1618-1696
    m 1649 **Mary Merriam** ....-1699
    XXV 56; XXX 56; XXXII 198;
    XXXVII 297
NH **WILLIAM** 1625-1677
    m 1648 **Anne Wyeth** 1630-1714
    XXXX 252

**TAYLOR-WILLISTON, see
WILLISTON**

TEAGUE
MD **EDWARD** c 1660-1697
    m c 1690 **Susan** ____ c 1666-
    p 1704
    XXXX 3

**TEBBETTS, see TIBBETTS
TEFFE, see TEFFT**

TEFFT/TEFFE/TIFT
RI **JOHN TEFFE** ....-1676
    m .... **Mary Barber** ....-1679
    XXXIII 284

TEMPLE
MA **ABRAHAM** c 1600-1639
    m .... **Abigail** ____ ....-1623/26
    XXVII 64; XXXX 434, 459
VA **WILLIAM, Sr** c 1660/65-1724
    m 1685 **Rebecca Tatum** ....-....
    XXXVIII 315

TEN BROECK
NY **WESSEL** ....-....
    m .... ____ ____ ....-....
    XII 113

TENNEY, see TENNY

TENNY/TENNEY
MA **THOMAS TENNEY** c 1614-
    1699/1700
    m .... **Ann** ____ ....-1657
    XX 56; XXXIV 257

TER BUSH/BOSCH/TER BOSCH
NY **JAN BOSCH/TERBOSCH**
    1626-c 1678 m 1663
    Rachel Farnelje/Vermilye 1637-
    a 1756
    XXXX 446

TERRELL/TERRILL/TURRELL/
TURRILL/TYRELL/TYRRELL
CT **ROGER TYRRELL** c 1610/19-
    1682/83 m 1627/43
    Abigail Ufford 1617-1682
    XVIII 137; XXV 9; XXXI 292;
    XXXVIII 300
VA **WILLIAM TYRRELL** 1629-....
    m .... **Martha** ____-....-.....
    XXV 179; XXVI 135
VA **WILLIAM TYRRELL** ....-1727
    m .... **Susanna Waters** 1639-....
    XXV 179; XXVI 138; XXX 228;
    XXXIII 217; XXXVIII 370, 371

TERRILL, see TERRELL

TERRY
CT/NY **RICHARD** 1618-p 1675
    m 1649 **Abigail** ____ ....-p 1686
    XXXI 253
MA **SAMUEL** 1661-1730/31
    m 1697/98 **Mrs. Martha**
    Boardman/Creden Crane
    c 1666-1743
    XXXIII 100
MA **SAMUEL, Sr** c 1632/33-
    1730/31
    m 1660 **Ann Lobdell** ....-1684
    XXXV 365; XXXVII 362

TERWILLIGAR, see
TERWILLIGER

TERWILLIGER/TERWILLIGAR
NY **EVERT DIRCKSEN** c 1630-
    a 1686
    m .... ____ ____ ....-....
    XXXIX 32

THACHER/THATCHER
MA **ANTONY** 1588/89-1667/68
    m2) 1635 **Elizabeth Jones** ....-
    p1667/68
    XX 129; XXIV 144; XXVI 70,
    126; XXXIII 196; XXXV 163;
    XXXIX 282
MA **THOMAS** 1620-1678 m 1643
    Elizabeth Partridge 1626/36-
    1664
    XI 169; XXX 218; XXXIII 44

THATCHER, see THACHER

THAYER
MA **RICHARD** 1601-1695 m 1624
    Deborah/Dorothy
    Mortimore/Mortimer 1600-

THAYER-Cont.
1630/95
XI 127; XIX 137; XXIV 93;
XXIX 104; XXXVII 336
MA **THOMAS** 1596-1665 m 1618
Margery Wheeler ....-1672/73
XVI 102; XXIV 84; XXXIII 165,
184; XXXIV 242; XXXIX 255

THIGPEN
NC **JAMES, I** 1627-1679 m 1652
Elyn ____ 1636-1688/89
XXXV 11; XXXX 124

THOMAS
MD **CHRISTOPHER** 1609-1670
m c 1632
Elizabeth Higgins (wid.) ....-
wp 1697
XXIV 55; XXV 225; XXVII 86;
XXVIII 6; XXXVII 193;
XXXVIII 246
VA **JOHN** ....-c 1675-76
m .... ____ ____ ....-....
XXXVII 339
PA **PETER, I** ....-1722
m 1686 **Sarah Stedman** ....-....
XXX 285
MD **PHILIP, Sr** c 1620-1674/87
m .... **Sarah Harrison** ....-a 1687
XXXII 12; XXXIII 209
VA **ROBERT** 1615-pr late 1600s
m pr p 1635 ____ **Massie**
pr early 1600-pr mid 1600s
XXXV 258
MD **THOMAS** ....-wp 1671
m .... **Elizabeth Barton** ....-....
XXXIII 191, 206
VA **WILLIAM Ap THOMAS**
1580/90-p 1635 m a 1613
____ ____ a 1613-a 1635
XXXV 258

THOMPSON/THOMSON
MA **ALEXANDER** c 1627-1695
m 1662
Deliverance Haggett/Hackett
c 1643-a 1695
XXXIX 222
CT **ANTHONY** 1612-1648 m c 1630
m1) ____ ____ ....-a 1637
V 57; X 150; XXXIV 315
NH **DAVID THOMSON, I** 1592-
1627/28 m 1613
Anyes Colle c 1592/95-p 1672
IV 115; XXXVI 211; XXXVII
373
MA **JAMES** 1593-1682
m1) .... **Elizabeth** ____ ....-1643
m2) 1644/45 **Susanna Blodgett**
....-1660/61
XXI 143; XXII 117; XXVII 102;
XXIX 300
NY **JOHN** ....-1688
m .... ____ ____ ....-....
XV 73; XXX 173
MA **JOHN THOMSON** 1616-1696
m 1645 **Mary Cooke** 1626-
1714/15
II 52; XVIII 149
VA **JOHN** 1636-1710
m 1657 **Sarah** ____ 1640-1696
XIII 92
ME/NH **WILLIAM** ....-1676
m .... ____ ____ ....-a 1676
XVIII 6
MD **WILLIAM** 1597-1649
m 1617 **Anne** ____ 1600-....
XXXVII 337

THOMSON, see THOMPSON
THORN, see THORNE

THORNE
MA/NY **WILLIAM** a 1617-p 1657
m1) .... **Sarah** ____ ....-....

THORNE-Cont.
    m2) ....? **Susanna Booth** ....-....
    X 129, 167; XXXII 200; XXXVI
    278

THORNTON
VA **LUKE** 1650-1726
    m c 1680 **Ann** _____ ....-....
    XXX 279
VA **WILLIAM, I** ....-c 1700/08
    m1) a 1642 **Elisia Billington** ....-
    a 1648
    m2) 1648 **Elizabeth Rowland**
    1627-1671
    XIV 33; XXIV 161; XXXV 40;
    XXXVII 351; XXXVIII 36, 141,
    298

THORP/THORPE
NY/NJ **THOMAS** ....-wp 1694
    m 1656 **Rebecca Milward** 1643-
    wd 1692/93
    XXVII 95
CT **WILLIAM** c 1605-c 1684
    m .... **Elizabeth** _____ c 1615-
    1660
    XXVI 219, 220; XXIX 91;
    XXXIX 330

THORPE, see THORP

THRALL
CT **WILLIAM** 1605-1679
    m .... _____ **Goode** ....-1676
    XVII 135

THRASHER
MA **CHRISTOPHER** ....-a 1679
    m ....
    Katherine/Catherine _____ ....-....
    XXX 37; XXXI 140

THROCKMORTON
RI/NJ **JOHN** ....-a 1687
    m .... **Alice** _____ ....-....
    XII 109; XIII 44
RI/NJ **JOHN** bp 1600/01-c 1683/87
    m ....**Rebecca Coville** ....-....
    XXXVIII 228; XXXIX 191

THROOP/THROOPE
MA **WILLIAM THROOPE** ....-
    1704 m 1666
    Mary Chapman 1643-1732
    XVII 48

THROOPE, see THROOP

THURBER
MA **JAMES** 1660-1736 m 1684
    Elizabeth Bliss 1657-1723
    XIV 84; XXXVII 71
MA **JOHN** ....-1706 m c 1648/49
    Priscilla _____ ....-p 1706
    XXXVII 71

THURMAN/THURMOND
VA **JOHN** ....-...
    m .... **Anne Morecraft** ....-....
    XXXVI 326

THURMOND, see THURMAN

THURSTON
MA **DANIEL** ....-1693 m 1644/55
    Anna Pell ....-a 1692/93
    XIX 166; XXXIX 184
RI **EDWARD** 1617-1707 m 1647
    Elizabeth Mott c 1627-1694
    XXXIX 241

TIBBETTS/TEBBETTS/TIBBITS
MA **HENRY** 1596-wp 1676
    m .... _____ _____ ....-....
    XXX 123

TIBBETTS/TEBBETTS/TIBBITS-
Cont.
RI **HENRY TIBBITS, Sr** ....-1713
  m 1660/61
  Sarah Stanton 1640-1708
  VI 56/63; VII 33; XXXIV 341;
  XXXV 312

TIBBITS, see TIBBETTS
TIBOUT, see TIEBOUT

TICHENOR
CT/NJ **MARTIN** c 1600-1644/82
  m 1651 **Mary Charles** ...-w 1681
  XIX 110; XXI 72; XXXV 72

TICKNOR
MA **WILLIAM** ....-1696/97 m 1656
  Hannah Stockbridge bp 1637-
  1665
  XXVII 151

TIDWELL/TYDEWELL/
TYDWELL
VA **RICHARD, I** ....-....
  m .... _____ _____ ....-....
  XXXIV 110

TIEBOUT/TIBOUT
NY **JAN** a 1656-p 1691 m ....
  Sarah Vander Vlucht ....-a 1687
  XXII 79

TIFT, see TEFFT

TILDEN
MA **NATHANIEL** bp 1583-1641
  m ....**Lydia Bourne (Huckstep)**
  1587-....
  XXIV 166; XXXVII 352

TILER, see TYLER

TILLINGHAST
RI **PARDON** 1622-1717/1718
  m2) 1664/**Lydia**
  Tabor/Taber/Mary Masters
  Tabor ....-1718
  XXVIII 12; XXXIV 320

TILLMAN/TILGHMAN
VA **CHRISTOPHER TILGHMAN**
  c 1586-.... m ....
  Ruth Devonshire/Dovenshire
  ....-....
  XXXVIII 105

TILLSON/TILSON
MA **EDMOND TILSON** ....-1660
  m .... **Joanne** _____ ....-a 1669
  XXXII 85

TILSON, see TILLSON

TILTON
MA/NY **JOHN** c 1620-1687/88
  m c 1641 **Mary** _____ ....-1683
  XXXII 48; XXXVI 14
MA **WILLIAM** c 1618-1652/54
  m2) .... **Susanna Stoddard** ....-
  1655/65
  V 99; VI 7/8; XXX 121;
  XXXVIII 206

TINE, see VAN TINE
TINGLE, see TINGLEY

TINGLEY/TINGLE
MA **PALMER TINGLE**
  1614-.... m 1635/40
  Anna/Hannah Fosdick/Fosduk
  1615-1681
  XXVII 60; XXX 200; XXXVII
  122

TINKER
MA/CT **JOHN** c 1618-1662
  m2) 1651 **Alyce Smith** 1626/29-
  1714
  XIII 52; XV 85; XVI 126; XXVI
  51; XXXV 310

TINKHAM
MA **EPHRIAM** 1615-1685
  m 1647 **Mary Brown** ....-....
  XXII 110

TIPPETT
MD **PHILIP** c 1660-inv 1706
  m ....**Mary** _____ ....-p 1708
  XXXIV 49

TIPTON
MD **EDWARD** 1618/20-1672
  m1) .... **Elizabeth** _____ ....-....
  m2) .... **Margaret Downing** ....-
  ....
  XXXII 171; XXXVI 32; XXXVII
  255
MD **JONATHAN** 1639-1757 (ae 118
  years)
  m1).... **Sarah Pierce/Rene** ....-....
  m2) ....**Mary Chilcoat** ....-....
  m3) .... **Elizabeth Edwards** ....-
  ....
  XXXII 171, 244; XXXVI 32;
  XXXVII 255

TITUS
MA **JOHN** 1627-1689 m ....
  Abigail Carpenter ....-1709/10
  XII 119; XXXV 50
MA **ROBERT** c 1600-a 1672/79
  m .... **Hannah** _____ c 1605-wp
  1672
  XII 119; XXXI 158; XXXIV 191;
  XXXV 50

TOBEY
MA **THOMAS** ....-wd 1710/14
  m1) 1650 **Martha Knott** ....-
  a 1689
  XIV 49; XXXII 50

TODD
CT **CHRISTOPHER** bp 1617-1686
  m c 1637
  Grace Middlebrook ....-1686
  VIII 20; IX 54; XI 126; XIV 93;
  XXI 93; XXIV 8; XXXIX 217
MA **JOHN** 1621-1689
  m .... **Susannah Hunt** ....-1710
  XX 22
VA/MD **THOMAS** c 1619/30-1677
  m a 1638/47 **Ann Gorsuch** ....-
  a 1697
  XV 117; XXXVIII 44; XXXX 15

TOLL/TOLLES
NY **KAREL HANSEN** 1658-
  1732/38 m 1683
  Lysbeth/Elizabeth
  Rinkhout/Rinkhard ....-....
  V 75; X 180
CT **HENRY TOLLES** c 1630-....
  m1) ....(div. granted 1767)
  Sarah _____ ....-....
  XXXVII 260

TOLMAN
MA **THOMAS** c 1608-1690
  m .... **Sarah** _____ ....-....
  XXXX 92

TOMLINSON
CT **HENRY** bp 1606-1680/81
  m a 1638
  Alice _____ 1608/18-1698 (ae 90)
  III 48; VI 84/97; VII 5; XVI 141;
  XXIX 336; XXXVI 114;
  XXXVIII 288

TOMLINSON-Cont.
CT **WILLIAM** 1643-1711
　　m .... ＿＿＿ ＿＿＿ ....-....
　　XI 50

TOMPKINS
CT/NJ **MICHAEL** ....-1690
　　m .... **Mary** ＿＿＿ ....-....
　　XIX 50
RI **NATHANIEL** 1650-1724
　　m 1671
　　Elizabeth Allen 1651-1714
　　XXVI 286; XXXV 34

TOMSON
MA **JOHN** c 1616-1696
　　m 1645 **Mary Cooke** 1626-1724
　　XXXV 170

TOOMER
SC **JOHN** c 1663/67-p 1710
　　Mary ＿＿＿ ....-....
　　XXXVIII 352; XXXIX 71

TOPPAN
MA **ABRAHAM** 1606-1672
　　m .... **Susana Taylor** 1607-1689
　　XVII 91

TORREY
MA **JAMES** c 1612/13-1665
　　m 1643 **Ann Hatch** 1623-c 1691
　　XXXIII 259
MA **WILLIAM** 1608-1690
　　m 1630 **Jane Haviland** 1612-
　　1639
　　XVII 31

TOUSEY
CT **RICHARD** ....-1674
　　m1) .... ＿＿＿ ＿＿＿ ....-1667
　　XXIX 85

TOWER
MA **JOHN** bp 1609-1701/02
　　m 1638/39
　　Margaret Ibrook 1617-1700
　　XIV 57; XXXI 144; XXXII 75;
　　XXXVII 182, 356; XXXVIII 116
MA **ROBERT** pr 1585/86-1634
　　m 1607 **Dorothy Damon**
　　c 1586/87-1629
　　XVII 69

TOWLE, see TOWLES

TOWLES/TOWLE
VA **HENRY** 1652-est. div. 1721
　　m 1668/69
　　Ann Stokely/Stockley ....-....
　　XIV 24; XVI 20; XVII 94;
　　XXVII 110; XXXV 348
NH **PHILIP TOWLE** 1616-1696
　　m 1657 **Isabella Austin** c 1633-
　　1719
　　XXXV 229; XXXVIII 9

TOWNE
MA **WILLIAM** bp 1599-c 1672/77
　　m 1620
　　Joanna Blessing ....-c 1682
　　XXXI 313; XXXII 277; XXXIV
　　160; XXXVI 25, 96, 143;
　　XXXVII 146; XXXX 303

TOWNSEND
NY **HENRY** ....-1695 m 1675
　　Ann/Annie Cole ....-p 1695
　　XXXI 136; XXXX 31
NY **JOHN** a 1615-1668 m ....
　　**Elizabeth Cole/Elizabeth
　　Montgomery** ....-p 1668
　　XIV 104; XXXV 211
MA **MARTIN** 1597-....
　　m a 1634 **Martha** ＿＿＿ ....-....
　　XXXIII 79

TOWNSEND-Cont.
MA **MARTIN** 1644-1697 m 1669
   Abigail Train/Grain c 1638-
   1690
   XVIII 148; XXXIII 79
MA **THOMAS** bp 1594/95-1677
   m ....
   Mary Newgate /Newdigate ....-
   1692/93
   XXX 59; XXXIII 317

TRACY
MA **STEPHEN** 1596-.... m 1621
   Typhosa/Triphosa Lee ....-....
   XVII 43; XXVI 148
CT **THOMAS, I** 1610-1685 m 1641
   Mary (Wilson) (Mason) (wid.)
   ....-c 1659/1721
   XIV 81; XXIX 121; XXXV 352;
   XXXVI 267; XXXIX 27

TRAFTON
ME/MA **THOMAS** c 1630-1706/07
   m a 1668 **Elizabeth Moore** ....-
   p 1691
   XXXII 124, 180

TRASK
MA **OSMOND** 1622-1676 m 1663
   Elizabeth Gally ....-1676
   XXXIX 57

TRAVERS, see TRAVIS

TRAVIS/TRAVERS
VA **EDWARD** c 1592-a 1663
   m c 1637
   Ann Johnson c 1620-....
   XXXVIII 203
MA **HENRY TRAVERS** ....-1648
   m .... **Bridgett Fitts** ....-....
   XXXIV 134

TREADWELL
MA/CT/NY **EDWARD** ....-1660/61
   m .... **Sarah** _____ ....-1684
   XV 56; XXX 92

TREAT
CT **RICHARD** bp 1584-1669/70
   m 1615 **Alice Gaylord** bp 1594-
   p 1669/70
   IV 72, 137; XV 28; XXXIV 201;
   XXXVIII 38; XXXIX 46; XXXX
   359
CT **ROBERT** 1624-1710
   m 1647 **Jane Tapp** c 1628-1703
   IV 137

TRESCOTT
ME/MA **WILLIAM** 1614/15-1699
   m 1643 **Elizabeth Dyer** 1625-
   1699
   XXXIX 187

TRIGGS, see TWIGGS

TRIPLETT
VA **FRANCIS** 1645-p 1700/01
   m .... **Abagail** _____ ....-....
   XXX 71; XXXV 46, 86

TROBRIDGE, see TROWBRIDGE

TROWBRIDGE
MA **JAMES** 1636-1717
   m2) 1674 **Margaret Jackson**
   1640/49-1727
   XXXV 312; XXXVI 84; XXXX
   44
MA/CT **THOMAS** 1598-1672/73
   m 1627
   Elizabeth Marshall bp 1602/03-
   1641
   XXXIX 302; XXXX 44
MA **WILLIAM** 1633/34-1688

TROWBRIDGE-Cont.
  m 1656/57
  Elizabeth (Lamberton)
  Sellivant   163_-1716
  XXXX 69

TRUAX/DU TRIEUX
NY **ISAAC du TRIEUX** 1642-
  a 1706 m ....
  Maria Williamse Brouwer ....-
  p 1706
  XXVIII 54
NY **PHILLIPPE** bp 1619-a 1653
  m .... _____ _____ ....-....
  XXXV 276; XXXVII 192

TRUE/TREW
MA **HENRY TREW, I** ....-1659
  m c/a 1644
  Israel Pike ....-1699/1700
  XXVII 166; XXXII 289;
  XXXVII 107; XXXX 407

TRUESDAIL, see TRUESDELL

TRUESDELL/TRUESDAIL
MA **SAMUEL** bp 1645/46-1694/95
  m c 1671
  Mary Jackson c 1652/53-....
  XXXVII 354; XXXVIII 304, 335

TRULL
MA **JOHN** 1633-1704
  m 1657 **Sarah French** 1637-1710
  XXV 135; XXVII 44

TRYON
CT **WILLIAM** c 1645-1711
  m1) a 1672/73 **Mary Steele** ....-
  ....
  m2) .... **Saint (Robinson)**
  Latimer 1656-1711
  XXXV 14; XXXX 432

TUBBS
MA **WILLIAM** c 1617-1688
  m1) 1637 **Mercy Sprague**
  a 1623-p 1688
  XXXV 310; XXXX 178

TUBMAN
MD **RICHARD** ....-1727 m ....
  Eleanor Staplefort c 1676-1727
  XXXX 46

TUCK
NH **ROBERT** ....-1664
  m .... **Joanna** _____ 1674
  XVIII 123; XXIX 160

TUCKER
MA **MORRIS/MAURICE** 1642-
  1662
  m1) **Elizabeth Stevens** 1639-
  1662
  X 31, 36, 72; XXX 99
MA **ROBERT** 1604-1681/82
  m .... **Elizabeth Allen** ....-....
  XIX 144; XXXIII 26; XXXX 378
VA **WILLIAM** 1589-1644
  m .... **Mary Thompson** 1599-....
  XXXII 149

TUFTS
MA **PETER** 1617-1700 m 1640
  Mary Pierce 1627-1701/03
  XVIII 117; XXXI 251

TUGGLE/TUGWELL
VA **THOMAS TUGWELL** c 1630-
  1684 m a 1661
  Mary Tarrant ....-a 1684
  XXXV 121

TUGWELL, see TUGGLE

TULL
VA/MD **THOMAS** c 1640-p 1697
   m 1666
   Mary Minshall c 1646-p 1677
   XXVI 283; XXVII 143

TULLER
CT **JOHN** ....-a 1741 m 1684
   Elizabeth (Case) Lewis 1652-
   1718
   XVII 153

TUPPER
MA **THOMAS** 1578-1676
   m3) 1634/36 **Ann (Anne)**
   Hodgson (wid) c 1588-1676
   XXXIII 215; XXXVI 161;
   XXXX 318

TURCK/TURK
NY **PAULUS JACOBSE TURK**
   c 1635-.... m 1660
   Aeltje Berentse/Barentse Coell
   bp 1640-....
   XXXIV 335; XXXVI 358

TURK, see TURCK

TURNER
CT **EDWARD** c 1623/33-1717
   m 1656 **Mary Sanford** ....-....
   XXXIII 164; XXXV 262
VA **HENRY** ....-....
   m .... _____ _____ ....-....
   XXXVII 325; XXXVIII 117
MA **HUMPHREY** c 1597-1669/73
   m .... **Lydia Gamer (Gainer)** ....-
   a 1673
   XXXVI 93
VA **JAMES** ....-a 1686
   m .... _____ _____ ....-....
   XXXVIII 317; XXXIX 31
MA **JOHN** ....-1705 m by 1647

   Deborah Williams ....-1676
   XXXIX 272
NH **NATHANIEL** ....-1646
   m .... _____ _____ ....-....
   XXIV 44
VA/NC **WILLIAM H.** a 1640-1696
   m .... **Katherine** _____ ....-....
   XX 139; XXXIII 41

TURNEY
MA/CT **BENJAMIN** a 1590-
   wp 1648
   m 1630 **Mary Odell** 1605-...
   VIII 28; XXXI 180

TURPIN
VA **MICHAEL** 1635-1677
   m .... _____ _____ ....-....
   XXX 201
MD **WILLIAM** c 1640-.... m 1668
   Margaret Ivory 1654-1721
   XXVIII 107

TURRELL, see TERRELL
TURILL, see TERRELL

TUTHILL/TUTTLE
MA/NY **HENRY** 1612-c 1650
   m .... **Bridget** _____ 1635/a/54
   XVII 135; XXI 19; XXV 33;
   XXIX 215; XXX 237; XXXV
   355; XXXVI 131
NH **JOHN TUTTLE, I** ....-inv. 1663
   m .... **Dorothy** _____ ....-....
   XXXIV 150
MA **JOHN TUTTLE** 1596-1656
   m 1626/28
   Joanna (Antrobus) Lawrence
   bp 1592-p 1659
   XXXIV 158
CT **WILLIAM TUTTLE** c 1609-
   c 1673 m c 1630
   Elizabeth Southcutt c 1608/12-

TUTHILL/TUTTLE-Cont.
  1684
  V 69; XII 65; XIII 76; XV 65,
  131; XX 9; XXIX 241, 338;
  XXXIII 61; XXXIV 43, 113;
  XXXVI 34; XXXX 27

TWIGGS
VA **THOMAS** ....-.... m ....
  Mary Southwood/Sutherd ....-....
  II 51

TWINING
MA **WILLIAM** c 1594-1659
  m2) 1652 **Anna Doane** ....-1680
  XXXIII 120

TWITCHELL/de TUCHEL
MA **BENJAMIN** 1599-1675/76
  m .... **Mary Riggs** ....-....
  XXX 264; XXXI 191; XXXIII
  293; XXXVII 80

TWOMBLY
NH **RALPH** c 1625-wp 1686
  m .... **Elizabeth** ____ ....-....
  XXI 119

TYDEWELL, see TIDWELL

TYDINGS
MD **RICHARD** ....-1689
  m .... **Charity** ____ ....-....
  XXXVIII 303; XXXIX 90

TYDWELL, see TIDWELL

TYLER/TILER
VA **HENRY** 1604-c 1672/79
  m1) a 1640 **Mary** ____ ....-....
  XXVI 177
RI/MA **JOB** c 1619-c 1700/01
  m a 1639 **Mary** ____ ....-p 1665

  X 267; XVI 44; XVII 9; XXVII
  27
RI **JOHN TILER** c1633-1700
  m .... **Sarah Havens** ....-p 1718
  XXXX 207
CT **PETER** ....-1712
  m1) 1671 **Deborah Swain** 1654-
  a 1684/88
  V 82; XXIII 8
MD **ROBERT, Sr** c 1637-1674
  m 1663 **Joanne Ravens** ....-....
  XVI 91
MA/CT **ROGER** ....-inv. 1674
  m .... **Ann** ____ ....-....
  XXXVIII 113
MA **THOMAS** c 1660-1703
  m .... **Miriam Simpkins** 1663-
  1703
  VIII 29

TYRELL, see TERRELL
TYRRELL, see TERRELL

TYSON
VA **JOHN** 1635-a 1690 m 1659
  Sussanika ____ ....-p 1692
  XXXIII 285

UNDERHILL
MA **JOHN, Sr** 1597-1672 m 1628
  Helene de Hooch c 1600-1658
  XXXII 244

UNDERWOOD
VA **THOMAS WILLIAM** c 1644-
  1751/52
  m2) .... **Elizabeth Taylor** ....-....
  VI 48/55
VA **THOMAS** c 1630-wp 1702
  m .... pr. **Elizabeth** ____ ....-....
  XXXV 202

UPDIKE/opDYCK
NY **LOURIS JANSEN opDYCK**
1600-1659 m p/a 1643
Cristina ____ ....-....
XXVII 82; XXXIV 139

UPHAM
MA **JOHN** 1600-1681
m1) 1626/28 **Elizabeth
Slade/Webb** c 1603/08-c 1670/71
(**Eliz. Webb** XXIV 26; XXXX
340)
XXIV 26; XXXII 269; XXXIII
130; XXXVIII 134; XXXX 123,
340, 342

UPSON
CT **THOMAS** ....-1655
m2) 1646 **Elizabeth Fuller** ....-
p 1671
XIII 24; XXVIII 29; XXXIV 57,
220; XXXVIII 130; XXXIX 122;
XXXX 7, 300

UPTON
MA **JOHN** 1625-p 1678
m .... **Eleanor Stuart** ....-1678
XIV 14

USHER
CT **ROBERT** ....-1669
m2) 1659 **Elizabeth Jaggers** ....-
....
XXXVII 286

UTLEY
MA **SAMUEL, I** 1615-1662
m 1648 **Hannah Hatch** ....-....
XXXII 195

UTTER
RI **NICHOLAS** a 1637-p 1722
m .... ____ ____ ....-....

XXV 208; XXXIV 185

VALENTINE
MA **JOHN** 1643-1724 m 1702
Mary Lynde 1680-p 1717
X 48
NY **RICHARD** ....-c 1684
m .... ____ ____ ....-....
XVIII 140

**VAN AACHEN, see VAN AUKEN
VAN AERTS DAALEN, see VAN
ARSDALE
VAN AKEN, see VAN AUKEN
VAN AKIN, see AUKEN**

VAN ALSTYNE
NY **JANS MARTENSE** ....-
p 1697/98 m c 1662
Dirckje (Dorothy) Harmensen
c 1628-p 1687
XVI 86; XXXIV 324

VAN ANTWERP/ANTWERPEN
NY **DANIEL JANSE** c 1630/35-
1717 m 1656
Maretje Greet/Groot c 1640-....
XXV 151; XXXIII 325

**VAN ARSDALE/ARSDALEN/
VAN AERTS DAALEN/VAN
ARSDALEN/ VAN OSDOL**
NY **SIMON JANSEN VAN AERTS
DAALEN** c 1629/38-p 1710
m a 1658/60
Pierterje Claessen Wycoff
bp 1640-....
VII 47; XXVI 183; XXVIII 64,
210; XXIX 227; XXXI 58;
XXXIX 162

**VAN ARSDALEN, see VAN
ARSDALE**

VAN AUKEN/VAN AACHEN/VAN AKEN/VAN AKIN
NY **MARINUS VAN AKEN** ....-
   a 1722/24 m a 1685
   Pieternella De Pre/Prez/Pue ....-
   p 1724
   XVI 133; XXV 109; XXXIV 65

VAN BARKELO, see BARRICK(LOW)

VAN BENTHUYSEN
NY **PAULUS MARTENSE**
   1624/25-1717 m c 1660
   Catherine Van Kleek c 1639-....
   XXXVIII 238

VAN BOSKIRK, see VAN BUSKIRK

VAN BRUNT
NY **RUTGER JOESTEN** ....-a 1713
   m 1657
   **Tryntje Claes Claesen
   (Harmonson)** c 1618-p 1688
   XXI 111; XXXV 289

VAN BUSKIRK/VAN BOSKERK
NY **LAURENS/LOURENS
ANDRIESKEN VAN BOSKERK**
   c 1640-1694
   m 1658 **Janetje (Jans)
   Barentsen** (wid.) ....-1694
   III 70; XXXVII 130

VAN CAMPEN
NY **GERRITT JANSEN** ....-....
   m 1659
   Machteld (Stoffels) Lodewick
   ....- ....
   XXX 290

VAN CLEEP/VAN CLEAF
NY **JAN VAN CLEAF** 1628-1699
   m a 1661
   **Angelica Lawrence/Engeltje
   Pietersen** ....-....
   XXIX 163; XXXIV 176; XXXX
   167

**VAN COUWEN HOVEN, see
CONOVER
VAN CULEN, see VAN CULIN**

**VAN CULIN/VAN CULEN/VON
KOLEN**
PA **JOHAN/JOHN** 1621-
   liv. 1704/05 m c 1667
   Anneken or **Anna** _____ ....-....
   XVII 21

VANDALE/VANDALL/WENDEL
NY **EVERT JANSE WENDEL**
   1615-1702/09
   m1) 1644 **Susanna Du Trieux**
   1626-c 1660
   XII 90; XXXVIII 200; XXXX
   308

VANDGRIFT
NY **JACOB LEENDERTSZEN**
   bp 1622-1691 m 1645
   Rebecca Frederickse ....-....
   XXX 208

**VANDENBERGH/VAN DEN
BERGH/VANDENBURGH**
NY **GYSBERT CORNELISE VAN
DEN BERGH** c1620-a 1685 m ....
   Lysebert Van Voorhoudt ....-....
   XXVI 164; XXXIX 299

**VAN DEN BOSCH, see (JAN W.)
BUSH**

VANDER BEECK, see
VANDERBEECK
VANDERBEECK/VANDER
BEECK/VANDERBEEK/see also
REMSEN
NY REM JENSEN VANDER
BEECK ....-1681
  m 1642
  Jannetje Rapalje 1629-p 1681
  XIV 38; XXX 168

VANDER BEEK, see
VANDERBEECK

VAN DER BURGH
NY LUCAS DIRCKSEN 1654-
  a 1670 m ....
  Annatje Cornelia Blackman ....-
  ....
  XXIX 161

VANDERHOOF/
VANDERHOOVEN/
VANDERHOVEN
NY CORNELIUS CORNELISSEN
VANDERHOVEN a 1651-1690
  m .... Metas Beekman ....-....
  XI 189

VANDERHOOVEN, see
VANDER HOOF
VANDERHOVEN, see
VANDERHOOF

VAN DE VEER
NY CORNELIUS JANSEN 1623-
  a 1703 m 1672
  Tryntie De Mandeville ....-
  p 1703
  XXXI 241; XXXVI 64

VAN DE WALKER/VAN DER
WERKEN
NY ROELOF GERRITSE VAN
DER WERKEN ....-....
  m .... Geetruy Jacobse ....-....
  XXXVIII 13

VAN DOORN, see VAN DOREN

VAN DOREN/VAN DOORN
NY PIETER VAN DOORN
  1609/15-1657/58
  m1) c 1634 Catherine Stelting
  ....- ....
  m2) 1657 Jannetje Ranchen ....-
  ....
  XXXIII 32; XXXVII 358;
  XXXIX 24
NY CHRISTIAN PIETER c 1635-
  a 1686 m 1657 Tryntje
  Cornelise Shubber ....- ....
  XXXX 410, 411

VAN DUZER/VAN DEURSEN
NY ABRAHAM PIETERSEN VAN
DEURSEN bp 1607-....
  m 1629 Tryntje Melchiors ....-....
  XXXVI 119, 209

VAN DYCK
NY HENDRICK JOHANNES
  c 1610-c 1687/88 m ....
  Duvertje Cornelise Botjagers
  ....-1652/75
  XXXI 63; XXXIX 238
NY THOMAS JANSE 1580-1665
  m .... Sytie Dirks ....-....
  XI 137

VAN ESSELTYN
NY MARTEN CORNELISSE ....-
  a 1705
  m .... Mayke Barnevelt ....-....

VAN ESSELTYN-Cont.
XXIX 300

VAN ETTEN
NY **JACOBUS JANSEN** bp1634-
c 1693 m 1665
**Annetje Arianse Van
Amsterdam** ....-....
VIII 6; XXXX 182

VAN FLEET
NY **ADRIAN GERRITSEN** ....-
p 1664/a 1686 m ....
Agatha Jans Spruyt ....-....
XXXI 289, 318

VAN GAASBEEK
NY **DOMINIE LAURENTIUS**
1644-1680 m 1673
Laurentia Van de Kellenaar ....-
1703
XXIX 334

VAN GULICK
NY **HENDRICK** 1625-1653
m .... **Geertruyt Jochen
Willekens** c 1625-....
XXXIX 306

VAN HOESEN/VAN HUSSEM
NY **JAN FRANZ VAN HUSSEM**
....-1667 m a 1645
Volkeatje Jurriaanse a 1625-
a 1703
XXXIV 334; XXXV 301

VAN HOOK
NY **ARENT ISAACSEN** ....-1697
m2) 1665 **Styntie (Christiana)
Laurens** ....-....
XXXVIII 249

VAN HORN
PA **CHRISTIAN BERENSTEN**
1630-1658
m .... **Jannetje Jansen** ....-1694
XI 182

VAN HUSSEM, see VAN HOESEN
VAN KEULEN, see VAN KEUREN

VAN KEUREN/VAN
CEULEN/VAN KEULEN
NY **MATTYS JANSEN VAN
CEULEN** 1602-1648/a 63
m ....
Margarette Hendrickse ....-
1675/a 81
X 222; XXXIX 101

VAN KLEEK
NY **BARENT BALTUS** 1609-
a 1659
m .... **Elggeyn Poulus** ...-....
XXXVII 100

VAN KORTRIGHT, see
COURTRIGHT
VAN KORTRYK, see
COURTRIGHT
VAN KOUWENHOVEN, see
CONOVER
VAN KUYKENDALL, see
KUYKENDALL

VAN LENT
NY **ABRAHAM VAN LENT
(RYCK)** ....-1689
Grietje Hendrick ....-....
XXX 245

VAN LOAN, see VAN LOON

VAN LOON/VAN LOAN
NY **JAN VAN LOAN** a 1656-p 1720

VAN RYPER/VAN REYPEN/VAN
RIPEN/VAN RYPEN-Cont.
    m 1667 **Pryntje Hermans** ....-....
    IX 46; XXX 154

VANSANT
NY/PA **GARRET STOFFELSZEN**
    ....-a 1706
    m .... **Lysbet Gerrits** ....-p1690
    V 78

VAN SCHAICK, see VAN
SCHOICK

VAN SCHOICK/VAN
SCHAICK/VAN SCOYOC/VAN
SKIHAWK
NY **CORNELIUS AERTSEN VAN
SCHAICK** c 1610-c 1669
    m1) a 1640/41 **Belitje/Isabella
    (Arabella) Hendrickse** ....-1662
    XXIX 399; XXXIII 163

VAN SCOYOC, see VAN
SCHOICK
VAN SICKELEN, see VAN
SICKLE

VAN SICKLE/VAN
SICKELEN/VAN SYCKLIN
NY **FERDINANDUS VAN
SYCKLIN** c 1635-1712
    m 1660 **Eva Antonis Jansen**
    1641-....
    XXIX 136

VAN SKIHAWK, see VAN
SCHOICK
VAN SUTPHEN, see SUTPHEN
VAN SYCLIN, see VAN SICKLE

VAN TASSELL/VAN TEXEL
NY **JANS CORNELISSEN VAN**

TEXEL c 1625-1704
    m .... **Annetyne Alberts** ....-....
    XXXVII 115

VAN TINE/
FONTEYNE/FUNTINE
NY **CHARLES FONTEYNE** ....-
    p 1687 m a 1658
    Katrina Baaly/de Bailie ....-....
    XXXIII 81; XXXVII 361

VAN VALKENBURG, see VAN
VALKENBURGH

VAN VALKENBURGH/
VAN BALKENBURG
NY **LAMBERT VAN
VALKENBURG/H** c 1616-c 1697
    m c 1642
    Annetje Beekman ....-1704
    XXII 102; XXXII 251; XXXIV
    331; XXXVIII 273

VAN VEGHTEN
NY **TEUNISE DIRCKSEN** ....-....
    m .... _____ _____ ....-....
    III 49

VAN VORHEES, see VORHEES
VAN VRANCKEN, see VAN
VRANKEN

VAN VRANKEN/VAN
VRANCKEN
NY **CLAAS GERITSE** c 1600-1669
    m1) .... _____ _____ ....-1662/67
    XI 56

VAN WIE
NY **HENDRICK GERRITSE** ....-
    1691
    m .... _____ _____ ....-....
    XXII 86

VAN WINKLE
NY/NJ **JACOB (WALLINGEN)**
   c 1599-c 1657 m c 1647
   Tryntje Jacobs/Jacobe ....-1677
   XIII 59; XXXIV 158; XXXVI
   164; XXXVII 283

VAN WORMER
NY **LAURENSE JANS** 1630/35-
   1686
   m 1666 **Anna Jans** (wid.) ....-....
   XXXVIII 95

VAN WYCK
NY **CORNELIUS BARENTSE**
   c 1630-p 1712 m a 1667
   Anna Polhemus ....-....
   XXXVI 69

VAN ZANDT/VANZANDT
NY/PA **GERET/GERRET
STOFFELSE VANZANDT** 1620-
   1705
   m2) ....**Lysbeth Geritse** ....-1706
   XXIX 58
NY **JAN** ....-1729
   m .... **Jannetje** _____ ....-1728
   V 125
NY **JOSEPH JANSE** ....-a 1753
   m .... **Seytje Marcelis** ....-c 1753
   XVII 152

VANZANDT, see VAN ZANDT

VARNUM
MA **GEORGE** ....-1649
   m .... **Hannah** _____ ....-p 1649
   XXXI 272; XXXIV 155
MA **SAMUEL** c 1619-p 1702
   m .... **Sarah Langton** ....-....
   XXII 137; XXXI 272; XXXIV
   154

VAUGHAN
MA **GEORGE** 1621-1694 m 1652
   Elizabeth Hincksman 1631-
   1693
   XXV 20

VAUGHN
MA/RI **JOHN** ....-p 1683/87
   m a 1638/44
   Gillian Lousar ....-1667/81
   XV 136; XXXVI 223; XXXVII
   202; XXXIX 104

VAWTER
VA **JOHN** 1665-....
   m .... _____ _____ ....-....
   XIV 48

VEACH/VEITCH/VEICH
MD **JAMES VEACH** 1628-1685
   m 1657 **Mary Gakerlin** ....-....
   XXXII 196

VEASEY
NH/ME **GEORGE** c 1635-a 1673
   m 1664 **Mary Wiggin** bp 1641-
   ....
   XXIX 376

VEAZEY
MD **JOHN** ....-c 1701
   m .... **Martha** _____ ....-....
   XXIX 383

VEDDER
NY **HERMANS ALBERTSE** ....-
   c 1713
   m .... _____ _____ ....-....
   VI 90/106, 91/107

VEEDER
NY **SYMON VOLKERTSE** 1624-
   p 1696/97

VINTON
MA **JOHN, Sr** c 1620-p 1662
  m .... **Ann** _____ ....-....
  XIV 70; XXXIII 24

VISSCHER
NY **HARMON B.** 1619-1693
  m .... **Hester Tjerkse** ....-....
  XV 29

VLEREBOME/SERVAES/
VLIEREBOOM
NY **TYS/or MATTYS**
(MATTHEW) SERVAES c 1632-
  a 1700 m c 1661
  Maria/Maritie Jacobze c 1642-
  p 1704
  XXXIII 180

VLIERBOOM, see VLEREBOME
VOKERTSZEN, see also
FULKERSON
VON KOLEN, see VAN CULIN

VOORHEES/VAN VOORHEES
NY **LUCAS STEVANSE** 1650-1713
  m1) .... **Catherine Hanson Van**
  Noortstrand ....-....
  m2) 1689 **Jannetje Minnes** ....-
  a 1703
  V 47
NY **STEVEN COERTE VAN**
VOOR HEES/KOERTS
(COERTEN) c 1600-1684/89
  m1) by 1636 **Willempie Roelfse**
  1619-1690
  V 47; XI 151; XXII 62; XXX
  247; XXXI 81, 287; XXXVI 203;
  XXXIX 9; XXXX 309

VOSE
MA **ROBERT** c 1599-1683
  m 1629 **Jane/Abigail Moss** ....-

1675
XVII 21; XXVI 45; XXX 77

VROMAN, see VROOMAN

VROOMAN
NY **ADAM** 1649-1730
  m1) 1678 **Engeltie (Angelica)**
  Bloom bp 1652-1690
  m2) 1697 **Grietje Takelse**
  Heenstraat ....-....
  XXVI 123; XXXIII 34; XXXIV
  156
NY **HENRICK MEESE** 1618-1690
  m 1648 **Geertruy Johannis** ....-
  ....
  XXVI 123; XXXIII 34; XXXIV
  156

WADE
NY/NJ **BENJAMIN** 1646-1699
  m .... **Ann Looker** 1649-1737
  VI 11/13
MA **NICHOLAS** 1616-1683
  m 1638 **Elizabeth Ensign** ....-
  1708
  XX 156; XXV 146
MD **ZACHARY** c 1627-a 1677/78
  m ....
  Mary Hatton/Henson ....-....
  XXVII 194; XXXX 306

WADHAMS
CT **JOHN** ....-1676
  m .... **Susanna** _____ ....-1683
  XXXIV 289

WADSWORTH
MA **CHRISTOPHER** ....-
  w.f. 1676/79 m ....
  Grace Cole ....-wp 1687
  V 123; XXI 11; XXV 187;
  XXXII 189; XXXIX 246; XXXX

WADSWORTH-Cont.
47
MA/CT **WILLIAM** .... -1675
   m1) .... **Sarah** ____ ....-....
   m2) 1644 **Elizabeth Stone** ....-....
   XVII 71; XXX 122

WAGGAMAN
VA **HENDRICK GILLISSEN**
   c 1620/26-1682 m 1666
   Frances ____ ....-p 1712
   XXXX 418

WAGGENER/WAGGONER
VA **JOHN WAGGONER** 1643-
   1715 m ....
   Rachel Ward 1653-a 1716/18
   XXXVII 188; XXXX 125

WAGGONER, see WAGGENER

WAITE, see WAITT

WAIGHT/WAITT/WAIT/WAITE
MA **JOHN WAIT** 1618-1693
   m .... **Mary Hills** ....-1674
   XXIX 122; XXXIX 92
MA **RICHARD WAIT/WAITE**
   1608/09-1668/69
   m c 1636
   Mary ____ 1606-1678/79
   II 33; XVIII 76; XXX 27;
   XXXIII 234; XXX 174
RI **THOMAS WAIT** 1601-1669/77
   m ....
   Eleanor Wardwell ....-p 1677
   X 95; XII 59; XIII 57; XXI 108;
   XXXI 70; XXXIII 36; XXXV 16;
   XXXVIII 344

WAKEFIELD
VA/MA **JOHN, Sr** 1614/15-1667
   m a 1638

Ann ____ ....-a 1691/1702/03
XXV 166; XXVI 170; XXXI 315;
XXXII 295; XXXIV 103
MA **JOHN** ....-1674/75 m ....
   Elizabeth Littlefield bp 1627-....
   XXXIX 108

WAKEMAN
CT **JOHN** c 1598/bp 1601-1661
   m 1628/29
   Elizabeth Hopkins bp 1610-
   1658
   XXXIV 194; XXXVI 111;
   XXXVIII 11

WALCOTT
MA **JOHN** ....-1638
   m2) .... **Winnifred** ____
   ....-p 1646
   X 135

WALDERNE, see WALDRON

WALDO
MA **CORNELIUS** c 1624-1700/01
   m c 1651
   Hannah Cogswell c 1624-1704
   XXII 131; XXIV 132; XXV 216;
   XXVI 257; XXXI 65; XXXIII 15;
   XXXVII 156; XXXIX 179

WALDRON/WALDERNE
NY **RESOLVED** 1610-a 1690
   m2) 1654 **Tanneke Nagel** 1624-
   ....
   XII 7
NH **RICHARD WALDERNE** 1609-
   1689
   m1) 1636 ____ ____ ....-c 1670
   XXXII 213

WALE, see WHALEY

WALES
MA **NATHANIEL** 1586-1661
    m2) .... **Susan Greenway** ....-....
    XXVI 108

WALKER
MD **DANIEL** ....-p 1702
    m .... **Alice** _____ ....-....
    X 79, 103, 115
MD **JAMES** 1603-a 1660
    m 1627 **Ellen Maybole** ....-....
    XXXIV 312
MA **JAMES** 1619/20-1691
    m ....
    Elizabeth Phillips 1619-1678
    XXIV 152; XXVI 105
PA **LEWIS** ....-1728 m 1693
    Mary Morris c 1667-a 1747
    XXIV 157
RI **PHILIP** c 1627-1679 m ....
    Jane Butterworth c1631-1702
    V 104
MA **RICHARD** c 1592/1611-1687
    m2) c 1630 **Jane Talmadge** ....-
    c 1639/40
    XXIX 66, 85, 225; XXXVII 178
MA **ROBERT** 1606-1687
    m c 1635 **Sarah** pr. **Leager** ....-
    1695
    XXXIII 250
MA **SAMUEL** 1642-1704
    m1) 1662 **Sarah Read** ....-1681
    XXX 166
MA **THOMAS** ....-c 1697
    m a 1661 **Mary** _____ ....-....
    XXX 212
VA **THOMAS** ....-inv. 1657
    m .... **Elizabeth** _____ c 1608-....
    XXXVII 305
RI **THOMAS** ....-1724 m a 1685
    Elizabeth Parris 1648-1742
    III 41

WALLACE, see WALLIS

WALLBRIDGE
MA/CT **HENRY** ....-1729
    m 1688 **Anna Amos** 1666-c 1751
    XIII 22; XXIX 280

WALLER
MD **JOHN** ....-1667
    m .... **Alice Major** ....-....
    XXXIV 18; XXXX 376, 377
VA **JOHN** 1617-....
    m ....
    Mary Kay/Key 1617-....
    X 280, 281
VA **WILLIAM, I** c 1635-a 1694/99
    m .... **Mary Allen** ....-....
    XXXII 229; XXXIV 330

WALLING
RI **THOMAS** c 1630-wp 1674
    m .... **Mary Abbott** ....-1669
    XXXI 99

WALLIS/WALLACE
ME **JOHN** ....-1690
    m by 1662
    Mary Phippen 1644-....
    XXXIX 17
MD **HENRY** ....-p 1699
    m .... _____ _____ ....-....
    XII 89; XIV 39; XVI 54; XVII
    104; XXVII 170
VA **ROBERT** c 1618-c 1643
    m .... **Rebecca** _____ ....-liv. 1648
    XXV 150, 177

WALTHALL
VA **WILLIAM** c 1608-p 1669
    m c 1656 **Anne Archer** ....-....
    XXXVI 314

WALTON
VA **EDWARD** c 1656-1720
    m c 1697
    Elizabeth (Mason?) ....-1717
    XXVIII 42
NY **THOMAS** ....-1689
    m 1671 **Esther Lawrence** ....-....
    XXIX 38
MD **WILLIAM** ....-a 1686
    m .... _____ _____ ....-....
    XVIII 71
PA **WILLIAM** 1661/62-1736/37
    m 1689 **Sarah Howell** ....-1749
    XXXV 217

WANDEL/DE WANDELAER
NY **JOHANNES DE
WANDELAER** c 1652/54-p 1720
    m 1675 **Sara Schepmoes** ....-....
    XIX 48

WAPLES
DE **PETER** 1645-1733
    m .... _____ _____ ....-....
    XXXVII 222

WARD/WARDE
MA/CT **ANDREW WARDE** c 1597-
    wp 1659 m....
    Hester Sherman bp 1606-
    wd 1665/66
    XII 75; XXX 225; XXXIII 197;
    XXXVI 261
CT **GEORGE** ....-a 1666
    m .... _____ _____ ....-....
    XXV 114
RI **JOHN** 1619-1698
    m .... _____ _____ ....-....
    II 55
NJ **JOHN** 1620-1694
    m .... **Sarah Lyman** ....-....
    XVI 80
CT **JOHN** 1625-1694

    m .... **Sarah Hill** ....-....
    XXXIX 150
MD **ROBERT** ....-wp 1709
    m ....
    Susanna Robinett ....-1698
    XXXVIII 236
MA **WILLIAM** 1597/1603-1687
    m1) .... **Elizabeth** _____ ....-....
    m2) .... **Elizabeth** _____ 1613/14-
    1700
    V 111; IX 47; X 36, 49, 50, 52;
    XIV 86; XVI 130; XVIII 35, 52;
    XXV 41; XXVI 188; XXIX
    164; XXXV 275; XXXIX 201
CT **WILLIAM** 1632-1690
    m1) .... _____ _____ ....-....
    m2) 1660 **Phoebe** _____ ....-1691
    X 89; XVII 72

WARDE, see WARD

WARDWELL
MA **THOMAS** ....-1646
    m .... **Elizabeth** _____ ....-1697
    XXII 36
NH **WILLIAM** 1604-....
    m .... **Alice** _____ ....-....
    XXI 10

WARE/WEARE
VA **NICHOLAS** a 1648-1662
    m a 1655 **Ann Vassall** ....-....
    XXXIV 81
ME **PETER WEARE** c 1618-1692
    m 1665
    Mary Purrington bp 1632/33-
    1719
    XXXII 114
MA **ROBERT** ....-1699 m 1645
    Margaret Huntinge ....-1670
    XVII 24

WATSON-Cont.
IV 76, 94
MA **JOHN** ....-1700 m ....
    Eunice/Emma Barker ....-....
    XVIII 141
RI **JOHN, I** ....-1728
    m .... **Dorcas Gardiner** ....-....
    XXVIII 100; XXX 107; XXXIV
    89
MA **JOHN** bp 1620-1711 m ....
    Rebecca Errington 1622-1690
    XXX 15; XXXIV 49
MA **ROBERT** ....-1637
    m .... **Elizabeth** ____ ....-1638
    XIX 14

WATTLES
MA **JOHN** ....-1676 m 1666
    Marie Goole/Gould 1651-1687
    XVII 41

WAY
MA **GEORGE** 1620-c 1690
    m .... **Elizabeth Smith** ....-1711
    XXV 133
MA **HENRY** 1583-1667
    m .... **Elizabeth** ____ 1581-1665
    XXV 133

WEARE, see WARE
WEATHERS, see WITHERS

WEAVER
MA/RI **CLEMENT** c 1592-1683
    m 1617
    Rebecca Holbrook c 1597-....
    XI 30; XXIV 27; XXIX 184;
    XXX 60; XXXIV 166
VA **SAMUEL, Sr** 1604-1709
    m .... **Elizabeth** ____ ....-1728
    XXX 236

WEBB
MA **ALEXANDER** 1559-....
    m .... **Mary Wilson** ....-....
    XV 134; XVII 128
MA **CHRISTOPHER** c 1599-....
    1689/90 m ....
    Humility ____ ....-1687
    XVII 128; XX 130; XXV 28;
    XXVI 65; XXVIII 162
MA **CHRISTOPHER** 1630-1694
    m 1654/55
    Hannah Scott c 1635/38-1718
    XV 28; XXVI 65; XXVIII 162;
    XXXIII 13
VA **JOHN** ....-....
    m 1673 **Mary Sanford** ....-....
    XXVI 237
MA/CT **RICHARD, I** 1580/1611-
    1655/76 m ....
    Elizabeth Gregory ....-1681
    XI 88; XXXV 361; XXXVII 31

WEBBER
MA **JOSIAH** ....-....
    m .... ____ ____ ....-....
    XIII 120
MA **THOMAS** c 1630-1690
    m 1655 **Mary Parker** 1639-1700
    XXIII 16

WEBSTER
CT **JOHN** 1590-1661 m 1609
    Agnes Smith bp 1585-1667
    XIII 73; XIV 37; XVI 64; XIX
    147; XXI 158; XXV 189; XXIX
    111, 350; XXX 42; XXXIII 57;
    XXXVI 98, 156; XXXVII 56,
    124, 194, 320; XXXIX 174
MA **JOHN** c 1605-1642/46
    m 1624/30
    Mary Shatswell c 1606-1694
    XII 44; XVII 62; XX 138; XXII
    5; XXXII 84; XXXIII 351;

WEBSTER-Cont.
XXXIV 167; XXXVI 104
MA **THOMAS** bp 1631-1715
m 1657
Sarah Brewer c 1636/37-p 1699
XVIII 91; XXIX 371; XXXII 174

WEDGE
MA **THOMAS** c 1640-1685
m c 1666
Deborah Stevens c 1640-1703
XXXIV 296

WEEKS/WICKES
ME/NH **LEONARD** bp 1639-
1707/08 m c 1667
Mary Haines c 1635-a 1679
XIX 145; XXXIV 48; XXXVI
126; XXXVIII 257; XXXIX 75

WELCH
MD **JOHN** c 1625-....
m2) .... **Mary** _____ ....-....
XXXIV 86
MA **PHILIP** 1640/43-....
m 1666 **Hannah Haggett** ....-....
XXVI 191; XXXVIII 232

WELD
MA **JOSEPH** c 1597/98-1646
m 1620
Elizabeth Wyse c 1600-1638
XXX 196; XXXVIII 73
MA **THOMAS** 1590-1661
m .... **Margaret Doreslye** ....-
1671
V 90
MA **THOMAS** 1626-1682
m .... **Dorothy Whiting** 1628-
1694
V 90

WELLES, see WELLS

WELLINGTON
MA **ROGER** c 1609/10-1697/98
m 1636/38
Mary Palgrave c 1619-c 1695/98
XVIII 63, 83; XXXVII 61;
XXXIX 165; XXXX 391

WELLMAN
MA **THOMAS** c 1620-1672
m c 1642
Elizabeth _____ ....-a 1672/73
XXXIX 305; XXXX 110

WELLS/WELLES
CT/MA **HUGH** c 1590-c 1645
m c 1619
Frances Belcher ....-1678
XXI 70; XXV 89; XXIX 361
CT **JOSHUA, Sr** ....-....
m .... _____ _____ ....-....
XXI 81
MA **NATHANIEL** 1600-....
m .... _____ _____ ....-....
XXI 173
RI **PETER, Sr** ....-p 1715
m .... _____ _____ ....-....
XXXIII 166
CT **THOMAS WELLES** c 1560-....
m .... _____ _____ ....-....
XXIX 361
CT **THOMAS WELLES** 1598-1660
m1) 1618 **Alice Tomes** ....-1646
m2) .... **Elizabeth Hunt** ....-1640?
XII 37; XXI 78; XXXII 185, 249;
XXXIV 20
CT **THOMAS WELLES** 1598/1605-
1660/66 m 1630
Abigail Warner bp 1614/15-....
X 28; XI 123; XXXIII 17
CT **THOMAS WELLES** c 1620-
1676 m 1651
Mary Beardsley c 1631-1691
XXI 70

WELLS/WELLES-Cont.
MA/RI **THOMAS** 1626-1700
　m c 1655 **Naomi Marshall** 1637-
　....
　XXI 173; XXX 216
MD **THOMAS, Sr** c 1637-1718
　m c 1684 **Frances** ____ ....-....
　XXXIII 302; XXXX 139
NY **WILLIAM** 1608-1671
　m c 1656
　Mary (Marie) Youngs 1619-
　1709
　XIII 87; XXV 23

WELTON
CT **JOHN, Sr** 1633-1726
　m 1667
　Mary Upson c 1651/53-1716
　XX 64; XXXIX 49

WENDELL
NY **EVERT JANSE** 1615-1709
　m1) 1644 **Susanna DuGrieux**
　1626/44-c 1660
　XII 90; XX 82; XXXX 308

WENTWORTH
ME/NH **WILLIAM** 1615/17-p 1697
　m2) **Elizabeth (Kenny)** ....-1697
　V 48; XX 88; XXXII 250;
　XXXVII 49

WERDEN/WORDEN
MA **PETER, I** 1569-1638
　m .... ____ ____ ....-....
　XXXV 298

WESSELL, see also EVERTSZEN
WESSON, see WESTON

WEST
MA **FRANCIS** ....-....
　m a 1660 **Susanna Soule** ....-....

　XXXIII 50
MA **FRANCIS** 1616-1692
　m 1639 **Margret Reeves** ....-....
　X 12, 19, 27; XIX 6; XXI 8;
　XXXIX 189
VA/MD/DE **GEORGE** ....-
　est.prov. 1707
　m .... **Susannah** ____ ....-....
　XXX 61; XXXIV 300
VA **JOHN** 1590-1659
　m .... **Anne** ____ ....-....
　XXXI 20
VA **JOHN** 1638/39-wp 1703
　m c 1660 **Matilda Scarburgh** ....-
　....
　XXXVI 228
MA/RI **MATTHEW** ....-p 1655
　m .... ____ ____ ....-....
　XXIV 117
SC **SAMUEL** und. age 21 in 1652-
　1701/06
　m .... **Sara Nichols** ....-....
　XXXV 95; XXXVII 167
VA **THOMAS** 1577-1618
　m 1596 **Ceciley Shirley** ....-....
　XX 127; XXI 23

WESTBROOK
NY **ANTHONY JANS (JANSEN)**
　....-.... m c 1659/60
　Osseltje Dircksz (Richards) ....-
　....
　XXIX 88; XXXVIII 305

WESTCOTT
CT **RICHARD** 1612-1651
　m 1634
　Joanna Baldwin 1616-1682
　XXI 65
MA/RI **STUKELEY** c 1592-1676/77
　m 1617/19
　Juliana Marchante ....-a 1670
　XXV 238; XXVII 120; XXX 78;

WESTCOTT-Cont.
   XXXV 166; XXXVII 127;
   XXXX 220

WESTERVELT
NY **LUBBERT LUBBERTSON**
   1620-1686 m 1645
   Gessie (Grace) Roelofse ....-1696
   XXXVI 32

WESTON/WESSON
MA **JOHN** 1630/31-1723 m 1653
   Sarah Fitch bp 1632/33-1685/98
   II 44; IV 157; X 229; XIX 27;
   XXXI 209

WESTOVER
CT **JONAS/JONAH, Sr** 1628/48-
   1707/09 m 1663
   Hannah Griswold 1642-1714
   XXVII 16; XXXVII 236

WETHERBEE/WITHERBEE
MA **JOHN** c 1642/50-wp 1711
   m1) 1672 **Mary How/e** 1654-
   1684
   m2) 1684 **Lydia Moore** 1660-
   1724/25
   XXIV 146; XXIX 205; XXXI
   282; XXXV 206; XXXX 258

WETHERILL
NJ **CHRISTOPHER** c 1646-1711
   m .... **Mary Hornby** ....-1680
   IV 85

WETMORE
CT **THOMAS** 1615-1681
   m1) 1645 **Sarah Hall** 1616-
   1664/65
   XXIX 68; XXXV 327

WHALEY/WALE/WHALLEY
MD **EDWARD** 1615-1718
   m 1668/69
   Elizabeth Middleton ....-....
   XXX 182

WHALLEY, see WHALEY

WHARTON
PA **THOMAS** 1664-1718
   m 1686/89
   Rachel Thomas (Friend) 1664-
   1747/49
   XXV 159

WHEAT
MA **MOSES** c 1616-1700
   m a 1640 **Tamzen** _____ ....-1689
   XXXVIII 238; XXXIX 25

WHEATON
MA **CHRISTOPHER** ....-1683/84
   m 1674 **Martha Prince** 1645-....
   XXXIV 276
MA **ROBERT** c 1606-1696
   m 1636 **Alice Bowen** ....-....
   XVIII 28

WHEELER
MA/CT **EPHRIAM** ....-c 1669
   m .... **Ann** _____ ....-....
   XVII 55
MA **GEORGE** 1600-1687 m ....
   Katherine _____ ....-1684/85
   XXVII 225; XXXV 97; XXXVI
   308
MA **JOHN** ....-1670
   m .... **Ann** _____ ....-1662
   XXX 33
MD **JOHN** 1630-wp 1694
   m .... **Mary** _____ ....-....
   XXVIII 186; XXXIII 205
CT **MOSES, I** 1598-1698

WHITE-Cont.
XXI 33, 124; XXXV 71
VA **JOHN, Sr** c 1650-wp 1722
m by 1673 _____ _____ ....-....
XXXIX 209
CT **NATHANIEL** 1629-1711
m1) c 1652 **Elizabeth** _____ ....-....
V 46
MA **RESOLVED** c 1614/15-1680/87
m1) 1640 **Judith Vassail** 1619-
1670
XVII 38; XXXVI 303
VA **RICHARD** ....-wp 1708
m1) .... **Ardry** _____ ....-p 1675
m2) .... **Sarah** _____ ....-....
XXXVIII 61
MA **THOMAS** c 1599-wp 1679
m .... _____ _____....-....
X 130; XI 97, 118, 132; XIV 125;
XX 36; XXVI 101; XXVIII 90
MA **WILLIAM** ....-1621 m 1612
Susanna Fuller ....-1654/75
XVII 38; XXXVI 303; XXXVII
148
MA **WILLIAM** c 1605/10-1681/90
m1) **Mary** _____ 1606-1681
X 174; XII 64; XXXVI 303;
XXXVII 163
MA **WILLIAM** c 1620-1673
m .... **Elizabeth** _____ ....-1690
XIV 45; XXXV 290

WHITEHEAD
NJ/CT **ISAAC** 1621-1691
m .... **Mary Brown/e** ....-....
XXXVII 217; XXXIX 293

WHITEHURST
VA **JAMES** ....-c 1719/20
m ...._____ _____ ....-....
XXIX 29
VA **RICHARD** c 1599-a 1654
m .... **Ellen** _____ ....-p 1654

XXXX 296

WHITFIELD
VA **MATHEW** c 1655-p 1708
m c 1680
Ann/Priscilla Lawrence c 1660-
a 1708
XXIX 187; XXXIII 275;
XXXVIII 55

WHITFORD
RI **PASCO** c 1640-1700
m .... _____ _____ ....-....
XXIX 81

WHITING
MA **NATHANIEL** c 1609/17-
1682/83 m 1643
Hannah Dwight 1625-1714
IX 34; XII 26; XIII 97; XXI 107;
XXXX 241
MA **SAMUEL** 1597-1679
m2) 1629 **Elizabeth St. John**
c 1605-1677
XXV 274; XXXIX 88
CT **WILLIAM** a 1613-1647
m c 1630
Susannah _____ a 1618-1673
VIII 18; XII 15; XIX 10; XXIX
282, 369; XXXVI 311

WHITLEDGE
VA **THOMAS** 1660-1729/30
m .... **Sibell Harrison** 1663-
a 1734
XXII 27

WHITLOCK
CT **JOHN** ....-1658
m ..... _____ _____ .....-.....
XI 100; XII 38

WILLIAMSON/WILLEMSEN-
Cont.
WILLEMSEN c 1637-w 1721
   m c 1678
   Mayke Pieterse Wyckoff 1653-
....
   XVIII 115; XXIII 82; XXXVIII
362

WILLIS
VA **FRANCIS, I** 1650/60-p 1726
   m .... _____ _____ ....-....
   XXX 101; XXXV 33
VA **HENRY** ....-a 1689
   m .... _____ _____ ....-....
   XII 11
MA **ROGER** 1640-1700
   m 1664 **Ruth Hill** 1644-1736
   XXXX 213
VA **THOMAS** c 1625-a 1670
   m c 1652 **Mary** _____ c 1630-....
   XXXVIII 353

WILLS, see WELLS

WILLISTON
MA **JOSEPH** c 1667-1747
   m2) 1714 **Sarah (Strong)**
   Stebbins 1681-1732
   XXXVI 181

WILLSON
MA **BENJAMIN** ....-....
   m .... _____ _____ ....-....
   XVI 129

WILSON
CT **EDWARD** ....-1684
   m .... _____ _____ ....-....
   XXXVII 287
MA **HENRY** c 1615/16-1688/89
   m 1642 **Mary Metcalf** 1618-....
   XIV 80

VA **JAMES** ....-1712 m ....
   Elizabeth Willis ....-p 1712
   XXXI 21; XXXII 57
MD **JAMES** ....-wp 1672 m ....
   Margaret Kidd ...-liv 1672
   VII 7, 45; XXI 110
CT **JOHN** 1618-1655
   m 1646 **Mary Clark** 1626-1652
   XXXVII 241
MA **ROBERT** ....-c 1685
   m .... **Deborah Stevenson** ....-....
   XXIII 11
VA/NC **ROBERT** 1629-1696
   m 1660 **Ann Blount** ....-1702
   XXXI 266
CT **SAMUEL** 1650-1729
   m 1679
   Phebe Middlebrook 1660-
   p 1686/1720
   XIV 74
MD **THOMAS** ....-1705
   m .... **Margaret** _____ ....-....
   XXVI 155
MA **WILLIAM** ....-a 1653
   m .... **Patience** _____ ....-1663
   XXVII 189

WILTBANK
DE **HELMANUS/HERMANUS**
FREDERICK 1625-c 1693
   m 1664
   Johnaken/Jane pr. **Hill** ....-
   1693/94
   IV 143; VII 28; XXXI 56

WILTSE, see WILTSIE

WILTSIE/WILTSE
NY **HENDRICK MARTENSZEN**
   c 1623-c 1712 m 1660
   Margaret (Meyers) Jansen
   c 1633-1704
   XXX 79; XXXX 60

WINN/WINNE/WYNN/WYNNE-
Cont.
    m1) 1655 **Martha Buttel** ....-
c 1670
    XXXIV 210; XXXV 65, 132;
    XXXVII 239

WINNE, see WINN

WINSHIP
MA **EDWARD, I** 1613-1688
    m2) .... **Elizabeth Parke** ....-1690
    XXXII 73

WINSLOW
MA **JOHN** 1597-1674
    m 1624 **Mary Chilton** ....-1679
    XXVI 218
MA **KENELM** 1599-1672 m 1634
    Eleanor (Newton) Adams 1598-
    1681
    V 89; X 194; XI 25; XV 86; XXII
    73; XXIV 54

WINSOR
RI **JOSHUA** ....-1679
    m .... ____ ____ ...-1655
    XVI 52

WINSTEAD
VA **SAMUEL** ....-a 1726
    m .... ____ ____ ....-....
    XXXI 231

WINSTON
VA **WILLIAM** ....-1702/06
    m .... ____ ____ ....-....
    XXXI 39; XXXIII 324

WINTER
MA **EDWARD** c 1643-....
    m 1669 **Deborah Golt** 1648-....
    XXXIX 185

MA **JOHN** 1552-1662
    m .... ____ ____ ....-....
    XXVII 197

WISWALL/WISWELL
MA **EBENEZER WISWELL** 1682-
    ....
    m 1721 **Anna Capen** bp 1696-....
    XXXIII 212
MA **THOMAS** ....-1683
    m a 1633 **Elizabeth** ____ ....-....
    XXXIV 11

WISWELL, see WISWALL

WITBECK
NY **JAN TOMASSE** ....-p 1696
    m ....
    Gertrude Andriese Dochter ....-
    ....
    XII 81

WITHEE/MACKERWITHEE/
MACRORY/
WITHEE, see MACKERWITHEE
WITHERBEE, see WETHERBEE

WITHERS/WEATHERS
VA **JOHN WEATHERS** 1658/60-
    1686
    m1) 1681 **Margaret Powell** ....-
    ....
    m2) c 1685 **Sarah** ____ c 1662-
    p 1687
    XXVIII 110; XXIX 90
VA **WILLIAM** 1636-1698
    m .... ____ ____ ....-....
    XXXV 75

WIXOM
MA **ROBERT** ....-w 1686

WIXOM-Cont.
    m 1654 **Alice** _____ ....-p 1686
    XXXV 102; XXXVII 144

WOLCOTT/WOOLCOTT
MA/CT **HENRY, Sr** bp 1578-1655
    m 1606
    Elizabeth Saunders bp 1584-
    1655
    VIII 32; XII 6; XXI 83; XXV 61;
    XXVI 156, 166; XXX 193; XXXI
    117; XXXV 146
MA/CT **HENRY, Jr** 1610/11-1680
    m 1641
    Sarah Newberry 1614-1684
    XV 61; XXX 193; XXXV 146
MA **WILLIAM** ....-....
    m .... **Alice Ingersoll**
    c 1630-....
    XI 110, 111

WOLVERTON/WOOLVERTON
NJ **CHARLES WOOLVERTON**
    c 1670-c 1746
    m 1697 **Mary Chadwick** ....-....
    XXII 56

WOOD
MA/CT/NY **EDMUND** 1578/80-
    1663
    m 1611
    Martha Lorne/Lum ....-....
    XXXI 186
MA **EDWARD** ....-1642
    m .... Ruth Mousall ....-p 1657
    XXIX 238
MA **HENRY** 1594-wp 1670
    m 1644/45
    Abigail Jenney 16__-1675
    XXXIII 141; XXXIX 328;
    XXXX 25
NJ **HENRY, Sr** 1603-1686
    m1) .... **Isabel** _____ ....-1675

(England)
    m2) .... **Alice** _____ ....-....
    XXXIII 201; XXXV 363;
    XXXVIII 57
NJ **JOHN** 1643-1705
    m .... **Sarah Branson** ....-....
    XVI 114
NY **JONAS** bp 1614-c 1660
    m1) 1635
    Mary Drake ....-....
    XXXVIII 322
NY **JONATHAN, I** 1658-1726
    m 1691
    Mary Titus 1673/74-1729
    XXXV 344
MD **JOSEPH** ....-.... m 1684/93
    Francine Herman a 1666-....
    XXXI 135; XXXIV 14
RI **THOMAS** ....-....
    m ...._____ _____ ....-....
    XXV 276
MA **THOMAS** a 1634/35-1684/87
    m 1654 **Ann Hunt** c 1637-1714
    V 73; X 238, 239; XXIV 42;
    XXXVII 317
MA **WILLIAM** 1582-1671
    m .... **Margaret Sawyer** ....-1659
    X 158

WOODBRIDGE
MA **JOHN** 1613-1695
    m 1639
    Mercy Dudley bp 1621-1691
    VI 12/14; X 107, 286, 287, 289;
    XI 7, 15; XIII 49; XV 100;
    XXXII 21

WOODBURY
MA **JOHN** c 1579-1641
    m2) .... **Agnes Debry** a 1629-
    1672
    XVII 80; XVIII 114, 117; XXXV
    70; XXXVII 159

WOODBURY-Cont.
MA **WILLIAM** c 1589-1676/77
    m 1616/17
    Elizabeth Patch bp 1594-p 1677
    XXXVI 108

WOODCOCK
MA **JOHN** c 1615-1700
    m1) .... **Sarah** _____ ....-1676
    IV 140

WOODFORD
CT **JOSEPH** 1636-1701/10 m ....
    Rebecca Newell 1643/44-a 1701
    XVI 73
CT **THOMAS** ....-1667
    m 1635 **Mary Blott** ....-....
    XVI 14

WOODHULL
NY **RICHARD** 1620-1691
    m 1645 **Deborah Crewe** ....-....
    XIII 45; XXXII 232; XXXIII 188

WOODMAN
MA **EDWARD** 1606-1692/94
    m a 1628
    Joanna Bartlett 1613/14-
    p 1687/88
    III 5; XXXI 97; XXXIII 56

WOODRUFF
NY **JOHN** 1604-c 1670 m 1636
    Ann Gosmer 161_-1670
    XXII 10; XXV 82; XXVII 74
CT **MATHEW** c 1633-1682
    m .... **Hannah** _____ ....-p 1692
    XXXIV 111

WOODS
MA **SAMUEL** c 1636-1717/18
    m 1659 **Alice Rushton** c 1636-
    1712

XI 22; XX 77; XXXIX 30

WOODSON
VA **JOHN** c 1586-1644 m a 1618/19
    Sarah Winston c 1599-1660
    XXIX 267; XXX 204; XXXVII
    342; XXXX 107

WOODWARD
MA **HENRY** 1607-1685
    m .... **Elizabeth** _____ ....-1690
    XI 21; XIV 74
MA **NATHANIEL, Sr** 1589-p 1673
    m1) .... **Margaret** _____ .....-....
    XXVI 133; XXXI 41; XXXVIII
    160
MA **PETER** ....-1685
    m ..... _____ _____ ....-....
    XXVI 153
MA **RICHARD** bp 1587/89-1664/65
    m c 1614/18
    Rose Stewart 1582/84-1662
    XXI 14, 29; XXIX 113; XXXIV
    242; XXXIX 345; XXXX 297
PA **RICHARD** 1636-1706
    m .... **Jane** _____ ....-p 1714
    XXX 53

WOODWORTH
MA **WALTER** ....-1685
    m .... _____ _____ ....-....
    XIII 25; XXII 116; XXXII 91;
    XXXIII 228

WOOLARD
NC **RICHARD** c 1645-1707
    m1) .... **Ann** _____ ....-c 1702
    XXIX 97

WOOLFOLK
VA **RICHARD** ....-....
    m .... **Elizabeth** _____ ....-....
    XXIV 165

WOOLFORD
MD **ROGER** ....-1701 m 1660/61
    Mary Denwood ....-....
    XXXII 173

**WOOLVERTON, see
WOLVERTON**

WOOSTER
CT **EDWARD** 1622-1689 m 1669
    Tabitha Tomlinson ....-....
    XX 45

WOOTEN
VA **THOMAS** a 1624-1669/70
    m ....
    Sarah (Jennings) Wood ....-
    p 1669
    XXXI 265

WORCHESTER
MA **SAMUEL** 1635-1681
    m 1659
    Elizabeth Parrott 1640-....
    V 94, 100
MA **WILLIAM** 1595-1662
    m1) .... **Sarah** ____ ....-1650
    V 94, 100; XVI 83; XXVIII 145

WORDEN, see WERDEN

WORLEY
PA **FRANCIS, Sr** 1672-p 1724
    m 1693 **Mary Brassey** 1673-
    1728
    XXXX 202, 454

WORRELL
PA **PETER, I** 1663-1722
    m .... **Susannah** ____ ....-....
    XXXX 2

WORTHEN, see WATHEN

WORTHINGTON
CT **NICHOLAS** ....-1683
    m1) c 1668 **Sara (Bunch)
    White** ....-1676
    XVI 121

WRIGHT
MA **EDWARD** ....-1691
    m .... **Elizabeth** ____ 1690
    XXVI 13
MD **JOHN** ....-est. prob. 1695
    m ....
    **Elizabeth Lewger/Lugar
    Midgeley** ....-....
    XXXI 73
MA **JOHN** c 1601-1688
    m .... **Priscilla** ____ ....-1687
    II 54; XX 153; XXIII 61;
    XXXVII 130
MA/NY **PETER** ....-p 1660/63
    m .... **Alice** ____ 1615-1683
    XXIII 22
VA **RICHARD** 1633-p 1663
    m c 1656/57
    Ann Mottrum 1639-....
    XXVIII 44, 48; XXIX 381; XXX
    235
MA **SAMUEL** 1613/14-1665
    m 1627
    Margaret Stratton 1604-1681
    IV 136; XXX 213; XXXVIII 114;
    XXXX 219
NJ **THOMAS** ....-1705/06
    m .... ____ ____ ....-....
    XXXX 109

WYATT/WIATT
VA **EDWARD** 1619-1690/98
    m 1644
    Jane Conquest 1622-1698
    XV 127; XVI 95

YOUNG/YOUNGE
MD **GEORGE, Sr** ....-1718
    m .... **Elizabeth** ....-....
    XXXV 321
MA **JOHN** c 1615-1690/91
    m 1648 **Abigail Howland** ....-
    1692
    XXXVIII 106
VA **LAURENCE** ....-p 1687
    m .... _____ _____ ....-....
    XXXIII 45
NJ **ROBERT** 1663-1726
    m .... **Sara Baldwin** 1665-....
    XII 90
ME **ROWLAND** c 1616/20-w p 1685
    m c 1647/48 **Joan Knight**
    c 1625-wp 1698
    XXXX 420
VA **THOMAS YONGE** 1579-
    p 1642 m 1619
    Mary Strachey ....-....
    XIX 62; XXXII 283

YOUNGS/YOUNGES
NY **JOHN** 1598-1671/72
    m1) 1622 **Joan Harrington/Ann**
    Lewington? ....-c 1630
    m3) .... **Mary (Warren)**
    Gardiner ....-1678
    III 62; XII 19; XIV 35
MA **JOSEPH YOUNGS** c 1605-
    p 1656 m 1623
    Margaret Warren ....-p 1669
    XXVII 167

ZEVIE, see SEAVEY

www.ingramcontent.com/pod-product-compliance
Lightning Source LLC
Chambersburg PA
CBHW031535260326
41914CB00032B/1813/J